Until We Meet Again

Until We Meet Again is a treasure chest with many hidden jewels awaiting the patient reader: the story of a long-distance romance in the age of postage stamps and letters, of a cooperative sibling partnership beyond the outer edge of Canadian settlement, and of the detailed survey work required in the construction of the CPR's subsidiary, the Columbia and Kootenay Railway. What makes this story particularly intriguing for me is that one of my heroes exerts his powerful influence on Karel's advancement: William Cornelius Van Horne, who became general manager and, later, president of the CPR as it was being pushed westward toward the Rockies.

— Walter Volovsek, Castlegar historian
Author of *A Railway from Nowhere to Nowhere*
Review from the *British Columbia Review*

Compelling and insightful. As two siblings engage in a restorative journey to Canada, we experience an intimate exposé into the hearts and minds of the enterprising Boissevain family. Through impressively researched and crafted translations, Green and Krijff reveal first-hand the Boissevains' correspondence; their business and political connections and influences; their family lives, aspirations and apprehensions; and the attitudes and social norms of the time. An intriguing view of the pioneer life, the landscape of Alberta, and the people that played a central part in the push westward of the CPR.

— Erwin van Asbeck
Great-great-grandson of Karel Boissevain

Reading this collection of letters is like travelling back in time. In particular, Heleen's words describe the rarely documented experiences of women living in Calgary, Ft. Macleod, Pincher Creek and Edmonton at the dawn of the twentieth century. The siblings' journey from Amsterdam to London to Montreal and their train trip west provides snapshots of influential people we've only met when sitting in school desks — people who were involved in opening the West and the beginnings of Canada, including CPR President William Van Horne. A meaningful addition to the social history of Alberta and Canada, this volume will be a treasure for those curious about early Canadiana and the CPR, and invaluable to researchers.

— Bonita S. Bjornson
Library manager, archivist
Gerry Segger Heritage Collection
The King's University, Edmonton

Until We Meet Again is a fascinating and insightful look into an outsider's perspective on prairie life in early Alberta history. Comparisons to the Boissevain siblings' world back home in Amsterdam are stark in nature, providing compelling observations of local characters and how they flicker in and out of Karel and Heleen's lives. Green and Krijff have found a rare treasure in these letters, painting an authentic picture of the newcomers' experience as they explore the pioneer West.

— Erin Benedictson
Associate Curator
Lougheed House, Calgary

Until We Meet Again

Scouting for the CPR's Crowsnest Line – 1891

Amsterdam's Boissevain Family Letters – Part 1

Jan Krijff & Karen Green

GRANVILLE ISLAND PUBLISHING

Copyright © 2023 Jan Krijff and Karen Green

All rights reserved. No part of this publication may be reproduced, stored in a retrieval system or transmitted, in any form or by any means, without prior permission of the publisher or, in the case of photocopying or other reprographic copying, a license from Access Copyright, the Canadian Copyright Licensing Agency, www.accesscopyright.ca, 1-800-893-5777, info@accesscopyright.ca.

Publisher's Cataloging-in-Publication data

Names: Krijff, Jan, author. | Green, Brenda Karen, author.
Title: Until we meet again : scouting for the CPR's Crowsnest line — 1891, Amsterdam's Boissevain family letters — part 1 / Jan Krijff & Karen Green.
Series: Amsterdam's Boissevain Family Letters
Description: Includes bibliographical references and index. | Vancouver, BC, Canada: Granville Island Publishing Ltd., 2023.
Identifiers: ISBN: 978-1-989467-46-6 (paperback) | 978-1-989467-47-3 (ebook)
Subjects: LCSH Boissevain family. | Crowsnest Pass Region (Alta. and B.C.)—History. | Railroads—Canada—History. | Dutch—Canada—History—19th century. | Netherlands—Emigration and immigration—History. | BISAC HISTORY / Canada / Post-Confederation (1867-) | HISTORY / Europe / Benelux Countries (Belgium, Netherlands, Luxembourg)
Classification: LCC F1035.D8.K75 2023 | DDC 970.004/3931/092—dc23

Editor: Jessica Kaplan
Copy Editor: Kyle Hawke
Book designer: Omar Gallegos
Proofreader: Rebecca Coates

Granville Island Publishing Ltd.
105 — 1496 Cartwright St.
#14354, Granville Island
Vancouver, BC, Canada, V6H 4J6

604-688-0320 / 1-877-688-0320
info@granvilleislandpublishing.com
www.granvilleislandpublishing.com

To my grandparents, who settled in southern Alberta just after the turn of the twentieth century, to farm near Brant, as did my parents, who 'let' me run the machinery.

Karen

A Message to Our Readers

These letters were written between 1891 and 1892, during the era of New Imperialism, at a time of European colonial expansion, and contain some racist comments about Indigenous peoples and others of various cultures; they were as wrong then as they are now.

Acknowledgements

The skilled hands, keen eyes, and purveyors of thoughtful support and professional assistance behind the building of this book are many. All of those we have relied upon are very much appreciated for their enthusiasm, curiosity and wisdom. Researchers and aides at various archives were invaluable in assisting us with providing photographs and hard-to-find documents. Starting with the Amsterdam City Archives and the McCord Museum in Montreal, we later found ourselves chatting with librarians at the State Library of Western Australia and corresponding with the Hampshire Genealogical Society in the UK, both making it possible to trace many names of people who played a strong role in the story.

This is especially so in Alberta, where we received advice and assistance from the archivists or curators at the Esplanade Arts & Historical Centre in Medicine Hat, the Galt Museum and Archives in Lethbridge, the University of Calgary, the Edmonton City Archives, the Lougheed House in Calgary, the Whyte Museum at Banff, and the archivist of the town of Wetaskiwin. Too many to mention are the folks that have developed helpful and informative websites, often about family or local history. One special mention goes to David Paley, who aided us by sharing his passion for French poetry.

Our friends have done what friends do — Ted Bal built the maps; Jan's sister, Nienke, helped with French translation and added her pointed critiques; and our dear friend Helen Hall listened a lot and read a lot of pages that needed a lot of changes. Their support has been invaluable.

To finish, we are grateful to work with the team of professionals at Granville Island Publishing, benefitting from their essential advice, editing and artistic flair.

Contents

Preface	xiii
Introduction	xvii
Chapter 1 All the Way to Canada!	1
Chapter 2 Our Land of Promise	19
Chapter 3 To the Far North-West on Velvet Couches	35
Chapter 4 Last Town on the Rail Line	57
Chapter 5 How Heleen Meets the Doctor in Pincher Creek	81
Chapter 6 Stake-Marker in the Crowsnest	119

Chapter 7
Forty Miles through the Snow   147

Chapter 8
Our Plan in Disarray!   181

Chapter 9
To a Convent and Dancing in Edmonton   209

Chapter 10
The Benevolence of Bigwigs   249

Reference to Volume 2   263

Images List   265

Archive Inventory List   269

Bibliography   271

Index   275

22d Decb. 91

Dear Sir,

Every time that I pass your name on an address or that I send one of your kind telegrams to my cousin at London, I think of your friendliness towards my son and daughter, who have found in you such a true staunch support in their Canadian experience.

They have really met with such a kind reception and assistance that I think Canada unrivalled as an abode of true hospitality.

We were glad to see that the main object of my son's voyage appears to have been attained, and that his health is much improved, which enables him to do his work under apparently difficult circumstances of climate and surroundings.

I took the liberty to address

A. R. Hosmer Esq
   Montreal

to you per [...]
for my dau[...]
presents, a[...]
for yourself [...]
of one of ou[...]
which genera[...]
the wherefo[...]
sweet wind[...]

The agent[...]
for deliver[...]
so that I [...]
get them a[...]
without any [...]
but should [...]
my daughte[...]
charge yo[...]
her box or y[...]

Believe m[...]
With kind [...]
for a happ[...]

Dear Sir,

Every time that I put your name on an address or that I read one of your kind telegrams to my cousin in London, I think of your friendliness towards my son and daughter, who have found in you such a true, staunch support in their Canadian experiences.

They have really met with such a kind reception and assistance that I think Canada unrivalled as an abode of true hospitality.

We were glad to see that the main object of my son's voyage appears to have been attained, and that his health is much improved, which enables him to do his work under apparently difficult circumstances of climate and surroundings.

I took the liberty to address to you per parcel express a box for my daughter, containing a few presents, and added to it a box for yourself containing a few specimens of one of our national industries, which generally finds favour when the cheerful bowl is mixed in the social wintertime.

The agents have got all particulars for declaration at the customs [exchange] so that I hope you will get them delivered at your house without any charge whatsoever, but should this not be the case, my daughter will reimburse any charge you might have paid on her box or yours.

Believe me, dear sir, with kind regard and best wishes for a happy Christmas and New Year.

Yours truly,

J. Boissevain

KLAB09193000021
[Jan Boissevain to Charles R. Hosmer, Esq., Montreal, Telegraph Manager, Canadian Pacific Railway]
Amsterdam, December 22, 1891

At Crow's Nest Pass

At Crow's Nest Pass the mountains rend
Themselves apart, the rivers wend
A lawless course about their feet,
And breaking into torrents beat
In useless fury where they blend
At Crow's Nest Pass.

The nesting eagle, wise, discreet,
Wings up the gorge's lone retreat
And makes some barren crag her friend
At Crow's Nest Pass.

Uncertain clouds, half-high, suspend
Their shifting vapours, and contend
With rocks that suffer not defeat;
And snows, and suns, and mad winds meet
To battle where the cliffs defend
At Crow's Nest Pass.

Emily Pauline Johnson

Preface

It was a small advertisement embellished with a pair of maple leaves in a Dutch daily newspaper that caught my attention. It was 1968, and Europe was rife with student uprisings and protests, such as those against the so-called Old Establishment and its conservative morals and attitudes. The advertisement was aimed at young people with a trade who could then live and work in Canada for one to two years. Then and there, I made a life-changing decision and took the bold step of accepting Canada's invitation. That same summer, Calgary became my new hometown.

While working in the food department at the Foothills Hospital, I was encouraged by one of the dieticians to pursue higher education. So, I went back to school (grateful for Canada's accessible education system) and I was eventually admitted to the University of Calgary. There, in the fall of 1972, I had the great fortune to meet (the late) Professor Herman Ganzevoort, one of the foremost authorities on Dutch Canadian history. After completing my degree in economics, I worked at a Canadian bank, which provided me the opportunity to become the bank manager in Resolute Bay.

A few years later, I returned to the Netherlands, where I completed a master's program in history at the University of Leiden. After obtaining my degree, I received an unexpected call from Herman asking whether I would be interested in writing a book about the first coordinated group of Dutch immigrants to Canada, who were to settle in Winnipeg, Manitoba. This was organized by the Committee for Immigration, its members being affiliated with the Dutch Reformed Church.

Accepting Herman's offer, I published my first book, *100 Years Ago: Dutch Immigration to Manitoba in 1893*. That was the first time that I happened to come across the name Boissevain, in documents regarding financial support for the Canadian Pacific Railway (CPR). It was not until I was doing research for my second book, *An Amicable Friendship* (published in 2003), that I came across a short but intriguing news story in the *Montreal Gazette*, dated September 10, 1895, announcing the appointment of Charles (Karel) D. W. Boissevain "from Amsterdam" as the new Consul in Canada, representing the Kingdom of Holland. The article further mentioned that William Cornelius Van Horne, then President of the CPR, had, in late October 1891, recommended Karel to work with a survey crew in the Crowsnest Pass area of southwestern Alberta. It was noted that Karel, who suffered from asthma, was "recruiting his health" and that Van Horne had said to him, "What you want is a course of Northwest air."

To my astonishment, I also discovered a tiny announcement in the *Calgary Daily Herald*, dated November 2, 1891, that included "K. [Karel] Boissevain and Miss H. [Heleen] Boissevain, Amsterdam" in the list of arrivals at the Alberta Hotel. To my great disappointment, and despite my piqued curiosity, further details of their stay and movements in Alberta (especially the details about Heleen's activities) escaped my grasp.

Shortly after the publication of my fourth book, *Dutch Gentlemen Adventurers* (published in 2014 and co-written with Herman), while strolling around Amsterdam I made an unexpected stop at De Bazel, the monumental building that houses the Amsterdam City Archives. While there, I could not resist a quick online search for the name Boissevain and the connection to Alberta, which was still on my mind. To my great surprise and joy, the search resulted in a list of letters written by members of the Boissevain family to and from Canada. After scanning through a few of their letters from 1891, which mentioned Montreal and Alberta, it was immediately clear to me that this was unique material. There was no question in my mind that this would be my next project.

The times when one could hole oneself up at a rickety desk in an archive are fading away. It was once a joy to sift through boxes of fragile, musty old documents that an author had once carefully penned, or to read strange handwriting with no tools other than a magnifying glass. Under new archival policies, the Boissevain letters were now only available in digitized form. This meant scrolling through the collection of documents and photographs from a desk at home, downloading hundreds of pages (from 215 letters!) and adapting to the modern way of revealing this wonderous tale.

Throughout the process of translation (which meant first typing out the contents of the original documents in Dutch), one develops a profound respect for the words and feelings of the writers; one dreads misjudgment or misinterpretation. In that way, the greatest challenge of translation is the preservation of the 'voice' of the writer. Our goal was to translate the Dutch into English, paying close attention to the culture, meaning, style and undertones of words and phrases. (A few poems written in Dutch, or short expressions in French and German, have, for the most part, not been translated.)

The small gaps in the letters here and there are the inevitable result of being unable to read what was written, whether due to damaged or aging paper or, of course, illegible handwriting. Overall, we have tried to keep as close as possible to the tenor of the letters.

Some letters included in this volume are incomplete and noted as fragments, while others refer to letters that were not found in the archives. Despite these relatively minor gaps, the existing letters contain such a wealth of personal, delightful and fascinating historical content that I felt compelled to share them with a wider public. These intimate letters, which the Boissevain family themselves had carefully preserved, are not only edifying but a pleasure to read. They are also, in the words of the late Professor Ganzevoort, "a great new historical resource in the jigsaw puzzle of history."

We hope that the authors of these letters, whose innermost thoughts we have disclosed, would have approved of the result.

The translation, a worthy, oft-times spirited, log-rolling exercise, I accomplished along with my loving wife, Karen, an Albertan, whose unwavering commitment made this publication possible.

Jan Krijff

Introduction

The letters of Charles Daniel Walrave (Karel) Boissevain and his sister Helena Mensina (Heleen)[1] about their year-long experience together in Canada have all the earmarks of a movie script — dramatic twists, hilarious anecdotes, unforeseen adventures, plenty of gossip and even a multinational love story.

It begins at home in Amsterdam, in the mid-autumn of 1891. Karel's asthma has reached such a severe state that, according to their family doctor, Constant Charles Delprat,[2] his best option is to "cut anchor and run" to Canada, as soon as possible, to recover his health. This is devastating news for Karel, his family and especially for his young fiancée, Willemina (Wil or Wim) de Vos, who must stay behind. Worry and anxiety about Karel's ill health, along with uncertainty for his future, are first and foremost on everyone's mind, so keeping in touch is essential. The way they do this is by frequent letter-writing.

The family was well educated, capable of expressing themselves clearly and producing informative letters. They were also able to afford both the postal costs as well as the cost of an occasional telegram. For Wil, Karel's departure is overwhelming and she desperately clings to this lifeline of letters to sustain her own health and heart. This is also true for Karel and Heleen's parents, Jan Boissevain and Petronella

---

[1] See Genealogy of Lucas Bouyssavy: www.boissevain.org, or https://www.genealogieonline.nl/stamboom-boissevain.

[2] Constant Charles Delprat (1854–1934): a well-known family physician; married in 1888 to Catharina Elisabeth Reijnvaan (1859-1954).

(Nella) Brugmans, especially since their daughter has accompanied her brother across the Atlantic. Their commitment to remaining connected to each other during the long separation gives rise to their regular and extensive correspondence.

As with all great stories, the setting (or in this case, various settings) is as much a part of the story as the conversations among the letter writers. In 1891, Amsterdam was a city that had rapidly grown from a population of 240,000 in 1860 to one of 430,000 in 1890.[3] Between 1880 and 1890, tens of thousands of people moved to the city in the midst of an economic crisis that had severely affected the countryside and northern provinces, more so than Amsterdam. Even though there was a better chance of finding work in the big city, unemployment increased and many people lived marginally in crowded and impoverished neighbourhoods.

To improve its dire housing and economic circumstances, Amsterdam began to focus on planning and redevelopment. This was realized not only by the building of new housing for the working class, but also through the creation of new neighbourhoods for the middle class. It became a new era for burgeoning commercial ventures, with newly developed districts for shopping (such as those in the city centre), as well as for factories and light industry. Ambitious and rapid growth also included the new building for the Rijksmuseum (1885), known for its collection of seventeenth-century paintings by Dutch masters; the now world-renowned Concertgebouw (1888) and the Amsterdam Centraal train station (1889).

This bustling and noisy city soon became home to an influential movement in the arts, spurred on by a literary group called the Tachtigers.[4] Drawing from the Impressionist movement in France, they were writers and poets who pushed for new forms and genres of literature and poetry, eschewing formality and championing the use of raw emotions in writing. Similarly, Dutch painters such as Vincent van Gogh and George Hendrik Breitner were also moving away from the old formality by instead focusing their attention on the common people. It is clear that Karel and Heleen were drawn to this movement, making many references and comments in their letters regarding the writings of the Tachtigers, as well as the up-and-coming painters of the new style.

During this period of social change and with the arrival of new commercial talent, fortunes were being made. Entrepreneurs profited through international finance and transit trade, as well as the trade in and processing of products from the various Dutch colonies. Many involved in these business ventures were part of the newly formed, arguably more progressive but certainly enterprising, elite of Amsterdam. By contrast, the old elite was slowly beginning to lose privilege and influence. Many of their trading houses had lost business or had failed due to a ban

---

3   H. Schijff, "Wonen op Stand in de Negentiende-eeuws Amsterdam," *Sociologisch Tijdschrift*, Jaargang 14, nummer 4, febr 1988.

4   Gerben Colmjon, *De beweging van tachtig, Een cultuurhistorisch verkenning in de negentiende eeuw* (Utrecht, Antwerpen: Aula boeken, 1963).

on trade with the United Kingdom during the Napoleonic War (1803–1815). In the aftermath, the movement in world trade had shifted away from Amsterdam to London. Moreover, new national laws pertaining to the operational requirements of municipal governments in the Netherlands were passed in 1851. One such regulation ensured that officials were elected by the citizens and that council meetings were held publicly. This brought to an end the centuries-old practices of nepotism and secrecy, causing the old elite to lose interest in running the city, thereby losing the influence it had once been accustomed to enjoying.

A new class of business leaders emerged who adopted modern business practices, such as new accounting methods and the use of modern steam-powered ships. This particular group of Amsterdammers also formed a new coterie which became closely interrelated through marriage and association. Many lived near each other in the large houses on the canals of Amsterdam's most fashionable areas, and of these, a number also owned country homes in the choicest areas of Holland. The Boissevains, a modern and socially minded family, belonged to this new, prosperous class.

As letters from 'home' often do, the Boissevain letters are filled with family stories and the goings-on of a busy household. Notably, there are numerous references to their Huguenot background, revealing more than a touch of pride about their family history. Their roots can be traced back to Lucas Bouyssavy, a Huguenot, who arrived in Amsterdam in 1691. He had fled the village of Couze, near Bergerac, in France, as one of thousands of refugees escaping the persecution of Protestants by the Catholic Church. Bouyssavy later became well established in Dutch society, as did many of the Huguenots who had also fled to the Netherlands. By 1891, the name Boissevain was attached to businesses such as shipping, banking, politics and newspapers. In light of this, the branches of this famous family tree now extend to many corners of the world, including Canada.

The letters also serve as a reminder of the consequential role that Dutch bankers played in the financing of North American railroads during the latter half of the nineteenth century. Among the illustrious cast of characters that appear in the letters, and a key figure in this story, is the banker A. Adolphe H. Boissevain,[5] Jan Boissevain's

[1] A. Adolphe H. Boissevain

5 Athanase Adolphe Henri (Adolf or Adolphe) Boissevain (1843–1921): second cousin of Heleen and Karel; banker and financier; owner of Adolphe Boissevain & Co. in Amsterdam and New York. He invested in the Bell Farm at Indian Head, Saskatchewan, established in 1882. (See Bell Barn Society, https://bellbarn.ca/.) He married Ottoline Henriette toe Laer (1844–1921).

cousin, referred to (only by the family) as Count Adolphe. Adolphe likely played a role in the decision for Karel to go to Canada, and his influence may well have reached those who held Karel's fate in their hands.

For some time, the Boissevain name had already been known to the residents of what is now known as the Golden Square Mile in Montreal. Adolphe's reputation spanned the international world of finance as early as 1879, when he was involved in the placement of a loan on behalf the Province of Quebec through the New York branch of the firm Adolphe Boissevain and Co.[6] In light of this transaction, he became known to the Bank of Montreal and, consequently, to the executive of the Canadian Pacific Railway. It was Adolphe's firm that supplied desperately needed financing for the struggling CPR in 1883, upon an appeal by its president at the time, Sir George Stephen[7] (formerly president of the Bank of Montreal). Stephen's appeal was directed to his "Amsterdam friends [who] were the first Europeans to invest in CPR shares . . .," thereby investing in what became known as the "second transnational railroad."[8] For this commitment, Adolphe was honoured by the CPR in 1885, when the Boissevain name was attached to a new settlement in southern Manitoba.[9] The CPR also named the village of Bienfait, Saskatchewan (incorporated on April 15, 1912) for Antoine Charles Bienfait,[10] a partner at Adolphe Boissevain & Co., Amsterdam.

Having pitched in during that period of financial strain in 1883, Adolphe also fostered what became a close relationship with William Cornelius Van Horne,[11] who succeeded Stephen as the president of the CPR in 1889. This friendship helped to facilitate introductions for Heleen and Karel, giving them access to some of the families of the upper echelons and new elites in Canada. Among these contacts were other top brass of the CPR in Montreal and some of the movers and shakers in Alberta.

This, however, was not the first time that Van Horne had given a helping hand to the Boissevains. In 1883, René R. H. toe Laer,[12] a brother of Adolphe's wife, Ottoline toe Laer, was appointed by the CPR as Agent for

---

6   *Algemeen Handelsblad*, April 9, 1879.

7   George Stephen, 1st Baron Mount Stephen (1829–1921): businessman, philanthropist, financier, president of Bank of Montreal, first president of the CPR.; first marriage to Lady Annie Charlotte Kane (1830–1896); second marriage to Lady Georgiana Mary (Gian) Tufnell (1862–1933).

8   See William Kaye Lamb, *History of the Canadian Pacific Railway* (New York: MacMillan, 1977), 93.

9   After an amalgamation in 2015, it became part of the municipality of Boissevain-Morton.

10 Antoine Charles Bienfait (1857–1899): banker; married to Marie Jeanne van Hemert (1868–1933).

11 William Cornelius Van Horne (1843–1915): president of the CPR; lived at the Van Horne mansion in Montreal's Golden Square Mile with his wife Lucy Adaline Hurd (1837–1929), daughter Lucy Adaline (Addie) Van Horne (1868–1941) and son Richard Benjamin (Bennie) Van Horne (1877–1931).

12 René Robbert Herman toe Laer (1843–1906): director of the Equitable, a life insurance company; first marriage in 1872 to Mildred Pollard Gaines (?–1880); second marriage in 1882 to Flora Christina Louisa de Jong van 't Woud (1863–1940). See Jan Th. J. Krijff, *Een Aengenaeme Vrientschap (An Amicable Friendship), A collection of Historical events between the Netherlands and Canada from 1862–1914* (Toronto: Abbeyfield Publishers, 2003), 125–6.

the European Continent. And at the Montreal harbour in 1884, Van Horne personally welcomed Daniel François Boissevain,[13] a nephew of Adolphe's who had purchased a quarter-section of land in Saskatchewan from the CPR, where he established Hilversum Farm, near the settlement of Cannington Manor. Heleen and Karel had probably heard about these family connections, but it seems unlikely that they had ever considered going to Canada for any reason.

Amsterdammers from birth, Karel (1866) and Heleen (1867) were two of the nine children of Jan (1836) and Nella (1838). Their eldest child, Gideon (1863), died in a tragic accident in 1881.[14] The other children, whose names appear often in the letters, from eldest to youngest, are Elisabeth (Li, 1864), Matthijs (Thijs, 1870), Anna (An, 1872), Petronella (Nel, 1873), Walrave (Wallie, 1876) and Maria (Mia or Miep, 1878).[15]

Nella was the daughter of Anthonie Brugmans, an Amsterdam lawyer and member of the senate of the Dutch parliament, and Elisabeth van Maanen, a daughter of the former Minister of Justice, Cornelis Felix van Maanen.

13   Daniel François Boissevain (1856–1929): farmer and rancher; married in 1886 to Alberta Mary Carman (1867–1894), who was originally from Newfoundland and with whom he had five children. In 1895, he married and divorced Mina MacFarland (1860–?) and in 1914, married Elisabeth Mary Ellis (1858–1929). See also Krijff, *An Amicable Friendship*, 128.

14   Gideon Jeremie Boissevain died on Thursday, August 18, 1881, in Amsterdam, after losing his footing and falling between the wharf and the *Prins van Oranje*, one of the ships of his father's shipping line. His body was recovered from the harbour the next day.

15   See footnote 1, Genealogy Boissevain.

[2] The Boissevain children: (standing, L–R) An, Karel, Heleen; (sitting, L–R) Thijs, Nel, Li, Mia; (reclining) Wallie

Within the family circle, Nella was known for being socially conscious and active, particularly in helping poor and disadvantaged families in Amsterdam. Once a week, from the house, she would hand out turf coupons (to be exchanged for turf used for heating and cooking), brown and white beans, and flour to a procession of those in need. This was simply part and parcel of her Christian upbringing. She also succeeded in handing down her passion for social justice to her children, some of whom became very active in social welfare. In many ways, Nella was a modern mother, especially for her girls, whom she encouraged to pursue their individual interests. She supported their independence, both intellectually and socially. For example, in 1899 Li became the first director of the Opleidingsinstituut voor Sociale Arbeid, the first school of social work in Amsterdam. Mia, the youngest, earned her PhD in biology in Zurich in 1903 at the age of twenty-five, one of the earliest women in the Netherlands to do so. Mia became a strong advocate for women's rights and played a lead role in organizing the 1915 International Congress of Women in The Hague.

Jan's mother, Maria van Heukelom, was the daughter of the banker Walrave van Heukelom. His father, Gideon Jeremie Boissevain, was the head of Boissevain & Co., which owned a relatively modest fleet of cargo ships and maintained a shipping route with the then Dutch East Indies. Eventually becoming the head of his father's shipping company, Jan initiated a new company in 1870, De Stoomvaart Maatschappij Nederland (SMN), which was known locally as the De Nederland. Under Jan's competent ownership, the firm reinvented itself for the new age, building a fleet of modern and fast steamships. He also proved to possess an enviable combination of shrewdness and diplomacy, successfully obtaining lucrative mail and freight contracts from the Dutch government. After its first lean years, the SMN became a large and profitable shipping company, with significant interests in the Dutch East Indies. Jan's letters reveal a man of considerable influence, well known in both commercial and the highest of political circles, as well as a board member of several social organizations. This busy life appeared in no way to interfere with his deep commitment to his family. His love for his wife and all of his children was often expressed with great feeling in his many letters to Karel and Heleen in

[3] Jan Boissevain and Petronella (Nella) Boissevain, née Brugmans

Canada. The letters also reveal a special bond between Jan and his clever daughter Heleen. As Karel put it, she and their father were "connected intellectually." While in Canada, Heleen was also determined to keep up to date on all that was happening in Holland, as well as to provide her father, in particular, with important updates on Karel's status.

As a young girl, Heleen attended elementary school, followed by the Fransche School. It was a private school providing secondary education for girls from the upper class; the language of instruction was French, with a focus on languages, history and geography. From the letters, it is clear that Heleen later became interested in medicine (she even considered doing some nursing work in Montreal) and that she had received some training in nursing.[16]

At home, the Boissevain children were surrounded by books, and Heleen certainly kept up to date by reading literature, poetry, newspapers and writings about politics and social movements. She also played the piano and was multilingual, which was an important part of her education and upbringing. Heleen's command of English was very good, evidenced by her easy way of mingling with the Canadians, most of whom only spoke English. Perhaps learning English was encouraged by the family's British nanny. Heleen had also mastered French and German and was studying Greek; her letters are clearly those of an intelligent and well-informed young woman.

Born one year before Heleen, a bit more is known of Karel's early years. After his primary schooling, he pursued a career in the navy, signing up as a Naval Cadet 3rd Class in September of 1880, at the age of fourteen. He spent about ten years in the navy, serving for a time in the Dutch East Indies, and was awarded a medal, the Expedition Cross, for his war service in Atjeh.[17] The records also show that a new assignment as Lieutenant 2nd Class aboard the HMS *Wachtschip* in Hellevloetsluis was cancelled on February 26, 1891. On June 1, 1891, Karel was granted a one-year leave of absence. This was followed by an honourable discharge as a Lieutenant 2nd Class on October 16, 1891,[18] shortly after his departure for Canada. Karel's very evident love of poetry and literature, frequently appearing in his letters, was likely fostered at home, and his facility with languages may well have been enhanced through his extensive training (in many disciplines) as a naval officer. Nevertheless, his true passion was writing.

[4] Helena (Heleen) Boissevain, wearing the fur hat

16   Her training was most likely completed at the Buitengasthuis, a hospital in Amsterdam, run by Dr. Jacob van Deventer and Johanna Paulina Reijnvaan. See also footnote 466 regarding Reijnvaan's book.

17   The Aceh (*Atjeh*) War (1873–1904) was a military conflict between the Kingdom of the Netherlands and the Sultanate of Aceh, at the northern tip of the island of Sumatra.

18   *De Tijd: godsdienstig-staatkundig dagblad*, p. 2, October 16, 1891.

Before ending his active service in April of 1891, Karel had become engaged to marry Willemina (Wil) de Vos. Wil was born in Amsterdam in 1869, into a family that belonged to the same coterie as the Boissevains. Indeed, both families even lived on the same canal, the Keizersgracht, the de Voses at #182 and the Boissevains at #717. Wil's late father, Hendrik de Vos, had been a partner of de Vos & Zoon, a firm established in 1750, which operated as an assurance broker and damage-claims assessor for foreign insurance companies. Wil's mother, Cornelia Leembruggen,[19] was born into a wealthy family of textile manufacturers in Leiden. Hence, Wil was used to prosperity, living in a grand house with her mother and two older sisters, Jo[20] and Cor,[21] supported by a staff of servants. There is little to find about Wil's life as a young girl, but is it easy to conclude that she was well educated, evidenced by her prowess with multiple languages and her musical talent. As a young woman of high social standing, she was also a seasoned traveller, having been to Italy, Germany, Switzerland and, in the summer of 1892, to Latvia (then part of Russia). This life of luxury travel in Europe, which included visiting spas and staying in grand hotels, came to an end when fate forced her fiancé to leave home, and with it came the possibility of settling down on the other side of the world, in Canada.

19 Cornelia Leembruggen (1844–1909): married to Willem Hendrik de Vos (1842–1878).

20 Johanna (Jo) Willemina von Möller de Vos (1867–1934), was married in 1889 to Friedrich Nikolai Otto von Möller (1854–1924). They lived in Villa Solitude in what is now Meijermuiža, near Wenden (now Cēsis), in Latvia, which was then part of Russia. They divorced and in 1909 Jo married Johan Constant Prins (1879–1957); they divorced April 25, 1916.

21 Cornelia (Cor) de Vos (1871–1945) married Carel Julius Prins (1884–1972), a dentist, in 1909; they divorced April 5, 1916.

[5] Willemina (Wil) de Vos and Charles D. W. (Karel) Boissevain

Why Delprat had suggested Canada as the place for Karel to recoup his health was a mystery for Karel, since, at that time, Switzerland was already en vogue as a location for the European elite to convalesce. It is also not clear how it was that Heleen came to be Karel's travelling companion. Was this decision initiated by her parents? Was it duty-driven or did it simply arise out of affection for her brother? The letters suggest that she may have just been the best equipped to care for him, given her nursing training and, perhaps, her strength of character.

Getting to Canada was the least of their problems. Indeed, it was a leisurely first-class voyage on a modern steamship from Liverpool to Montreal. Travelling within Canada, however, was quite a different cup of tea. While Van Horne had ensured that they were taken care of by the CPR — which provided luxury coaches for many of their long journeys — after only a few nights at the Alberta Hotel,[22] recuperating from a brief illness, it was high time for Karel to head south to join the CPR survey crew. Heleen joined Karel on his long journey by train and stagecoach southward to Fort Macleod, about 180 kilometres away, where he would connect with the survey crew that had left Calgary a few days before, bound for the Oldman River.

One of the most enjoyable aspects of poring over letters is discovering how the personalities of the writers are reflected on the pages. Karel was an aspiring writer, or at least a prolific one. He could at once write detailed descriptions about places and people while simultaneously, and in sharp contrast, sharing his personal thoughts and imaginings in an often labyrinthian manner. His new role as a survey stake-marker was not easy sailing. Karel now found himself working with men who were used to the rigours of physical labour, often in temperatures well below zero. When he had enough ink on hand, he produced letters about the starkly primitive conditions of a survey camp in the Crowsnest Pass area of southwestern Alberta. He included within his stories a few small sketches showing floor plans of the tents, minute details of the process of surveying for a railroad line, and descriptions about crossing icy rivers in the challenging terrain. He also peppered his letters with the names of many famous and infamous locals. Under the guiding hand of railroad engineer Noel Brooks[23] of Sherbrooke, Quebec, Karel does indeed learn a bit about surveying and eventually earns his stripes, so to speak. At the time, Karel could not have foreseen that the back-breaking work of the survey crew along the north side of the Oldman River was ultimately in vain. The proposed route for the railroad was eventually shifted to the south side of the river in 1898 and was completed the following year.

Leaving Karel to rough it in various survey campsites, Heleen enjoyed the hospitality offered to her by some of the most prominent people of

---

22   See announcement "K. Boissevain, Miss H. Boissevain, Amsterdam" among the list of hotel arrivals, *Calgary Daily Herald*, November 2, 1891.

23   Noel Edgell Brooks (1865–1926): CPR division engineer and Karel's boss; married to Marion Ryley (1863–1946).

the region. Her travels to various towns in southern Alberta, as well as to visit Karel at different campsites, were made possible by stalwart stagecoach drivers and 'seasoned' buggy drivers, along with occasional escorts by the Northwest Mounted Police. This sort of travel, for a woman alone in that era, was considered all novel and modern,[24] but still may have been whispered about by the more conservative. Heleen's letters provide a distinctive perspective into the lives and lifestyles of wealthy ranchers and city dwellers, of those living in harrowing conditions on First Nations reserves, and of nuns in a convent northwest of Edmonton, in what is now known as St. Albert.

A welcome element in the letters are Heleen's views about the women that she met in her travels, one of whom, Kathleen Wilkins[25] of Calgary, became her close friend. Many of the women about whom Heleen writes have rarely been mentioned before in historical documents, perhaps overshadowed by stories about their husbands. The apparent dearth of writings about women of this time period applies equally to women in both Canada and the Netherlands. For this reason, the footnotes contain the names of all the women they met, as well as names of the wives of the men that are mentioned in the correspondence. Heleen's letters also resonate with some earlier writings about Canada by women of means. Perhaps the most comparable in tone and style are the memoirs of Irish-born writer and feminist Anna Brownell Murphy Jameson (1794–1860), who fully and pointedly related her experiences while living in eastern Canada in 1838.[26]

The frequent letters that Heleen and Karel received from Jan, as well as the precious few from Nella, are both supportive and instructive, while demonstrating a tireless devotion to the welfare of all of their children. Despite their worries about "the odyssey of the Canadian Boissevains," they ensured that Karel and Heleen were privy to the stories of family life back in Amsterdam. Their letters give a glimpse of the social activities and the circumstances and circles in which the whole family lived back home. There are tales of the siblings' ups and downs, the vicissitudes of grade-school life, the culture of a university fraternity, and the preparations for social gatherings, all experiences which differ from today, though only in setting and style.

Many stories from Jan and Nella are about their wide circle of family and friends, both in Holland and abroad. Jan's personality emerges through his letters, not only as a devoted father but also as the ultimate 'rainmaker'. With a huge network of business contacts, including close

---

24 Lillias Campbell Davidson, *Hints to Lady Travellers* (London: Lliffe & Sons., 1889). See also Lady Ishbel Aberdeen, Countess of Aberdeen, *Through Canada with a Kodak* (Edinburgh: W. H. White & Co., 1893).

25 Katherine (Kathleen) Hollingsworth (1867–1942), in 1891, married Ernest Drummond-Hay Wilkins (1859–1938), then a railway mail clerk who later became a lawyer. They lived in Wetaskiwin, Alberta.

26 Jameson's letters are published in a book by Gerardine Bate Macpherson, *Memoirs of the Life of Anna Jameson* (Boston: Roberts Bros., 1878). See also M. Susan Birkwood, "Different sides of the picture: Four Women's Views of Canada, 1816–1838," Faculty of Graduate Studies (London: The University of Western Ontario, January 1997); Rachel Herbert, *Ranching Women in Southern Alberta* (Calgary: University of Calgary Press, 2017); and Lady Ishbel Aberdeen, *Through Canada with a Kodak*.

relationships with those in the highest levels of government, he writes candidly about his business dealings, thereby giving insight into how he so successfully managed his shipping company. Along with the serious bits of news about business, Jan also displays his sense of humour and his calm directness. With Heleen, he also privately reveals his concerns about Karel's future, greatly valuing her good sense. In contrast, the letters written by Nella are very sparse; information about her activities and well-being were usually to be found in letters written by others. Not surprisingly, she was worried for the safety of her daughter in that dangerous land and, of course, Karel and Wil's relationship.

Throughout this time, Wil was waiting in the wings — or rather, under the wings of Jan and Nella and, of course, her own family. Her longing for news of Karel, and from Karel, was often too much to bear. The frequent letters to her from Heleen, who was so faithful about ensuring that Wil was kept as up to date as possible, were a godsend. The poignant few (sometimes lengthy and almost illegible) letters from Karel that arrived in Amsterdam from the Crowsnest were nearly all that Wil needed to keep her going. Despite her youth, and through her strength of character and her own strong social circle, she faithfully wrote long chatty letters, giving both Karel and Heleen news of home, her adventures, funny stories, her family and a great deal of comfort.

Heleen stayed on the prairies for nearly the entire winter of 1891–92, experiencing the severity of the cold and admiring the power of the warm Chinook winds. Just before Christmas, she said goodbye to Karel and her new friends in the southern prairies to settle for the next few months in Calgary. There, she stayed once again in the relative luxury of the Alberta Hotel,[27] a sandstone building that still stands today. These early days of this posh hotel have been described by others as a "male mecca," especially for well-to-do cattle ranchers and businessmen, from whom Heleen took great pains to distance herself when they gathered in the lounge. Maybe this is the reason that during her stay in Calgary, Heleen doesn't mention the name of Meinard Sprenger,[28] one of the ranching businessmen who was often in town. He was a wealthy, educated Dutchman who ran a real estate business out of his 'office' at the Royal Hotel (a few short blocks away) and also owned the Domburg Ranch at Carseland, sixty-seven kilometers southeast of Calgary, bordering the Siksika Nation.[29]

As time went on, Heleen's 'enthusiasm' for Calgary waned. With the news that Karel would be soon leaving his position at the camp, she was

---

27   The Alberta Hotel, a luxury hotel, opened in 1890, and although it is no longer a hotel, it remains as one of the oldest structures in present-day Calgary, located at the corner of 804 First Street SW. See *Alberta Register of Historic Places*, Alberta Hotel, Calgary: https://hermis.alberta.ca/ARHP/Details.aspx?DeptID=1&ObjectID=4664-0255.

28   Meinard Jacob Iman Sprenger (1860–1951), born in Middelburg and died in Oostkapelle, the Netherlands, was a rancher and early Calgary real estate owner best known for his collection of First Nations artifacts from the Blackfoot, now housed in the Zeeuws Museum in Middelburg. In 1904 he married Monica Agnes Pitcaoin Duncan (c.1877–c.1968).

29   The Siksika (Blackfoot) Nation is one of the four Indigenous nations of the Siksikaitsatapi (Blackfoot Confederacy), whose traditional territory is the northwestern plains of North America.

on the train back to Montreal by March 1, 1892. Karel was expected to arrive a few weeks later.

Perhaps the writers of these letters could not have imagined that their correspondence would survive for 130 years, let alone turn out to be of historical relevance, providing a wealth of new, often personal, insights into the lives of many pioneers of Canada at the end of the nineteenth century. Their letters reveal a stark contrast between the powerful elites in eastern Canada and the rising influential entrepreneurs of the North-West Territories. The events they describe and people they mention have formed part of the world that we now live in. Moreover, this is a personal story. It is about their lives and family in Amsterdam and the people they met in Canada, those who helped them and those who hosted them — from the humble to the high and mighty.

Letters are among the most significant memorial a person can leave behind.

— Johan Wolfgang von Goethe

Chapter 1

All the Way to Canada!

Karel breaks the sad news to Wil and, making their tearful goodbyes, Karel and Heleen, accompanied by Jan and Nella, travel from Amsterdam (via the port at Vlissingen) to London, where the siblings board the Sardinian in Liverpool, bound for Montreal.

KLAB04554000171-172 [Karel to Wil]
Amsterdam, September 28, 1891

Dear, Dear Wim,

You must prepare yourself for a huge disappointment that lies ahead for both of us. My health, which, up until now, I thought to be very robust despite slight indispositions, appears to be badly undermined.

Yesterday evening I arrived home all right, thoroughly tucked into the carriage with blankets and jackets; I also slept last night with closed windows, again. Thijs was home and we slept in the same room, but it seems that the precautions and prudence no longer help anymore.

I took an early train to town and consulted Delprat. He examined me very thoroughly and found my situation serious, at least in the face of the nearing autumn with the damp and cold, etc.

Papa and Mama are also very upset about it. They had been worried more often than I had, but this, however, they had not expected; it came on so suddenly.

[6] Dr. Constant C. Delprat and Catharina (Coba) Elisabeth Reijnvaan

Mama will come to you at Veenenburg[30] tomorrow to tell you precisely all about it. Then you can even cry out loud together. Have patience until that time, my darling, and keep your spirits high; we need them in order to fulfill our duties, and I trust that we will support each other in this.

Give my regards to Uncle[31] and Miss Doswell,[32] your deeply loving Karel.

KLAB04555000288-289 [Karel to Wil]
From home [Amsterdam], Tuesday morning [September 29, 1891]

My darling, darling Treasure,

Our verdict was pronounced yesterday evening by Delprat. As soon as possible, I must make a sea voyage [to Canada], where I am to stay in the clear air to keep the asthma under control. What this will mean for the two of us, my darling, I dare not to think.

I begged to be sent away to Merano or San Remo,[33] or some place where at least I could see you now and then. It was to no avail. I must now remain in my room and take care not to catch a cold, and I cannot go

---

30 Veenenburg is a country estate in Lisse owned by Willem Leembruggen (1851–1899).

31 Willem Leembruggen is a brother of Wil's mother; married to Alida van Embden (1854–1898).

32 Jane Doswell (1833–?): born in Beckington, Somerset, England; housekeeper of the family Leembruggen.

33 Merano is a spa resort in northern Italy and San Remo is an Italian resort town on the Mediterranean Sea.

outside anymore. When we see each other again, it will also be to say "Goodbye."

Oh! Wim, Wim, who could have thought that! I am so sad and hope that I can keep under control so that you can have some support from me in these last days.

It is forbidden for me to talk a lot. The only thing that remains for me to do is to speak with you by this means. And still, I will be so busy these days with preparing for the move that I will hardly have time for a short letter. This one, I will send with Mama. Be brave when you face her. She is also so terribly saddened, and I am so afraid that her nerves will overcome her. Do not succumb to the sorrow and let us remain confident in a better future.

All the way to Canada! How did Delprat come up with that? And I am so afraid that once I am there, I might never be able to return. Let us not fear the worst. Perhaps I will recuperate quickly and you will get back a strong, healthy man. If that is so, then everything might have turned out for the best.

Tomorrow, if we have both calmed down, I would love very much to see you for a moment. I will be up and dressed and can receive you and, even though I am not allowed to say many words, a handshake would not harm me.

Mama must go to the train now. Bye, darling. Do not let your spirits wane and just think, after the rain comes the sunshine.

Bye-bye, sweet Wim; I love you dearly. Your Karel

P.S. Perhaps Heleen will come with me. That would comfort me a bit.

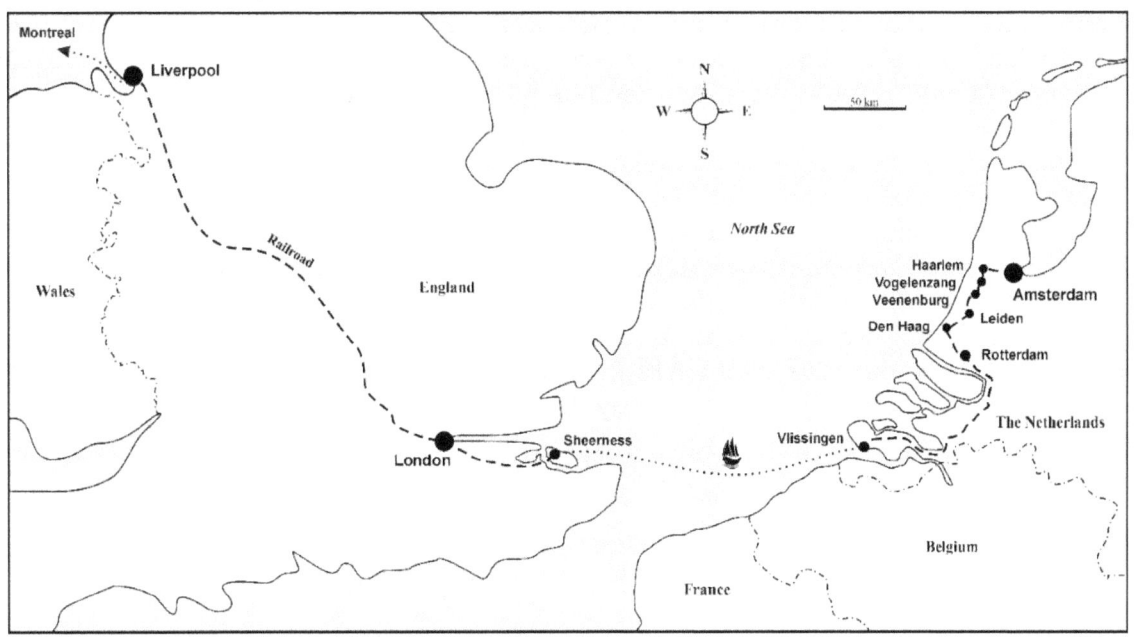

[7] Map: Amsterdam–Vlissingen–Liverpool

A32074000136–137 [Heleen to Wil]
Vlissingen to Sheerness, England, Sunday, October 4, 1891, 3:30 p.m.

Dear Wil,

We had a beautiful crossing, and it seems as if he breathes more freely at sea. Thijs greatly helped us this morning. We saw Nel and Mia in Haarlem and, further along, the three others.[34] At the station in Rotterdam, Hosang[35] and Cornelis[36] joined us in the wagon and rode along until the next station. It did him good to have seen loyal, affectionate friends, if only for just a moment. The sea is now so calm that not even Mama has any hint of sickness. We are sitting cozily together on deck, enjoying the peace, the lovely weather and thinking about you.
    Bye, darling, I will write from London. Bye, dear Willetje, your Heleen.

KLAB04555000173–76 [Karel to Wil]
Royal Hotel London, October 5, 1891

So long as we are still in Europe, I consider our parting not yet a *fait accompli* and will not compromise in my determination to continue with our correspondence.
    I also have a lot to tell you. And even if I hold back everything that would flow out of my pen about gentle words revealing my sorrow and my love, I could still fill many pages with what my mind now proposes to make our situation the least unbearable. Self-composure is therefore our motto, over and above our sorrow, but also the manifestation of our love. I tried to explain this view to you in our last painful conversation, but I fear that I have only succeeded in part. What does your mother say about this?
    On warm days during a long walk in the dunes, Papa tended to forbid we children talk about the heat in the hope that we would think about other things. Therefore, we too must reduce the suffering about my parting by minimizing our lamentation about it. These days, I think, I have given over to it too often and, because of that, I find that I am less resilient, with no strength to rebound, but I will regain my buoyancy. I have to, for the sake of our futures. Also, my dearest, you need a diversion, and I am thinking, that is, racking my brains, about what might be the best way to get a such a diversion.

---

34 The "three others" could refer to their siblings, Li, An and Wallie, the youngest. If so, they may have been at the next train station after Haarlem.

35 Johannes Frederik Hosang (1864–1919): Navy Lieutenant 2nd Class at the time, later retired as Rear Admiral, unmarried.

36 Willem Cornelis (1866–1924): Navy Lieutenant 2nd Class, later obtained the rank of Captain Lieutenant, unmarried.

See, for you, I do not believe in an 'outside distraction' through a change of surroundings, by travel or sport. The best way to express my wish is to say that for each of us, something must be found so that during this time apart, our lives are fulfilled, so fulfilled that the thoughts about each other's own suffering or sorrow is precluded. That, I hope I shall find in Canada in 'the struggle for life', in both direct and indirect ways, that is, in the battle for my health and for my daily bread. And how might you find that?

I wholeheartedly hope [it would be] as a matter of course, not by taking one or another occupation by the horns for the sake of distraction, and because of [the distraction's] own will, it will never absorb you; but through deep reflection upon the seriousness of life, about the calling that every person has in order to contribute their small bit toward the creation of a good society, you shall avoid taking on a task or a small task, not completely avoid — I mean not your whole day — but still give a good part of your big heart toward [the cause]. Or perhaps is this too much to say and not necessary. From a long distance, I cannot influence these decisions in detail, and leave this completely to the wisdom of you and your dear mother.

I am also thinking about her, before I depart from Liverpool. After arriving in Canada, I shall write a few words. Her winter will also be completely different than we had expected. She was very much in a good position to encourage our happiness, often putting aside her own interests and comfort. She has shown herself to be a dear mother in our fortune, so I have no doubt that she will also be of great support during our sorrow.

You will, nevertheless, not completely withdraw from the pleasurable Amsterdam society life. In the beginning, your mind may not be attuned toward dinner talk and theatre flirtations, but I still hope that you will play the role of a 'young and pretty widow'. But now and then, your old laugh shall be heard in the salons of the Herengracht and Keizersgracht and in the foyer of the brothers van Lier.[37] It is not necessary for [your younger sister] Cor to always go out alone; and when you have studied the history and geography of Canada in the mornings and have comforted the suffering of human nature in the afternoons, you deserve an uplifting diversion in the evenings.

I also hope very much that you will keep visiting my parents at their house and that you will become intimate friends with my sisters. They think, I believe, that you have kept strong in the face of great sadness, and they are full of regard for your unselfishness, that you only thought of my affection and not about the distressing collapse of the beautiful house in Spain.[38]

---

37 Known then as the Grand Théâtre in Amsterdam, managed by the Van Lier family.

38 The "collapse of the beautiful house in Spain" is likely a metaphor for Wil's loyalty to Karel and her choice to focus on his feelings instead of on how her world is crumbling around her.

As you have already been informed, our crossing was lovely and my night was reasonably good. Happily, in London there was no fog. To boost my spirits somewhat, I did not stay moping in the hotel, but bravely went out. I spoke little but looked around a lot. Papa and I did not find Cousin Adolphe (who had seven letters of recommendation prepared for me) at his office, only Daan [Gideon].[39] Now, before dinner, Papa and Helena have gone again to him, to thank him and to ask for some more information.

Bye, dear, dear Wimmekind, *deinen Gotte befohlen*, your most loving, Karel.

A29670000032-35 [Heleen to Li]
North Western Hotel, Liverpool, October 6, 1891

Dear Li,

Just a word to let you know that I received your letter of October 4. Mr. Noltenius,[40] a gentle, amiable, grey-haired man, handed it over to us at his office on the third floor — dark stairways, stuffy. At first sight, Liverpool is just as horribly sombre, dirty and ugly as it has always been described; I am glad that we do not have to stay here long, but the journey here was very enjoyable. A delightful salon-carriage, with lunch served while underway. Mama enjoyed it very much and thought it a pity when we reached our destination.

I am really beginning to get used to the idea of Canada. In the cities there, it is very cultured and with pleasant society, especially in Montreal. Yesterday evening, we had a very enjoyable visit from Daan [Gideon] who gave us much courage and loved Canada even more than the United States. There will be a lot of French spoken, and the hospitality great. Papa and I went to Count Adolphe to thank him for the letters of introduction, and also to learn some more about various people.

These days with Papa and Mama are still lovely pauses between the whirlwind of partings and preparations in Amsterdam and being away for such a long time. On board, I also spoke, particularly with Papa, about this, that and the other, like we do once in a while. That has given me much peace, because I believe that Papa no longer sees the future so bleak as in those first moments of bewilderment. Now, during these last days, it constantly surprises me that I still have so few things to ask,

---

39 Daniel (Daan) Gideon Boissevain (1867–1940): nephew of Adolphe, then manager of the office of Blake Boissevain & Co. in London; two marriages, first to Elvira Thekla von Schiller (1882–?) in 1901, divorced in 1923, and second in 1923 to Woutrina Johanna Jacoba de Bordes (1900–1981, Orlando, Fl.). Adolphe Boissevain had formed a partnership with the Blake Brothers and Company of Boston, bankers and brokers.

40 Herman Heinrich Noltenius (1838–1908): agent of Norddeutscher Lloyd; married to Theodora Hermanna Castendyck (1837–1907).

even knowing that once there I will certainly often face difficulties, about which I would love to have advice from Mama and Papa. But I also still enjoy the same feeling of complete security that I always have while travelling with Papa.

I do not write much about Karel's health because there is so little to say about it now. At least he is not worse off than in Amsterdam, and he says that the nights are quite reasonable. Of course, the worst remains, that is, the fear that he will not be careful enough or that another influence or development will worsen his ailment. I am happy, so long as I do not see any symptoms of it.

October 6, 1891: Luckily, he has become a little bit more careful, and slowly he will also get used to all those things that he has to watch out for. He really misses smoking, but he sees for himself that it is better [not to] and that eating makes him much less short of breath.

I had my hair shampooed! A lovely and smart establishment where at least seven ladies were taken care of at the same time by countless neat girls.

Slowly, we have come to the conclusion that it is an extremely lucky moment in time to go to Canada, because all kinds of new and interesting things will be happening there. Among other things, Canada and [East Asia][41] would like to have a faster mail connection, [in particular] between Japan and England, via Vancouver and [Hong Kong]; all of the magazines this week have one or more articles about Canada. How disheartening for Jan Faber[42] that he did not know this. He is nevertheless a good-natured, although strained, young fellow.

Did you folks still do something for Mrs. de Vos' birthday? We had thought about it but did not have the wherewithal to mail congratulations.

Bye, dear Li. I must still thank you for all your trusted help during these last days at home. It was so lovely to leave all that packing to you, and I would never have been able to let anyone other than you have the freedom to do it alone. Now, I have actually done a little bit myself.

In Antoinette's[43] first letter she wrote a great amount that was also intended for you, but I read it only yesterday. Tell her, therefore, that you know that she also wrote to you about her work and so forth.

Much love to everyone, your Heleen.

---

41   The CPR had had shipping service since the 1880s, with routes from Vancouver and Victoria, B.C., to the so-called Far East, the first port of call being Hong Kong. In 1891, the CPR, at Van Horne's behest, reached an agreement with the British government on a contract for subsidized rail–sea mail service between Britain and Hong Kong, via Canada, with a new name, Canadian Pacific Steamship Company (CPSC). See Pieter Pigot, *Sailing Seven Seas: A History of the Canadian Pacific Line* (Toronto: Dundurn Press, 2010).

42   This is likely Johannes (Jan) Arnold (Faber) Boissevain (1854–1918): director of the Hollandsche Stoom-gipsfabriek (plaster manufacture), Amsterdam.

43   Georgina Antoinette Fruin (1864–1929): writer; later lived with Willem Hendrik Cox (1861–1933), a medical doctor and director of the psychiatric hospital in Den Dolder.

KLAB04555000177–78 [Karel to Wil]
Liverpool, October 8, 1891

Dear, dear Wil,

My last word in Europe is a word of farewell for you, just like my last spoken words to Father and Mother will soon be "Give Wil my love."

Soon the irrevocable parting will come and thus begin the big ordeal; so, I will control myself and remain quiet. Let me say again now, dearest darling, that I adore you very, very much.

Wim, I thank you for the lovely time spent at your side; every place that we visited together is a fond reminder, the reminiscing about it a lovely sensation for my soul.

You had asked for my advice about the choice of books that you plan to read. I shall think about it sometime. For now, I suggest Dickens, reread *David Copperfield* and read *Bleak House*. During my journey, I will read *The Old Curiosity Shop*.

But Wim, I did not want to write to you about that. My last words are about our love. In my following letters I shall not write much about it, intentionally avoiding even the mention of it. But I hope that you can read between the lines that which I shall not dare to write. I shall write to you approximately every month.[44]

Farewell, stay brave, and keep on believing in our reunion. Your most loving, Karel.

A32074000138–139 [Heleen to Wil]
On board the *Sardinian* at Moville, Irish coast, October 9, 1891, 7:00 a.m.

Dear Wil,

We are on the grand journey and, initially, it is going quite well. However, during the night he was quite short of breath, but that was not unexpected after all of the misery of the last departure and the horrendous coal smog and commotion in Liverpool. Now, this morning, it is a lot better again; and when you read this, we will already be well out to sea and we are feeling that the longer it takes, the stronger we become. I gave him your letter and it did him a great deal of good. He asked me to sincerely, warmly, thank you: "Wil, Wil, words are so unpleasant when I write to you. I constantly think of the way that I saw you for the last time, so courageous, so strong. Keep it up my darling."

Li and Thijs will make sure that you see their cards. A warm kiss from Heleen.

---

[44] This prescription was on Dr. Delprat's orders.

A28335001453-54 [Heleen to Mother and Father, no salutation]
Sardinian, October 17, 1891

This morning, I walked [the deck] for quite a while, talking with Mr. [J. E.] Gordon,[45] a Scot, not family of the famous general but rather from two other generals. His wife knew Sir William Mackinnon.[46] He also grumbled about the education in English schools, even having a strong Dutch notion about it, wanting to keep his boys at home and letting them go to day school. With much praise, he also told me about the work of Mr. Bernardo[47] in London, who cares for dozens of children taken off the streets every year; all of them who are suitable for it are sent to Canada. There, everything for them is prepared. Many of them are taken in by families of farmers and are then under the oversight of the clergy and the state. Others will go to a colony in the west that was founded by him, where they will be schooled in agriculture and trades. Mr. Bernardo started twenty years ago as a medical student and gets his money from voluntary contributions.

This evening there will be a 'great' entertainment — no, a dreary program, with lots of music, all of it terrible. There are a number of sales clerks, etc., on board who keep the piano going, warm-hearted souls with whom we have no problem. Everyone keeps themselves at a distance so that we, ourselves, must approach them, even though they are all very familiar with each other and sometimes boisterous.

I have not yet told you that the fruit was so wonderful. I have never eaten such big grapes. The pears have lasted and are delightful. The stewardess was nothing if not enthusiastic about them and could not understand that during the bad days, I had no appetite for them.

Saturday evening: We had 'the entertainment' (!) for the benefit of an orphanage in Liverpool. It was organized according to passenger class. The second class was invited to it and all of them showed up. A full house! A just-married music master and his wife had the lion's share and sang and played on all sorts of instruments and in all sorts of styles. In between, I talked a little bit with our Scot, who again was very normal and told me the story of how he and his wife got together. "Love at first sight." Declaration by letter. Refusals, etc., etc. The object of his choice: a bundle of shapeless clothes, like Mrs. D. van Hall,[48] with a face that had once been lovely, but now is drowsy.

45 Source: Passenger list of the *Sardinian*, Montreal, the *Gazette*, p. 8., October 19, 1891.

46 Sir William Mackinnon, 1st Baronet, CIE (1823–1893): ship owner and businessman, with interests in India and East Africa; married to Lady Janet Colquhoun Jameson (c.1834–1894).

47 Thomas Bernardo (1845–1905), born in Ireland, is most often associated with the "home child" movement, moving tens of thousands of homeless, orphaned and poor children to Canada in the late nineteenth century; married to Syrie Louise Elmslie (1842–1944).

48 Debora Cremer Eindhoven (1843–1906): married to Maurits Cornelis van Hall (1836–1900), a lawyer, banker and politician.

[8] Dr. Ernest Black

In the meantime, I am sitting on a bench at the back of the ship, writing. Tomorrow the letters will go with the pilot-boat and I will include this one. Dr. [Ernest] Black[49] will come to Holland at the end of December, or thereabouts, and I shall give him a card with your address.

Perhaps Thijs can take him to Arti[50] or to a sale of paintings. He cares more for new art than for old art and he can tell you that he has seen us in Canada. He claims to enjoy reading Dutch books and I shall give a few names of books to him. Do you know which bookseller in London sells translations of Dutch books? Uncle Karel[51] knows for sure and now I would like to know, even though it is not for the moment but for later.

October 18: This morning I walked for some time, talking with another acquaintance of Karel's. Dr. Duncan[52] is a curious man who constantly tells stories and blathers on, proclaiming a very sensible, good-life philosophy, but who also tells the most unusual tales that are almost unbelievable. He spoke a lot about his distinguished acquaintances and patients and is very amicable with Karel. He is racking his brain to find Karel a healthy, honourable and lucrative job in Canada.

It is a lovely morning. We sat with pleasure on deck in our chairs, with blankets, and enjoyed the lovely sight of the tumbling water and curious lights playing on the forested hills of the coast.

Karel is also almost free of asthma, although the people on board, especially the ladies, still have a bit of sympathy for him and find him frail. Two friendly young ladies told me that various relations of theirs had come to Canada because of asthma and were now fully, or nearly, better.

Tomorrow we arrive in Quebec [City], but I do not know if we will have time to visit because we have to take care of our luggage while it is being unloaded, and we can stay only a few hours or so.

I already feel exhilarated by the Canadian air. All the misery of the first days at sea is forgotten and I remember only the lovely hours in the storm when I watched the ocean around me surpass itself. We are in good spirits.

Bye, dear Mama and Papa, Li, Thijs, An, Nel, Wallie and Miep. Much love for everyone from . . . Helena.

49 Dr. Ernest Black (1860–1934): physician in Australia; married on the Isle of Man, June 24, 1890, to Isobel Minnie Anderson (bap. 3, Feb. 1863–1938). After living, studying and working in Edinburgh, London and Paris, he moved back to Australia with his new wife in 1892. Described in his obituaries as "a man of great activity," he became the principal medical officer for Western Australia and president of the Central Board of Health. During WWI, he served in France (1914–1915) as a major in the Royal Army Medical Corps, later co-writing the book *War Diseases and Pensions*. In the last years before his retirement, he practised as a specialist in Sydney.

50 Arti en Amicitiae (Arts and Friendship) is an artists' society in Amsterdam which started in 1839.

51 Charles (Karel or Uncle Karel) Boissevain (1842–1927): brother of Jan Boissevain, journalist; married to Emily Héloïse Macdonnell (1844–1931).

52 Dr. George Cuthbertson Duncan (1852–1935): Canadian physician, surgeon, collector of art and violins.

A07095000001–4 [Karel's 'notes']
Aboard the *Sardinian*, October 17, 1891

This morning we sailed between Newfoundland and Labrador. Calm weather and cold. Ice on the deck and snow on the mountains of the coast. We made good headway and hope to be in Quebec tomorrow. The people on board have become friendlier. The stormy days with all their misery are forgotten, for now. I remember only the brief moments on deck, wrestling against the storm to remain standing, in awe of the gigantic waves when the ship was in the trough, when I saw the waves threatening high above me, or when I was being lifted upon a wave with the thundering mass of water behind and around me and seeing bottomless depths into which the colossal waves plunge and break with inner joy and fascinating sounds. I have felt the untamed power of the sea and, thereafter, all the helplessness of a seasick mortal, as did most of the other passengers.

    At least there is a lot of socializing, as the Canadians are beginning to feel at home and are praising their land. The fall is beautiful there, which we can now see as we approach Quebec. The hills are glowing in their beauty from the red leaves. It does not look like our autumn. No soft melancholy here and no sad musings. The colours are clear and shining, a deep red, with a clear blue sky, no false spring and not a trace of haze.

KLAB04555000179–182 [Karel to Wil]
On the St. Lawrence, *Sardinian*, Sunday, October 18, 1891

Dear Wim,

It has not yet been a month since I mailed my farewell greetings to you from Europe, but the time that has passed seems to me longer than a month and, anyhow, I wish to send you a sign of life at the end of this first stage. And thank you especially for the lovely idea to provide a few sentences for me en route from your lovely, lovely hand, which has lightened my load during my voyage.

    I hope that you do not expect to be kept up to date with all of the ups and downs of my health situation. I cannot and am not allowed to do this. I can tell you only in a few words that I am doing reasonably well, not yet the feeling of being on the way to full recovery but, nevertheless, I do believe that I breathe more easily now than in Amsterdam.

    We now have the sea voyage behind us and are sailing on the broad St. Lawrence with both sides of the coast shining in our faces and with a fresh southwestern wind and clear sunshine over the blue waves. We had stormy weather that delayed our journey. With favourable weather we could have arrived on Saturday the 17th. Now we will be in [Montreal] on Monday the 19th around noon. I surely hope that you have not been worried this

Sunday and Monday and that you will also remain courageous, despite this small setback.

We, Leentje and I, are in good spirits. For the time being, we will be staying in a good hotel, probably the Windsor Hotel, and shall spend our first days seeing the city and delivering our letters of introduction. From what I have heard from our fellow passengers who are familiar with Canada, it seems that Cousin Adolphe has indeed recommended us to influential men and I very much hope that, with their help, I will succeed in finding work this winter in Montreal. Delprat has predicted that my recovery will be a matter of endurance and much patience. Therefore, during these first weeks, I shall not overtask myself in the cold air of Canada, a taste of which I already had this morning on deck, which was to my liking. How nice it would be if, afterwards, once again with an unconstricted chest . . . Stop! No future dreaming, no building castles in the air. Self-control, young man!

One of our co-passengers is a London insurer of about my age (± thirty) who is getting married in Canada. He has not seen his bride in two years and the ceremony is set for this coming Wednesday. When we were in the middle of the ocean and we were chopping through the high waves, progressing so slowly, he feared that he would arrive too late for the ceremony. Nevertheless, it seems to me that those two may well look at each other awkwardly during the first days of their honeymoon. In two years, one can change a lot; even if that change has turned out for the good, one still has to get used to it, but if the souls live close together, one can even start to love the other's shortcomings.

We had pleasurable travel reading material: (1) the last issue of *The Nineteenth Century* [magazine], from which I read a piece by Gladstone as well as a piece about Sir Thomas More, which I especially recommend for your attention (by the way, the issue does have various good pieces); (2) *The History of the Dominion of Canada*, not very informative; (3) the verses of More, with the dramatic songs dedicated to green 'Erin'; (4) an anthology of the verses by Paul Verlaine,[53] which Thijs forwarded from Liverpool and in which we found delightful, beautiful things.

Now it is Sunday morning and on the long tables in the salon lie the Common Prayers, the Holy Bible and the hymnbook, ready for the 10:30 a.m. service. There are two ministers on board who were seasick during the whole crossing, and I fear that the repercussions will show up later in their sermons.

Right now, I have a lot more need for a word of incentive to battle and to labour than one of thanks for rescuing us from danger that was not there, but rather only in the disturbed brain of seasick clergymen, *mais nous verrons*.

How are Papa and Mama enduring the separation from their son and daughter? You can better observe this than our brothers and sisters (and perhaps do a lot to cheer them up), because Papa was extremely upset

---

53 Paul Marie Verlaine (1844–1896): French poet; married to Mathilde Mauté de Fleurville (1853–1914).

about having to bid farewell to Leentje. He loves her so deeply; they are so connected intellectually, but Papa did hold his own at the departure. During those days in London and Liverpool, he constantly walked arm in arm with her and searched every so often for an excuse to stroll with her alone.

Sunday afternoon: church was not so bad. There was no preaching, but two clergymen, one young and one older, read alternately prayers and chapters from the Bible, and that was quite edifying. Four hymns were sung by the whole congregation. That sounded very lovely. We read Luke 10, in reference to a collection of passages, and a chapter from [Isaiah], in which, among others, "because my ways are not your ways, nor my thoughts your thoughts, and so spoke the Lord." I no longer know it precisely, but it is a nice chapter; also a few nice psalms, amongst others, #90.

Now at 3:00 in the afternoon there is once again a kind of study group, in which a young lady with glasses is holding a lecture about the Christian mission in China. The subject does not appeal to me, therefore I preferred to talk with my sister. Later, I must walk a half-deck to take a breath of air because I have to keep my lungs in training and should not be enticed, by the lovely sun and the beautiful water and the magnificent coast in all its splendour, to settle into a lounge chair, reading and dreaming.

These days I have been rereading a passage in Musset[54] that I knew well, but now it touches me very deeply:

[Musset: "La Muse" excerpt]

Le coup dont tu te plains t'a préservé peut-être,
Enfant; car c'est par là que ton coeur s'est ouvert.
L'homme est un apprenti, la douleur est son maître,
Et nul ne se connaît tant qu'il n'a pas souffert.
C'est une dure loi, mais une loi suprême,
Vieille comme le monde et la fatalité,
Qu'il nous faut du malheur recevoir le baptême,
Et qu'à ce triste prix tout doit être acheté.
Les moissons pour mûrir ont besoin de rosée;
Pour vivre et pour sentir l'homme a besoin des pleurs;
La joie a pour symbole une plante brisée,
Humide encore de pluie et couverte de fleurs.

[Excerpt translation]

The blow of which you tell has perhaps saved you,
Child; for, by this means, your heart has opened.
Man is but apprentice and sadness is his master
And none can know until he suffers.
It is harsh law but a law supreme,
As old as the world and fate,
That we must know misfortune to be baptized
And that this sad price must be paid by all.
The harvest must have the dew in order to mature;
Man must have his tears in order to live and feel;
Joy has a broken plant as symbol,
Still wet with rain and covered with flowers.

Oh, my love, must this for us also be, must the time come that we bless the day when I was sent away from everything that I held dear?

---

54 Alfred Louis Charles de Musset-Pathay (1810–1857), French dramatist, poet, and novelist. The translation into English is by David Paley at http://www.poemswithoutfrontiers.com. He has shared his passion for poetry and has given his permission to share this excerpt.

I doubt, and I will still doubt for a long time, but still, who knows? Dear, dear Wil, let us remain hopeful and believe in a better future and let me know soon when you speak through your letters: "Wil has regained her resilience and once again conducts herself courageously." Do I now come under the category of 'inevitable topics' when you are visiting or receiving visitors? I beg of you that you do not talk too much about me with those who are indifferent. Here, I feel as if I am the object of trite pity and I find it awful.

Bye, my darling. Think about the words of the psalmist [Longfellow]:[55] "Let us then be up and doing, With a heart for any fate; Still achieving, still pursuing, Learn to labour and to wait."

Farewell, for many, many long days, my darling. Did you read between the lines what I do not dare, what I am not permitted to say in so many words? And do you feel on your forehead the kiss that I, with blessings, send to you? Bye, loving heart. Karel

A07095000001-4 [Karel's notes continued from October 17]
Aboard the *Sardinian*, October 19, 1891

Arrived at Quebec at eleven o'clock in the morning, but still a few hours to go to the fortress on the rocks. Oh, what an old village and how dilapidated.

[9] Citadel from harbour, Quebec City, QC, about 1890

---

55 *A Psalm of Life: Reflections* by Henry Wadsworth Longfellow (1807–1882), American poet.

Mr. and Mrs. McC. met us on the other side of the city and escorted us back to the hotel, where we parted, then a few minutes later we went through a second door to arrive in the dining room, where everyone was seated at a different little table, and where we had to eat our meal.

The evening before, I had also promised a Scottish teacher to go with her to the Presbyterian church; and so, we went to the church. The church was full when we arrived and the congregation was singing. I followed the teacher to her bench beside the platform (no pulpit) and from there I had a good view of the congregation members preaching. It is curious, the difference in the physiognomy in the various churches.

The singing also has a completely different character. In the English Episcopal Church, everyone evidently appears to strive toward a correct manner, proper kneeling, bowing your head gracefully. To sing on key or, rather, to not sing at all. We could already hear the singing from afar. It seemed that for most of them their objective was, especially, to sing their hearts out; it also seems that the choir had to exert all of its power to manage the individual singing styles so as to keep them in harmony.

And then there was the prayer. Young Reverend G. from B. stood up at the right moment and gave the inspiration with much feeling; he expressed himself as someone who was struggling. He reminded me of Robert Elsmere[56] after the first talks with the squire, trying to fight the rising doubt with a tenacious grip on the inextricable truth in the beautiful words of the Bible. Also, [he had] the same boyish figure with the thin face and the searching, 'far-sighted' eyes. After the prayer, there was the strange thumping and cooing of a reformed congregation. Afterwards, during a blessing of song, there was a soft reminder to understand the message and to draw comfort from it. It was a well-known hymn:

> Art thou weary, art thou languid,
> Art thou sore distressed?
> "Come to Me," saith One, "and coming,
> Be at rest."

Indeed, it was sung with the best intentions. The sermon referred to Maria and Martha, an encouragement for the ladies to not be consumed with homemaking, but rather to nurture a spiritual life in their families. About the ideal home, he was indeed eloquent, but the audience heard, as always, Martha's side and whispered, shaking their heads about Martha's objections. The sermon was also left to the inspiration of the moment, and it seemed as if he could hear the arguments and even thought to refute them.

The teacher stayed for Bible lessons, and for companionship and out of curiosity, I stayed with her, so I had the opportunity to meet

---

56 Robert Elsmere is the main character of the novel *Robert Elsmere* by Mrs. Humphry Ward, first published in 1888, about an Oxford clergyman who begins to doubt the doctrines of the Anglican Church after encountering the work of German rationalists.

Reverend G. He was still full of the subject of his sermon. I mentioned my astonishment that he urged simplification from a material life, while I found life here so positive in comparison with the Old World. But he said how pathetically few married men were devoted to their homes and, like a real man, he blamed it solely on the women.

A32005000361-362 [Wil to Heleen]
Amsterdam, October 20, 1891

My dear Heleentje!

You cannot know how relieved and happy your telegram from yesterday made all of us. I would so much like to embrace you sometime, now that you are safe and well, having arrived with him there. Be honest. Were you both also not a little bit afraid when it stormed so much? I endured terrible fear and I believe that your mother and father were also very strained by it.

 Now, we are so thankful. Now it should go well and, since he also experienced some relief in the sea air and you were not seasick yourself, I think that is what "well" must have meant. I am also so thankful to you for everything. Then, I did not say it enough. Everything was also so unnatural; I did not think enough about what you were sacrificing for me and could only think: "She is allowed to go with him! And she will have a big responsibility and difficult days." All of it did not register with me well enough.

 Thank you also for the postcard. How awful when he was short of breath, again. However, it did me good to hear that he had my letter and that it did not upset him. I found it so awful that he had written to me twice, so nicely, and that I could not answer anymore. Please also write to me sometime about how his mood is. I hope somewhat more cheerful, but his last letter was already more hopeful. When he starts feeling a little better, he will also become faithful for a full recovery and that is a big step forward.

 This morning, I was briefly at Keizersgracht 717 [the Boissevain home] to talk a little bit about the happy news and to be thankful together after having been saddened together. Otherwise, about the latter, I can assure you that we are certainly much better. However, I am from time to time still in tears, but that is more about one or another memory, about a saying of his or something that he did, and more a sense of melancholy than sadness. You were right about what you told me before your departure. It gives me an imperturbable happiness to know that he loves me and to carry the awareness that he loves me above all. I was so afraid that all of that would be disturbed because of the sorrow, but it did remain and, therefore, even though I can sometimes be sad, I am

[10] Boissevain home: Keizersgracht 717

not unhappy. Let him know this when you think that it can give him some peace to know that I am uplifted by his love. I did not dare to write him something like this, and it is so awful [for you] to have to take care of him, but I did not want to start to ignore his last wishes and advice.

I got a very lovely letter from [my sister] Jo, wherein she said that she would gladly suffer more pain "so long as it could help us," because one quickly becomes used to physical suffering. She also described to me how everything gains value through such a monotonous life as that of an invalid, and how much she enjoyed her autumn walks, how much she learned to value nature, though she can so seldom enjoy it. They are soon going to Stockholm via Berlin in order to avoid a long sea voyage. Mama asked me if I had the desire to try to see her there, but to be honest, I would rather stay home for once, in familiar surroundings, and when [Jo] comes back, I will appreciate her return all the more. Also, Mrs. Viruly[57] invited me [to visit], but I refused for the same reasons.

Soon I will go with Mama and Nel to the cooking school to inquire about both of us taking lessons there. I believe that we would be busy with it for two mornings. Furthermore, I do not yet want to schedule my time before I know the dates. The hours for singing lessons (and perhaps

---

57 Aegida Johanna Elizabeth Viruly Ledeboer (1833–1907): married to Theodorus Pieter Viruly (1822–1902), an entrepreneur, senator and large landowner with four children, two of whom are daughters Aegida (Gidia) Johanna Elizabeth (1863–1944) and Helena (Heleen) Cornelia (1869–1948), both unmarried.

the course from Berlage⁵⁸) are already booked, and then I shall talk with Suze⁵⁹ about the Kindervoeding.⁶⁰

Cor now knows an Italian poem and some verbs, but the latter have not yet taken hold, such that I now have her translate sentences in which they appear. Yesterday, after a five-and-a-half-month rest, I had my first piano lesson. I had practised with mistakes and the timing was a little bit of my own making, but otherwise [my piano teacher]⁶¹ was quite satisfied. Uncle Jan⁶² claims that I play much better than before, but that is not true. At your house, I had learned to play a little bit more [comfortably] for others and now I am not so afraid of him anymore, which is why I had always stumbled.

[Jeanne] des Tombe⁶³ wrote very nicely asking for our portrait, and then yesterday came another letter thanking us for it. She is extremely friendly and is sympathetic.

Do you know already that Tol Waller⁶⁴ has sent that photo of the ditch by the hill to your parents, the one she took at your parents', when we teased her so much and chattered about colour and light? Nice, eh?

And now, until we see you again in the next letter. Much love to Karel and a friendly kiss for you, from your Wil.

P.S. I have already seen a stamp with the very young Queen, but I have not acquired any yet.

---

58 Dr. Hendrik Petrus Berlage (1856–1934): architect; married to Marie Bienfait (1864–1937).

59 Helena Suze van Hall (1869–1928): married in 1893 to Gijsbert van Tienhoven (1867–1900), lawyer.

60 The Vereniging Kindervoeding (Society for Child-feeding) supplied hot meals for poor children, especially during the winter season.

61 Sarah Bosmans-Benedicts (1861–1949): pianist and pedagogue; wife of Hendrik Nicolaas Bosmans (1856–1896), principal cellist of the Royal Concertgebouw Orchestra of Amsterdam (as it is now named).

62 Johannes Leembruggen (1838–1928): civil engineer; unmarried brother of Wil's mother.

63 Jeanne (Jennie) Frédérique Baroness des Tombe (1863–1944): a friend of Karel and Heleen's; married in 1885 to Jan Lodewijk Willem Baron van Hardenbroek van Lockhorst (1862–1921), at one time mayor of Nederhemert.

64 Catharina Rutgera (Tol) Waller (1868–1931), unmarried.

Chapter 2

Our Land of Promise

Now in Canada, Karel and Heleen make their way from Quebec City to Montreal, where they stay at the Windsor Hotel while awaiting news from William Cornelius Van Horne regarding Karel's job prospects, as well as getting to know who the 'top dogs' are.

```
A28335001455-58 [Heleen to Mother]
Windsor Hotel, Montreal, October 21, 1891
```

Dear Mother,

Yesterday evening, close to 6:00 p.m., we arrived [in Montreal] in a downpour after a wet cold day on the river. We have since spent most of the time downstairs in the warm salon and have had an enjoyable time with our friends, [Drs.] Black and Duncan, and Miss Maude Grange Kingsmill.[65] We exchanged cards. She asked me to come and visit her if I was ever in Toronto and I shall do that, for sure. I hope very much that you will become acquainted with Dr. Black. He has promised to visit you when he comes to Amsterdam (end of December to beginning of January). He will take down the names of some books and perhaps send them to Amsterdam.

In case a letter for me arrives from England — London or Douglas (Isle of Man) — could you or Papa please open it and list the titles of the

---

65 Maude Grange Kingsmill (1871–1942): a teacher, recorded by the University of Toronto graduate list as Mrs. Edmund Wragge, 96 Madison Avenue, Toronto; married to Edmund Carlyon Wragge (1872–1972), lawyer.

books and mail them to me? If you happen to be sending a chest and the books are not too expensive, then you could send them. You must also try to become acquainted with his wife. She has stayed behind in England, but in talking about her, there is so much affection and admiration that, according to me, it is reciprocal. He is, I think, as tall as Papa, really blond, with a very long beard, and he appears very young. He would very much like to see the hospital of Mendes de Leon.[66] You could certainly help him with that. I told him that he also may call in the evenings, having the best chance of finding someone at home. He told us yesterday some nice details about locks. He can forge and make locks and has, for his hobby, a workplace in the basement of his house.

It is a pity that we are away from Vogelenzang. It would be so good for Wallie to learn smithing from dear Ruigrok[67] during the vacation.

October 22: I cannot get things done because I have been so busy. Yesterday, I had to take a break due to a visit from the two gentlemen Meredith,[68] sons of Sir William [Meredith].[69] In Quebec, we had visited their father, an amiable eighty-year-old, particularly spry for his age. Lady M. was out and we stayed only a few hours in Quebec City. He had promised to write to his sons. One is in business, stiff and a bit shy. The other is a lawyer, very jolly and lively. In a very friendly way, they both invited Karel to come to lunch at their offices and would like to take us on a trip. Both are unmarried. They were barely gone (we had received them [at the Windsor Hotel] in a very proper ladies' reception room downstairs) when there was Mr. Hosmer[70] again. Delightful meeting him. [He is] small, with a slightly dark complexion, a black goatee and pronounces the *s* as *tsh*. He is very lively and quick in his movements, takes a great interest in Karel and has already made plans with Mr. Van Horne. Karel will visit Mr. Van Horne this morning, who was out of town yesterday, and shall speak with him then about the plans.

The hotel is exceptionally good and lovely, but terribly expensive. On the fifth floor, we have two very decent rooms with an adjoining door, a pleasantly large bed, big clothing closet, vanity with large mirror and drawers, canapé, easy chairs, etc., etc. Everywhere it is heated too warmly, but we keep the windows open so that it is made very comfortable. We have a beautiful view of the whole city and the river and the hills in

---

66   Dr. M.A. Mendes de Leon (1856–1924): gynecologist, Amsterdam; married to Anna Mathilda Teixeira de Mattos (1862–1937).

67   Ruigrok is the name of a well-known family of blacksmiths and fence-makers that operated until well after the Second World War, in the village Vogelenzang and area (near the Boissevain summer house, Teylingerbosch).

68   Frederick Edmund Meredith (1862–1941), lawyer and chief counsel to the CPR, married to Anna Madeleine Van Koughnet (1863–1945), and his brother, William Henry Meredith (1849–1895), director of the Bank of Montreal, never married.

69   Sir William Collis Meredith (1812–1894): Chief Justice of the Superior Court of Quebec; married to Lady Sophia Naters Holmes (1820–1898).

70   Charles Rudolph Hosmer (1851–1927): businessman and chief of telegraph office for the CPR; married to Clara Jane Bigelow (1852–1926).

the background. Behind us is the Mountain, which is enchantingly lovely now with all the autumn colours. We walked up a short way on it yesterday and from time to time stood still, full of admiration.

We are going to bed early because the evenings are uneventful. We also do not want to sit upstairs in our rooms because we do not want to make our rooms too warm for the night. Downstairs, there is also a sort of concert, with many guests in all of the drawing rooms. [Tomorrow morning] we will get up early and then walk for a bit.

October 22: A troublesome thing for travellers here is that the trunks are terribly thrown about. My large trunk had come open on board, one padlock completely gone and the other clasp loosened. Of the black 'HB', both locks are either broken or gone. Everyone on board complained about it, except those who had already expected it and had equipped everything with extra locks on the inside and thick leather suitcases. If we are still going far away to the west, I fear that the purchase of a strong suitcase will be inevitable.

To have things washed costs a dollar a dozen, large and small mixed together. Terribly expensive! Yesterday evening, we came by a house where some Chinese were ironing. We went inside to ask for a price list. They spoke little English, but it went fine anyway. The small pieces were cheaper, but the large pieces, again, were very expensive.

It is a pleasure to walk through the city, broad streets and sidewalks, trees almost everywhere, and the residential area mostly resembles the left side of the Vondelstraat [along the Vondelpark in Amsterdam]. High staircase straight up [to the front door] and another door underneath. Many large buildings and a countless number of churches. Around our hotel there are eight, within a few steps. You see churches here like bars on the Nieuwmarkt.[71] The houses are not tall and there is so much light in the city that even without sunlight it is easy to find your way because of the high mountain in the back, the river in the valley and the straight streets. It is completely different than Quebec, which is more like a southern French village, with terribly steep roads without paving, or sometimes covered with long planks like our attic, and then, once again, there will be a wooden stairway. Quebec also looks dead and empty; only the panoramic views over the wide river and the beautiful, lush hills are lovely.

Here, it is just like at home now, the time of rain and bad weather and they seriously advise us to go to the west until Christmas. We would really like it if we could stay for a time on a farm. That would be, at the same time, healthy, cheap and most interesting. In any case, we will stay here for a week to make plans.

Mr. Hosmer is the boss of the telegraph for the CPR and telegraphs the whole day with pleasure. He also asked if he could wire something to Holland for us, something we might gladly accept later on. Now he bombards us with local telegrams, such as just a minute ago, to tell us

---

71   One of the well-known squares in the centre of Amsterdam.

that Count [Adolphe] had responded "Many Thanks" to his telegram about our arrival.

It is not a structured story that you get to read! I feel that my letter is hanging together like dry sand, but a lot is still so strange. Sometimes, I cannot even believe that we are here for such a long time. Travelling for me was once so synonymous with having carefree pleasure. Now, it is also so strange (among all the pleasure and interest of the journey) to wonder, from time to time, whether this [travelling] is good for Karel. Would it be best to stay in Montreal, or must we go further on, etc.? I am glad that he is so free from shortness of breath these days. He is still coughing, but less so than on board and walking seems to tire him less; at least, I can easily get him to go walking.

I am beginning to long very much for some letters. We found a letter from Tol and *De Nieuwe Rotterdammer*.[72] In one of the American newspapers, we read something about a collision of a Dutch warship in the Channel. Was that the *Koningin Emma*?[73]

The watercolour by Thijs has acquired commercial value. We had to pay a dollar for it [at customs] and the chest had to be opened in order to show how lovely it was! We had to spend a lot of time at customs in order to get all of our things together. I stayed with the watercolour while Karel looked for the rest and dragged it around. Dr. Black kept me company in the meantime. He had only one suitcase and was quickly ready, while his brother-in-law, Mr. Anderson,[74] had to search for a long time.

October 23: This morning we had a visit from Mrs. Van Horne and her daughter, who asked us to dinner for tomorrow, but then we will be eating at the home of Mrs. Angus.[75] This afternoon we rode with Miss Angus, [and had] tea at her house. Lovely, warm-hearted people, five daughters between twenty and thirty-five, of which two are married, and three younger sons.

Much love to everyone from your Helena.

A32074000132–135 [Heleen to Wil]
Windsor Hotel, Montreal, October 21, 1891

Dear Wil,

Here we are in Canada, our 'Land of Promise'; the journey has gone well and now the recuperation can start. Yesterday evening, I gave your last letter to Karel after 6:00 p.m., when we arrived. He very much regretted that I had not given it to him in Quebec, before we disembarked from the

---

72   *De Nieuwe Rotterdamsche Courant*, a liberal paper established in 1843.

73   On October 10, 1891, a steam-powered warship, HNLMS *Koningin Emma der Nederlanden*, went on exercises in the Atlantic Ocean, with no known record of a collision.

74   Arthur Scott Anderson (1865–1918) from the Isle of Man.

75   Mary Anne Angus (née Daniels) (1834–1913), married to Richard Bladworth Angus (1831–1922), board member and vice-president of the CPR.

ship, because he could still have answered it in his letter that he had mailed from there. Now he has to wait again for another month. He could only ask me to tell you that he is so very much thankful for the lovely letter and would have liked to respond to so many things that he must now postpone. I am also very sorry now that I did not give it to him sooner, but I did not know that he was going to mail his letter in Quebec, and only regarded Montreal as our point of arrival.

The last beautiful days on the ocean did him quite a bit of good. He is hardly short of breath anymore, but he remains quite depressed; it is sometimes difficult to recognize my older, jolly brother. To see the beautiful new land, and all of the unfamiliarities on board and here on land, is naturally much less uplifting for him (who has already seen so much) than it is for me, who time and time again is enthralled with looking out over this beautiful and lovely land. The fall colours are indescribably stunning, not faded and melancholic like in Holland, but glowing and full of light, even on a rainy day like today, and we do not have to go by train to Haarlem or to Baarn to see them, because the whole town is full of trees, along streets, in gardens and in parks.

This morning, Karel delivered our introduction letters. Some people were out, but others received them very courteously, especially Mr. Hosmer. He had already been informed in advance by Cousin Adolphe. Yesterday evening he came to the hotel, inquiring as to whether we had arrived, and received Karel this morning like a good friend. Pretty soon, close to 5:00 p.m., he will come for a visit, just like 'Lady' Angus and her daughter. It is such a nice feeling to be so warmly welcomed here.

After coffee, we walked up the mountain a bit and enjoyed the lovely view of the woods, city and river. When we got home, we discovered a card from Mr. Arthur Piers,[76] the father of the lovely children on board. He is also connected with the CPR, and upon our arrival here, his wife introduced him to us right away.

Our arrival was quite miserable because the weather was exceptionally cold and wet. We spent a lot of time at customs with our many suitcases, but they helped us very well and politely. For the watercolour from Thijs, we had to pay a dollar and the trunk had to be forced open in order to let them see it.

Our acquaintance Dr. Duncan is also here in the hotel and always comes to sit with us at meals. He is always busy talking and is always quite courteous, but I would love to know how many of his stories are actually true. He says that he came here to perform an operation and now he seems to be very nervous about that decision, but it is postponed time and time again, and to me that seems apocryphal. In Quebec, he bought a pink and a black pearl that he showed to everyone. He also has an interest in famous violins and bows, and claims to be on intimate footing with

---

76 Arthur Harry Brymer Piers (1851–1930): secretary to Van Horne and later manager of the Canadian Pacific Steamship Company; married to Mary Amelia Jarvis (1851–1947), with children Nora Diana (1879–1979), Isabel (1884–1970) and Arthur Stapleton (1885–1962).

almost all the celebrities that ever lived in Rome, etc., etc. During the journey, it was quite amusing to hear his stories, but I do hope that we manage to lose him here.

Wil, I very much long to hear something from you. I so often think, "What a shame it is that Wil is not here," and I very much feel how often you must long to do what I do and to be what I am. Then I would also like to fly to you, just once, to give you courage and comfort, because you will go through so many dispirited moments when it is so difficult to rid yourself of your own sad thoughts and to participate in what happens around you. When all other things seem so purposeless and you are so indifferent to them, then I would like to take you again in my hands and say, "Be brave, my dear Wil." Every pain that we endure with humility gives us the strength for what life has in store for us, gives us a longer life, and teaches us to do more for those who love us. I would also very much like to help you figure out how to fill your days a bit, because work is really always the best comfort and that will be especially so difficult for you, because everything you wanted to do is now so useless.

I do hope that Karel will start learning Italian again, with verve, and then we would be able to read Dante together. That, I would so much like to do and it is so difficult.

Afternoon, October 23: The first days here have been busy days and the sea journey already seems to be long ago. At 2:00 p.m., we saw all the 'Sardinians' again, at least many of them. Mr. Paterson,[77] one of the passengers, got married in the church here and we went to watch. Very 'high-church priest' in a beautiful cassock like a Roman Catholic, with a choir, cross and so forth. We met Mrs. Piers, who was most engaging and who took us along to meet with her husband. In that church, it was so funny, just as if we were at home, to see so many acquaintances here bowing, nodding their heads and exchanging a few words. Mrs. Piers will most likely be of service to Karel in finding work.

This afternoon, Karel was also at Mr. Van Horne's, an amazing chap who was extremely busy. Karel had to wait an hour and a half with a number of other people who also wanted to talk to him, an astonishingly smart man who uses few words. He will certainly be of much service to us. Karel was much more cheerful when he came away. [Van Horne] had laid out the prospect of getting to work soon, probably in the far west, near the Rocky Mountains. During these months, the climate must be much better there than here, but Karel dreads having a lazy life there, of living like a lazy patient and, therefore, I very much hope that he will get work there.

The air here is, needless to say, so delightful. I have never felt so light and perky, and Karel is beginning to feel that way, too. I already also feel a bit like a local here. Just a while ago, I took Karel to Mr. Hosmer's office and walked back alone through the (already well-known to

---

77   William Brockie Paterson (1864–1905): actuary of the Norwich Union Life Assurance Society; married Ethel Maria Lamplough (1869–1936) on October 23, 1891.

me) St. James Street. A lady asked me the way to the post office and I was proud to be able to point it out exactly!

With a warm kiss and very much love to your mother and Cor, your loving Heleen.

A28335000707-712 [Karel to Father and Mother]
Montreal, October 24-26, 1891

Beloved Mother and dearest Father,

Yesterday afternoon, we received Papa's letter of October 13, for which we both thank you very much. Heleen was somewhat disappointed that none of her sisters had written to her, the last letter being dated October 5, so that one lets eight days go by without sending anything. We found a letter from Cateau [Tilanus][78] to Heleen, and a newspaper. It appears that Uncle [Niek][79] is not sending [*Algemeen Handelsblad*[80]] newspapers. It deserves consideration to follow the original plan of sending clippings, or the complete paper if there is an important news item. I believe, or rather know, that [Heleen] likes to be informed about everything that is going on in the family circle. Life here, which really amounts to being constantly ready should I need care and in watching over my situation and the progress with my health, will certainly not completely occupy all her thoughts. Now things are still okay; the new land interests her very much and she enjoys all of the new and unexpected things. Later on, when we are settled somewhere and we live our lives from day to day as she has accepted, she will try to fill her life with all sorts of activities. Please everyone, make this easier for her by also sharing Amsterdam life fully with her. She was so at home with that, even though it did not satisfy her, and she will miss the intellectual elements of her circle of acquaintances.

For myself, I fear that I will not keep my interest about what is going on there at the cooking-point. For sure, she will; and I do not, as yet, quite see how this need for complete and comprehensive information about the goings-on in Amsterdam will be satisfied. Who will take up the task of writing chronicles? It could not suffice, for one who accepts the job of writing, to sit down one morning each week and start to think about all of what has happened. With each event, one would have to think right away, "Ah, what kind of impression would that make on Heleen? How shall I tell her about this? In what context?" Methinks, even a daily notebook

---

78   Catharina (Cateau) Johanna Tilanus (1866–1948): nurse; married in 1918 to Jan Hendrik Zeno Koch (1859–1940), commercial agent.

79   Nicolaas (Uncle Nic/Niek) Jacob den Tex (1836–1899): lawyer; married Hester (Aunt Hes) Boissevain (1842–1914), sister of Jan.

80   The *Algemeen Handelsblad* was originally a liberal newspaper, oriented to Amsterdam, that started in 1828, merging in 1970 with the *Nieuwe Rotterdamse Courant* into the present-day *NRC Handelsblad*.

would be a help to the chronicler's memory. But, above all, he or she must think a lot about Heleen, with thoughts of her life, so all of what comes from the outside that affects them, *per se*, will be good for the correspondence. Dare Nel do this? Does Li have the time for it? Does Thijs see any chance of keeping it up? Please talk about it in the family circle and let me know the result of the to-and-fro of the conversation.

We are very pleased about what you have said regarding the meeting with Holt.[81] Was it, after all, Alfred, whom you had met previously, or how was the quid pro quo resolved?

Also, thanks for the letters. One chatty letter from a colleague who did not yet know anything [about my departure], a word of farewell from the elder van Stockum,[82] very kind. We are shocked about a telegram in the *New York Herald* about the collision of a Dutch navy ship, seriously damaged, and look forward to more details about it.

On Monday, October 19, we arrived at 11:00 a.m. in Quebec after two beautiful days on the river. A short visit with the old gentleman [Sir William] Meredith, [about] eighty years old. Very friendly, wrote to both of his unmarried sons in Montreal to receive us and to welcome us here. Sightseeing and departure in the evening. The city is located, for a large part, against the hill, upon the top of which sits a fortress. Wooden planks pave the sidewalks, a lot of mud and poorly built houses, but everywhere there is electric light.

During the night, we were anchored when the moon was gone, since the water had become unsafe. With daylight, anchors aweigh! The river is not so picturesque, flat land, but now and then there are beautiful light effects on the trees that shine in colourful autumn splendour. Maple trees and red oak. Cloudy sky.

[October 20 at about 5:00 in the afternoon]: We arrived in rainy weather and paid $1.05 for the import of Thijs' watercolour. The nails of the crate were removed. Otherwise, no problems with customs. Checked into our hotel rooms and suites, fifth floor, 448 and 450. Arrangements made for one week at $7.00 per day.

It seems that I have been introduced to the important people of the country:

Hosmer: Chief of the telegraph service of the CPR. Small, lively little chap, says *tsh* for *s*, very courteous, loves familiar gestures with people that he knows very well, like poking in the belly and slapping on shoulders. Sent a long telegram to Adolphe, which he most likely has sent to you, who introduced me at the St. James Club,[83] where I am now

---

81 Philip Henry Holt (1830–1914): founder and owner, with his brother Alfred (1829–1911), of Alfred Holt and Company and the Ocean Steam Ship Company, later the Blue Funnel Line. Philip was married to Anna Booth (1833–1899), and Alfred was married to Catherine Long (1841–1865) and later to Francis Long (1846–1913).

82 Dirk Johannes van Stockum (1826–1908): lawyer; married to Sophia Clara Emilia Lastdrager (1837–1915).

83 The St. James Club is the oldest private business club in Montreal, established in 1857, then situated on St. James St., now called Rue Saint-Jacques. The Club Saint-James (as it is now known) stands at the corner of Union and René-Lévesque.

sitting to write. He has visited us a couple of times at the hotel and is extremely helpful, but for the time being he cannot do anything to advance my situation.

Sir Donald Smith[84]: A 'top dog', was not in his office; I left my letter there. Heard nothing from him. Shall just go another time. Lady Smith is in Europe.

Lord Mount Stephen is with his wife in Europe.

Charles Drinkwater[85]: Secretary of the CPR, sympathetic reception, was out of town, shall visit Heleen, bachelor.

[Richard Bladworth] Angus: Director of the CPR, tall, stiff, bearded Englishman, posh family. Yesterday, to her great pleasure, Heleen rode around town with his unmarried daughter. There are about seven children. We will be dining there this evening. It will be the first time that I will be dressed in white tie and tails [in Canada]!

William C. Van Horne: President, CPR, one of the most powerful men in the country. An intellectual colossus, the stature of Mr. Hooft Graafland Dedel,[86] with a bit more girth. Says very little but does more and, when he does speak, it is to the point. A large head with piercing steel-grey eyes. He will help me, for sure.

This is an unfavourable period of the year regarding the climate in Montreal. The day of our arrival was also the last of thirty-one [consecutive] summer days. Now it will remain damp and quite cloudy until the first snow falls. I have been advised to first go a bit further west, and I have notified Van Horne of my wish to also find work there. He will have a small bit of his powerful brain ponder upon it; this afternoon I will hear about my fate.

Shortly, we will be lunching at the home of the young Meredith, a lawyer who visited us a little while ago with his older brother (of the firm Middlemist and Meredith). Also, Mrs. and Miss Van Horne visited us and Helena will go on an afternoon tour with the latter.

Montreal is a pleasant city. Built on the river against the hills, one can easily find their way. Many handsome public buildings. A lot of churches. You can find as many churches [here] as pubs at home. Three side by side and on both sides of the street, all with lovely towers or steeples. A quite nice sort of park crowns the mountain behind the city and, on both sides, you can see the beautifully constructed church tower. The hill is not high and, therefore, the city is not that deep [below],

---

84 Donald Alexander Smith, 1st Baron Strathcona and Mount Royal (1820–1914). Heleen refers to his negotiations in 1869 at Fort Garry (in present-day Manitoba) with Louis Riel. He was the man who drove the last spike of the Canadian Pacific Railway on November 7, 1885, at Craigellachie, B.C. He was married to Isabella Sophia Hardisty (1825–1913), an aunt of Isabella (Belle) Clarke Hardisty Lougheed, the wife of James Alexander Lougheed, Calgary, Alberta.

85 Charles Drinkwater (1834–1908): secretary-treasurer of the CPR and former private secretary to Prime Minister John A. MacDonald; was married to Sarah, born in 1850.

86 Jhr. Ferdinand Hooft Graafland (1836–1901): lawyer; married to Jkvr. Anna Hillegonda Dedel (1838–1914). *Jhr.* and *Jkvr.* are abbreviations for *Jonkheer* (male) and *Jonkvrouw* (female), respectively, titles of Dutch nobility.

but the river is quite long. So, in size, the city is therefore very spread out. Looking across the river, in about the centre of the city, is St. Lawrence Street, or Rue St-Laurent. Eastwards, downriver, everything is French. Westwards, everything is English. I am very much surprised by this partitioning and shall try to find out the reason for it. Of course, religion plays a part in the division, with much success.

Of our fellow passengers on board the *Sardinian*, only the ones that we befriended are still in the city. Along with their three lovely children, Mrs. Piers reunited with her husband here (who is also part of the CPR) and is very thankful that I played with his six-year-old son on my knee, off and on board ship. His patronage/intercession could become helpful for me.

Dr. Duncan and Dr. Black are both staying in the Windsor Hotel and we see them now and then. [Duncan] introduced us to Dr. Fenwick,[87] the oldest doctor in the country and a great collector for the museum here in town. He led us through part of his collection. Heleen will probably have already written about it. With Dr. Black, who has become a great friend, we have taken a tour and a walk. Very pleasant. He is a young man of thirty-one years and was married last year. A big man, with a soft, attractive face and long brown silky beard. Never wears an overcoat, never drinks wine or strong liquor and does not like dancing, but likes to read a lot and has a lot of ambition for his profession. His speciality is women's illnesses, and a specially equipped hospital in Perth, Australia, appears to have asked him to manage it. He has already worked for a long time in Australia and loves the country very much. He wanted me to go there. He is a pleasant conversationalist with refined manners and has a very logical approach in his arguments.

Sunday morning, October 25: Yesterday, Mr. Van Horne was on an inspection of the house that he has had built, so therefore I cannot tell you with any finality about my plans. There will be a new track constructed by the CPR in the Rocky Mountains at the level of Banff, an extension of a local track, and I could perhaps join the staff of engineers who will be going there to survey. That will most likely save travel and accommodation expenses, and would be instructive. However, it is as yet undecided, so therefore do not spread the word around. You understand how much this makes me smile, to get work right away.

Sir Donald Smith is back from a trip; an old man with a snow-white beard; he visited us, yesterday. We have his carriage at our disposal and will go this evening to dine with him. At 2:00 p.m. we have lunch at Mrs. Van Horne's, and I shall postpone the mailing of this letter until after the lunch party. Perhaps I will find out more, then.

This morning, we had a very cozy breakfast with Dr. Black, who is visiting all of the medical facilities, hospitals, museums, etc., and who shared his critique with us. There seems to be a corps of very bright medical doctors, especially surgeons.

---

87 George Edgeworth Fenwick (1825–1894): chief surgeon at Montreal General Hospital; professor of surgery at McGill University; married in 1852 to Eliza Charlotte de Hertel (1826–1907).

I am doing quite well. The air is lovely, very dry. Heleen cannot brush her locks, or rather, the brushing does nothing, because you generate so much electricity from it that when she stops brushing, her hair flies all over as if the wind has taken it.

Except the possible postscript, I will say goodbye for now. Give our greetings to everyone. Write me a lot about Wil, and may you stay strong. Heleentje is doing fine. She is very cheerful and enjoyable and that is delightful to see. I wish that I could reach that point!!!

Many greetings from her and your loving Karel.

P.S. One day later than yours, we got [An's] and [Li's] letters of the same date. Many thanks! Things are looking good. Li can write about whatever she wants to write; I actually find it lovely that letters from her are addressed to me. Normally, Heleen and I will let each other read our letters anyway. It is too bad that An did not break her foot, then she would have a lasting souvenir from Teylingerbosch.[88] Sourpuss!

Monday, October 26: The dice have been cast! I have a desire to work in the open air and will find that by surveying the terrain of a railway from Fort Macleod into the Rockies. The work will be done through James Ross,[89] a big contractor here. I will be placed under his chief engineer, along with ten or twenty others. This evening I spoke with one of them, Brooks, a young Englishman with a pleasant appearance. He will go to Ottawa this evening and will arrange to meet us there tomorrow night on our way to Calgary. I will leave Heleen there for the time being and will likely join the rest of the party there. Then, if I find the situation in Fort Macleod such that it is suitable for Heleen to get there with some decorum, I will let her know and she will arrive on her own. Everyone that I talk to has been terribly busy, therefore I have no details about the matter, such as the time span of the work, salary (eventual), etc. Between us, I believe that Van Horne is sending me out to determine whether I am a 'cockney' or a 'hackney'; if the latter, he will help me and if the former, he will drop me. I am convinced that I will do my best to earn a positive first impression.

We will travel three or four days in the train with Brooks, and he (who worked the whole previous winter under Ross in the same area) can tell us about everything then. In the beginning, we will incur some expenses. They advised us to buy a fur [coat], but for the time being I think that I can make do with my winter coat and our fine rugs. Once there, the means of transport will be open carriages, and then one has to be pretty warmly outfitted. Leentje ordered a warm riding habit. I will try to rent a horse for her there. Then, while we are working, she can visit us and

---

88   Teylingerbosch is a summer house of the Boissevain family, located in Vogelenzang, rented from the Barnaart family. It was purchased by Willem Barnaart in 1807 and, in 1817, he was awarded the title of Jonkheer.

89   James Levison Ross (1848–1913): civil engineer; director of the CPR; businessman, art collector and philanthropist; said to be the largest shareholder of the CPR. He oversaw works on the CPR west of Winnipeg and on the Calgary and Edmonton Railway. He lived on the Golden Square Mile in Montreal and was married to Annie Kerr (1847–1915).

[11] Noel Edgell Brooks, seated left

bring painkillers and chocolate. Along with this mailing, I am sending some maps of Canada that I found very handy for general use. It makes the correspondence easier when one has a general idea of the location. Glue one onto a piece of carton to protect against wear.

This afternoon, I will talk to Van Horne and Ross. We will be leaving already tomorrow evening. Here, we leave our summer clothes, letter boxes, and other unnecessary things, three pieces all in all, and the rest we will haul along. By telegraph, I will also let you know that our address will be as follows:

> Care of: C.R. Hosmer
> Manager Telegraphs, CPR
> 4 Hospital Street, Montréal

He will always know where we are and, if he is absent, a secretary who knows us takes care of everything for him.

Before we depart, I will write to Count Adolphe with a word of thanks for our introduction letters; they were for the best of those who could be of help to us in this country. The dinner yesterday with Mr. Donald Smith was very enjoyable. I was seated between Mrs. and Miss Van Horne and had a good time. The luxuries of 'Mr. Donald' surpassed everything that I have ever seen in any particular house to this day. One [room] is furnished like a Japanese temple — that little luxury must have cost him more or less $400,000. A Japanese man came over to install it, a nice man who spoke seven languages and painted very well.

The Van Hornes, father and daughter, both paint quite nicely. They, as well as the Smiths, have a beautiful collection of paintings. Several Corots,[90] a Daubigny,[91] a Mauve,[92] a Bosboom,[93] a big painting by Thérèse Schwartze,[94] the mother with a boy and girl sitting on each side of [her] upon a bench against a wall. It was nice to see our old friend there again. In his atelier, Van Horne had a sketch by Thijs Maris,[95] which [Maris] later used for his painting of the hill with the tree trunks.

From here, we will take introduction [letters] with us to 'the Northwest'. It will be hard for me to leave Leentje behind, alone; she is not dreading it and I have faith in the Canadians. They appear to be fine people.

Now goodbye, elders. With full confidence that I will soon get my health back, I will go west. Also, keep yourselves well. Perhaps I will not write often, but I will be thinking about you a lot.

Embraced in my thoughts, your most loving Karel.

KLAB4554000083-84 [Karel to Wil]
Windsor Hotel, Montreal, October 26, 1891

Dearest Wil,

We have now been in Montreal for a week and will leave here tomorrow. Folks have received us warmly and after delivering our letters of introduction, various ladies came to visit us at our hotel and also brought *cartes de visite* from the whole family: Papa, daughters and, in this case, the son. Then an invitation followed that we accepted on the condition that there be only a few guests and at not too late an hour. Anyway, I can do much

---

90   Jean-Baptiste-Camille Corot (1796–1875): French landscape and portrait painter.

91   This is probably Charles-François Daubigny (1817–1878), French painter of the Barbizon school and arguably the first Impressionist; married to Marie-Sophie Garnier (1817–1890).

92   Anton Mauve (1838–1888): painter from The Hague School and the Laren School; married to Ariëtte (Jet) Sophia Jeanette Carbentus (1856–1894).

93   Johannes Bosboom (1817–1891): painter from The Hague School; married to Anna Louisa Geertruida Toussaint (1812–1886), a writer.

94   Thérèse Schwartze (1851–1918): well-known artist; married in 1906 to Anton Gilles Cornelis van Duyl (1829–1918), chief editor of the *Algemeen Handelsblad*. This painting, *Mother with two children on a bench in a church*, is now in the collection of the Montreal Museum of Fine Arts.

95   Matthijs (Thijs) Maris (1839–1917): painter, etcher.

more here than over there in the dampness. De Génestet's[96] lamentation ["Zomertochtje"] was perhaps, for his time, a witticism, but after a summer like the last, one may say it is a quite true description of the sentiment of the average folks, but not that of the affluent Dutch.

Our letters landed us into the very best set of Montreal people, gracious, decent, cultured people. We were especially drawn to the Van Hornes. He is an intellectual colossus, a man for whom the whole city has enormous esteem because he manages large undertakings so courageously. He is the president of the Canadian Pacific Railway. Charles Drinkwater, to whom I was also introduced, is the secretary, and [Richard] Angus, one of the directors. Just the opposite to us, here the president, vice-president and secretary are those who do the work and the directors, 'Board of Directors', are the money-folks who oversee and approve the balance sheet once each year. If Papa were here, he would most likely be named 'President of the SMN', and Baron [George August] Tindal,[97] 'Director', along with all of the other members of the board.

She [Van Horne's wife] is a good housewife, extremely modest and idolizes her husband. [They have] two children, a boy of fourteen and a girl of twenty. One had died, who would now be eighteen years old. The father paints quite nicely. He has never had lessons but has developed his own talent well. He has a beautiful collection of modern art and is currently busy with the reconstruction of the new house, because this one has insufficient room for his paintings. It was pleasant in the strange surroundings over lunch to chat about Mesdag[98] and Israëls,[99] Breitner[100] and Mauve, and to see a very good copy of Rembrandt hanging [there] and, upstairs in his atelier, to see a sketch by Thijs Maris and a couple of nice pieces of Delft pottery!

They are very proud of their Dutch heritage. In the United States, this is seen as patrician. The grandfather of this William Van Horne was a minister of the Dutch Reformed Church in New York and his mother, who was French, for the first time brought blood other than Dutch into the family. The young girl [Addie] was a day or three in Amsterdam on her way home from the Berliner Art School, so we could therefore touch on points in common.

One day, [Addie] took us for a tour in her carriage, along with Mr. Hosmer, manager of the telegraph for the CPR. That man is also quite a character. He lives for his work and he enjoys having daily close contact with the entire world within the reach of his hands, like the keys of a

96 Petrus Augustus de Génestet (1829–1861): poet and theologian; married to Henriette Elisabeth Jaqueline Bienfait (1824–1859).

97 George August Baron Tindal (1839–1921): chairman of the board of the Stoomvaart Maatschappij Nederland (SMN); chamberlain to Queen Emma; married in 1905 to Jkvr. Julie Claire den Tex (1853–1937).

98 Hendrik Willem Mesdag (1831–1915): painter; married to Sina (Sientje) van Houten (1834–1909), also a painter.

99 Jozeph Israëls (1824–1911): painter; married to Aleida Schaap (1843–1894).

100 George Hendrik Breitner (1857–1923): painter and photographer; married to Maria Catharina Jesphina Jordan (1866–1948).

piano. The long telegram that he was so kind to send to Cousin Adolphe shortly after our arrival must also have given you some pleasure.

One of these days, probably tomorrow, October 27, Hosmer shall telegraph our address to London and, undoubtedly, Adolphe will cable it to Amsterdam. To make sure, I have written it here once again:

>Care of: C.R. Hosmer Esq.
>Han: Telegraphs CPR
>4 Hospital Street, Montréal

He is a small nervous chap, with a cheerful face, lively eyes and a little black moustache, who speaks rapidly and indistinctly, just like one of his own machines. And to be certain, he constantly asks (indeed, every five or six words), "D'ye know what I mean?" He pronounces *s* as *tsh* and is constantly in motion and grips the person with whom he is speaking by the bottom of their coat or thumps him on the side or gives a pat on the shoulder. With all of that, he is very considerate and friendly. "Make my office y'r home, drop in at any time youtsh like. You know wh't I mean?" He is married, probably with a coloured woman,[101] whom he never appears with. At any rate, he speaks rarely about his wife. Today, for the first time, she invited us at an hour that we could not possibly manage and so late that it was nearly impossible to reciprocate.

Tomorrow evening, we leave for Calgary. In that area, there are various railway lines under construction and one is in the planning stage. You will find one and another of these things on the map that I have already sent to you via Mama. With a group of engineers, I shall be surveying the terrain for a new railway line that is to go from Fort Macleod into the Rocky Mountains. This provides me with the work in the open air that was prescribed for me. Without that regimen, living only a rich man's life of late hours now and then, etc., I will never get better. Now I have the hope that it will soon turn out for the better. The air already does me good. I feel that I am able to breathe easier.

From Ottawa (the capital of the Dominion) to Calgary is three or four days' travel with Mr. Brooks, soon to be my workmate on the prairie and in the mountains. He will be able to tell us a lot about the details of the project, about what kind of life we will have, sleeping accommodations, etc. I am very hopeful that Leentje will find good quarters in our area. When she is alone, the winter evenings will be long for her. But she is in good spirits and I think that with the fresh cold and lots of exercise in the open air, it will be to bed with the sun and up with the sun. The Canadians seem to me to be a decent sort of people with whom we will get along very well.

If I do it this way, writing to you like writing to a very close sister and making no allusions about an intimate relationship, I think that it will serve to allow for writing only monthly, which already feels terribly

---

101   Karel's assumption (evidently based on race and class) is not only inaccurate but unsettling. This applies also to his comments about Indigenous peoples.

long. (That is, if I adhere to it, which I have not yet done). Perhaps, in any event, camp life will offer little opportunity for writing. Then Helena shall fill in for me. I read with pleasure that you were helpful to Li with the unpacking of [the proverbial few sticks of furniture in her move to the Jordaan]. I hope that my admittance into the camp will give me a lot of hard and busy work and will be the best diversion also for you.

Fare thee well, greet your loving mother and sister warmly. From your affectionate, loving Karel.

Chapter 3

To the Far North-West on Velvet Couches

Karel is to join a survey team that is scouting terrain for a potential CPR rail line from Fort Macleod to the Rocky Mountains. He and Heleen leave Montreal by train, bound for Calgary, in the North-West Territories.

A28335001459–60 [Heleen to family]
Montreal, October 25, 1891

Today was an interesting day. It has been decided that we will go to the 'far North-West' tomorrow evening. Now at a tear, buying thick clothing and repacking because our summer clothing and excess baggage will be left here. I went with our two doctors to the big hospital, kindly received and showed around by a head nurse. Dr. Black asked everything for me so that I would be well informed. I became acquainted with many other doctors. They would gladly take me on if I wished it. For Karel, we ordered a coat made of woollen blankets, which is very chic here and, at the same time, practical, warm and light; and for me a riding habit, because I will have to ride a lot (or ride behind one). If I were to stay here, I could also ride every day on a horse. I have had many offers of horses that I can use.
    Bye now! In a hurry, your loving Heleen.

P.S. Four days travelling onward, four days for the letter to return, certainly therefore, there will be no news for ten days. Let everyone know. [Added later:] We had the best seats reserved in the middle and a beautiful view with the river in the distance.

A28335001560–61 [Heleen to Papa, October, no date]

On the railway map, you can follow the whole trip and see how ~~far~~ close we are to Fort Macleod. Just before our departure, we received yet another letter from Wil and the *Fairplay*[102] with Karel's article. It is nice that it has drawn so much attention. What does our government say about it? Are you looking for someone else to take the matter in hand? Wil wrote to us many particulars about it. Very nice, and now for sure we will quickly get a letter from you.

In the beginning, it was so strange to travel without you and to have so much more responsibility, but I am starting to get used to it. Karel is doing his very best to make it easy for me and we have, so far, neither forgotten nor neglected anything.

I am now very happy that we are so quickly out of Montreal and that Karel has this work that will certainly do him good. What has also surprised me is that, indeed, so many people find healing and health in this hard life. I do not have to write anything other than what is absolutely true and, here, no one is surprised that he chose this life.

I also have a very favourable impression of Mr. Brooks and I am convinced that also, without ladies, a good tone will prevail under him, better than in the gentlemen's lounge on board. Karel is now also, from time to time, in really good spirits, with the prospect in view of exerting himself and of making himself useful.

Over the last few days, we had a very nice time with Dr. Black. He did not like his hotel, so he also came to the Windsor. As a parting gift, he gave me a very useful handbook about nursing, from which I can certainly learn a lot. His father is an archdeacon in Australia, but not rich. Dr. Black paid for all of his studies from fellowships, which he obtained by working hard. He has an unlimited drive for study in his own profession and, this year, he was awarded three degrees, for which, earlier, he was too young to receive. (He is thirty-one.) I very much hope that you can be of assistance to him and his wife when they come to Amsterdam, for example, by recommending him to Dr. Delprat and other doctors. He does not initiate a conversation about his profession and, at first, I thought for a while that he did not care about hospitals and doctors.

It is a woefully sloppy letter that you will get, but a train remains a train, even in this delightful country. We have been riding since 7:00 a.m. along the lake, and at every turn, it's once again delightful. Sometimes, when the mountains are bare and only covered with short red ground-covering plants, it looks like Scotland with the heather. A Scot in the wagon also thought so. Yesterday, we met a nice young man who had travelled a lot and now has a five-year contract with his cousin's bank in Vancouver. Such days as these in the train are lovely; Mama would enjoy it.

102   *Fairplay*, a British international shipping magazine, founded in 1883.

Bye, dear Papa, this letter should perhaps be torn up. A warm embrace, from your Helena.

A29670000028-31 [Heleen to Li]
On the train between Montreal and Calgary.
Wednesday morning, 7:30, October 28, 1891

Dear Li,

Busy and interesting days are behind me and now I will start so many new things again. I shall try to write a bit of that which I had almost no time for in Montreal. We have left all of our summer clothes behind in the Windsor Hotel, along with many books in the large chest, which was too damaged to travel with, the hat box and a crate that we also received there. It was a lot of work to repack everything in one day, but at about three o'clock, after it was all done, Addie Van Horne came to pick me up in her carriage to go shopping.

It was horrendous weather, rain and snow, and the sloping asphalt streets were so slippery that it was very difficult driving, but I was glad that I did not have to walk. I bought a large stand-up collar made of sable fur to go over my ears for $15.00, and 'over-socks', which are large, coarse socks that folks wear over their shoes and that give you some chance of keeping your feet from getting too cold. I ordered a riding habit and she helped me with the fitting, because I hope to get to Fort Macleod.

There is no railway, yet, but we have been recommended to a prominent gentleman who has a large house and hundreds of horses. For the time being, I will stay in Calgary, a small town on the CPR line, four days' train ride from Montreal and two days from Vancouver. We have free train tickets for everywhere, both there and back. Mr. Van Horne has made everything as pleasant as possible for us. His family makes me think of the family Tak v. P.[103], father and daughter both broad and heavy and folks of deeds more than words. Both families paint, he with great speed and a good eye for colour and light.

The landscape is lovely here, at every turn, small lakes set between rugged groups of hills; slim-branched birches, some still with the last glowing-orange autumn leaves, and firs in the foreground; then and again, a small creek, and once in a while, a small house on the lake that appears Lilliputian. Around [the lake] there are many trees that have been chopped down and often the train must stop, like it is now, and then I can write quickly with a bit of ink.

Mrs. Van Horne is a bit intense, but very friendly and appears quite clever and tactful. Since her marriage, the mothers on both sides and

---

103   Johannes Pieter Roetert Tak van Poortvliet (1839–1904): Minister of the Interior; married to Christina Louisa Henriette Geertruida van Oordt (1850–1879).

a sister-in-law live with them. They have a mass of paintings — two Rembrandts, Rubens, Thijs Maris, etc. — that give the illusion of being in Holland.

Time and time again he tried to fool us, but we know our masters very well. They are very proud of their Dutch heritage, have read Motley[104] with great interest, and listened attentively to the stories about our little queen. Addie is the only girl; there is also a boy of fourteen or fifteen. When I get back to Montreal, I would like to see them very often. They interest me more than the Angus family, who are very friendly, rich and good-natured, but who seem to be a little dull.

As always, I am charmed the most by the eldest gentlemen. Sir Donald Smith has me completely enthralled. He is the perfect host, even during the absence of Lady Smith, and he is so enlightening when he speaks, mostly as he explains one or another proposition or principle. My other neighbour at the table was Sir George Baden-Powell,[105] the English representative who is to settle the dispute over the Bering Sea with the Americans. He gave me all sorts of examples of Sir Donald's excellent qualities: how, thirty years ago, only by nature of his personality, he had quelled a dangerous revolt in a new province, his experiences with Indians in the interior, and so forth. Sir George has been in The Hague for the North Sea fishing disputes and I was glad to be already so well informed about it. He also asked why the Zuiderzee had not been reclaimed and I told him about the plans. He is a lovely, jolly man and spoke a lot about his life and his journeys to find seals.

North Bay [Ontario], 12:30 p.m.: We are stopping here for a quarter of an hour. There is a large station and various wide streets with small wooden houses, a wooden church, a stone school under construction and a friendly wooden hotel. It is located on a splendid lake. We walked through the streets to the edge of the woods.

I have become acquainted with one of the young engineers [Noel Brooks] that is travelling with us. He boarded the train last night while we were sleeping. Karel first met him in Montreal. We had breakfast with him in the dining car. He is a pleasant, energetic and robust young man, who has already done this work for six years. His parents live in Sherbrooke, Canada. He writes home each week and always has books with him — novels and a couple of deeper ones. I heard a little bit more from him about their work. They will start close to Fort Macleod (pronounced 'Makloud'). They have tents for one or two persons, a cook, ponies to carry the baggage, wagons, and horses for the people. There is one head engineer, four young engineers and fifteen workers, all of them pleasant,

---

104   John Lothrop Motley (1814–1877): American author and diplomat who was married to Mary Elizabeth Benjamin (1813–1874). Two of his books are *The Rise of the Dutch Republic* (New York: Harper and Brothers, 1856, 3 vol.) and *The History of the United Netherlands* (London: John Murray, 1860, 4 vol.).

105   Sir George Smyth Baden-Powell (1847–1898): married to Frances Wilson (c.1863–1913). In June of 1891, he was appointed joint commissioner, Representative of the Canadian Dominion, concerning fishing rights and the condition of seals in the Bering Sea. Britain and Canada reached agreement with the USA in 1892.

vigorous men. Sundays will be mostly for resting, except in the event that bad weather threatens and the work must be finished. Sometimes they can receive visits by ladies for a few hours, but to travel along with them is too difficult. I now hope that I can get to Fort Macleod quickly.

Thursday, [October 29]: My second night on the train was even quieter than the last one. It almost does not jolt, and it is so quiet without busy stations or oncoming trains. When we stop, I wake up for a moment, see out of my window that the sun has not yet come up, and go back to sleep as soon as the train moves again, after one or two minutes. As soon as it becomes light, I get up to be the first one in the toilet room. Behind my curtain, I wrap myself in my big ulster dressing-gown, my feet in slippers, step out of my couchette and into the aisle and, from the upper couchette that is free, take out my clothing and bag and walk in between all the curtains to the ladies' lavatory at the end of the wagon. Then, I am fresh and ready when it becomes beautifully light. My bed is then tidied, folded upwards, and once more I find the two velvet couches facing each other like in a Zandvoort wagon.[106]

When the gentlemen are also ready, we go to the other end of the wagon, to the smoking room that ends in a balcony, and because our wagon is the last one, we have a lovely view from there. This morning everything was frosted over, the big Lake Superior spreading out to the left. Clear blue sky. Lovely!

Much love, your Heleen.

KLAB04554000185–89 [Karel to Wil]
Winnipeg, October 30, 1891

(*In a corner of the dining car that is being switched to another platform.*) Dear Wil, perhaps this letter will be left for a month, but I have to write to you now and then. Once occupied, I shall have to train myself to write less, and still, during the long winter evenings in the tents of our camp, it will be so tempting to talk with you on paper.

I must still mention the safe receipt of two letters, the last one via Helena, the one she gave me after her arrival in Montreal. It is so moving to receive a "Welcome in Canada" from your side, and it is such a sweet letter. I carry it with me and reread it when I am in low spirits and I am inclined to let my arms go limp when I ask myself: "To what purpose do I live and strive?" Nothing other than the prospect of misery ahead. I also thank you for your letter of October 16, the last news from home that we received before our departure from Montreal. I concluded from your letter that the Salonica case[107] is still being discussed these days. That pleases me. I would have loved to spend some time on the preparation and possibly, later on, on the execution of the case. It just did not happen.

106   A beach wagon, wooden, with two plank seats facing each other.
107   This is probably about the 1890 fire in Salonica, Greece, where a Jewish community was destroyed.

Whenever you have the opportunity, thank Jo and [Otto] for their kind offer. I do really appreciate it that your friends help you by looking for activities of the mind and of the heart. I very much hope that you have found the opportunity to visit the children's hospital with Miss van Gorkum[108] and the Kindervoeding with Suze Van Hall. Both ladies' pursuits have my full sympathy. Do you know that I also once visited the children's hospital for a few days to teach a fifteen-year-old boy math and languages in preparation for his high school exams? He was the son of a former Prussian officer and was very much scandalized when I tried to get him to sympathize with the songs of revenge by Paul Déroulède![109]

Anneke introduced me to a matron, an older lady from a noble family,[110] and a couple of young nurses. The children's hospital does not give the visitor a creepy or nauseating sensation. It put me in a melancholic mood to see all those little, young sufferers, for which life gives so little joy and yet still so much suffering to come. I know very little about the Kindervoeding. Now and then, I went to pick up Heleen after she had served food in the morning at Rapenburg [in Amsterdam], and once went inside where, on low, long tables, the steaming bowls of soup or *hutspot*[111] were set, and the hungry mites raised a dirty finger if they still wished to have another full plate.

Can you find Winnipeg in Gerard Keller's[112] book of prints? We arrived here at 10:00 this morning and should have, according to the timetables, departed at 2:30 p.m. During this time, the cars were thoroughly cleaned and aired (a lot of dust accumulates on a train after three days of rolling through the prairies) and I took advantage of this opportunity to do some shopping. I purchased a large piece of India-rubber mat to use as a ground cover for sleeping in the tent. This guards against the damp from the ground. Further, I have an inflatable pillow, two woollen blankets, sheets and pillow-covers so, therefore, I am very well equipped. At the station, I met Mr. Hogg,[113] who is the chief engineer of our party and, therefore, my future boss. Pleasant appearance.

We had lunch in the city, and, upon our return, we were informed that due to the delay of an American train, our departure would be postponed until quite a bit later. We went for another walk and, later on, wrote some letters. Now it is 5:00 p.m. and I hear that we will not depart

---

108   Sara Jacoba Susanne Caroline van Gorkum (1868–1946): in 1893 married Adrianus Slotemaker (1862–1935), a lawyer at the courts.

109   Paul Déroulède (1846–1914): French author and politician.

110   Jkvr. Pauline Clasina Elisabeth Berg (1831–1901), unmarried.

111   *Hutspot* is typically mashed potatoes, carrots and onions served with sausage.

112   Gerard Keller (1829–1899): writer and journalist; author of *Amerika in beeld en schrift: Canada*, a book with prints, drawings or wood-etchings/engravings, and text (Amsterdam: Elsevier, 1870); married to Carolina Cornelia Allot (1831–1898).

113   Alexander Lauder Hogg (1845–1906); chief engineer in Alberta for the CPR; married in 1886 to Isabella Elsie Rhind (1851–1939).

before 8:00 p.m. The main rail line, the Transcontinental, has only a single track, and therefore one cannot send us on our way at random because of local trains in the area.

[Calgary] Tuesday, November 3: Do you remember the song from *The Right Honourable* that Len sang while playing his banjo? This poignant negro melody with the refrain, in plaintive tones and melancholic final words, "And may the world go well with you!" Well then, we heard this whole song sung by a lady yesterday evening in the drawing room of the hotel. Imagine, I was wholly unprepared to be in the company of such a large number of people, and was sitting quietly at a table with Heleen when calling cards were handed to us from Mr. and Mrs. McCaul.[114]

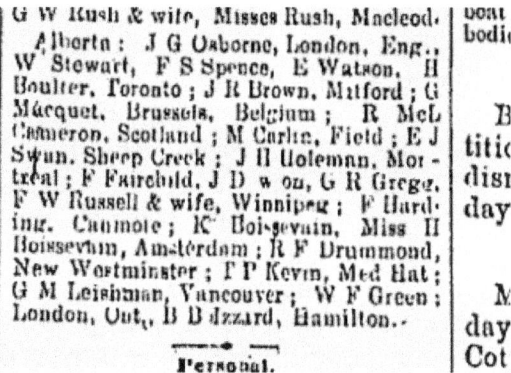

[12] Alberta Hotel arrivals, *Calgary Daily Herald*, Nov 2, 1891

For the last few days, I have not worn linen, nothing other than wool; no colour, no starched cuffs; I have not shaved for one week, partly because of the four days on the rails, partly because I have been ill for two days, and partly because I would like to keep my beard while in the wilderness. *Enfin*, I look like you would not give a penny for me. Helena, in comparison, is in a light grey summer dress, carefully coiffed and casually leaning against the back of an elegantly upholstered rocking chair. Helena, I might say, is enchanting. We were unable to discourage a man, who has lived in Fort Macleod for five years, from talking to us; anyway, we had to ask him about local arrangements. After talking for an hour and getting what we wanted to know from him, I was only thinking about a convenient way to end the session when the man let us know that he loved music and asked whether Heleen would perhaps play something. Heleen did play the piano, Schumann, Chopin, etc. In order to relieve her, a thin, tall lady was fetched, who turned out to have a very lovely voice and, with her, another three friends came along so that the small drawing room was filled to the brim and I felt ashamed about looking like a buccaneer. But it was pleasant to hear a song that Lord Arden[115] so enjoyed!

The good Leentje looks after me so loyally and I am such an ill-mannered patient. I now am sick to my stomach and these days I am in a really bad mood. It is enough to drive you crazy, now that I am held up day after day in this stifling-hot hotel due to a trivial stomach-

---

114   Charles Coursolles McCaul (1858–1928), a lawyer and author, moved from Lethbridge to Calgary and joined the firm of James Alexander Lougheed in 1891. In 1887, first married in Lethbridge to Frances Greenwood (1860–1943), and in 1921 to Eugenie Marie Lachapelle (1885–1952).

115   Lord Arden is the main character in *The Right Honourable*.

wretchedness, especially just before I can live healthily in camp life. And I so badly wanted to leave! The idea that, over there, they have already installed themselves, etc., and are already working without me; and now I will arrive like a real ninth wheel on a rail car.

There will be four engineers:
- Hogg — the boss
- Brooks — our friend, the trailblazer who leads the way; I hope that I will share a tent with him.
- Clercks — who I do not know, yet.
- Drury[116] — who must still spend a lot of time with the railway that is currently under construction and will perhaps come later, or not at all, to our project.

You can see on the map that I mailed to you which way we will have taken from Calgary, eastwards to Dunmore.[117] There we will stay for half a day, from ten in the morning until six in the evening. (It is a village with about the same number of souls as in Vogelenzang.) At 6:00 p.m. we will board a sleeper car on the train heading southwest to Lethbridge. It will arrive there at 4:00 in the morning; the people who are sleeping on the train will be left alone until 9:00 a.m., when the stagecoach with four horses will come around to take us (in twelve hours) to Fort Macleod (pronounced 'M'claud'). The rail line, Calgary-Macleod, is not, by a long shot, as far along as the other one; they have reached the point where they are repairing bridges.

This morning, we received a lovely package of letters. Heleen received a warm, kind letter for which I also thank you.

Yes, my love, I feel that I have found my place in this country and I can feel this clearly and that gives me courage.

Je ne sais où va mon chemin
Mais je marcherai mieux si ta main
Serre la mienne[118]

Be it then only in thoughts.

After everything, Jo is indeed a sweetie to sympathize with our feelings. She has suffered after her wedding; it would give her some peace if she could know that you would rightfully have a few years of happy marriage. But we will never get this guarantee and there are no longer astrologers and dream-readers to find in this century of science with whom to cast our horoscopes. Perhaps the Redskins practise this craft. I will

---

116   Edmund Hazen Drury (1859–1917): from 1890–1893 was division engineer and acting chief engineer of the Macleod branch of the Calgary and Edmonton Railway; married to Ethel Morris Austin (1873–1956).

117   Dunmore is a hamlet that is located in Alberta — then a district of the North-West Territories — within Cypress County, located 2.6 kilometres southeast of Medicine Hat's city limits, on Highway 1 and the Canadian Pacific Railway main line.

118   Louis Charles de Musset-Pathay; translation: "*I don't know where my road is going, but I know that I walk better when I hold your hand.*" https://www.goodreads.com/author/quotes/224009.Alfred_de_Musset

look into it. The women that I saw were old and ugly enough to serve as witches in some fairy tales of the world.[119]

November 6: It is already more than a month since we parted, a month that seems like a year to me. Today, I am up for the first time after a few days of being bedridden. Gastroenteritis!! It is very unfortunate; just now I would have been working, and perhaps a vigorous fresh-air cure would already be healing my asthma. While I am lying ill here in Calgary, the engineers are already busy over there with the surveying and every day is one lost. But I can see that it would be foolish to start for the first time in camp life with unstable health and I have to be very strong before roughing it.

Our letters are well taken care of. They are being readdressed, as you know, to Mr. Hosmer, our lively telegraph-friend. He mails them in a linen envelope as a 'value parcel', by registered mail, as we would say, to his agent in the place where we are and, therefore, that is why we get them quickly and securely. Normally he telegraphs in advance about what he has mailed, so that we know what we may expect from the mail.

Heleentje looks after me these days with exemplary care. We were specially recommended to the manager of the hotel; in that way, Heleen has it easier. She toils and drudges all day long and she is constantly thinking of new delicious treats to make me better, studies in many books, consults with various authorities, and is always positive and caring. [Ends here]

KLAB09193000004-9 [Father to Karel and Helena]
Amsterdam, October 30, 1891

Dear children,

Just as I had predicted, the letters you had sent arrived yesterday, Thursday morning. During our breakfast, Helena's letter arrived, which was enthusiastically opened and read, and later Karel's letter, which I read aloud at lunchtime. Further, I immediately wrote a couple of words to Wil, who is in Berlin with her mother to see her sister (who is travelling to Stockholm) for a few days. Karel's letter to Wil was mailed to Berlin later in the day, taken care of by Cor.

Well, well. This journey is nothing to sneeze at when one rolls on the Atlantic with the gigantic storm winds of the equinox, indeed completely different than on a journey to Java. Poor Helena! How much you must have longed for a short pause in the persistent rolling! Luckily this suffering will soon have been forgotten and that during the last days of your stay

---

[119] The term *Redskins* (in Dutch *roodhuiden*) was widely used in the Dutch press at the time. It is still used in North America in a few contexts but is recognized as being disrespectful to Indigenous peoples. To refer to the Indigenous women in the manner that Karel used is an affront to their dignity and ignores the realities of the harsh environment in which they lived. The word *squaw* is also being purged from use.

on the ship you had the benefit of meeting with quite respectable types among your fellow passengers.

Yesterday, I also received a telegram from London (or no, it was already the day before yesterday) while having dinner at Aunt Hes' [Hester den Tex Boissevain] on her birthday, where your upcoming departure to Calgary was shared. Having been informed by Daan [Gideon Boissevain] from London by telegram (also from maps in travel books) that Calgary is a city with a good future, not too far from the Rocky Mountains, a place for supplying the mines and the agricutural regions of the area, perhaps a future like Chicago!

I think that you will receive this letter there and I hope that you will by now have acclimated somewhat by the time that you have read these sentences. Of course, it is in many ways still primitive there, due, in part, to the mixture of primitive people and the lack of ultra civilization; of the magnitude of America, a real Amsterdammer cannot imagine it.

The birthday of Aunt Hes was extremely gay, with van Eeghen,[120] Quack,[121] etc., in the newly renovated living room, and the table full of all the gifts for the silver anniversary. Thijs dined at Uncle Karel's, where it also was very lively.

On Nella's birthday we all went to the fifty-second performance of *De Doofpot*, where we heartily laughed at the parody of the decorating of the monument at the Dam [Square]. There was a scene of a teacher at the children's cantata, who appeared as a lifeguard and had difficulty in making clear to the recalcitrant youth the necessity of swimming in school, and still many other relevant jokes.

I do not know whether we have already written to you that on Sunday we walked together from Hilversum to Baarn and that Mama also came along. She enjoyed the beautiful fall colours of the landscape, and even though she was very tired, it still did her a lot of good. As much as possible, I try to provide healthy diversions for her. I am at home quite often in the evenings, and then we talk or read together.

I am also trying to organize gatherings for some young folks once a week. They would come at about 8:30 p.m. to talk, play cards — a mixture of things — all kinds of music or something like that, and about 11:30 p.m. they would return home. It is still only a plan, but I am trying to get the family in on it. I would like to give as few dinners as possible and avoid going out.

Also, I have a building plan for a new house in the Vondelpark. I seriously doubt whether anything shall come of it, but it occupies Mama's thoughts with a pleasant topic.

As for me, I am doing quite well. I sleep reasonably well and feel energetic and ready for my work. The worst things are all those enquiring friends and acquaintances, and that endless repeating of the same

---

120 Anne Willem van Eeghen (1827–1892): sugar merchant, banker, politician; married to Johanna Louisa den Tex (1830–1904).

121 Hendrick Peter Godfried Quack (1834–1917): professor, lawyer, economist, writer of history; married to Clasine Thérèse van Heukelom (1841–1923).

banalities. I spoke about it with Wil and Mrs. de Vos, who told me that they already know in exactly which order the queries and condolences will be.

For his first appearance, the new mayor[122] did fine in the eyes of the council members. Mrs. Meinesz will not get into her house until the end of November.

Rotterdam has now appointed the [former] mayor of Leeuwarden, Lycklama à Nijeholt.[123] Our friend Havelaar[124] would have loved to have been appointed, but only if he were to have received some money. However, everyone who knew Rotterdam advised him not to take up the mantle, with [an expected] income of [only] 8,000 guilders.

I visited Ruys[125] in Rotterdam, who is housebound due to a bruised arm. On his way back from London, he fell on the Zeeland boat when they were passing by the *Wandelaar* [light ship] and he thought, therefore, that they would not yaw anymore. A rogue current threw him off his legs. He was very thoughtful about your departure. He liked the potatoes from Keuss,[126] but found nine guilders a lot of money. (Keuss only charges us seven guilders, so he maintains odd principles that Mama finds, in any event, understandable and fair.)

Cateau Waller[127] has given us a very nice painting — but I believe that I have already written to you about it.

With flying colours, Ko den Tex[128] became a member of the Provincial Council and shall already participate in the November sitting.

Mr. J.T. Cremer[129] has been chosen by us as the President of the Board of the KPM;[130] however, he has had influenza for fourteen days, so he has not yet been able to serve.

From Genoa, Tiedeman[131] wrote a friendly letter to tell us that if the climate in Canada does not suit you, he recommends St. Paul, as he says

122   Sjoerd Anne Vening Meinesz (1833–1909): mayor of Amsterdam, 1891–1901; married to Jkvr. Cornelia Anna Clasina den Tex (1852–1928).

123   Petrus Lycklama à Nijeholt (1842–1913): mayor of Rotterdam, 1891–1893; married to Catharina Elisabeth Margaretha de Kok (1841–1914).

124   Carel Eduard Havelaar (1842–1912): lawyer; married to Mauritia Catharine Arnoldine Swaving (1845–1931).

125   Willem Willemsz Ruys (1837–1901): ship owner; married to Maria Cankrien (1840–1932).

126   Cornelis Henricus Keuss (1842–1892): merchant in potatoes, at Spuistraat 96, Amsterdam; married to Catharina Dijkman (1839–1924).

127   Catharina (Cateau) Rutgera Waller (1837–1913): artist who studied in Amsterdam; wife of Nicolaas Gerard Pierson (1839–1909), Minister of Finance, 1891–1894; close friends of Jan Boissevain.

128   Jhr. Cornelis Jacob (Coo/Ko) den Tex (1855–1907): member of the North Holland Provincial Council from 1891–1898; first married to Catharina Josephine (Cateau) Biben (1858–1889); remarried in 1892 to Miss Eva Ketjen (1862–1929).

129   Jacob Theodoor Cremer (1847–1923): entrepreneur in tobacco; politician; married to Annie Herminie Hogan (1854–1924).

130   Koninklijke Pakketvaart-Maatschappij (KPM): shipping company in the Dutch East Indies.

131   Nicolaas Jacob Tiedeman (1838–1909): Consul General in Genoa; representative of the SMN; married to Jkvr. Magdelena Maria de Jonge van Ellemeet (1851–1936).

it is known to be 'windless'. He has a brother-in-law there, Henri van Ellemeet[132] (Seven Corners, Moore's block, St. Paul, Minnesota). Just put the address in your little memorandum book — *on ne sait jamais ce qui peut arriver*.

For the last few days, we have had very refreshing weather with a high barometer reading, in any event, cold.

The ice-clearing [issue] will come up at the next sitting of the Provincial Council. The members of the council propose a maximum subsidy of 12,000 guilders. We shall see if that will come through. *Dieu me garde de mes amitié*, because all of the too-zealous members of the Chamber of Commerce will perhaps spoil the matter through proposing that nothing is to be paid for by the shipping industry, while the subsidies, in particular, are only available when the interested parties, through their own contributions, deliver the proof that they really take the matter to heart and that it is actually necessary.

Warm greetings from your loving Father.

A28335001461-68 [Heleen to Father]
Calgary, November 1–2, 1891

Dear Father,

In one day we went through the whole month of November, with its wild rainstorms and wet streets, and now we are high and dry in snow and ice. It was the most remarkable experience, the long train trip. We left Montreal in October colours. Slowly, the landscape became duller; along the track the trees were burnt, and the young trees and small shrubs grew between the cooled stumps and bare dead trunks.

After Winnipeg, where we enjoyed the whole month of November in one day, we woke up in the morning to snow. The balcony was slippery, the windows frozen, and it seemed at first that we were on the ocean. In the twilight, the endless white rolling plain seemed to move. Later, I also heard from other people who lived on the prairie that it also seemed to them to be an ocean, but with an unending deadness without sound.

About animals, we also saw no trace, only a few prairie chickens high in a tree. Those birds are not very skittish, so that when there are seven in a tree, one can shoot several, one after the other, before they fly away.

These last days in the train, to me, took much longer than the first days. Looking out of the windows was not a pleasure anymore; only at sunrise and sunset was it again beautiful, but everyone else was too cold to look at it. Karel lay in bed, because the brave young man was not feeling well from all the time in the train and the unfamiliar food.

---

132 Jhr. Jan Hendrik (Henri) Adriaan de Jonge van Ellemeet (1848–1918); married to Mathilda Eliza Moore (1862–1936).

To let his illness run its course, he is now still lying down for a bit in a comfortable, spacious bed here in the hotel. It is not serious, but his stomach was quite out of sorts and made him feverish, which is really not pleasant while travelling.

Our travel companions, the gents Hogg (chief engineer) and Noel Brooks (his birthday is on Christmas Day), will leave us in Dunmore, from where they will take another train close to Fort Macleod. I hope that Brooks will become a good friend of Karel's. He is calm, level-headed and honest, which inspires a lot of trust. He is, I think, about five years older than Karel, needs a lot of time before he speaks, but then, it is always *ad rem*. He smiles cheerfully and readily, and during the journey was, for us, genuinely friendly and thoughtful, which made my long stay on the railway very pleasant.

I think that many good people live in Canada. Mr. Niblock,[133] who we were to see in Medicine Hat, came to visit us a few stations earlier. He was just touring around for his vacation but will recommend us to other people. And now, already this evening, we will be visited by Mr. Lougheed,[134] senator of Calgary, who will in turn connect us with his associate in Macleod. Everyone treats us as if we were part of their own family.

We arrived here eight hours too late, due to a delay in Winnipeg, but because of that, at a more humane time of day, that is, at 10:00 in the morning instead of 2:00 at night. The hotel is close to the station.

[13] John Niblock,
president of hospital board (1890)

133 John Niblock (1849–1914): assistant superintendent of the CPR; served as president of the Medicine Hat Hospital Board from 1889 to 1895; first marriage in 1871 to Isabella Sleter (1851–1890); second marriage in 1892 to Clarissa Alma Atwood (1856–1942).

134 Sir James Alexander Lougheed (1854–1925): son of a carpenter; raised in Ontario; became a lawyer and later a senator from Calgary in Ottawa; knighted for his service in WWI. He was married to Lady Isabella (Belle) Clarke Hardisty (1860–1936), a daughter of William Lucas Hardisty (1824–1881), a Hudson's Bay fur trader, and Mary Anne (Ann) Allen (c.1840–1930). In 1891, the Lougheeds had two sons, Clarence Hardisty Lougheed (1885–1933) and Norman Alexander Lougheed (1889–1963). See *Dictionary of Canadian Biography*: http://www.biographi.ca/en/bio/hardisty_isabella_clarke_16E.html. See also The Hardisty Family Legacy, Lougheed House at https://www.communitystories.ca/v2/conflicting-loyalties_allegeances-contradictoires

We walked toward it over the cracking snow and were immediately given rooms; I put Karel quickly into bed. I then went for breakfast, still with our travelling companions, all of whom also ate here. The food here is exceptionally good. Lovely fish from the lakes, excellent milk, butter and eggs, good meat, and capable preparation, but the service, by a pair of fresh and cleanly dressed girls, goes slowly.

After breakfast, a bit of bickering with Karel, sending a telegram to Montreal, and then Heleentje went alone on her way to the office of Mr. Ross, where she hoped to find the party of engineers who were to be soon departing. Mr. Brooks had given us a letter for one of them. The clerk of the hotel showed me the way (1.5 miles) and it was not difficult to find because there are few roads here. It was quite cold, low frost-filled air into which the glittering snow rose in a mountain of mist, but it was pleasant to walk fast without having to move out of the way for someone, because there was no one. In the beginning, I had to rub my ears to keep them from freezing and because I wanted to save my collar for the extreme cold.

First, in the street, there are many stores of which some are posh, with two floors and decorated facades; many others are small, genre de Wit,[135] with a geranium and hanging plant for one window; for the other window, the name of the occupant, in large letters, such as "Ti San-Hai Chinese Laundry" or "Boarding House." How the latter is managed in such a property, I do not yet know.

Gradually, the houses became scarcer, but the plank sidewalks still went on, and I, too, at a quick pace, as if I had only an hour to go to Grandmother's[136] and Aunt Gerarda's[137] and back. All the houses were shrouded in mist and out of it appeared a big wooden building that I soon recognized as the one that was pointed out to me by the hotel clerk, the 'Barracks', which I was to keep to my left. So, I chose the road on the right, around a corner, and indeed I saw the large bridge over the frozen river beside the railway bridge and I knew that I had gone the right way. Although there were five black footpaths through the endless snow, without hesitation, I chose the direction of the rails and, within a few minutes, saw a hut on the railway bank. I climbed up, despite two barking dogs that ran toward me. I knocked on the door and a bearded face looked through the window and opened it up. He redirected me to the next house, a red-painted wooden one that, with its small windows, reminded me of a circus tent. On the other side was a door. I knocked again. "Come in." And I stood in the small office, a corridor along a counter. Behind, the tough old face of a man in shirtsleeves said that Mr. Drury was on

---

135   Simon de Wit is the name of a grocery store that was on Weesperstraat 62, Amsterdam, later becoming a chain of supermarkets that was taken over by Albert Heijn in 1973.

136   Elisabeth Susanne Gerardine van Maanen (1805–1895): maternal grandmother of Karel and Helena's, married to Anthonie Brugmans (1799–1877), a lawyer and recipient of the Militaire Willems-Orde, the highest of the nation.

137   Huyberdina Gerarda Punt (1849–1937): married to Jan's brother, Jacob (Ko) Pieter Boissevain (1844–1927), who became the chief of the import-export firm Reiss & Co.

the rails for a few days, but "Please, sit down!" Passing the glowing stove, I sat down in a leather armchair beside a desk. On the envelope of the letter was yet another name, in case Mr. Drury was not present, belonging, luckily, to the inhabitant of the office. I say 'inhabitant' because, from my chair, I saw through the open door a separate corner with a bed, washbowl and clothing rack.

Mr. Couchon[138] read the letter in the meantime and was very amiable and said that the party [of engineers] had already left Calgary, yesterday. Mr. Drury was only travelling along until the end of the train line and probably would come back on Tuesday evening. Whether he will still go to the surveying party is not yet decided. He advised us that it is better to take the route through Dunmore. From there we should take the night train to Lethbridge, and from there, probably a coach to Macleod. The difficulty now is to find out on which days the coaches go, because we can indeed rent another carriage and horse, but that is very expensive. He telephoned yet another person, and for that he went to another hut. We also talked a bit about this, that and the other, and then I took the way back.

About one thing I am glad is that the crew was already gone. Now, there is no way that Karel could go along, and I have more of a chance to first get him healthy.

The clouds remain the same nasty grey, but the air here is stimulating anyway, and it was a joy to run back over the cracking snow and to not slip. I found Karel quietly sleeping and went to the dining room to partake of some bread, ham and milk. The entrance, or in other words, the vestibule, of the hotel is also a smoking room and a sort of club, which is always full of smoking Canadians. But they are not noisy, and so I have no problem with it.

Upstairs in the hotel, it is very cozy. There are three small salons. I am writing now in the largest of them, 5 × 3.5 metres, with two windows on the long side and, in between, a mantlepiece with an empty hearth. Left, on the smaller side, is a window and beside it in the corner, a reasonably playable piano. A small square table in the centre, 65 × 65 cm.

Along the wall, there are comfortable canapés and easy chairs with carved wood and red velvet. The first day it was boiling hot everywhere but, thanks to our boldness in the opening up of the windows and the turning of many knobs, it is now a pleasant atmosphere. Up to now, I have seen three ladies and a number of gentlemen, but the latter seldom come into the salons. A lady, Miss Williams, has a book of classical music and plays reasonably well.

From time to time, Indians ride by on ponies, wearing large floppy 'robber-hats' and strange clothing. Most of them look shabby, especially the women, who wear a sort of bag and walk along the street picking up rags. On the train, we sometimes saw a few of their tents, miserable rags around a stick. Luckily, there are no negro servants, but there is a

---

138 Nalon Couchon, clerk of the CPR. Source: *Henderson's Manitoba and Northwest Territories Gazetteer and Directory* (Winnipeg: Henderson Directory Co., 1894).

negro guest who dines with a very proper lady. That still looks strange to me.[139]

Karel is much better today. He got up and went out to enjoy a little bit of the fresh air. It is much clearer weather. We can now see several stone houses and a wooden church. The sun is coming out and it will thaw this afternoon.

We got a telegram back from Montreal, and a *Rotterdammer*, but no letters. Each time, it is a pity to walk away before the letters have reached us. I so hope that something will still come tomorrow before we depart.

My plan is, namely, to go along with Karel to Macleod. There is a hotel there and in the first days it may be possible to visit him in the camp, while, later on, there will be few chances, as they will be many days of travel away.

I think that this letter can be circulated, even though I have not written it with that intention, because between caring for Karel's health and hurrying to get ready as soon as possible, I was a little bit flustered and wrote haphazardly. Many warm greetings to all our good friends from both of us, your Helena.

November 2, 1891: Now, just for a moment, a chat. I wish that I could get an answer at the same time, because it is so different than I had imagined. It seems so strange to travel around now for my own pleasure and, after all, I still find it difficult to turn down all the friendly people here. As things now stand, I think that Karel will stay in camp for at least a few weeks. After the first days, I will not be able to see him; that does not matter to him nor to me, because I am convinced that he will have the life and the companionship that will be very good for him. I was very pleased to notice that he is also very taken with Brooks and can imagine himself learning a lot by example from him, while previously, he did not like to be friends with, or in the company of, people to whom he felt inferior.

Regarding myself, I do not dread being alone among all these good Canadians, but I think that it is a pity that this separate life is, of course, so much more expensive; I fear that all of the outings that these brave people think of to amuse me will also not be cheap. I do believe that I will always be able to ride the train for free and I also think that I should take this opportunity to see so much beauty and things of interest, and perhaps not let it pass. On top of that, everything is still so vague. If, after a week or so of surveying, Karel sees a good opportunity here or there, then it could certainly be that he will start something different.

---

139 At this time in the Netherlands there was little known of the Indigenous peoples of Canada. Heleen's description of the dress of the men and women was indeed accurate, as was her comment about the teepees. In this regard, both she and Karel expressed concern about their treatment and conditions. Despite the two of them having progressive and modern views, however, they also made disparaging comments about black train porters and hotel workers; Karel even cautioned Wil about seeing them, revealing his harsh beliefs. The roots of their deep-seated prejudices, while not uncommon, are unclear, as both Heleen and Karel were unlikely to see or meet the very few black people that lived in Holland.

I end this hastily because we were surprised this evening by a visit from Mr. and Mrs. McCaul, who are also staying in the hotel, until their house in Calgary is finished. They have lived for five years in Lethbridge and he for a long time in Macleod. They will recommend me to many people there in the neighbourhood, in villages and on farms. They also told me that beyond Fort Macleod there are still a few villages and many houses, so, I could travel that way for some time along with the camp, at least until they get to the mountains.

They are most enjoyable young people. He has read *The Right Honourable*,[140] many works of Ibsen,[141] and was very happy with *The 19th Century*[142] that I loaned him. Unfortunately, they heard me playing [the piano] and now I have to do it for them again. Afterwards, another lady was fetched who could sing. Still a few more folks came in and there was no opportunity for a nice chat anymore.

In all likelihood, we will leave tomorrow evening and then the real roughing it will begin. Hurray! Karel is truly better again and I am as healthy as a fish.

I wish that I had more time for writing; that will come later and now I must not go to sleep too late. With an affectionate kiss, your Helena.

A32074000140–41 [Heleen to Wil]
Alberta Hotel, Calgary, Canada, November 3, 1891

Dearest Wil,

This morning, to my great pleasure, a large package of letters arrived, and from that I will first answer yours, because I had already longed to do just that. It has done me quite a bit of good; so much courage and energy came out of it that it fired me up again and gave me hope for the future. Today, Karel was especially down again. During the long train ride here, his stomach became upset, and now we have had to stop for a couple of days before continuing on again. He is not at all short of breath and there is absolutely no reason to worry. It is just only a little unpleasant; he longs so much to work that this sitting weighs heavily on him. That is why the letters were such a welcome distraction.

I believe that you are quite right to go neither to Jo [in Russia] nor to Heleen Viruly[143] [in Gouda], but to stay quietly at home and to fill your life with regular activities, as you would bravely do. What lovely things

---

140 Justin McCarthy and Mrs. Campbell Praed, *The Right Honourable: A Romance of Society and Politics* (New York: Appleton and Co., 1888).

141 Henrik Johan Ibsen (1828–1906): Norwegian author and playwright; married to Suzannah Daae Thoresen (1836–1914).

142 Robert MacKenzie, *The 19th Century: A History* (London: T. Nelson and Sons, 1880).

143 This is probably Helena Cornelia Viruly (1869–1948), an unmarried daughter of Theodorus Pieter Viruly (1822–1902), a politician, owner of the soap and candle company De Hamer in Gouda, and Aegidia Johanna Elizabeth Ledeboer (1833–1907).

you have written from Jo's letter, and so much love, along with a little sadness, is shown to us in so many aspects.

If you ever get to live in Canada, then your music will give you much pleasure here. Yesterday, I played a little out of a book that I found, and then had to play all of those old things for different people that we got to know, with fingers as stiff as a rod and on a piano that was very limp in the middle, and almost rusted solid on the end, but they thought it was lovely, anyway.

An English lady sang that negro song from Zenobia in *The Right Honourable*, and it turned out that Mr. McCaul had read the book. This gentleman is a lawyer and prosecutor here. This afternoon, he came to pick me up for a walk, even though he is very busy because he has been away for a month and now he must bring everything up to date. He has a friendly, kind wife and two small children. He loves reading, music, and even draws, and is very satisfied with life here in the far west and would not even live in a big city again. Mrs. McCaul does many things herself because maids are very expensive and know little.

It was lovely to walk, beautiful mild weather, even thawing a bit. The sun came through the light cloud cover and beautifully lit the faraway mountains behind the shadowed hills close by. We walked up to the smaller river of Calgary that was half-frozen, and where a couple of boys were skating. I got a much greater impression of the city, which is built in a triangle along the two rivers that merge here. I saw a few very large houses, those of a judge and a lawyer. We met a detachment of mounted police on beautiful big horses. I yearn to ride horses here. It looks so wonderful.

November 4: I wrote a long letter to Papa with an orderly story of how we are faring here. He will certainly let you read it. Today, I also wrote to Kees[144] and Mary[145] and shall now end because I cannot think about any more sentences. Much love from Karel, who is doing, yet again, a lot better than yesterday. Tomorrow night, we are once again on our way.

Warm greetings to your mama, and Cor, and a warm kiss from Heleen.

A32005000366–69 [Jan to Karel and Heleen]
Amsterdam, November 6, 1891

Dear children,

Grumbling sometimes helps. This morning at breakfast, I had let loose about the strange notion of travellers who make us wait so long for news (since we so much wished to know how the reception had been in Canada), and see, just as I was going to my office, something fell in the mailbox

---

144   Cornelis Anne (Kees) den Tex (1867–1916): eldest son of Aunt Hester; manager at the Stoomvaart Maatschappij Nederland (SMN); married in 1903 to Martine Henriette van der Waarden (1875–1961).

145   Maria (Mary) Boissevain (1869–1959): married in 1888 to Cornelis van Eeghen (1861–1949), banker.

and I came back inside with the so-welcome letters from October 24–26, and both small maps of Canada, etc.

I am very satisfied with the news. You could wish for no better reception. Adolphe and Daan [Gideon] have given good advice. A smart, lively young man such as Mr. Hosmer to give you directions, and the bigwigs of society to give you a wave in the right direction.

I heartily hope that Karel will give an impression of energy and competence. That they will come to know both of you as decent, civilized and, hopefully, amiable young people. And so now, the die is truly cast.

On Nella's birthday, while she was toasting you, you got your first job, "Helper" of the Chief Engineer of the contractor, James Ross, during the construction of the railroad from Fort Macleod into the Rockies. In our wonderful *Imperial Atlas*, I found this 'fort' marked at the end of a branch of the Canadian Pacific that runs southwards between Dunmore and Medicine Hat. It is located at 49°45'N 123°22'W and is, according to my rough estimate, 250 English miles, measured along the railway, from Calgary, therefore eight or ten hours' travelling.

I understand that Calgary is the only place in the area where one can get good accommodation with certainty, and wholeheartedly approve that Helena is first going there. I trust that further arrangements will be made by both of you with consultation and discernment. May God give his blessing upon it! That is no trite exclamation, but the expression of my inner conviction that Providence has been laid within the hearts of the people who can lead the weak and fallible to their full development.

Now, something else. Thriftiness is good, but you must equip yourselves very well for life in the wilderness. There must be a fur coat; and if you do not have one by the time you have received this letter, then have one sent to you from Montreal or Calgary.

We spent yesterday evening looking at a number of photographs[146] from British Columbia that were sent to me from Mr. Jan van Eeghen.[147] Beautiful nature, glaciers, waterfalls, canyons, gigantic trees. It helps us to imagine the surroundings where you most likely are. 'Exploring parties' of the Canadian Pacific, which were working on laying bridges and making snow-sheds, etc., were also photographed.

I think that you will get details from others in the family about the illness of Uncle Toon.[148] It is an infection of the large intestine, from which Oosterwijk Bruijn,[149] van Ogtrop[150] and others have also suffered, and

---

146   In 1887, the CPR commissioned William Notman & Co., Montreal, to photograph the progress of the railway and the spectacular scenery of the opening of the West of Canada, showcasing the arable land and the route through the Rocky Mountains to the Pacific Ocean.

147   Jan Herman van Eeghen (1849–1918): banker, art collector; member of H. Oyens & Zn. Bankers, part of the Dutch CPR syndicate; married to Anna Maria du Mée (1862–1949).

148   Pibo Antonius (Toon) Brugmans (1840–1891): lawyer; unmarried brother of Nella; uncle to Heleen and Karel.

149   Pieter Adolf van Oosterwijk Bruijn (1837–1900): lawyer; married to Marie Elize Schiff (1846–1923).

150   Lambertus Johannes Gerardus van Ogtrop (1840–1899): lawyer, judge, politician; unmarried.

from which they also recovered after a long convalescence. With plenty of morphine and absolute rest, there is hope for a full recovery. Two nurses take it in turns.

Grandmama is keeping herself brave. She has a bad cold and is somewhat feverish and stays in bed. I spoke with her this afternoon. She sends her greetings to both of you and is convinced that you will find your way in Canada because you know your foreign languages and speak decent French, which is very much appreciated in Canada.

Uncle Sebald[151] came to see his sick brother, played a round of cards with us in the evening and was very quiet. Mama is doing very well, fortunately. We both have been very dismayed by the sudden serious condition of Uncle Toon. However, we are becoming encouraged again and your letters have now completely cheered us up.

A.C. Wertheim[152] stopped me at the stock exchange and said, "You probably have good news!" I read part of your letter to him. The kindness of this friend was indescribable.

At the Provincial Council [of North Holland], which met this week, the ice-clearing item was on the agenda. In the commission, of which I am also a member, heated debates were held, the conclusion being that the proposal to provide a subsidy of 12,000 guilders per year for twenty-eight years was supported unanimously. However, part of this proposal is to share in all of the costs of the ice-clearing operation, not only the fixed costs. We then still have a chance to reduce the fixed costs, e.g., lower interest rates, no insurance or something like it, or to provide exemptions [from certain taxes] for the shipping industry, while, in this proposal, the operating costs during the 'frost season' must, in any case, be paid by the shipping industry.

Due to the passing of Mr. Maurits Insinger,[153] there must be an election for his senate seat. Most likely the decision over the matter will be dealt with no sooner than fourteen days, at which point a meeting will be held for that purpose. In the meantime, we are not sitting still.

I am greatly perplexed about the building plans. Architect van Gendt[154] spent an evening with us after first having inspected our present house. He has discussed everything with us and concluded that we absolutely need more breadth for our lot. Also, he wanted different terms, all of which were expensive. I would like for him to calculate [the costs] and then decide. But look, now Mr. Schmidt[155] comes to tell me that he wants

151 Sebaldus Justinus Brugmans (1842–1893): lawyer; unmarried.

152 Abraham Carel (A.C.) Wertheim (1832–1897): banker, politician, philanthropist; married to Rosalie Marie Wertheim (1839–1909). The first public park in Amsterdam, Het Park, was renamed Wertheimpark shortly after his death.

153 Maurits Herman Insinger (1825–1891): banker, politician; married to Jkvr. Henriëtte Agnes van Loon (1825–1902).

154 Adolf Leonard (Dolf) van Gendt (1835–1901): architect; married to Elisabeth Frederica van Elten (1838–1901).

155 Andries Christiaan Nicolaas Schmidt (1857–1919): wholesaler in wines; married to Elisabeth Sabel (1856–1914); lived on Keizersgracht 711.

to buy the terrain beside it and must know how much breadth I would like to have. Therefore, an instant decision with insufficient information. On top of that, Mama and Elisabeth made it clear that they are completely satisfied with our present house, so long as I do not buy [anything else] and that I absolutely do not long for anything other than to live quietly where I am. So, you can imagine that my enthusiasm for renovation is not great.

This afternoon, Wil is coming here for lunch and to look at the photographs of Canada. Then we shall discuss who will take on writing the desired gossip letters. It is perhaps fitting work for Nella (daughter), especially when it also serves to improve her Dutch.

Uncle Karel has asked for your address in order to send you the *Handelsblad*, and he will definitely do it.

In the *London & China Telegraph* is a story about a case involving the Java Agency, against an English bank, regarding an advance of £11,000 to Brand,[156] who signed for the Java Agency. The management in London wanted to repudiate that debt; however, they have already been ordered to pay the [bank] for the second time.

[Our ship], *Burgemeester den Tex*, with Kees on board, arrived in Batavia today, one day before mail day. All is going well with the ships. The 'Holt' with whom I was on friendly footing all those years is Philip and not Alfred. The latter I met for the first time in my life on October 8, 1891. Our negotiations continue. He has put something on the table that was irrevocably refused by us. Now he talks about an arrangement for export duties only. I demanded, upon the condition of working together, that he send a trusted person to Java who will work along with our agent, in order to keep the cargo from spoiling.

All the best to both of you, as always, your loving Father.

---

156 Jean Daniël Brand (1873–1942): agent for the KPM; married to Anna Catharina Müller (1881–1967).

Chapter 4
Last Town on the Rail Line

Karel and Heleen finally set out from Calgary, ultimately riding with the crew on a coal freight train from Dunmore bound for Lethbridge. Bundled in fur, they travel by stagecoach to Fort Macleod, then further to the surveyors' camp.

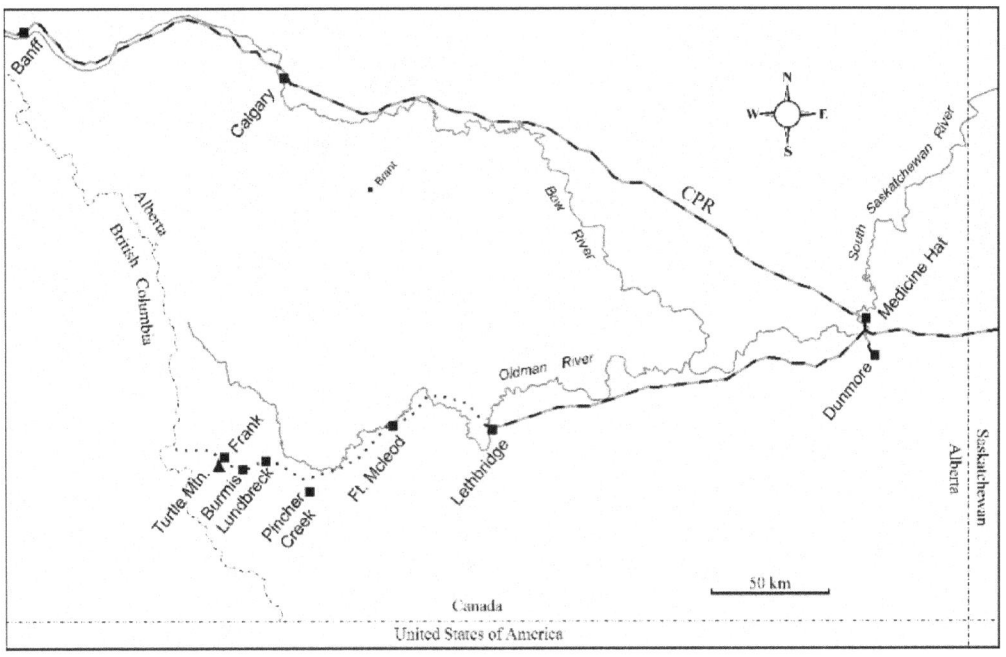

[14] Map showing Calgary and rail lines to towns in southern Alberta

A28335001469–72 [Heleen to Mother]
The Lethbridge House [Hotel], November 9, 1891[157]

Dear Mother,

Yesterday evening, we arrived here after the most unusual train journey, from Calgary to Dunmore, from 2:00 at night until 10:30 in the morning. We had a wonderful carriage from the CPR, not a sleeping car but still comfortable. In Dunmore, we inquired about the train to Lethbridge, a rail line for coal that ends there, and we heard that besides the regular night train, there is also an empty coal train that departs at 11:30 a.m., with one passenger-wagon attached. Dunmore is nothing more than a station, wooden hotel, store and a few shacks, so we enthusiastically seized the opportunity to exchange a nasty, slow train-day on the prairie for a good night in a hotel [in Lethbridge].

[15] **Lethbridge House Hotel**

Our rail carriage was very unusual, with a circus-caravan door in the front, in the back and on both sides. Along the wall on both sides was a high bench, on which pillows and blankets showed how the men had recently slept there. The back end of the carriage was taken up by an old-fashioned stove and two wooden platforms under a sort of spire-like lantern. On the platforms were chairs for the conductors and the

---

157 Heleen had originally dated this letter "November 8," being confused by the time of journey that started at 2:00 a.m. on November 9.

'brakeman'. Their upper bodies disappeared from our view in the lantern light and the seemingly disembodied legs were a very comical sight. Our fellow passengers were an old, tall travelling salesman and a young coal-worker. The benches were long enough that two people could easily lie on them and, during the ten-hour journey, that suited us well. We passed not a single station; only at 4:00 p.m. did we stop at a small house for supper, dried fish and a kind of cake with currants and cloves. On the prairie, we sometimes heard a shot fired by the conductor, who was trying to shoot prairie chickens while the train was underway.

After 4:00 p.m., the lamps were lit. A small petroleum lamp on our side and, behind on the floor, two lanterns, which were taken outside at the switches by the [conductor and brakeman]. The stove was fully stoked up because it had become cold outside. It snowed and we had so much headwind that we arrived two and a half hours late, but in the circus wagon, it was comfortably warm.

We arrived at 9:30 p.m., and a short walk over the freshly fallen snow (it was no longer snowing nor storming here) brought us to the hotel. In the lobby there is again a large stove surrounded by robust smoking chaps, a dining room and a billiard room that leads to the lobby. Upstairs is a very neat, small salon with a coal stove, two canapés, rocking chairs, etc. Everything is shabby, a few fake oil paintings in frames on the wall. Also, there were a few people who were getting warm or writing, but when I came in, a place was readily made for me and a nice chair was drawn up beside the stove. We went downstairs for a cup of tea and, with it, bread and lovely strawberries in their own juice.

Our small bedrooms, across from each other on the third floor at the end of the hallway, are fresh and proper. We both slept wonderfully, had our breakfast in a full dining room (very good porridge and lamb chops) and soon, that is, 9:00 a.m., we will go with the coach to Macleod. The chief engineer, Lumsden,[158] should also be here and will ride with us. He arrived on the night train, which was four hours late! Karel is keeping very strong! I see to it that he gets whipped eggs and milk now and then, and that he swallows very bravely!

Bye, Mama, much love to everyone. I am healthy and in great spirits. A warm kiss from your Helena.

KLAB045540000192-94 [Karel to Wil]
The Lethbridge House, Lethbridge, Alberta, November 9, 1891

Dear Wil,

From the last town on the rail line before we actually go into the wilderness, I shall finish this letter, even though I can only mail it from Macleod, where I will have access to my suitcase. Heleentje travels

---

158   Hugh David Lumsden (1844–1922): supervising engineer; married to Mary Frederica Whitney (1859–1926).

along everywhere, nothing fazes her and she finds everything to be just fine. You should have seen us yesterday, arriving here on a freight train. Not even! A train of empty coal cars that was being taken back to the mine district to be filled with coal! We reserved seats in the employee wagon and left at 11:00 a.m., instead of leaving at 6:00 in the evening on a real train, because otherwise we would have had to stay the whole day in the minuscule town of Dunmore.

There were two benches along the length of the wagon that covered a portion of the sides. The part of the bench located close to the door was covered with bedding, a couple of dirty pillows and the blankets of the employees who had previously slept on it. This was quickly tidied up and I installed Heleen in a corner where she felt comfortable. Behind the benches were two large side doors which, luckily, were mostly kept closed. Between them stood a stove that, later in the evening, was stoked to become red hot. There were also two large side-cupboards, with a narrow passage between them that led to the door at the other end. On top of the cupboards stood chairs, so that the occupants of them had the opportunity to follow and control the movement of the train by watching through the windows.

As you can see, we had two fellow travellers who, in turns, smoked and slept. Halfway there, we had lunch, which consisted of fried fish and, afterwards, berry pie, in a comfortable wayside inn, where Helena's neighbour, the stoker of the train, despite the best of intentions, was pitch black. Later on when it got dark, several more men boarded the wagon, from various small stations, all black and shabby and smoking heavily from small pipes, who told each other tall tales around the glowing stove, and who had a dog with them that they left to howl and bark for amusement. This was too crass for me, and when I requested that they stop with that, it was immediately over.

Now I am here (contrary to the posh writing paper) in a small country hotel, where ten to twenty men with high boots and coarsely woven hats stand and smoke pipes in the entrance

[16] Lethbridge House letterhead with Karel's diagram of train

hall around the stove. It is where the coach will soon come around to take us to Macleod, close to which I hope to find the surveying party.

In the meantime, I wish you well. I will take good care of myself when Heleen is not here anymore. Say hello to your lovely mother and to Cor for me. Yours truly, your fervently loving Karel.

[Written later:] Now I am in Macleod, my last evening with Heleentje. We are both dead tired after six hours of being jolted in a coach with four horses and fording two rivers (stone cold in the rivers), and in the morning, I will reach the camp. Wonderful! It is cheerfully freezing weather and I must become better. Give these latest tidings to everyone at home. I have not written a decent letter to them in a long time and once camp life starts, I will also not do it for a while. The Canadians remain decent folks, also in the wilderness.

Farewell my whole love, Your Karel.

KLAB09193000009 [Father to Karel and Helena]
Amsterdam, November 10, 1891

Dear children,

At the stock exchange, I received a telegram from Adolphe that says "cousins leave Calgary for Fort McLeod [sic] in high spirits," from which I understand that you have learned that the situation in Macleod allows for Helena to go along. How lucky for both of you! The telegram gave me a huge amount of gratification. Here, there is nothing special going on.

With Uncle Toon, all things considered, it goes reasonably well, and he was allowed to eat an oyster today.

I am ready to go with Captain T. Bakker[159] to London to finalize a charter for the SS *Celebes*,[160] which perhaps will be chartered for six months by Furness.[161] At this time, however, there is no telegram; therefore, it will probably be too late to leave today.

It was very pleasurable for me to reread your last letters. What a friendly and hospitable welcome you received in Montreal! I am meditating on sending a small Christmas present to Hosmer and hope that he is not a teetotaller, because I will probably send him some choice Curaçao, etc.

In my thoughts, I will now often be with you in the vicinity of Fort Macleod; and the photographs of Jan van Eeghen are actually so diverse that I can picture the surrounding environment very well. Think about us without worry. I am highly confident that Mama shall keep herself well, and our home life is very peaceful and cozy. All of the children are doing their best to make our lives pleasant.

---

159   Captain Teunis Bakker (1842–1891 in London): married to Neeltje Verheij (1848–1921).

160   SS *Celebes* is one of the steamships of the Stoomvaart Maatschappij Nederland (SMN), as are the following ships, also mentioned in the letters: SS *Koningin Emma*, SS *Prins Alexander*, SS *Prins Hendrik*, SS *Prins van Oranje*, SS *Prinses Amalia*, SS *Soenda*, SS *Voorwaarts*, SS *Prinses Wilhelmina*.

161   Furness Withy & Co.: British shipping company, headquarters in Hartlepool.

On Sunday, we had a family procession to the Walloon Church[162] to hear from a proposed successor for H.E. Valès;[163] we stood with seventeen Boissevains on the little Walenplein, but the general opinion was that he would be no improvement.

This afternoon, I went to the exhibition in Arti, where I saw a half-dozen paintings that I viewed with much pleasure, and our family art-expert, Thijs, also seemed to be in agreement with me.

Now, it is 4:00 p.m. and no telegram as of yet; therefore, I will not go to London today. Always, your loving father, J.B.

A32074000142-47 [Heleen to Wil]
Fort Macleod ("pronounced Mkloud"), November 10, 1891, Tuesday 5:00 p.m.

Dear Wil,

A large part of the journey is complete, and I am delighted to be able to tell you that Karel has pulled it off very well. And that tells you a lot, because travelling here is no small matter. Sunday evening, or rather, night, at 2:00, we left Calgary. The night train brought us into Dunmore at 10:30 a.m. On the way, we again had breakfast in a dining car. From Dunmore to Lethbridge, it was the coal train that I have written about to Mama. A good night in Lethbridge and now, today, a journey by coach (!), for four persons inside and one beside the driver. The baggage goes on top and is tied to the back. The sidewalls consist partly of materials that are attached above and below but, on the side, it is somewhat drafty, with small windows in the door with two panes, one of which was missing. A quite cold coach, but we were prepared and had even thought about sitting outside, so were therefore equipped with furs, blankets, etc. Furthermore, there was company, a big, broad [man], a skinny travelling salesman and an unappealing little lawyer. Karel, who takes on unlikely proportions in his fur, and the big gentleman, were both seated on the front bench and I opposite in the middle, between the two skinny ones. The big man, who was also in a comfy fur, had great pleasure making fun of the skinny one, who found it cold. They were good friends who travelled often together and their manner was very civil and pleasant.

The journey started along the coal mines. We saw the black holes in the mountains and the wagons that were waiting for their load while the ponies grazed. It was cheerfully sunny but bitterly cold; we progressed slowly because time and time again the rope around the baggage came undone and we had to stop to fasten it again.

---

162   The Walloon Church (Waalschekerk) is a Protestant church in Amsterdam, along the southern stretch of Oudezijds Achterburgwal canal, on the Walenplein. The building dates to the late fifteenth century and has been in use as a Walloon church since 1586.

163   Henri Etienne Valès (1838–1890): minister of the Walloon Church, Amsterdam, from 1869–1890; married to Suzanne Marie Martin (1842–?).

After some time, we neared the Oldman River and our travel companions warned us to put our legs on the bench, because the river was deep at some spots and we would get water inside during the crossing. With much hilarity in these new experiences, we heeded the warning and held our feet and blankets up. The river was split by a small island and not very deep, but there was a strong current, so the carriage was pulled along at an angle. The bottom was rocky and the bumping and jolting of the rickety coach caused me to imagine all of us floundering in the river. Then, we landed on the island with a strong jolt.

The second part was less bumpy but deeper, and our careful preparations turned out to be essential. On the other side, the road was very steep and, from time to time, the horses had to stop for a moment to catch their breath, and then, sometimes, the coach would begin to roll backwards, something that gave our big friend a reason to spur on the horses with a louder voice.

In the meantime, we had the most amusing conversations. The salesmen made constant commentary about each other and found it delightful when I agreed with them. They were much more like gentlemen than the little lawyer, who was, nonetheless, also polite and harmless. We told [them] about Holland; they knew nothing other than that there must be some kinds of ditches and canals. The skinny one (trading in confections such as candies and cakes) loved music very much, had heard many operas, and had even heard Adelina Patti.[164] I recommended that he use van Houten's cacao[165] for his chocolate factory.

Just before our stop, we had to cross the river again, which was full of small ice floes, but it was shallower, so that we got almost no water inside. At noon, we stopped at a small house, where we found an excellent meal and a lovely warm stove. The deaf boy who brought the food inside evidently found that to be a very nice job and brought every cup or plate one by one. He even brought the empty cups in first, only to take them away afterwards to pour the tea into them. We were also not in a hurry and warmed ourselves comfortably near the huge stove (the 'big friend') that was vigorously stoked with logs.

At 1:00 p.m., we climbed back into the wagon again, which, with the fresh horses, brought us at a full trot into Macleod by 3:30 p.m. The hotel seemed to be abandoned, insofar as there was no one there, but the hall was nicely warm and the skinny one discovered a parlour upstairs, to where he led me. After that, he fetched a pail of coal from downstairs with which he reawakened the smouldering fire. In the meantime, the big one and Karel unfastened the baggage and brought it into the house. Eventually, a fat innkeeper appeared downstairs and, upstairs, his daughter was full of apologies that the bedrooms were not yet made up because they had had

---

164   Adela (Adelina) Juana Maria Patti (1843–1919) was a Sicilian-French nineteenth-century opera singer, married three times.

165   Van Houten's Chocolate Factory was established in 1815 in Amsterdam. The brand name still exists. Also at this time, Bensdorp Royal Dutch cacao was offered for sale at Bentley & Co. in Lethbridge.

so many guests this morning. I got a room bordering the parlour with a door in between, and since I am the only lady there, it was like being in an apartment just for me. My toiletries, which had hung outside on the wagon in my bag, were frozen, as was the water in the pitcher. I allowed them both to thaw near the stove.

November 12, 1891: Yesterday, I brought Karel to the camp and left him behind there. I am glad that I have seen how he is situated and now I feel much more comfortable about leaving him there to fend for himself. In every tent is a small stove with a pipe, so that it is nicely warm and not stuffy. In the eating tent, I got a very good cup of tea with apple pie, and everything looked tasty and clean. With respect to the food, it is certain that he will want for nothing.

It never rains in the winter here and the beautiful, clear, dry weather that we now enjoy will probably continue throughout the winter.

To An, I wrote a long description of our journey to the camp. For you, who have crossed through so many snowfields in Russia, it would not have been that new, and those sleds are perhaps even more comfortable than our spring wagon. But Karel enjoyed it immensely and also, for me, it was an unforgettable day.

Also, it was a lovely feeling to be at the end of unhealthy train journeys and hotel life. Karel was afraid that he would be a nuisance to the others [in the camp] but, to the contrary, I believe that they will receive the new fellow very cordially and will be happy with the variation in companionship and the atmosphere in the tent. Brooks shall certainly take good care of him; he, who for a year had taken care of his ailing sister, and therefore knows what a not-all-too-strong person is up against. Today the camp moves to a nearby hamlet, Pincher Creek. Soon I will also go there and then will see Karel again, quite often.

[17] Survey wagons in Oldman River, Alberta

I am very glad that I went along with him straight away. To take the coach journey alone would have, for both of us, been less gratifying and, if still in Calgary, it would have been difficult for me to keep informed of his movements.

Bye, dear Wil, now we are on the right track. A warm kiss from Heleen.

A29662000043-52 [Heleen to An]
Macleod, November 9-12, 1891

Dear An,

An evening of beauty! My little self is keeping warm, almost unnoticeable in a bunch of buffalo hides and coyote pelts, as we move forward at a fast pace through the soft, cracking snow. The proud, rugged, glittering snowy mountains weaken slowly in the falling shadow, while the world glows behind it in changing colours. And, in front of me, the wide softly rolling plain, so still, so pure, as if with its own light, gives a silver-copper glow to the silent, clear, softly darkening hill. And there, the moon, not shining, but as a lit face. Oh, I cannot describe the wide, pure, soulful stillness that changes slightly everywhere without movement; the young, beautiful earth so close to the faraway, gentle heaven!

"You're not cold, Miss?" sounds a voice from the pelts in front of me. "No, thanks, Macdonald, quite comfortable." A quicker hoofbeat beside me and our scout exchanges a few words with Macdonald, who shortly veered the four-in-hand from the trail. Still continuing at a fast pace, the journey onward is no longer unnoticeable, but the suspension is excellent and, however steep the slope, however deep the snow, the brave little horses do not hesitate. Further, the darkening mountains appear whiter and lighter; look, there is the moon; timidly, the stars begin to peep toward the tireless earth, glowing like mother-of-pearl.

Again, a turn, slowly into a deeper ravine, and in front of us the large wooden bridge that was completed yesterday to the great satisfaction of the brave coachman, who permits himself to make a remark: "I guess it would kill many a horse to feel this water tonight." The glistening shards of ice that float six miles an hour down the small stream illustrate his point and the scout is completely in agreement with him. A short distance walking, while the rider speeds forward to open the large gate, is then again followed by speeding our way up the hill at a steady pace through the vast plain. "Hope you'll have less cold the next time," now says the voice from the left fur in front of me, who has already made many comments, possibly from the fear that I will drop off to sleep. He also enjoys the beautiful sunset but must rub and slap himself often to stay warm. My answer, "If it is as bright as this, I do not mind the cold," appears to have surprised him. A half-hour later, he points out to me the approaching lights of the barracks, and his mate adds to that, "It

[18] Macleod Hotel, Fort Macleod, Alberta

is only three miles now." Within twenty minutes, we reach Macleod and the scout helps me out of the animal skin and to climb down.

The asthmatic innkeeper (the spitting image of Jorksveld[166]) approaches me in the hall with the most welcome message that "the fire is burning in the parlour." So it is, indeed, and after a few minutes, the innkeeper's son also comes in to light the lamps.

November 11, 1891: Dear An, I have not answered your lovely letter from the beginning of October, at all, and I found your last Teylingerbosch and new cat stories, in any event, the most interesting. Now you will get as a reward a story of one of the most thrilling days that I have experienced.

At 10:00 in the morning, Karel and I were seated in a spring wagon, by the courtesy of Major Steele,[167] chief of the police post at Macleod. Karel had planned to go alone, but one of the policemen who was joining him told us that the camp was only three miles out of Macleod. That was only a short trip, and I could easily go with them and come back in the afternoon with the team. Therefore, I right away put on a lot of warm clothes and took a seat beside Karel among the numerous animal hides in the back of a sort of high tent-wagon, without the tent.

166   This is probably Steven Jansen van Jorksveld (1844–1910): married to Cornelia Spurius (1842–1922).

167   Major General Sir Samuel Benfield Steele (1849–1919): then chief of the Northwest Mounted Police (NWMP) in Macleod; married in 1890 to Marie-Elizabeth de Lotbinière-Harwood (1859–1951).

The coach box, also a broad plank just as high as ours, was taken up by the two policemen in pelts, upon which a copper button, which tried in vain to give a military appearance, was visible among the black, curly fur. We got acquainted with our guide, or 'scout', Captain Denny,[168] the most polite, congenial talker, who made me think of the navy officer Posthumus Meyjes,[169] but much older. He sits on his horse like he grew up on one and rides without spurs, lash or crop. It was wonderful weather, nicely cold but little wind, no trace of a cloud.

The wagon had wonderful springs that we soon experienced, because once past the few houses of Macleod, it went straight down over a stony surface. Further on, the road became quite even and the snow also made it a smoother ride. Karel and I enjoyed this trip indescribably, particularly in comparison with yesterday's jostling in a drafty coach. At first it was somewhat cold and I lowered my thick shawl over my face, but the landscape became so beautiful that, from time to time, I shoved it away; and slowly the sun became so warm that I did not think about a shawl anymore.

Here, the prairie is hilly, like enlarged dunes. The dry, yellow grass grows everywhere through the snow and, in the sun, it takes on surprisingly gentle, varied colours. The snowy mountains slowly appeared in splendid majesty, the high, sharp-sided, glittering peaks above the widespread, deeply pleated coats of snow.

We sat as if we were in silent adoration of the all the beauty. Here and there large herds of cattle made an appearance, at first as if telegrammed on the large white fields:

(. . – .) (.) = in front (–) = profile

We passed the bridge, which had just been finished, and were pleased to not have to cross the fast, half-frozen stream. Thereafter, we soon left the track and followed our scout, who, without any fear, rode on and formed a nice silhouette as he stood still at the top of a hill and, with his hand, showed our coachman the way.

The camp was further than we had thought, but at 11:30 a.m. we suddenly saw it ahead of us in a lovely little valley. A large dining tent and

---

168 Although the letters of Heleen refer to "Dennis," this was undoubtedly Sir Cecil Edward Denny (1850–1928), once a captain and sub-inspector with the NWMP. In 1881, he became an Indian Agent and worked later as a scout. Among many other things, he was appointed Chief Archivist of Alberta, serving between 1922 and 1927.

169 Reinier Posthumus Meyjes (1860–1939): naval officer; married in 1891 to Petronella Adriana Agathe Wurfbain (1867–1955).

two small sleeping tents, a wagon and three ponies were scattered under a group of high trees. The entrance required exceptionally skillful horsemanship. From quite a steep slope, the team had to take a corner and then again, turn around to pass over a small bridge above a deep trench, but Macdonald, our experienced coachman, did it with great dexterity. He hardly uses the lash but has many different ways of whistling, by which he lets his brave horses know what he wants them to do. In the camp was a cook and someone who was disabled. The engineers were further away, probably about six miles. They had staked poles along their way. The luggage was brought into Brooks' tent. We warmed ourselves in the dining tent and, after a short deliberation, decided that we would go to look for the engineers.

Again taking our seats in the coach, we move on through thick and thin, with no trail to follow anymore but only sometimes a bunch of stray tracks; but our guide leads us beautifully along the short stakes. Sometimes it declines very steeply and, all of a sudden, the coachman asks us to get out with the remark "We may come down all right, but in case of an accident, it would be just as well if you were outside." We need no second invitation and watch with interest how the coach journeys downward through the deep snow. One horse stumbles but comes up again on his feet. Macdonald stays in the driver's box, but the other one jumps off and hangs on the back of the coach to slow it down. At the bottom of the ravine, we take our seats again and begin the climb up the other side at a gallop.

We then drive through fairly high brush, like English broom but not so prickly. We approach the river again and, with that, the Indian camps of the 'Bloods'. The camps look very poorly. The dwellings are mostly a bundle of sticks that form the skeleton of a tent. At night, woollen blankets, which serve as clothes during the day, are draped around them. There are a few small wooden houses, but for us they would be no more than a small booth, without windows and not always with a door. Even so, these are the best kind of Indians of Canada. They farm the fields along the river, [where they grow] oats, potatoes and wheat; they also look a little bit less shocking than the begging Indians at the railway stations.

In the meantime, we have already travelled more than six miles, the stakes absent since the last ravine, and still no engineers are in sight. The scout, who is far out in front, comes galloping back and signals us to a halt. He acknowledges that he lost the trail and goes to ask the Indians for information. He runs off again to flag down a few Indians who are calmly galloping on their ponies. The news that he brings does not help us very much. Yesterday, the "whites" were seen in this area, further inland. Therefore, we have probably followed the old trail of yesterday. What now? It does not matter very much to us to find those men. Tonight, they will come again back to the camp and Karel can wait for them there. But now, we are certainly ten miles away from it and the horses need to drink.

[19] Women of the Kainai Nation (Blood Tribe) on travois, Ft. Macleod

```
The scout tells us that we are only three miles from the Indian
Agency, where Mr. Springett¹⁷⁰ will gladly give us some lunch. With much
pleasure, still a way to go!

A28335001473-76 [continues on]

We keep the strange, meandering river in view and now drive a pretty good
trail toward the Indian Agency, a gathering of four or five good wooden
houses. The agent is out with the doctor, but his servant receives us
hospitably, stokes up the stove and prepares a luncheon for us of cold
meat, bread, butter and tea.
     Afterwards, we walk around a little bit with the [scout, Denny], who
tells us many interesting things about the Indians. He was an [Indian]
agent for several years and knows their language; many of the Indians
that we see know him and approach him.
     The Indians live in the Reserved Territories, fertile areas which
have been set apart for their use. On top of that, from the government
they receive three pounds of meat 'per head' every two days, and four
```

170 Arthur Richard Springett (1861–1914) was the Indian Agent for the region, Treaty No. 7 Piikani (Peigan), married in 1893 to Evelyn Cartier Galt (1865–1950).

dollars every year. The money is paid out twice each year. At that time, they come all together to the pay office; it must be an entertaining spectacle, the many hundreds of Indians on ponies, sometimes a man and three children on one animal, but they all ride.

It is difficult to distinguish a man from a woman, as they both often wear a red handkerchief around their heads, not decorative like the Javanese, but worn like our cleaning lady usually does while she dusts the rooms. Two stiff braids hang out of it on the forehead. The face is painted bright vermilion and dark yellow. The multicoloured woollen blanket is held around the waist with a rope or a belt, and at the top with the hands. Small children are put on the back of the women in woollen blankets, now and then shored up so that it looks like a hood. A little bit of leg that sticks out of the blanket is within a kind of pants made of woollen blankets, seamed with a thick thread on the outside. Men and women wear rings, armbands and large ear-hoops or earrings. On top of the red handkerchief, the men often wear a floppy felt hat that looks quite absurd. They speak little, also amongst each other, but make horrendous facial expressions. Most of them live only from the government allowances. Sometimes they try to steal cattle, such as the day before yesterday when one was caught red-handed. He then shot the police officer, whose throat was singed, whereupon another officer shot the Indian. The Indians where we are now are very peaceful. Our scout shows us the butcher shop from which the meat is handed out every other day.

We warm up again inside and are ready to take on the return journey. They now know the road exactly, and in a shorter time than it took for us to come, we see the camp again. At the agency, we had also heard that the engineers had crossed the river, no wonder then that we had not found them. I say goodbye to Karel in the camp and ride toward home by myself in the back of the carriage, as I had described on the first page.

This letter is so strange, with two beginnings. I shall tell you the reason for this. 'Description [Letter No. 1]', I firstly had in my head, but when I wanted to write that one, I saw the little lawyer from the coach, who I had already found unpleasant and who was constantly waiting for me. Especially now that I was alone, I did not want anything to do with him and so I started writing right away, and wanted to let my pen flow without stopping, to give him no opportunity to say anything. That I could do with a new story and, therefore, I began No. 2. My trick worked. He said something that I answered without looking up, and then he disappeared to the Elysian Fields.

Before that, I also had to get rid of yet another man. A broad Norwegian (genre vom Rath[171]) in a natty corduroy travel suit and new high boots came in and started speaking with me, in French, to tell me that he was very well known here and would be happy to be of service. Karel had talked to him in the morning, and I was, therefore, not surprised and not thinking

---

171 Heleen is making the comparison to Edwin Julius Wilhelm vom Rath (1863–1940), an Amsterdam sugar merchant, art collector and patron of the arts, unmarried.

him of any harm, but soon it appeared that he was not completely sober. In turn, he spoke French, English, German and Danish, and each time asked me the same thing, etc. He was, even so, a good-natured fellow who would not hurt a mosquito, and when I saw how he behaved, I thanked him nicely for his good intentions and said that I would most likely not need his assistance, since I knew the language of the country and had many friends. I also told him that I intended to get back to my writing. With much bowing and scraping, he did leave me in sole possession of the parlour.

Later in the evening, a new guest arrived, a very young girl with her escort, Mr. Burns.[172] They came from Calgary along the direct way and had ridden seventy-five miles in a buggy with one horse that day. The man's right wrist had been broken three weeks ago and was still in a bandage. Therefore, most of the time the girl had driven, but at the dangerous places, for example, Mr. Burns had taken the reins with his left hand, such as while crossing the river that was full of ice. The horse reared up in the water from fear of the cold shards of ice and the bank was steep and slippery. Mr. Burns acknowledged that he had no idea of how he made it to the other side. A pleasant, agreeable Canadian, he also knew Mr. Hogg. The young girl was on her way to her married sister at the agency in the south.

The maid [from the hotel] also came to chat, thinking that I "might feel a little lonely." She and her sister have been working here for four months. She was a dressmaker in Winnipeg but the salary here is much higher, forty dollars per month! Her sister cooks. She serves upstairs and downstairs and is very busy. The cleanliness, therefore, leaves a little to be desired, but she is well intentioned. At my request, the dubious sheets were immediately exchanged for others, which, according to her were "quite new and have never been under anybody." At least they looked somewhat clean, and I found it easier to believe her. This morning, I asked for some hot water and freshly washed my glass and pitcher and dried them with my own hand towel.

If I were to stay here for a while, I would also certainly get my own plates and cups cleaned, but I will most likely be gone again soon. Captain [Denny], the scout, was here at breakfast and told me that yesterday evening a man had come with news from the camp. A half-hour after us, the engineers had come back. Today the camp is to be broken up and will be moved toward Pincher Creek. I have [introduction] letters for Mrs. [White] Fraser,[173] who will certainly allow me to stay [with her],

---

172 Patrick (Pat) Burns (1856–1937): rancher, businessman, politician; married in 1901 in London, England, to Eileen Louisa Francis Anna Ellis (1873–1923).

173 Elizabeth Sage Retallack (1862–1908) is the daughter of Francis Retallack, the aide-de-camp for Governor General Head; married to Montague Henry White Fraser (1854–1927), inspector with the NWMP. In 1900, he joined the Canadian Mounted Rifles in South Africa. Henry dedicated a window to his late wife in the Anglican Church of Agassiz, British Columbia. In 2019, a special gravestone was placed for Henry in a ceremony dedicated to his service as a member of the NWMP. See also http://www.rcmpveteransvancouver.com/dedication-of-a-stone-of-remembrance-inspector-montague-henry-white-fraser-o-50a-north-west-mounted-police-july-13-2019-1100-old-agassiz-cemetery.

and I plan to go there soon. But today, I am staying here to wait for letters. By telegram, I know that letters arrived for us in Calgary at the same moment that we steamed away, and they could be here [in Macleod] this evening.

Now, I might as well just end this letter here. If you wish, you could certainly share some of it around. Much love for everyone, and also from Karel. Bye, An, a warm kiss from Heleen.

A32005000370–73 [Wil to Heleen]
Amsterdam, November 11, 1891

Dearest Heleen!

A little while ago, I received a letter from Li with the news that a telegram had arrived, saying that you two had left for Fort Macleod.

Comparing this with the date of Karel's latest letter [October 27], four days before the journey and thus around November, it follows that nine days have gone since you arrived in Calgary and before you departed for Macleod. I hope that this indicates that Karel first sized up the situation and discovered that you could perhaps very well live together, that he can come home to your house every day and, therefore, that he has gone to pick you up. Oh, I so hope that it is not what we somewhat feared, that with constantly changing locations [he] could not take a lady with him and that you are, therefore, separated from each other for long periods. In that case, I think that it would be so lonely for you, partly out of the feeling that you have no particular work and partly out of the feeling that you cannot be of use to him every day.

But now, perhaps everything is coming together and he has his dear sister as a loyal companion. Oh, Heleentje, I am so thankful to you for everything (!), also for the lovely words and feelings expressed in your letter. Yes, sometimes it is still very difficult for me, but the good news from Canada balances it out. So long as he gets better, I believe that I will still be thankful for everything that has happened. How wonderful that he, finally, not only breathes better but also has his courage back. It is just like Karel, after setting a goal and a promise to do something, to blossom once again.

For someone like him, it was so hard to be treated like a patient and, in his letter to me, he also wrote that he had faith in his recovery once again. I regret very much that I did not write somewhat sooner, but I wanted Karel to get my first letter and did not dare to be disobedient and write within a month. Now, he himself has shortened the time limit and I think that is a good sign. Don't you think so?

We had a big 'letter dinner' when I dined at your parents' last Friday, in order to look at the photographs in the evening, which were recently sent by [Jan Herman] van Eeghen. Over dessert, Papa began (then

I, then Thijs, then An, and then I again) to read parts of our letters from both of you. (I was allowed to read the one from you to your mother beforehand.) In that way, we got an overview of all the news that had flowed out of your pens, and that was truly considerable. How lovely it is be so well brought up to date on everything that is happening over there! And never think, "Oh, I have nothing to write about!" — everything interests me. Even when you gave me a description of all the furniture in your room, I still like it, because you two use it, after all!

How sweet the Montrealers have been to you both, truly exemplary. I do not know if we Dutch people would be like that. Friendly, oh yes, but when it is not a courtesy visit, but looking for a job, would we be so obliging and helpful?

What you have written about Dr. Duncan (who is certainly an adventurer), the old professor, and your own talent for dealing with people, I find quite amusing. Perhaps you would be able to find work in a hospital over there. But you shall probably have a lot to do in your household. Write to me if you would like to get the *Maandblad Voor Ziekenverpleging*[174] or preferably something else of that kind.

How awful that your Uncle [Toon] Brugmans is sick! I did not wish to speak about it in my letter to Karel because I did not know whether your parents had already written about it. It is especially difficult for your mother. He just started to improve somewhat and now, the new worries again. We would like to hope that the worst days of his illness are over, but it was a difficult thing for her to deal with, and for your kind grandmother, who, despite her eighty-seven years, still came to his bed time and time again. However, sorrow never comes alone. It seems that when one is already suffering, still something else will follow.

Li and Nel ate here on Monday evening and afterwards we went to the *Soirée dramatique et litteraire* of Mme Thénard.[175] This was the first time that had I attended anything like that and saw so many acquaintances together again. The recitations were really amusing. However, we have heard something funnier from her before. Her *causerie sur la mode* was, of course, not complete, but she said interesting things and, while she otherwise talked of everything in long, long sentences, every time there was a *trait d'esprit* or a *bon mot*, she paused for a moment to give us the opportunity to digest it. Only, it was so annoying that she was so convinced about the truth of what she claimed that she must have said 300 times in that discourse, "*C'est évident.*" Also, she did not spurn the use of *évidemment* and *naturellement* for things that were, indeed, not so self-evident. When she followed by performing a piece from *Deux Orages!*,[176] she

---

174   This monthly magazine began on September 15, 1890, a sign of professionalism and the modernization of nursing.

175   Jenny Thénard (1847–1920): French comedienne; played at the Odeon Theatre in Amsterdam, entry fee ƒ1.99.

176   *Deux Orages!* is a comedy written in 1882 by Eugène Bertol-Graivil (1857–1910), a French journalist and writer.

actually ended again with "*C'est évident.*" Tin [Boissevain][177] and I said, at the same time, that she was glad that she could say "*C'est évident*" one more time. Thijs, Tin, Gi [den Tex],[178] van Marle[179] and van Notten [Notje][180] were seated behind us. The latter came to talk to Mama during the intermission, very sensitive and lovely, said Mama. He did not want to take the chance of upsetting me in front of all those people, which I doubly appreciated. I do not understand Gi very well. He has not yet said anything about Karel and also has not approached me. I always think of him as a sort of brother and now he is so strange, but van Notten can also relate better to the situation. His engagement is still a secret, but many do know about it, it seems. The girl, Doude van Troostwijk, is a cousin of Jet Schiff.[181] She recently began to take riding lessons. Cor often goes to the Schiffs' and got to know her there.

Don't you think that it is nice that Thijs, Gi and Tin have become members of the Senate?[182] I think that is just the right thing for Thijs and think that he will do well. From Isaac da Costa,[183] who was visiting here on Sunday, I heard how nicely Thijs had adorned the table for the V.O.N.D.E.L.[184] dinner. He is the president and had decorated the menus with drawings and citations from Dutch poets, and all of the name cards were handwritten, with mottoes and anecdotes for each. Da Costa had found, among other things, his signature, "T Boissevain," in a corner of his [card]. Isaac da Costa is a good fellow. He is so friendly; one can see right away whether he really means something, and he was particularly sympathetic.

Yesterday, we were at Veenenburg. We had been thinking about it for a long while. Mama had not been there for a long time and felt a little bit guilty (not about the journey to Berlin), but certainly dreaded this chicken run. We breakfasted at Veenenburg and then went for the afternoon and evening to Uncle Marinus'[185] [at Duinlust]. One of my cousins had to stay in his room and the youngest heir came after lunch on tippy-toes,

---

177 Rutger (Tin) Jan Gideon Boissevain (1870–1945): lawyer, director of Kas-Vereeniging (which in 2002 became KAS BANK N.V.); married in 1901 to Sybilla Frederike Franzisca Maria Wilson (1875–1949).

178 Gideon (Gi) Mari den Tex (1870–1916): son of "Aunt Hester"; general manager of the Surinaamsche Bank between 1903–1906; in 1896 married his cousin Anna (An) Maria Boissevain (1872–1916), Karel and Heleen's sister.

179 Jan Constant van Marle (1864–1918): lawyer; married to Cornelia Anna Jacoba Vening Meinesz (1877–1965).

180 Unico Hendrik (Notje) van Notten (1868–1928): lawyer; married in 1894 to Wilhelmina Louisa Doude van Troostwijk (1869–1939).

181 Agatha Henriette (Jet) Charlotte Maria Schiff (1873–1950): married in 1894 to Ernst Franz Insinger (1870–1939), Lieutenant-General.

182 Illustrissimus Senatus Studiosorum Amstelodamensium, the Senate, is the administrative body of the Amsterdamsch Studenten Corps, equivalent to a student association at the University of Amsterdam.

183 Isaac da Costa (1867–1943): studied law at the University of Amsterdam; unmarried.

184 V.O.N.D.E.L.: the Literary Debating Society of the Amsterdam Student Corps; named for the famous Amsterdam poet, author and playwright, Joost van den Vondel (1587–1679).

185 Marinus Leembruggen (1848–1925): also a brother of Wil's mother, who lived at the country house, Duinlust, beside Veenenburg in Lisse.

with his astonished blue eyes, to partake of his sandwich and chocolate drink, while Auntie [Alida], Mama and I were seated around him. With a serious face, I was told that I was sitting on "Bet's chair," and when I sat on another chair and asked about whose chair it was, the answer was "Mien's," in the same chastising tone. I do not know whether I am now in his bad books about that, but not only was I refused a kiss but also a hand, and that, even without wearing my lorgnette! He was certainly regretful afterwards and followed us, but quickly turned around when I wanted to come toward him. Still, he is a nice little tot; too bad that Karel did not see him.

To be at Duinlust was so strange to me. I had never thought to return to Teylingerbosch when I had left there sobbing, or that I would ever be happy there again. And after all, with my letters from both of you in my pocket, I can be calm and cozy there with them, without having to justify the fears of Uncle [Marinus], who had determined that his house would always hold something unpleasant for me.

Tomorrow, Cor's guest, Aunt Caro,[186] comes for breakfast and dinner. Today, we go to Mrs. ter Meulen's,[187] and Saturday, Uncle Marinus comes. You see that we have quite a varied life and sometimes it's even bustling.

My blouse is finally finished. On Monday, Li put it to the test and this morning I gave it the finishing touch. It took a very long time, but often days passed without being able to work on it. I missed Karel's help with the hemming of the tie, but it is ready, after all.

I believe that Maria B. P.[188] is expecting a baby. I already suspected it when Karel and I were last there. Charles was already so fretful and concerned for her; she walked so carefully and slowly when I last walked with her. Also, Bertha Zimmerman[189] (who once, with [her sister] Line,[190] took [Maria] under her wings to go to the Concertgebouw) had told Cor that Charles only went along because [Maria] felt so poorly. And Bertha also said that Charles, time and time again, alluded to their house as becoming too small, which Marie found very annoying. She said nothing to me, so don't write about it. I am betting that she has also not told your mother. How lovely it will be to see Charles as a father. Hopefully, poor Maria will come through it fine. She must look so awful.

Line Zimmerman will soon move to Hoorn, just the right wife for the mayor of a city! How nice for Guus that he will see his comrades from time to time.

186 Johanna Jacoba (Caro) de Vos (1824–1899): married to Isaäc Warnsinck (1811–1857), architect.

187 Antonia Elisabeth Trakranen (1821–1908): married to Jan ter Meulen (1815–1896), assurance broker.

188 Maria Barbara Pijnappel (1870–1950): president of the Dutch organization for women's suffrage; married in 1891 to Dr. Charles Ernest Henri Boissevain (1868–1940), owner-director of the ammonia factory Van der Elst & Matthes.

189 Bertha Zimmerman (1870–1905): married in 1902 to Arthur François Emile van Schendel, Sr. (1874–1946), Dutch author.

190 Jacoba Elisabeth (Line) Baroness van Rhemen van Rhemenshuizen (1869–1951): sister-in-law of Bertha Zimmerman; married in 1890 to August (Guus) Eduard Zimmerman (1861–1926), one-time Mayor of Hoorn.

It was recently mentioned in the paper that Hosang was transferred to a guard ship at Willemsoord. And yesterday, Auntie [Alida] Leembruggen said that she heard from the van Stockums that Bram[191] had to stay on his ship for a long time in one place; they were very worried.

From Willem Coster,[192] I got a lovely letter out of Funchal in Madeira. He speaks very nicely about Karel. He says, among other things, that even though he has only known him for a short period, Karel has made such a good impression on him, and ended with "I love him." Furthermore, he said he would leave Madeira in the middle of November and would travel slowly overland toward here. He feels somewhat stronger, but the coughing is the same and "it goes no better with me," he says. "If I felt that I would get better, then I would have still remained here. The way I feel now, I would rather be in the city." In short, as if he wished to say, "I would like to die at home." A melancholic end, but you should not focus on that, as such.

Adio, dear sister, much love from Mother and Cor, also to Karel. Say a few words to him for me, and receive a warm kiss from your loving Wil.

A29662000049–52 [Heleen to Mia, or Miep]
Macleod, November 12, 1891

Dear Miep,

I still have to thank you for your amusing letter with the description of the fun you had riding, etc., and I shall now start with telling you what a beautiful walk I had in Calgary.

Karel was still in bed; I had been hotel-bound for a long time and I longed for a brisk walk. I first went along the road that I had walked earlier with Mr. McCaul, on a proper sidewalk toward the Catholic church,[193] from there, a turn and over the bridge. The river was open again. The water flowed lustily and was so clear that I could count every little pebble on the bottom. It was beautiful warm weather, so I had happily left all the coats at home. On the other side was the hill that I was planning to climb, where a sandy trail zig-zagged up the hill. Soon, I left [the trail] in order to climb straight up to the top over the hard grass. Quite often, I stopped to catch my breath and to look toward the city at my feet, and every view encouraged me to climb higher and to also look out from the other side. My expectations were not dashed because, at the top, I had my first full view of the snow-covered mountains. I walked

---

191   Abraham (Bram) Jacob van Stockum (1864–1935): married in 1906 to Olga Boissevain (1875–1949), a daughter of Uncle Karel and Aunt Emily. At the time, he served as Lieutenant 2nd Class aboard the unprotected (that is, unarmed) cruiser HNLMS *Koningin Emma der Nederlanden*.

192   Willem Coster (1857–1892): administrator; unmarried, had been ill and eventually died on March 15, 1892.

193   St. Mary's Church, a sandstone structure completed in 1889 (replaced in 1955), is the predecessor to the one at what is now 219 Eighteenth Avenue SW.

some ways toward them, but the wind at the top was very cold and, without my coat, I did not dare to walk against it for a long time.

It was a pity to turn my back on the lovely view, but the city also lay beautifully on the other side, as in a bowl surrounded by hills, which were only broken in two places by the rivers. My ridge was on the city side and thickly wooded with quite high trees, firs and others; and on top grew a mass of dune thistles and a low sort of pussy willow, which was sometimes a beautiful reddish brown. I picked some of them and stuck them in my hat. After a short walk, I found it so enjoyable that I had no desire to go back the same way; a steep path led me to the bottom. I followed that and it brought me toward the river. Along the water, I could now reach the bridge again, but I knew that there was also another bridge (see bridge II) at the other end of the city and wanted to try to reach that one [by walking] straight through the open field, because here, the river made a bend toward the city and the field looked walkable. Well, I soon stood before a gate of that abominable barbed wire that they also have here, but I could easily go underneath it and I could not do any harm to the stubble field that I came upon. I passed a small abandoned house and then a small farm with a hay rack, where a pair of barking dogs and two small children looked at me with surprise.

I walked yet another short piece and, all of a sudden, I found myself standing again in front of the river, which runs [in a deep gorge] there, and therefore I had not seen it. I did not like having to turn back. I was now between the two bridges and wanted to walk the unfamiliar way. I therefore followed the river to the right. It went very easily until [I reached] the place where the water flowed so strongly from the mountains that I had to make a choice, the high hilltop, which sometimes broadened and made a much longer curve, or to pass right along the water where there was no path. I had no time to lose if I wanted to be home at 1:00 p.m. to deliver the soup for Karel.

A couple of jumps and a little bit of muddling along the slippery clay wall brought me to the edge of the water. There was just enough room to walk, alongside tracks

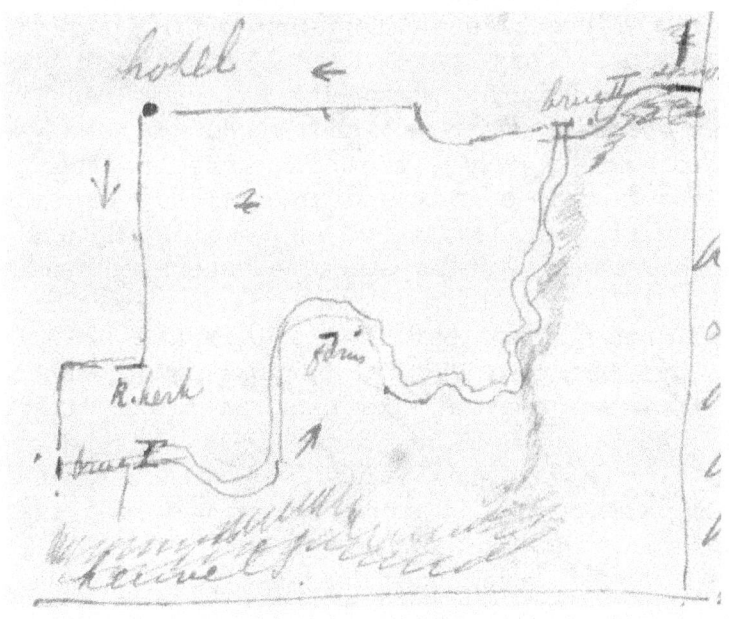

[20] Heleen's drawing of a map of the Bow River in Calgary for Miep

of hooves that proved that a pony also had tried not long ago. I hoped that I would not come across him, because there was certainly not enough room for two. The rocky hillside coming upon me looked threatening, but I had to really focus on my footing and sometimes to grip the earth with my hands to keep from falling into the water. Sometimes, there was a piece of wider land, where brush was growing. There I found an enormous carcass of a buffalo, the legs still draped with skin, but the rest was bare bones. Furthermore, at every turn the ground was strewn with various separate buffalo bones and, as in the dunes, from hares and rabbits. Once again, the flat ground disappeared and I had to climb a few metres up and along the slope. The river was very winding and time and time again, when I thought I was approaching the bridge, a new curve took me further from my goal. Once, I came to a large, flat piece of land upon which was an extensive stretch of bushes. Now, in the winter, it was not difficult to break through it, but the branches were so thick that I was standing right in front of a pony before I had seen him and his two friends. It was an entertaining little tour.

It is too bad that Karel could not be there. I finished all the same by, indeed, reaching the bridge and then going for a moment to Mr. Ross' office in order to hear if there was any word about the engineers, and was already home by quarter to one. I then told Karel a splendid story about my adventures. I still have the red branches on my hat.

Bye, Miepsje, maybe I will still add something here tomorrow when I have the letters. They arrived [here in Fort Macleod] today, Thursday, but it is Thanksgiving Day, an inconvenient, unexpected Sunday in the midst of the week; the post office was only open for an hour in order to give out the mail. I, who did not know that, did not receive anything. It is a precarious thing to go to sleep before I have read the long-awaited letters, but I have been brought back to my good mood by having a very pleasant dinner with Mr. and Mrs. Gigot,[194] German Canadians with six charming children, from one to fifteen years. Mrs. Gigot often has no maid and so does everything herself. The girls of twelve and thirteen years can also cook and one served very nicely after the dinner. They are also learning French and music, and all ride one by one on a docile horse. The oldest boy, fifteen, had been hunting with his own gun that he proudly showed to me. The girls were excited when I told them about the children's dance parties at home and they found it very difficult to go to bed before I had told everything about them. But nevertheless, they went right away at the first warning, without procrastinating! The boy had fourteen dollars in the bank that he had earned by delivering meat for the butcher on Saturday afternoons, and he did not understand why his parents and I laughed about the idea that he could be doing the same work in Frankfurt or Amsterdam.

Now, for sure, it ends. Goodnight, Miepje, many warm kisses from your loving sister, Heleen.

---

194   Edward-Francis Gigot (1847–1928): Hudson's Bay Company employee; married to Rosina Ness (1857–1921).

A33091000001-03 [Heleen to Grandmother Brugmans]
Fort Macleod, Prov. Alberta, November 12, 1891

Dear Grandmother,

Where I am now is very far away (but in some aspects I seem to be closer to you, or at least with your memories), especially in light of the manner in which we travel. The railway has not yet reached every town here, not by a long shot. Long distances are instead covered by stagecoach and wagon or, in a more aristocratic way, in one's private coach drawn by four horses. I cannot deny that the latter way of travel is very much to my liking, and I am quite pleased that our very good letters of introduction have provided us with the best coaches in town. We have letters from Mr. Van Horne (the 'big man' of the railway, also of Canada) for the chief of the police force in every town. Those gentlemen represent the government and have a number of mounted policemen, etc., under their command.

Yesterday, I took Karel to his camp on the prairie. At ten o'clock, Major Steele's empty coach, with suspension and with the best four-horse team, arrived [to pick us up]. Two police soldiers on the bench of the coach and a guide on horseback came along to help us find our way. Is that not a distinguished way of travelling? In any case, it was a lovely way to see this beautiful land of snow. We enjoyed the view of the high snowy mountains and the magnificent wild prairie. It was admirable how the experienced coach driver handled the four-span over thickly overgrown hills and through the deep snow in the ravines.

We encountered a large herd of free-range cattle and a few Indians on their swift ponies. The camp was situated in a sweet valley, well protected. I left Karel there and by 6:00 p.m. was back in the hotel.

This afternoon I received a visit from Mrs. Steele, a very cultured lady, and we dined at the home of Mr. and Mrs. Gigot, very friendly German Canadians, and their six very well brought-up children. Mr. Gigot speaks both English and French very well and has a penchant for collecting old books. He also has a very nice old Dutch edition (dated 1751) [published by] Johannes Enschedé of Haarlem, of a travel story in Canada with lovely old prints. He also showed me a very beautifully illustrated Latin Bible that is dated 1628 and bound in wood.

The meal was also extremely delicious, just like a Dutch menu: ox-rib soup with genuinely delicious peas she had preserved herself and which tasted as if they had been freshly picked; nicely cooked potatoes, without the peel; lettuce with unsurpassable mayonnaise; and a sago pudding with peaches. We sat cozily at a round table with a floor lamp. One of the daughters, twelve years old, helped with very nice service after dinner. It is, therefore, not even close to being in the wilderness here.

Would you be so kind as to give my heartfelt greetings to Uncle Toon, with the same for Uncle Menso[195] and Uncle Sebald, should he be in town?

195 Menso Johannes Pijnappel (1830–1906): barrister and solicitor and senator; married to Helena Catharina Justine Brugmans (1837–1876).

Also, please share my best wishes with Miss Lanting,[196] and believe me, dear Grandmother, I remain your loving Helena.

A28335001477-78 [Heleen note to Mother]
Macleod, November 12, 1891

This letter, which I had left unfinished in order to add that we did indeed go travelling and that Karel was better, I could not find in the end. Now, it has shown up, again, from between the envelopes and is now in my hands.

Now, I can add to it that Karel remained in bed until Saturday. Sunday, [he] was much better and withstood the tiring journey very well. He still looks a little bit peaked, but that was already so for a long time and I am convinced that camp life will strengthen him.

About myself, I walk every day. My strong, healthy frame feels much better during the day, much more energetic and stronger than in Amsterdam. I am tired at night and sleep like a rose! Even the Canadians here are surprised that I can withstand the cold so well and do not shrink from their way of travelling. They are honoured that a Dutch lady visits their land and seem also to be pleased by it, and seem to find it an honour to be of service to me. The only people that I found less pleasant, such as those about whom I have written to An, were the ones who were strangers.

Bye, dear Mother, with a warm kiss, your loving Helena.

---

196   Dieuwke Lanting (1850–1923): a house servant.

Chapter 5

How Heleen Meets the Doctor in Pincher Creek

Karel learns the ropes of surveying and of camp life while Heleen spends her days with the "who's who" of Pincher Creek. Back home in Amsterdam, Wil and the Boissevains struggle with feeling disconnected from the travellers, while life, in alls its ups and downs, continues on.

A29670000022-27 [Heleen to Li]
Pincher Creek, November 14–15, 1891

Dearest Li,

At another place again after a lovely four-hour ride over the prairie in the same coach as the one we took to the camp. We passed two creeks, or little rivers. One was frozen so hard that one half of the coach stayed on the ice while the other wheel fell to the bottom through a crack. That was a crazy feeling, being tilted, but luckily no water came in. Once on the other side we climbed a hill by a sunken path that, way back when, was once a riverbed. There lay a thick layer of stones as large as the heads of children.

It is beautiful weather, warm sunshine, no wind, but the people here find it cold. They also claim that they find it remarkably brave for a lady to travel [alone] here, and tried to scare me yesterday evening with chilling stories of people and coaches that had been swept away with the stream. But they were mostly light coaches with one horse, driven by people who were not very capable; my trust in Macdonald and his four-horse rig remains unshaken. My arrival here was like that of the Marquis van Carabas.[197] My 'tom cat' is a corporal of the [Northwest Mounted Police] who was waiting in the street when we arrived. He knew who I was without my telling him and walked ahead to the hotel[198] to announce that an eminent lady, well known by all the supreme commanders of the 'Force', had come to honour them with a visit to their humble homes.

[21] Alberta Hotel in Pincher Creek: white building behind the Union Bank

I was immediately guided to a private sitting room. Two children and lots of stuff were cleared away and the stove was stoked up and, a few minutes later, a tray with a full tea was set on the table for me. In the meantime, my tom cat was looking for Mrs. White Fraser (who was not home) and was set to bring her here, right away. He had already found her husband, the commander of this area, and had also put him on the search, because "Mrs. is the boss" and Mr. does not dare to receive strangers in the house without her. My tom cat assured me, in the meantime, that they know very well who I am and that Karel is working with Mr. Hogg. I think that Karel was here yesterday.

I had a really fun day in Macleod yesterday. I experienced only one disappointment, which is that the letters had not yet arrived as I had hoped. I had to leave again before I could get them and now it will take another four days before they can be delivered here, because the mail only comes here twice each week. I now hope to stay here [in Pincher Creek] a bit longer and shall then, in any event, receive them.

I wanted to wash handkerchiefs yesterday (twenty-three were dirty again) and to write letters, and started with the first. Downstairs, in a kind of wash-shed, where the coal is also stored, I found the tub and soap. On the stove stood a large bucket with water, and outside at a spot where it was freezing cold, wires were strung to hang the wash. This was all very fine, only it was made less enjoyable by a large wagon

---

197 Heleen cheekily compares herself to the Marquis of Carabas, a fictional nobleman in the fairytale of *Puss in Boots*. Puss in Boots is the hero of the story, of course.

198 Alfred Thomas Connelly (1862–1924) and his twin, Albert Charles Connelly (1862–1908), opened their Alberta Hotel in Pincher Creek around 1887. Alfred was married in 1890 to Elizabeth Cline (1862–1941), and Albert was married in 1891 to Elizabeth Reardon (1872–1959).

of coal that was being unloaded into the shed, which was not conducive to the cleanliness of my wash. Later on, I got an iron and a small table (which I cleared) in the dining room in front of the kitchen and, then, I bravely blazed away at it.

At two o'clock my adjudant in Macleod, Captain Denny, who was our scout to the camp, told me that the court session was going ahead. As it happened, I had already learned that a man was to be sentenced that day for stealing horses, and I had let it be known that I wanted to attend. My adjudant had objected, because ladies were not normally allowed in the courtroom. I was, therefore, more or less surprised when it now seemed to be possible anyway. I rolled my unironed handkerchiefs into a bundle and a moment later strode with my guide to the courtroom.

The door of the wooden building creaked open and we were inside. The group of ranchers in front of the door made room to let me through to the centre of the room, where I sat down on a wooden chair. What I saw next gave me the impression of a charade. In the background was a kind of stage with hastily painted coulisses and I recognized right away that this was the same room where, last evening, a ball was held. (More about that later.)

At the spot for the prompter, but above and on top of the stage, sat Judge Macleod,[199] a very distinguished gentleman, presiding at a table that was encircled at his feet by three gentlemen, namely the clerk and two lawyers in robes. Left of the judge, in the witness stand, sat the accused, a white merchant with a cunning look, the back of his head in a crosswise bandage. At the same height as me, a little bit closer to the side wall, sat two Indians amongst a troop of policemen.

The victim [of the robbery] was questioned. Afterwards, one of the Indians had to testify. Meanwhile, the other one, well guarded, had to stand outside. The [Indian] witness, a large, well-built man with lovely features, but weakened and sick, ill due to a month of imprisonment, carried himself with difficulty to the witness box, where he received a chair. A 'half-breed'[200] interpreter also joined and the questioning resumed.

I found it to be a most interesting case. The [two] Indians had stolen the horses, but claimed that they were made to do it by the accused [merchant]. Earlier, the [Indians] had told a different story, and now, this one sometimes was contradicting himself and his story was yet again different from that of the other Indian. He spoke in long sentences that were conveyed in a only few words by the interpreter. The general opinion was that the white merchant was guilty, but he had a well-known family

---

199 James Farquharson Macleod (c.1836–1894), for whom the town of Fort Macleod was named. He was a lieutenant-colonel in the militia and commissioner of the NWMP. In 1887 he became judge of the Supreme Court of the Northwest Territories and was married in 1876 to Mary Isabella Drever (1852–1933).

200 The term *half-breed* (now considered offensive) was used by the Canadian government in the late nineteenth and early twentieth centuries to refer to people who were of mixed Indigenous and European ancestry. The term was also used to refer to Métis residents of the North-West Territories.

in the east; his lawyer knew how to draw out all kinds of contradictory evidence from the Indians and the jury let him go.[201]

Afterwards, I visited the judge's wife [Mary], a fairly tall, slim beauty with half-grey hair, who already has been here in the region for many years, often without a maid, as now, and who longs a bit for sufficient help. Two other ladies also joined us and the inevitably trivial conversation was quite unusual. Mrs. Macleod once had a good maid named Janet,[202] who is an industrious soul and has accumulated a nice fortune, owns a few houses and some cattle, but still serves, and is soon to go to England for a few months to see her family. Janet had slept the previous night at Mrs. Macleod's before leaving for Montreal. The guestroom was occupied, but there was a bed made for her in the dining room, just like in the salon for the male guest. In the morning, Janet did as she would have done at home, started the stove, etc. But at first she could not find the matches, and figured that they must have been in the salon. The male guest got up, but also could not find them, after which he returned to bed and then Janet herself indeed found the matches in the salon.

[22] Mary Macleod

One of the other ladies, Mrs. Saunders,[203] a jolly Irish woman whose husband is also a member of the police (and who cooks better than [Mrs. Macleod]) invited me for tea at her house in the barracks. Through the double door, we came directly into the living room, a spacious room with three windows, a desk, a large canapé, tea table, children's toys, etc.; a lovely, playful, good-natured baby of about eight months; and a very sweet, lovely child of two, who appeared to be very sick with an awful cold. In the evening, it turned out to be the mumps.

201   The outcome of this "charade" may have been due (at least in part) to the resentment that the Indian witnesses felt toward being cross-examined, "which they interpreted as an accusation of lying." Source: Christopher James Marsh, "Scouts and Seizers: Community-Oriented Policing in Blackfoot (Niitsitapi) Communities of Southern Alberta, 1874–1919," PhD diss. (University of Saskatchewan, 2020), 172.

202   Janet (Jennett) Sanderson (c.1859–1915), domestic aid and entrepreneur, married in 1898 to William Elwood Swain (c.1854–1930), rancher.

203   This is probably Caroline A. Sanders (née Jukes) (1850–1938): married to Colonel Gilbert Edward Sanders, NWMP, then inspector of D Division, Macleod (1863–1955).

Another lady came knocking at the door when I was alone for a moment in the living room. I opened the door and we introduced ourselves. Mrs. Macdonell[204] was also married to a policeman and, just like all the other ladies, she had not found me at home and had left calling cards. She asked me to visit her after the tea. She was in deep mourning about her father-in-law, sister and brother-in-law, and did not go out. Nevertheless, a few lieutenants (who had heard that there was a footloose and fancy-free lady) came by in the evening and did their very best to act just like their European counterparts, without the slighest idea of how annoying I have always found that genre of insect. For them, in any case, there was very little gained by it. They were just really very congenial, simple boys, who could more easily deal with a wild horse than a young lady, and could tell of interesting riding adventures. The conversation also touched upon the ball from the evening before. One of them had been there in his grey suit for only half an hour; one of the ladies had not gone, because she had had to watch her house since the maid had gone [to the ball]. All in all, eight ladies had been there!!

Mrs. White Fraser stopped by [the hotel] in the meantime. To her regret, she could not take me in tonight because there are so many people [in the town] for the large Freemasons' meeting. I now have a very good room in the hotel, above the parlour, the only one with carpet. The bed linens are clean and fresh and the maid is very accommodating. New guests arrive continuously; even though the hotel was already full when I came, there is always still a place to be found.

I think I will just close off for now and go freshen up for supper! All of the ladies who are coming will be half-frozen and shaken from the icy rivers, while I did not feel at all cold and enjoyed my trip. Long live a healthy constitution!

Lots of love to everyone, Heleen.

```
KLAB04554000195-97 [Karel to Wim]
Beaver Creek, the [Walrond] Ranch,[205] Saturday evening, November 14, 1891
```

204 Heleen, ever the accurate reporter, may be forgiven for having lost track of who was whom. Mrs. Macdonnell is Mary Sophia McGillis (c.1860–1939), married to Alexander Roderick Macdonell (1840–1906), then a superintendent with the NWMP. After his death she remarried in 1912 to Colonel William Frederick Wallace Carstairs (1860–1945). In May of 1891, Mary's sister, Margaret Louisa (Lucy) McGillis Jarvis, passed away. Mary's other loss was of Antoine Chartier de Lotbiniere Harwood (1825–1891), the brother of the husband of her other sister, Mary Charlotte McGillis de Lotbiniere Harwood, who was married to Robert William de Lotbiniere Harwood. The reference to the mourning of the "father-in-law" remains a mystery, as her father-in-law died in 1842, two years before her husband was born.

205 The Walrond Ranch was one of the earliest and largest ranches in southern Alberta, established in 1883 by Dr. Duncan McNab McEachran, a veterinarian, with financial aid of Sir John Walrond Walrond, of Middlesex, England and other British investors. McEachran was also the president and general manager. It is most likely that "the boss of the farm" was McEachran. Sir John Walrond had died in Cannes in 1889. See Edward Brado, Cattle Kingdom: Early Ranching in Alberta (Vancouver: Douglas and McIntyre, 1984) 133.

Dear, dear, dear Wim!

So loveable, and as dear to me as never before in our best times; so dear to my heart that I, like a fool, now feel the tears in my eyes, while I can finally spend a little time in surroundings you will never really come to know, that will always be strange to you, and where I, happily enough, will never have to take you. God willing.

I am writing now at the farm, mentioned at the top of this page, a line you probably missed reading, with my forgiveness. Oh, Wim, it is still very strange for me here. At the moment, I am sitting at a long table with (beside me and across from me) three men in shirts and patched clothing, Canadians passing through. Around the huge column stove sits Walrond, the boss of the farm, a tall, lean, pleasant and congenial man, hospitable and also courteous; Brooks, the youngest engineer; and a threesome of other bearded and unshaven farmhands of the boss, who has a sizeable cattle ranch. Our camp is pitched three minutes from here and since there is so little space in the tent, I have come here to write for a bit. Saturday evening, folks are less hasty with going to bed and so I came here right after supper. Our daily schedule is as follows:

Up at 6:30 a.m.

7:00 breakfast: porridge, bread, pastry, tea or coffee, ham, beans, potatoes and applesauce

Between 7:00 and 9:00: wagons hitched, horses saddled, instruments loaded and clothing put on

8:30: toward the survey area! The first day we walked there and arrived at 10:30, but we had left at 8:00, and therefore found it quite a walk — two and half hours! But then the work was about to begin. Levelling, chain-measuring, using a theodolite,[206] etc.

1:00 p.m.: halt. Wood chopped from neighbouring shrubs, fire built; I haul water from the river beside us in the kettle that we brought with us and boil it to make tea. Done and dusted.

I fetch a small box that holds large loaves, cookies and apple pie. All very good, but everything is frozen, of course. So, we have to melt the butter over the fire, defrost the bread by toasting it, and then the frozen pie is our dessert. After a half an hour, we begin work anew (you understand that there is little time to rest during lunch) and, until 5:00 p.m., we again measure some miles. Always onward, onward!

At 5:00 p.m., we march to the camp where, at 7:00, a delicious supper is waiting. First, a moment in the tent to wash our hands, and thereafter to the cook's tent, where all fourteen of us find a seat at a long table. How good such warm pea soup and a tomato dish can taste, after such a day. It is then that one finally realizes what one's physical needs are. At such a moment, all that you are aware of is the pleasure in your stomach and

---

206   A theodolite is a survey tool of uncertain origin, attributed to the sixteenth-century mathematician Leonard Digges. It is used in the field to obtain precise angular measurements for triangulation in road building, tunnel alignment and other civil engineering work.

on your palate; everything else falls silent. I would have liked to have put it to the test, that just at the moment I was to set upon eating, it would be made known that you were waiting for me a few miles away. I bet that I would go immediately, but that I would regret it.

After supper, the engineers start to do the calculations from their observations, and at 9:30 p.m. they all retire to their bunks.

Here is a floor plan of the tent: a canvas with a pole in the middle, at more or less the height of a man, against which rests the stovepipe that goes up through the top of the tent and to the outside; *b* is the stove, *c* a table with places for two people (who then have to sit on the chest that contains the instrumentation and drawing materials, etc.), and *e* is a small box containing straw and glass-lamp chimneys, upon which the jointly shared lamp stands, and beside the box there is a pail of water from which the men can fill a washbasin with a scoop — also drinking mugs. In the morning, the stove is quickly lit by the first one awake and the pail is set on it to melt the water, because it is, of course, frozen stiff during the night. Figures *h* and *i* are the various places for our mattresses; *f* is the chief engineer, Hoggs, nicknamed Chief; *g* is Brooks; and *h* is Clercks, a thirty-eight-year-old engineer whose wife and six children live elsewhere. I am *i*, but with little bedding in comparison to the rest.

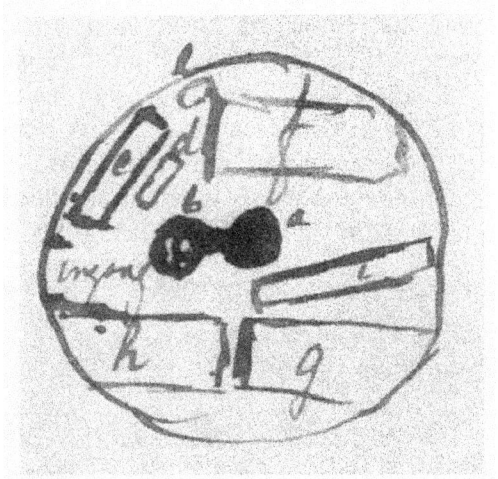

[23] Diagram of CPR survey camp tent, drawn by Karel

I think that Helena has already written one thing or another to Amsterdam about Macleod and our ride to the camp, and perhaps has even described the camp. By the time you have received this letter, perhaps I will already be somewhere else, because this work will not keep us busy until the middle of December. By then, the snow will be too high in the mountains.

Today, November 14, we are camping across from the last settled place, Pincher Creek, that Helena will try to reach and where she perhaps will visit me tomorrow. It would be nice to see her one more time before we go into the wilderness for a month. In case she comes, I will give her this letter. If not, then I will stay with my normal practice and you will get it after a while. It is very healthy living here. Every day there is beautiful freezing weather, nicely warm in the afternoons because of the gentle sun and at night deeply under the bedcovers.

Oh, Wim, I am getting so healthy; dare to have some faith with me in the future, oh, darling. Signed, your most affectionate Karel.

A29662000033-34 [Heleen to An]
Pincher Creek, November 15, 1891

Dear An,

Let me know by return post the name of the white dune flower of which Miss Scherpenberg[207] had such a bunch in that flat glass vase. We also found many of them on our last walk through the dunes and we knew the name very well, but now I have forgotten.

Yesterday evening, I was at Mrs. White Fraser's, a beautiful, distinguished, gifted and sweet lady. She showed me ninety different wildflowers that she searched for this summer and painted; and therewith, I found many of our dune flowers, among others, three kinds of *pyrola*, our white, a yellow and a very nice red one.

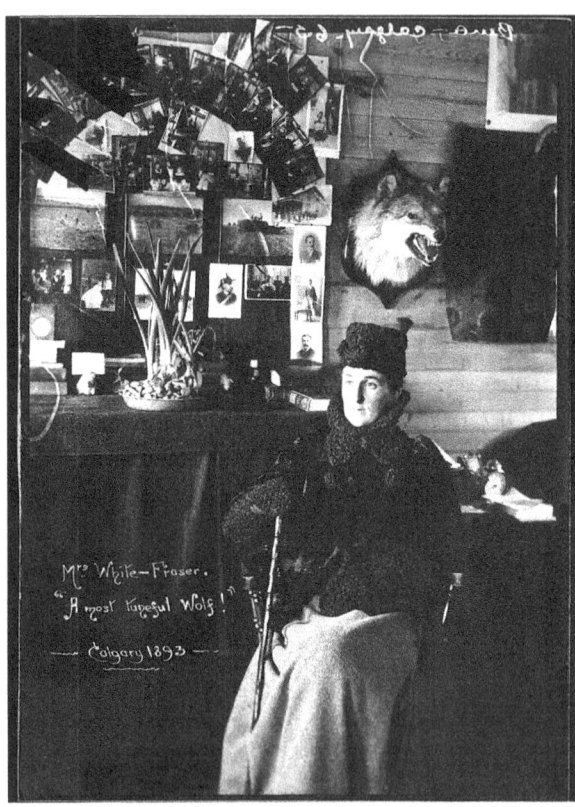

[24] Elizabeth S. White Fraser

[25] Inspector M.H. White Fraser of the NWMP

She also paints very prettily and has plans to send a complete collection of flowers from here to the upcoming world exhibition in Chicago [in 1893]. The flowers are much larger than those in the dunes. I would very much love to be here in the summer. Dune violets are also in abundance here

---

207 Maria Cornelia van Scherpenberg (1856–1950): married in 1892 to Daniël (Daan) de Clercq (1854–1931), engineer and director of a chemical manufacturer, socialist and activist.

(but there are no fragrant, delightful anemones), as are wild roses, dune roses, and also, on old paths, lilies, a few chrysanthemums, etc.! She knew most of the names, but those that I have asked you about, she would also like to know; I thought it was so awful that I had forgotten them when I once knew them so well. She is a member of a botanical society and you would enjoy walking with her. She must sometimes wade up to her knees in the water in order to gather the water plants.

She also sang for me, and it was a great pleasure to hear her. She had had a dinner for all of the distinguished Freemasons, who had meetings there in the evenings. For this, she was dressed in a kind of tea gown of green velvet with an overlay in the front and wide sleeves of pink sura.[208] Also, at her house, everyone arrives straight through the front door into the living room, a spacious square room, half-dining room, half-salon, the wooden walls charmingly hung all over with watercolour paintings and sketches of her own. Two standing petroleum lamps with large soft yellow shades, parasol stand, a beautiful piano and lots of books and magazines on the small tables.

She is English and, a few years ago, she met Mrs. Campbell-Praed.[209] The evening flew by. It was a quarter to twelve before I went home. In the meantime, it had snowed heavily and the quiet white night was breathtakingly beautiful.

I have not yet spoken to Mr. White Fraser. Yesterday, he was very busy, but he will visit me today. I hope that you understand which flower I mean, because I do not dare to give a description. They grow in damp areas and it seems as if each one comes separately out of the ground.

Bye, Anneke Tanneke, a warm kiss from Heleen.

A32074000153-56 [Heleen to Wil]
Pincher Creek, November 15 [1891]

Dear Wil,

Just now, Karel left again for the camp after a short visit here, and I will tell you right away how he is getting along there. I was surprised by how well he looks! The bags under his eyes had disappeared, he had quite good colour and his eyes were much clearer than before. It is a tiring life: getting up at 6:30 a.m., stoking the stove, thawing ice in order to take turns washing in a bowl, lovely hot breakfast in the food tent, and at 8:00 on the march; then walking and taking measurements until 6:00 p.m. The lunch goes with them on the cart and when there is water and wood nearby, tea is made; otherwise, they do not drink.

Back in the camp, they eat and then the engineers start busily calculating and drafting by lamplight. Karel cannot yet participate in

---

208   Sura is a kind of embroidered linen.

209   Rosa Campbell Praed (1851–1935): an Australian novelist.

that. For that matter, he would still be too tired now, because ten hours of walking through the snow is quite a tiring activity for him. The first day that he was there, the camp was in the process of moving. Karel walked with the engineers to the worksite, which was two and a half hours further on, and from there they kept going on for the whole day. At 6:00 p.m. they went back to the camp, but nobody knew where it was and it was beginning to get dark. Karel was dead tired. They took driving the wagon in turns, which he also did for half an hour, but he was glad when someone else drove again because it was horrendously cold. Mr. Hogg, the chief engineer, has a horse but does not like riding very much, and sometimes Karel can ride it home.

Karel brought much too much baggage and the others made quite of lot of fun of him about it. He brought sheets and pillowcases, but they are too cold and freeze at night. He sleeps well, the food is very good, and of asthma, no trace! I certainly believe that it will do him good. Gradually, he shall also become used to the fatigue that still weighs on him.

Today is Sunday. He came here with a few folks to get a doctor for one of the workers who is sick. I was reading here in the hotel when I suddenly heard his "Hup. Hup." I flew to the balcony and indeed, there he was, in a fur and hat. I had been feeling just a little bit disappointed because Mr. White Fraser had told me that he had no clue where the camp was and I was therefore afraid that I would not see him for a long time. It is now such a blessing to know that those first tiring days have suited him well and that he can take part in the work.

From now on, it will certainly continue to go well. This work will probably last until the middle of December, but much will depend on the weather. Sometimes it is much milder in December than it is now; in that case, they will keep on working.

Only on Sundays is there any opportunity for me to see him, and most likely, next week will be the last one when I can reach him. I will probably return to Calgary to make a trip from there to the coast. I have free passage on the train and I strongly desire to greet the Pacific Ocean.

Karel and I will meet each other again in Montreal, unless he makes other plans in the meantime. It is just as well that you are not here instead of me, because it would be of little benefit to you, anyway.

Our address still remains c/o C.R. Hosmer, 4 Hospital Street, Montreal.

With a warm kiss, your loving Heleen.

A28335001481-84 [Heleen to Father]
Pincher Creek, November 16, 1891

Dear Father,

Karel has now been in camp for four days, and yesterday I spoke for an hour with him and received his first impressions. It is a hard life, much harder and, especially, much more tiring than he had thought, but I believe that it is very good for him.

A half-hour after I had left him behind, the engineers had come home tired and spoke little. It appeared that the tent to where Karel had brought his luggage was the one for the engineers, and that they were not really happy with the new guest. It was cozy eating all together in the large dining tent. The workers are all young guys, many of them also more or less gentlemen, and there is very little distinction between them and the engineers.

After dinner, all the engineers started the intensive calculation work by the light of the only lamp in the engineers' tent, and Karel kept the fire going in order to gaze at it. By 10:00 p.m., all were in bed. At first, Karel was laughed at for his linens and pillowcases that are absolutely too cold and impractical. The next morning at 6:30, he started the fire to melt ice for washing, had a lovely warm breakfast and then they were on the march.

After two and a half hours they were at the last pole from the previous day! At that time Karel thought, "That is quite a walk, but see, it just started." With great diligence, everyone started working right away, and Karel participated in the 'chaining'.

Mr. Hogg went ahead to point the way and, along his way, had them post poles with flags! Following that route, the engineers had to take height and angle measurements, so the progress was slow. It went on that way until 1:00 p.m., then wood was chopped and a fire made. Water was boiled to make tea and they had lunch. After half an hour, again forward, working uninterrupted until 6:00 p.m. Karel was already dead tired, but the camp still had to be reached, which in the meantime had been moved to an unknown place. There was a wagon with the team, and Karel also drove it for a while, but it was so cold after sunset that he was very glad when someone else took over. They already had made plans to spend the night elsewhere when the camp was finally found. That evening Karel was too tired to think about anything and happy that he did not have to do the engineering work. For all that, he slept very well, and bravely worked side by side with them again the next day, with astonishing satisfaction that he could do so without being completely worn out.

Sunday, he came to Pincher Creek, where I had arrived the previous day, and I was surprised at how good he looked. He, himself, also thought it surprising, because he had found all those days very hard, but still felt quite well, and was even convinced that it will do him good and that he will become accustomed to the fatigue. I believe that there is no better cure conceivable for him. He must now go on, despite the fatigue, and he now sees that he can do things as well as any other could, which he had earlier thought to be impossible.

Sometimes, at one o'clock, there is no firewood within reach, and so there is nothing to drink for the whole day, also something that he had previously thought simply impossible. He also noticed that the other engineers find those things quite normal and make no complaints whatsoever about it. They are not aggressive in instructing him but, like shipping folks with a rookie, let him learn everything by experience and without giving explanations. He must now watch closely and be ready for anything. For now, everything is a tremendous effort for him and he has no opportunity to write. At first, do not expect too many letters from him. It is quite a pity that this is not the beginning of a good career for him, but after this probation, it should be much easier to start something else. I keep correspondence going with Addie Van Horne, hoping by this to keep her father's interest alive, because, without cooperation with the CPR, it is futile to start something here.

For myself, I am like the boy who had to learn how to deal with being afraid — always expecting to feel lonely but, up until now, I have always been able to answer "No" when folks ask me, "Do you not feel lonely?" Here, I have again met such kind people that I wish that all of you could get acquainted with them. To An, I wrote about Mrs. White Fraser, a sweet woman who, from time to time, made me think about Aunt Su[210] and Mary [B.], if you can imagine the two of them combined. She is dark, with a gorgeous complexion, the eyes of Mary and the bearing, manners and musicality of Aunt Su. Kingsley[211] is her hero. She loves reading a lot and speaks French beautifully. Her husband is already getting grey, but still looks very young with his fur hat; says little; adores his wife; has the mettle of Grandfather [Anthonie] Brugmans; took part in the war in Afghanistan[212]; and boldly holds the reins of an untrained horse at the front of a sled, as I noticed today. Mornings and afternoons, he comes to pick me up with a sled and two horses. One was a riding horse that had to be 'broken' as a draught horse. It was very cold, but lovely. We flew over the fields and frozen rivers. We could see a snowstorm in the mountains, again and again approaching and moving away.

I ate again at their house with a rancher from the area, a pleasant, jolly English gentleman[213] (who was also in Amsterdam and Russia, not that long ago) who always seems to have accidents with riding, and once again, yesterday, he had overturned his carriage and all. A few months ago, his leg was frozen and now he has a wooden one, with which he can manage very well and can still ride a horse. I have never seen anyone so jolly, with such an infectious laugh. The four of us had the greatest fun about nothing.

210   Susanna (Aunt Su) Catharina Cruys (1849–1927): married to Eugen Carl Gustav Bunge (1847–1894), merchant.

211   Charles Kingsley (1819–1875): minister, professor, social reformer, and novelist (perhaps best known for his novel *Westward Ho!*); married to Frances Eliza (née Grenfell) Kingsley (1814–1891), biographer.

212   Heleen is referring to the Second Anglo-Afghan War (1878–1880), which was fought between the British Raj and the Emirate of Afghanistan.

213   James T. (Jimmy) Routledge (dates unknown): former trooper, Regiment #45, No. 2 Troop of the Cowboy Cavalry; "Top rider on the Stewart Ranch, though one-legged. Sadly, he later committed suicide." See Gordon E. Tolton, *The Cowboy Cavalry: The Story of the Rocky Mountain Rangers* (Vancouver: Heritage House Publishing Company Ltd., 2011).

I still do not have the letters. They could now arrive within two days.

How sweet of Pa Quack to be so kind to you. I shall now forgive him for not bidding me farewell. When does his book come out? Tell him once more that I am counting on it.

I think that I will likely stay here for a week; then, I will stay at a place further on that is at a farm with pleasant people. After that, it is "Adieu, Karel" and then out on adventure.

Do not let Mama become worried. I travel alone with the Mounted Police teams and do take very good care of myself. Much love from your Helena.

A32005000376-381 [Father to Heleen (incomplete)]
Amsterdam, November 16, 1891

Dear Helena,

Since I wrote to you the last time, the day before I went to London, a lot has happened. On Friday, I came back and had received good news about Uncle Toon. Saturday the 14th, the day before yesterday, I came home from the office at 5:30 p.m. and found Elisabeth waiting for me, who told me that the situation had suddenly worsened. I drove immediately to the Herengracht and went directly to the sickbed where the good brother lay with his eyes closed, breathing with difficulty, with still longer pauses, but apparently not suffering. At 7:00 p.m., he was no longer with us. Mama was there at 2:30 in the afternoon when he became very short of breath. That was the beginning of the end. She had a difficult and *éprouvant* day. The nurse called right away for Doctor Bos,[214] who arrived at 4:30 p.m. and determined that an eruption must have taken place in his intestines, immediately upon which a complete loss of strength followed.

Grandmother was informed about the situation. I talked to her before and after the death and found her in a good state of mind, with the detachment of feelings that one notices with very old people, as if she is clinging to Mama, whom she hopes will help her with her loneliness. Also yesterday, Sunday, [Grandmother] was still reasonably well, and today somewhat weakened, but toward evening, she recouped again, a bit.

I mourn our brother Toon with all my heart. He was a loyal friend to me; we had many differences in our outlooks on life, but never had a quarrel or any hostility. I knew that he was deeply attached to his sister and he was heartily interested in all of you. Even on his last sickbed, he thought of you and Karel with love. Uncle [Menso] Pijnappel and I are his executors. [Toon] has (besides some bequests, amongst them to Pijnappel and his children) left a yearly income for living expenses to Sebald and his father's assistant, Suwerkrop.[215] Of the remainder,

---

214 Dr. Johannes Jacobus Bos (1842–1908): general physician; medical director of the Equitable Life Insurance Company of New York, unmarried.

215 Claus August Wilhelm Suwerkrop (1833–1904): office assistant.

Mama and Grandmother are the beneficiaries. The library is bequeathed to [the City of Amsterdam], but Matthijs can select a few books. All of the commotion and the rigamarole of announcements, visits, and so forth, are continuing without disruption. Sebald has come over to visit. Uncle Menso is very busy, as always.

Miss Lanting is very shocked, completely distracted. It seems that he made her difficult life bearable.

Mama is doing reasonably well. She does not sleep so well, but I still hope that she will not be set back too far by this new shock. The funeral will be this coming Wednesday at the Oosterbegraafplaats.[216] [Cornelis] Felix and Otto van Maanen[217] are coming [from The Hague] for it. His friends, Ogtrop, Sillem,[218] Kemper,[219] Koopmans,[220] Elias,[221] de Vries,[222] etc., are deeply touched and extremely sympathetic. We have had good moments during their visits.

Rahusen[223] invited us this evening for his birthday, along with Tienhoven,[224] Quack, etc. Mrs. Tienhoven came by herself this afternoon and was very sympathetic. Also the hospital directors, Dr. Zeeman,[225] van Deventer,[226] etc., gave us the impression that they had a lot to be thankful to him for, through his tenacity and his sincerity, and through his considerable steadfastness.

It will be a good memory for you and Karel that he was so especially sympathetic and compassionate regarding your departure [to Canada]. He belonged to the few who did me a lot of good with their sympathy, without being priggish. The papers mentioned him with praise and, from various sides, I hear how much he was honoured at the courts and the bar.

216 Oosterbegraafplaats is the main cemetery in Amsterdam.

217 Cornelis Felix Theodorus van Maanen (1829–1899): Solicitor General of the Supreme Court; married in 1860 to Wilhelmina Johanna Louisa Heller (1829–1868); second marriage in 1888 to Dodonea Jacoba Cats (1850–1905); brother to Otto Antonie van Maanen (1841–1916), colonel of the Artillery, unmarried, retired. Both men are cousins of Nella Boissevain.

218 Jerome Alexander Sillem (1840–1912): lawyer, politician, historian, unmarried.

219 Jhr. Gerrit de Bosch Kemper (1841–1912): Secretary General, Ministry of Waterworks; married in 1870 to Henriette Adriana Waller (1849–1884); second marriage in 1888 to Johanna Adriana Baroness van Fridagh (1852–1933).

220 Wilhelm Cnoop Koopmans (1837–1895): manufacturer; married to Louise Catharine Joosten (1844–1891).

221 Wouter Hendrik Elias (1845–1896): judge; married to Anna Maria Hulshoff (1851–1911).

222 Jeronimo de Vries (1838–1915): clergyman, poet; married to Alida Maria Jarman (1838–1902).

223 Eduard Nicolaas Rahusen (1830–1913): lawyer and senator; unmarried.

224 Gijsbert van Tienhoven (1841–1914): Minister of Foreign Affairs from 1891 to 1894; married to Anna Sara Maria Hacke (1846–1921).

225 Johannes Zeeman (1824–1905): family doctor and pioneer in medical statistics; married to Maria Anna Catharina Elisabeth Rahder (1836–1921).

226 Jacob van Deventer (1848–1916): chief medical director in 1892 of Meerenberg, a psychiatric hospital in Santpoort, the Netherlands; married to Antonia Wilhelmina Stelling (1852–1916).

Toon Pijnappel[227] is severely shocked, since he had, just last summer, spoken so frequently with his godfather, and had turned to him, even with all of his gymnasium-level [high school] wisdom. It is a strange feeling for me that someone whom I had hoped would remain behind (upon my death) as a support and adviser for my children has now died before me.

Aunt Hester and Gie den Tex are also extremely shaken by this. Mama Brugmans has received no one other than the grandchildren and Aunt Hes. Maria, [young] Karel's wife, is now bound to her couch in relation to an event that will take place in March, about which she looks upon with apprehension, so we did not meet with her. There is certainly a bit of 'bad luck' in our relations with the 'Karels'. We were to eat at Charles [young Karel] and Maria's, but he became indisposed and had to put it off. Then we were supposed to be eating at Charles [old Karel] and Emily's on Sunday, and now we must decline due to this bereavement. We asked them one evening to come to see the photographs of Canada, but then, they had to go to a philharmonic concert.

Thursday, I was in London with Captain Bakker (not your captain, but a younger T. Bakker) and closed a contract for the SS *Celebes*, which will sail for six months between London and Halifax, Nova Scotia, and so will come somewhat into your area. I travelled on Wednesday, the day of a severe storm, but had more trouble with it on land than on the sea; therefore, I feel strong enough for a journey over the Atlantic, if that becomes necessary.

Wallis[228] and I spent a day together and we lunched in a 'pure bread' shop that was not as good as the 'aerated bread' shop[229] where we had eaten before. Arriving home, I found your letter of October 28, which had been written on the train, at the office and it did me good. I am truly thankful to those hospitable, warm Canadians, and also to Adolphe for his introductions that completely hit the mark. You wrote wonderfully to me. Keep on going, then I will feel assured that you are not holding anything back. Before I get rid of it, I will let Mama read it, and when Dr. Delprat visited me, I read part of it to him as well. He is also very satisfied with how things are going and with your new entourage. We will prepare a hearty reception for Dr. Black and his wife, and Dr. Delprat will have the honour of being his guide in the medical world.

[Ends here.]

---

227   Pibo Antonius (Toon) Pijnappel (1875–1935): son of Menso; nephew of Toon Brugmans; editor of *Propria Cures*; was described as an armchair scholar and bibliophile.

228   Thomas Wallis, born "Wallace" (1836–1900), owner of the firm [Francis C.] Keller, Wallis & Co., Southampton and London, agents for the North German Lloyd Steamship Co. and the Stoomvaart Maatschappij Nederland, Amsterdam. He was married in 1856 to Eliza S. Shepherd (1838–1873).

229   This may refer to the Aerated Bread Company, Ltd., of Fleet Street in London, which developed the process of using carbon dioxide as a leavening agent.

A29648000029–34 [Heleen to Thijs]
Pincher Creek, November 19, 1891

Dear Thijs,

Do you remember my stories about my 'Black' friend[230] on board the *Sardinian*? If yes, then overcome your hostile inclinations toward my friends that are not known to you, or at the very least, help me to fulfill a promise. Prepare yourself for a difficult task. Get up early. Eat a hearty breakfast. Collect all of your patience and perserverance. Take your walking stick and leave your house. Aim your footsteps toward the Rokin, go in and ask for an English translation of Couperus' *Eline Vere*.[231] Then, let the always-astonished clerk search in every catalogue, and telephone in every direction, until he knows when he can obtain a good copy, neatly bound. Let him put the charges in my name and send the invoice to Papa at home. If, after a full exploration, it turns out that no English translation of *Eline Vere* exists, then try to get a translation of *Max Havelaar*,[232] which, for sure, does exist. And, if you have one of the books in your hands, then neatly paste the enclosed sheet of paper in the front of it. Wrap it tidily and take it to Keizersgracht 717 to a safe spot, such as Papa's letter rack, and when my Black friend visits our house, present him with the book. Explain to him the expression "for diligence and hard work" and, if needed, translate the rest of it for him. If the piece of paper is too big, then you can cut off the two [sentences] at the bottom and the top and paste them in separately. I had promised him a reward if he translated a verse about Bosboom[233] and he really made quite something of it.

Here, I cannot do much with the study book that he gave to me because the village [of Pincher Creek] is very small. Walking is dangerous due to the wild cattle that always attack people on foot, and it is not very easy to find a room for ladies. Because of this, I have mostly stayed at home for the last few days and received quite curious company:

1. Mr. Jacob[234] (son of an archdeacon and court preacher of [Queen] Victoria herself), previously was a navy officer, drifting for the last twenty

---

230 This is a joking reference to Dr. Ernest Black.

231 Louis Marie-Anne Couperus (1863–1923): novelist and poet; wrote the novel *Eline Vere* in 1889; married in 1891 to Elisabeth (Betty) Wilhelmina Johanna Baud (1867–1960).

232 A novel written in 1860 by Multatuli, a pseudonym for Edouard Douwes Dekker (1820–1887), a Dutch writer and civil servant in the Dutch East Indies.

233 Johannes Bosboom (1817–1891): artist known for his paintings of church interiors; married to Anna Louisa Geertruida Toussaint (1812–1886), novelist.

234 Augustus Jacob (1839–1893): formerly a Royal Navy captain; "The deceased officer, who was on the retired list, was in charge of a mine in Alberta, about 12 miles from Pincher Creek. He rode to the last-named place to get food, and left on horseback on his return journey, against the remonstrance of friends, as he insisted the men need provisions. As nothing was heard of him, search was made, and his body discovered. It was evident that being unable to ride he had pushed-on on foot and had been frozen to death." Source: *South Wales Daily News*, January 5, 1894: "Naval Captain Frozen to Death." He was buried in the Fairview Cemetery at Pincher Creek.

[26] Augustus Jacob

years, sometimes on his feet again after excessive drinking, and then, again, *sans le sous*. Now, he is writing comic, ironic verses, two of which he read to me.

2. Mr. Carlidge, looks like master Dirken,[235] started as a missionary, afterwards an interpreter, bricklayer, orderly, carpenter, and now a plasterer in the church here. He knows the [Native] language and gave me a dictionary and grammar book about it, and will also teach me more about it.

3. Tom Jones, a London street urchin, brought here by a rancher and then left to fend for himself. Now he works here and there for someone or another. His foot was frozen after wearing a damaged boot for three days. They will keep him in the hotel until he is well. He had never been sick and thought that now his end was near. I bound his foot and gave him a book (the history of Canada), after which he felt better about life.

We all eat together in the hall downstairs. The meals are all the same: tea, cakes and sometimes beefsteak. At noon, it looks like dinner; then there is sometimes soup, beefsteak, potatoes, a kind of wobbly bean, and two sorts of dessert, pudding and cake. Always tea. It is so funny to see all those big men eat so many sweet things. They hardly speak with each other, but some have long conversations with me, wanting to know everything about Holland, and they are very proud when they know that Holland is not the same as Germany, but are always surprised that such a small country has a distinct language.

I hear the most delightful stories about wolves and bears. Mrs. White Fraser herself lived for two years in another house a little way outside of the village. At night, she was often alone at home and would have to get up to chase away ten or twelve wolves who were howling around her house! Now they do not come so close to the city anymore, but at the ranches, there are still a lot of cattle killed by them.

It is very enjoyable to be with the White Frasers and the days fly by. They are both very likeable, musical like Aunt Su and affable together. He is cheerfully quiet, like Uncle Niek and Karel den Tex, and finds it delightful to laugh at her, but also has a hidden, unlimited admiration for her, time and time again starting stories about her excellent qualities, which she must then finish.

---

235 Marinus Dirken (1838–1919): teacher in Vogelenzang; married to Maria Albertina Staphorst (1844–1880); remarried to Janke Meijer (1861–1922).

They often disagree and that always provides an opportunity for some fun. If I help her, we prove to be right; often an encyclopedia or an almanac is fetched, in which we can find all the answers.

The house is truly Canadian. Through a built-on double door, where coats and overshoes hang, you enter into the living room. The front part is a salon and the back part is a dining room, evidenced by a square dining table; a covered plank *au fond* against the wall, upon which is beautiful silver and glassware; an improvised *chaise longue*; and a bookcase with much-read books. In the front half is a built-in cupboard without the doors, a piano, three different easy chairs and (against the wall here and there) are covered planks used as tables alongside a few very small, real tables with smoking paraphernalia and newspapers beside the chairs. Lots of photographs and watercolours by her. A gigantic stove in the middle of the right wall warms the whole house. When you come in, the bedroom is on the right, and is eaten up by a huge English bedstead; behind it is the dressing room, without any light, then through two doors toward the bedroom and the dining room, and halfway behind it, is the kitchen. That is all. They have a kitchen garden where they grow wonderful vegetables. Many growing plants in the room, three dogs, and a sweet kitty like our Ho-14 who died from tuberculosis. The whole description of the house perhaps does not interest you, but is more interesting for Mama and Li, so let them read this part in particular.

Today and tomorrow, the White Frasers are off to Macleod with the team. I received a message from Karel that they are still in the old camp, fourteen miles from here. I had ordered a team and a policeman in order to bring some goods to the camp, if I could find it, but now I shall wait until they come closer.

By the way, it is not cold today like it was the first days, when it was 28° Fahrenheit and it froze fast during the day. (Here they use a spirit thermometer because mercury would freeze.) The 'Chinook', a mysterious warm wind from the mountains, is blowing now, which only appears on this side of the mountains in a specific region. It is a strong wind. The first night, I was awakened by the shaking of my bed and the house, but it is a treasure of the land that otherwise would be uninhabitably cold.

Bye, Thijsie dear, thank you in advance for the task that I have imposed upon you, and a warm kiss from your loving sister, Heleen.

A32005000386–387 [Father to Heleen]
Amsterdam, November 21, 1891

Dear Helena,

A lovely letter from you from Calgary, dated November 2. I did empathize with you, followed you during your walk to the engineers' office over the snowy plain; that made me think about my walks this winter when the [naval ship] *Queen Emma* was stuck in the ice; I also placed myself in your situation while Karel was ill and everything fell upon your shoulders.

It is fortunate that the ice fog cleared again and that you could leave for Macleod in high spirits.

I will write you again soon, a long letter, even though I have absolutely no time at the moment, since all [the time] that I can wrest away from De Nederland [Stoomvaart Maatschappij] is taken up by Uncle [Menso] Pijnappel, who wishes to consult me about a variety of measures in respect to the passing of Uncle Toon. This applies also to Louis van Heukelom,[236] with the same sort of conferences in respect to the passing of Aunt Louise van Heukelom,[237] for whom I was the co-trustee. It is a kind of involvement that is 'very distasteful' for me, but when duty calls, your avocation must wait.

I wanted, however, to not postpone writing to you, so that you should not worry when the expenses are greater than you would wish. You should be comfortable. At first, Karel will probably not earn any money. But I am so happy that the primary objective will be reached, that you — in fairness and with understanding — should not have to be too concerned about your expenses. As soon as it is necessary, I will supplement your credit. Up until now, I have only paid $100.00, once.

Furthermore, I heard from cousin [Count] Adolphe, senior, that he will soon go to America and may also come to Montreal. You will hear from him when he is there, and then you may get into contact with him by telegraph. Also, when he is in New York at the office of Blake, Boissevain & Co. (Hosmer knows the telegraph address), he could get back to you, if you have something to say or ask of him.

While I was at the stock exchange, Eduard Rahusen[238] showed me your letter that had delighted him very much. You have struck the most charming tone with him! Bravo, *à ces traits là je reconnais mon sang!*

Now, dear child, *Gott befohlen!* Warm greetings to Karel, your loving father.

A28335001485-1490 [Heleen to Mother]
Pincher Creek, November 22, 1891

Dear Mother,

Karel has just left again for the camp. Yesterday, he came with a buggy, actually 'a buckboard', that had to be repaired, and so he had to stay here overnight. We had a very pleasant evening together. He is beginning to get very used to camp life and has never felt so healthy. He said, "I

---

236 Lodewijk Casper van Heukelom (1849–1920): banker; married to Anna Hillegonda van Outeren (1849–1924).

237 Louise Victoire van Heukelom (1818–1891), unmarried.

238 Eduard Nicolaas Rahusen (1830–1913): lawyer and member of the Provincial Council of North Holland and the Senate.

feel like another person. It is so lovely to go to sleep and to know for sure that the next morning I will not be short of breath!"

But on the other hand, life is not particularly pleasant. The people are somewhat coarse. They take no pleasure in their work, and on top of that, it is also a hard life with this early winter. Up to now, Karel has been in the tent with the engineers, but they expect that Drury, also an engineer, will soon join them; then Karel must move into one of the two tents for the workmen. He says that he does not mind that so much, but those men are sometimes quite rough, and what Wallie would call 'uncouth'. Karel does their work, 'chaining', quite clumsily, of course, and I believe that he sometimes has a tough time, even though he says nothing about it. 'Chaining' is the measuring of the [proposed] rail track with a chain, 100 feet long, that is dragged over the ground, and then, at every 100 feet, a pole is driven into the ground. These poles are made along the way and the number of completed feet are marked on them. One engineer measures the difference in height from one point to the other. The other one, the planar angles. They have now reached quite difficult terrain and must try many different routes before they continue. The day before yesterday, I went to visit them to bring some clean clothes for Karel and to bring some medicine for a sick man. Perhaps, I also did it so that I could read Papa's letter from October. Four letters that have gone to Calgary have not caught up with us yet, and now, last Wednesday, the mail only brought Papa's letter to Karel, and I yearned so much to hear something from home.

Howsoever it is, I went to the Lower [Waldron Ranch], to where the camp is close by. Mr. White Fraser could not take me, since he had to go to Macleod, but he ordered another carriage for me, namely a 'buggy', which is a kind of chaise on four wheels without a cover, with two burly horses. My driver was Mrs. Briet, a strapping half-Irish gal, well known in the area for her courageous riding and knowledge of horses. It was beautiful mild weather, but I was still warmly clad with fur and blanket, because it might have been late before we were back home. There we went, me not completely at ease without a man to control the horses. The mounted policeman who was to come along was not yet ready, but would follow us later. Mrs. Briet, stereotypically Irish (wearing a red knit cap, of which the fringes got in her eyes, like long ponytails), told all kinds of amusing stories about her adventures — how she had ridden eight horses when she moved here from Ontario; how she had ridden bucking ponies, etc. After a nearly an hour, we arrived at the home where we would wait for the mounted policeman, crossing the small river and stopping in front of the house.

We received a friendly welcome from the rancher,[239] a French-Canadian who enjoyed speaking French with me. The Irish [woman] became impatient because the soldier did not show up, and a son of the rancher announced

---

239   Moise (Mose) La Grandeur (1835–1900) and his wife, Julie Livermore (1856–1937), were ranchers and owners of a stagecoach stopping place at the junction of the Pincher Creek and the Oldman River.

that he would be willing to point us the way over the river. In the meantime, I was quite fond of my mounted policeman and was very happy when he arrived just in time.

At great speed, we were again going forward: the two horsemen (one of them on a bucking pony) were in front. Down, through the river, and then again at a gallop up the rocky hill. I was terrified because the road was unbelievably bad, the trail too narrow for the wide-wheeled buggy and the horses very fiery. The river that we had to cross was very wide but, for the most part, frozen. Only in the middle did the water flow quickly, luckily without ice floes. It did not look at all appealing, and Mrs. Briet and I called to the mounted policeman that if he didn't think it was safe, we would rather turn back. But the riders arrived safely on the other side and called to us that it was "all right." Therefore, again forward we went over the slippery ice. Then, quite a drop into the deep water — the horses urged and whipped to make the high step onto the ice on the other side. One leap of the buggy and we were safe and dry on the other side. In the meantime, the horses were a bit excited and the [Irish woman] was certainly tough and courageous, but not very steady with the driving.

Continuing on, things went fine for a good hour, but then with a momentary startle of one of the horses, they both took off. We had just arrived at the higher plain and they could therefore, without imminent danger, run for quite a long way. With all our might, together we held the reins that constantly threatened to slip out of our hands; it seemed that their speed was slowing, when, on top of it all, the reins broke. The buggy tipped. First, Mrs. Briet fell; the reins got away; the horses disappeared. How I fell, I do not know exactly; in any case, it was on my left hand, free of the carriage and on my face. Lucky that I have such an unappealing nose, which is now only scraped and swollen, but certainly not broken. The gal was not hurt at all. She rubbed me with snow until I came to, and you cannot imagine what a crazy feeling that was, in the middle of the snowy prairie, with that funny face in that red hat in front of me. She had to tell me the same thing again and again before I could understand that it was all true and not a frightening dream. Finally, the horses came back under the hands of the mounted policeman, who had ridden to the Waldron Farm to get help and to warn Karel.

My nose was bleeding, but not severely, and that was soon stemmed. The horses were harnessed again. Mrs. Briet mounted the horse, and the mounted policeman came to sit with me and to drive the buggy. In that way, we arrived safely at the farm. I profited from my first-aid kit and the bandage that I had brought along. I told them how to wrap my wrist and how to put it in a sling.

Karel soon arrived. I read Papa's letter with a lot of pleasure. We had a nice meal of I-don't-know-what. The sick man was improving and very delighted with his medicine. Karel was doing very well, but soon the return trip commenced because the weather was threatening and we wanted to be back before dark. The mounted policeman came to sit beside me again and, in the beginning, everything went as planned. The river was crossed safely. Slowly the wind came up, but that did not hamper us. The road was very steep and even more dangerous, as evidenced while on a very difficult, rocky slope, by the buggy overturning; I again fell out, very neatly, and tumbled down the slope.

    Be brave, Dear Readers, I am telling it myself, just like Sinbad the Sailor. I hurt nothing other than, perhaps, the same wrist; the man jumped out of the buggy and did not hurt himself. The horses were quite calm and the buggy was not broken. At the bottom of the hill, we climbed in again. By now the snowstorm had started, not very heavily but straight at us, and I was very happy that I did not have to ride and could protect my eyes with the red shawl and muff. I suggested staying the night at the Frenchman's, who had already invited us that morning, but the soldier wanted to bring the horses home, and in any case, I also longed to see a doctor for my arm, which was becoming very painful. In the meantime, we were continually going forward through densely falling snow. How the man found the trail, I do not know. To me, everything looked like one endless white plain. We only went the wrong way once, for a short stretch, and sooner than I thought, we saw the light of the barracks.

[27] Pincher Creek polo team: (L–R) William Humfrey, Louis Garnett, Dr. Herbert Rimington Mead, Jack Garnett

Was I ever glad to be in the hotel! Dr. Mead[240] very quickly diagnosed my arm, a very bad sprain, bound it with opium and warm water, and found it quite an entertaining case. Upstairs, I ate supper and retired early in order to recover from all that shaking and bumping.

Now, two days later, I can see that my arm is on the mend. Nothing is broken, but such a sprain can take a long time, especially without [Mezger].[241] In the beginning, it was quite painful, but now I have it in a splint and that helps very much. The doctor wraps it every morning and, in the evening, the maid does it; she is inexperienced but very willing and good-hearted and helps me very kindly. And with that, this story is over. When you read it, I am already safe in Montreal!

With a big kiss, Your Heleen.

A28335001491-1494 [Heleen to Father]
Pincher Creek, November 23, 1891

Dear Father,

Would you please first read the enclosed letter to Mama [November 22] and see if it will not upset her too much, should she read it before she knows that we both are again in safer surroundings. Probably, in about fourteen days, I will be again in Calgary (on the CPR line), and will then travel alone by train, first to Vancouver and then back to Montreal.

Karel will stay at work until about Christmas and will then also come to Montreal. I will feel sorry to leave here because the White Frasers are such very enjoyable people. Yesterday, I was again with them for a half-day. First, I went to the [St. John's] Anglican Church, where Mrs. [White Fraser] played the organ. Quite 'high church', the service was sung for the most part, the cross at the altar and a sort of mass, a tiny church, well-filled with twenty-five people. It was lovely mild weather, but the wind was blowing hard — it sang much louder than the hymns and the congregation together.

I was a little bit worried about Karel, who had left for the camp at 9:30 a.m., especially because the camp was moved the day before yesterday and therefore he had to search for it. First to the old spot, four hours from here, and from there he needed to find the trail, if it had not been buried under the snow. His buggy was in good shape and the pony was a quiet, safe, secure mountain pony. Since the weather had remained clear yesterday, I trust that he has safely arrived.

---

240   Herbert Rimington Mead (1859–1898) was the first practising physician of Pincher Creek; married to Louisa MacPherson in 1882, later divorced; second marriage in 1892 to Edith Smith (1853–1945).

241   Johan Georg Mezger (1838–1909) was a renowned medical doctor and masseur, known amongst European royalty as having treated Elisabeth of Austria (famously known as Sisi), for example. He was married to Maria Helena Reelfs (1851–1872), and his second marriage was with Pieternella Johanna Borsius (1851–1919).

In the afternoon, Mr. White Fraser came to fetch me. I stayed with them the whole evening. There also was Lieutenant Baker,[242] who I had met in Macleod, and the four of us argued a lot about Sunday's rest and boredom, the value of setbacks, 'Looking Backward Astronomy', etc. Mr. Baker had once been very poor, on the edge of destitution, but still had not been unhappy. Baker and Mrs. WF went to the evening church service and I stayed behind reading with Mr. WF. I got a book by a Frenchman who claims, on scientific grounds, to know how the life of the souls will continue in other beings, who, after earthly death, remain in the ether around the planets, and who will finally end up in the sun. Not very deep, but sunny, good observations and a good conversation-starter.

Mr. White Fraser found poverty especially lamentable and, for himself, found it very difficult to be religious. In Liverpool, he was so struck by the misery on the streets that it had spoiled his pleasure of coming home.

Back from the church, supper and afterwards still a little bit of music; it was 11:30 p.m. before I thought of going home. Mr. Baker brought me to the hotel, where everyone was sleeping. A good opportunity to practise using my right hand by itself. My left arm is progressing well. Dr. Mead came over today for a long visit to make small talk. Very pleasant. His mother lives in Bruges [Belgium] with his seven-year-old daughter. I had heard from Mrs. WF that he is in the throes of getting a divorce; his wife must be of humble origin. It is extremely interesting to get to know so many different people.

Bye-bye. Do you know that I have not yet received a letter from you? Much love from your Heleen.

A29670000013-14 [Heleen to Li]
Pincher Creek, November 23, 1891

Dearest Li,

I received with great pleasure your letter of October 30. It was lovely to be brought up to date with everything, the October birthdays, the Harry episode, the Norwegian experience. Brave to just step into the church,[243] and nice that Wil will go along with you in the evenings. I am very curious about whether you will continue to go and how the Norwegian sailors behave around the ladies.

I am so sorry about Uncle Toon's illness, but I trust, since I have not received a telegram, that he is recuperating. But it must have been anxious days for Grandmother and Mama, and perhaps will cause Toon some

---

242 Montague Baker (1859–1913) was an officer of the NWMP who also served in the South African Boer War; married to Edith Horton (1872–1944).

243 House owned by the Norwegian Seamans' Mission on the Prins Hendrikkade, Amsterdam; designed as a church, library and pastorie.

concern for the future. Tell him that I send warm wishes to him for a complete recovery and that he must walk a lot.

Long live Reverend Richard![244] A lovely prospect for more fellow churchgoers for Papa and Mama.

Long live the Frisians who married the Wertheims![245] Very proper Christian family, and Menalda[246] is a nice fellow. The family will also be delighted with that.

Would you please deliver the enclosed cards to Jo? I do not have an envelope that fits. I also think it a nice idea that Kareltje Schorer[247] comes to our house and know you will do him some good. He will probably enjoy a lot of the social life in Amsterdam.

Will Bentveld[248] be sold?

Li, I wish that you knew the White Frasers. The more time I spend with the two of them, the more energetic I become. They have been married for nine years, no children, and are so affectionate with each other! She is twenty-seven years old and was engaged for two years. At home, she was the oldest girl of nine children. Her oldest brother died from the yellow fever in Hong Kong. Her home is in Cornwallis, where she attended various clubs and maintained correspondence with clever people, among others, a critical essay club, the members of which from time to time would write a critique about an assigned book, coming together once each month to read aloud and review the essay. (Would Nel like to start something like that?) She took a nursing course and received her diploma within one and a half years. She tried to start a Shakespeare reading club, but that failed. She easily speaks and even sings French. Those Canadian songs, about which Pa Quack spoke, I have not yet uncovered. Various people have known about them quite well, and have also heard them, but did not have them on hand. For that, I think that I must be in Quebec.

This afternoon, I saw a nice collection of Indian artefacts at Dr. Mead's, a decent man who has made his house extremely comfortable with all the Indian beadwork and masses of bearskins. His mother lives in Bruges and made a few watercolours of the bell tower and those lovely old buildings and little cityscapes.

Have you folks seen the full eclipse of the moon? Here, it was very clear.

---

244 Jacobus Jeremias Richard (1823–1897): reverend of the Netherlands Reformed Church; married to Anna Jacoba Maria Gertruida Nieuwenhuis (1826–1877).

245 The Wertheims were Dutch Jewish financiers and bankers; A.C. and Karel Wertheim were good friends of the Boissevains.

246 Anneus Menalda (1862–1942): manager of Koninklijke Nederlandsche Beiersche Bierbrouwerij, which existed 1864–1926; married in 1892 to Johanna Sarah Wertheim (1871–1921), daughter of Karel Wertheim.

247 Jhr. Karel Johan Schorer (1870–1942): studied law in Amsterdam and graduated in 1895; likely a friend of Thijs, and also wrote for *Propria Cures*; married to Johanna Henriette Reinoudina van Eysinga (1876–1946).

248 This is the estate known as Groot Bentveld, now a national monument within the municipality of Zandvoort.

The day before yesterday I had a visit from the notables. It was hilarious. The blacksmith,[249] an incredibly stupid Hun,[250] who thought that Holland or the Netherlands was a province of Germany, between Austria and France, was terribly Prussian, and spoke clipped German. But he was very good-natured and talked with me, staying one and a half hours. Yesterday, he came again to bring the newspapers.

How is it going with the Cootjes[251] and Fräulein [Eva Ketjen]? Say hello to everyone for me and congratulate Coo for his seat in the Provincial Council. Soon a representative of the [North Holland] Provincial Executive?

Bye! With a warm kiss, your Heleen.

P.S. Many thanks for the portrait of Antoinette!

A29670000015–17 [Heleen to Li]
Pincher Creek, Alberta, Canada, November 26, 1891

Dear Li,

Yesterday was a great mail day for me, letters from Antoinette and Aunt Su, enjoyable and warm-hearted, very friendly letters from Addie Van Horne, and two from Mama.

What a very sad time with Uncle Toon's illness. It must have been very tough for you to keep things going at home. I would have loved to have been two people, to have been there and here at the same time. It was certainly comforting that there were two good nurses there. And then all those endless day-to-day worries, like little Miep, who is being a bad sort and renouncing her Huguenot blood. Would it not be better if someone looked over her homework and quizzed her lessons? In the beginning it would cause a fountain of tears, but slowly it would go automatically and less miserably than that of periodic despair. There are so many children whose homework is always looked over by their parents: see van Hasselt, Bakels, and Karsten.[252]

Antoinette's letter seemed pluckier and more cheerful to me than before, considering the circumstances. I am very happy that she does her work and that it is not disappointing for her.

249   This is probably Charles (Karl) Conrad Schoening (1854–1938): rancher and blacksmith, married to Johanna Wittkopf (1861–1943).

250   The word *Hun* can mean fighter or barbarian, probably referring to the ancient tribal leader Attila the Hun (434 CE–453 CE). Heleen uses the word as a disparaging comment about Germans, in particular, Prussians, who have a reputation for being coarse, aggressive and untrustworthy, and who sought to gain dominance in Europe, including having initiated the Franco-Prussian War (1870–1871).

251   The "Cootjes" are Ko den Tex and his young son, Cornelis (Coo/Ko) Jacob Arnold den Tex (1889–1965).

252   Families of Anne Karel Philip Frederik Robert van Hasselt, Heer van Empe (1839–1908), engineer and board member of the SMN, and Anna Aleida Houwink (1848–1929); Professor Herman Thomas Karsten (1839–1915) and Antoinette Ludovica Françoise de Melverda (1850–1931); merchant Johannes Adrianus Bakels (1841–1892) and Margaretha Cornelia Nieuwkamp (1849–1917).

Toos Kremers[253] still remains a difficult problem. Why would it be a solution if the father [a carpenter] were to begin working for the Salvation Army? Must he then leave his children? A consolation that Piet is cared for.

Will you stay with Mrs. Pierson? I would find that very nice and I would so much like to hear from you about how she is doing in The Hague. Mrs. van Tienhoven must still be forming her impressions of the [capital city].

Are you getting impatient that I only have questions and chat, and say nothing? Now then, it is a crazy sort of life here. The nature is grand in every direction: the endless, undulating prairie; the high, formidable mountains; the sudden, harsh cold; and then again, as if by magic, the warm, heavy wind shrieks along the windows and makes the houses shake. The people in their tiny 'log huts' seem to be so powerless against all that force, and then there is me, especially with my one useless arm. Because of it, I cannot do anything that looks like real work, and therefore, I lead my usual normal life of books and thinking, which is such an odd contrast with my surroundings.

The room where I sit most of the time is the craziest residence, 2.5 by 7 metres. Along the long side, very close to the corners, are two narrow windows. In the centre of the other long wall is a stove that constantly goes out when the wind blows. The short sides are taken up with a sort of resting couch that serves as a bed at night, because, very often, four or five men also sleep here. A table with drawers and a mirror; beside the window, a small table with tablecloth; halfway before the other [window], a wooden chair; and a rocking chair with a lot of nails over which I hang my rug, which looks so posh.

The man from the hotel always comes here to write his invoices, and in the evening, it is often full of people who are reading or writing. For that, a couple of chairs are taken from the bedroom. The walls that had been whitewashed are now very dirty, and a few days ago a visitor touched up about ten holes. The woodwork is unpainted.

A28335001493-94 [continues on]

I am the only one who ever opens a window, but I do it, and also quite often. Now it is difficult for me because there is no lead [weight] in the windows and therefore something must always be shoved underneath it.

My little bedroom is the same size as Wallie's, if you do not account for the room between his bed and the window. It is just exactly filled by the bed, washstand and suitcase. I make sure that the window is always

---

253 Catharina (Toos) Johanna Kremers (1877–1960) became a nanny and married in 1900 to Jan Cornelis Zwitselaar (1872–1945), an office clerk. From the records, it seems that the parents of Toos, Carel Johannes Kremers (1853–?) and Jacoba Smit (1851–?), were struggling, evidenced by often moving the family from one address to another. One of Toos' sisters, Femmetje (1880–?), left home for Vlissingen in 1891, as did her brother, Pieter (Piet) Johannes (1879–1940), who also left that year for Gorssel. In 1899, Pieter became a patient in Meerenberg, a psychiatric institution in Bloemendaal. This is just one example of the type of situation that Li was faced with as a social worker in the desperately poor Jordaan district.

open during the day and sleep very well if my arm lets me rest. I have a very pleasant doctor and, I believe, a capable surgeon. The opium and water bandage has now been taken off and he has strapped the arm with black clay-like, camphor-stuff on thick linen. I only use the splint during the night and, in the daytime, I have almost no pain anymore. But he says that it will take a long time before I can use it normally and I am sorry about that, especially for riding horses. I would just like to be able to do that right now, as it would be very easy to reach the camp.

Yesterday, I met Mr. John Garnett,[254] the spitting image of John Bienfait.[255] He lives on a ranch with two brothers (of which one is married), and has lived here already twelve years; but he remains informed about everything in the Old World. In contrast with his [brother], he holds his refinement in esteem and does the rough work out of necessity. I had a recommendation letter for him, but before he knew [of it], he had already asked me to stay. I will probably go there next week.

He also slept here for the night, and stayed for a long time yesterday afternoon to talk with me. He is one of the three magistrates. He was sorry that there was sometimes such a commotion and he expected salvation through different liquor laws. Overnight, there was again a huge racket and a guy was arrested and sent to Macleod. But really, in Amsterdam there is always just as much noise, maybe not in the home but indeed on the streets, so I am not very bothered by it.

By the way, I can always stay at the White Frasers', where I feel completely at home. Mr. [WF] cannot refrain from playing with knives and corkscrews at the table, to the great exasperation of Mrs. [WF]. He and I had fun about the idea of serviette-ring races and pillow fights. They are both crazy about Papa's latest portrait, and he right away got in the mood to let his beard grow, to which his wife and I strenuously objected. He told me about his previous flames and how, for one of them, he had carried a medallion around his neck; he also had the name of another one tattooed on his arm. He swears that he is fifteen years older than his wife, but is sometimes still unbelievably boyish.

Saturday morning, November 27: Yesterday there was only a little bit of wind and lovely, mild spring weather. I went to look around in the neighbourhood and had a lovely walk along the creek, which gently rippled and was almost completely thawed. I walked through nice little bushes and, for the first time, heard a Canadian bird whistle, and picked some nice thistle and other fluffy heads and ended up . . .

---

254 John (Jack) Garnett (c.1848–1898): rancher; remained unmarried and died of typhoid fever in the RCMP hospital during the Klondike Gold Rush. He was buried in the RCMP cemetery in Dawson City, being the only civilian. A few years later, the Garnetts gave up ranching and left the area; the fine house that they had built was destroyed by fire in 1898.

255 John Bienfait (1865–1922): engineer; married to Clara Suzanna Fangman (1868–1946).

A28335001553-4 [continues on]

. . . passing many nosy but peaceful cows from a farm. The gate was opened for me and a man took me along and through many gates, and then further to where he could point out the way to go. He was a friendly Englishman, who thought that I was also English and found it enjoyable to talk a little bit about the "Old Country." The main street of the village was filled with loose horses, about thirty or forty belonging to the Indians who had come to trade with the Hudson's Bay Company. Mama would have had little pleasure here. There are no sidewalks, not even paved roads, and there are always loose cattle on the road.

Monday morning [29 November]: Yesterday, it was just like spring. Almost no wind and very mild. I went out for a walk and lay for a while in the grass in order to comfortably enjoy the beautiful view.

This evening I saw a prairie fire in the distance. Here, that is the greatest bugbear for the people. When one is seen within the vicinity of the town, everyone must help to extinguish it. That is done by striking at it with bags of wet sand, and carriages with tons of water, riding back and forth. It sometimes takes very long, and it is scary and tiresome work. The last time, some folks hid in basements and behind crates, to the great outrage of the brave ones that did help. The burned hillsides create beautiful indigo colours against the gold-brown living prairie.

For now, my plans are as follows:
- Wednesday, December 2 or Thursday, December 3: to the Garnetts'
- Monday: back here
- December 8: to Macleod and then to Calgary, where I hope to be on the 12th, but might not be earlier than the 14th or 15th.

If the weather is good, I will go to Banff or Vancouver, returning to Montreal, again, around the new year. After December 15, I will be, in any case, in reach of the telegraph and railway.

My arm is progressing well, and my headache is over. The last reports from Karel were quite good.

Much love to all, from your Heleen.

KLAB09193000011 [Father to Karel]
Amsterdam, November 27, 1891

Dear Karel,

Now you are at your destination and, I trust, at work upon your arrival. I heartily wish you health and courage — paired with the customary prudence — and I have the firm conviction that you will come back to the civilized world as if reborn from your Canadian camp life.

Your letter from Calgary gave me a lot of enjoyment. Keep writing with an open heart. I feel everything about your impatience during your periods of illness, but you can imagine how thankful we are that Helena is still with you.

We are still strongly affected by the loss Uncle Toon, and of all the sadness of the friends at his passing away. I told you that he was still thinking of you with love. So, here is the situation. In his will of October of this year, he bequeathed 1,000 guilders to each of my children; however, this number is double for you and Helena. I will, therefore, one of these days, collect 2,000 guilders for you and try to invest it profitably. At the beginning of the year, you will receive a statement from me in which you can see what is in the account.

I do not have time for small talk, but I hope to write with more detail, soon. Everything is fine with us. Only Mama continues to be bothered by sleeplessness, so I have moved into your room.

Many greetings also to Heleen, to whom I will not write for this mailing. Your loving Father.

A32005000384-385 [Wil to Heleen]
Amsterdam, November 27, 1891

Dear Heleentje!

What a good caregiver you really are for Karel. He was so thankful for everything you did for him when he was sick, and especially that you had such patience when he was ill-tempered. Yesterday morning, I received his long letter, to which he kept adding a little bit, time and time again. At the same time, one of yours arrived at 717 [Keizersgracht, Amsterdam], and when I went there in order to read Karel's travel stories, your letter had just been forwarded to me. Your mother was at your grandmother's and therefore missed the visit from Mrs. Pierson, who had come over for the wedding of Anna Gunning[256] and Dr. Bonebakker. Mrs. [Pierson] was lovely; she spoke so nicely of you and was so friendly.

I am so glad that Karel was not short of breath in Calgary because otherwise it would have completely dispirited him, even though it was, nevertheless, a big disappointment. It must also be very tough, still hankering for work and having so much ambition to that end. But it is better to be strong before the journey starts. I imagine that it will be quite a rough expedition, all that sleeping in tents during the cold weather; hopefully, he is strong enough.

How kind of those people to invite you to their farms. I so hope that when you go from one to another you can keep an eye on him from time to time, and that you have someone for yourself with whom you can talk about home. Otherwise, it must be quite an unsettled life, and therefore you cannot take anything in hand to do for yourself when the surroundings change every time.

---

256   Anna Elisabeth Gunning (1867–1899): married in 1891 to Adrianus Bonebakker (1863–1947), medical doctor.

A while ago, I was at your grandmother's and found her upstairs in the front room in the company of your mother, who softly told me not to stay too long. [Grandmama] speaks somewhat haltingly, sometimes so because of her cough; yet she was so well supported in her sorrow and looked so reverent and lovely. But she has become a little bit thin around the mouth, which gave me such a sad feeling. It is still remarkable how dignified she remains.

That same day, it was last Monday, I ate at your parents'. I found it wonderful to be in the midst of the family again. Nel stayed with your Aunt [Annette] Kruseman,[257] while Suze [Kruseman][258] was at Marie Kam's[259] playing nanny for one of the [two] little Kams. The good-hearted Nel likely found it somewhat boring, I fear.

After dinner, Thijs had to go, but before that, at the table, he was already in fine form. He then took five large chrysanthemums (which were standing in a vase on the mantle) and stuck them in his buttonhole. This yellow boutonnière reached his ear, and therefore they had to be put back in their place. Furthermore, he told us what Karel had written and, during dinner, I got the story about his visit to the old Mrs. Beuker,[260] which you have certainly heard about in fine detail. Your father asked if we knew the saying "Frugality with diligence builds homes like castles." When everyone answered in the affirmative, Li protested. She found that your mother had practised thriftiness and your father diligence, and so ended with "Why do we not live now in a castle?"

Finally, during the lemon custard, it was announced that there was to be no chocolate custard. Beforehand, everyone had promised not to crack any jokes about it. Thijs had already announced that he would crack vulgar jokes at every chocolate custard, and so he was doubly denied the prospect of making a wisecrack.

In the evening, [Coo] den Tex came and said some nice things about little Coo, and then Papa brought me home. He did not want me to be fetched by the porter again. Nice, eh?

A32005000382–383 [continues on]

The Kindervoeding suits me very well. However, after my first stint, my hands were very swollen because of the heavy pots; but I shall get used to it. Only, sometimes I am afraid to drop such a load (with a good amount of *hutspot*) on the head of one of the children. Something that I also

---

257 Annette Jeanette Henriëtte (Boissevain) Kruseman (1835–1894): widow of Reverend Hendrik Lambertus Kruseman (1831–1871).

258 Suzanne (Suze) Kruseman (1864–1944): author of children's books, under the name S. Gruijs Kruseman; married in 1902 to Pieter Gerrit Gruijs (1866–1947), First Lieutenant, Infantry.

259 Maria Kruseman (1862–1959): sister of Suzanne; best known as the first social worker of the Netherlands; married to Jan Benjamin Kam (1860–1932), architect.

260 Jeanne Marie Louise Petronella van Rossum (1810–1892): was married to Jan Hendrik Beuker (1800–1877), insurance broker.

like are those greasy little handshakes. A few children really mean it. One boy said from the bottom of his heart, "Thank you very much, Miss!"

But there was one girl that I did not like, right away. She was already somewhat older, did not look very poor or hungry, and was a constant pain in the neck, so much so that others were also caught up in her troublemaking. Now, the rule is No talking, but telling them to stop does not help much, so we had to keep intervening. The second time, after I served the girls, I saw that child picking at her food; she was evidently not hungry. She had nearly finished her plate and she was again fooling around, which I had already forbidden her to do, many times. When I asked her if she still wanted to have something, "Heck no, Miss," and somewhat later, when she had scraped her plate completely clean, I said, "When you are ready, get up and go away so that the other ones can take a seat." "But Miss, I would really like to have some more, Miss." I had to give it to her, of course, and she started pestering once again, [eating] very slowly, on purpose, in order to stay with her comrades and to keep being wicked. Finally, she was done and I saw that she was now giving thanks. When I had served two [others], I asked her why she did not make room. "Heck, Miss, I must still give thanks".

Agnes ter Meulen,[261] to whose attention I brought [the girl], will keep an eye on her and tell us about her. There was also a sweet little boy who did not know the way home, and his little brother and sisters were [already] gone. He did not dare to cry, but those big dark blue eyes were so touching! Happily a boy came in with the message "Your sis is still in the street," and away went the little man with a brightened-up little face.

The last time, the smell of the cooking food was somewhat strong, but happily they opened the windows a bit; otherwise I could not do the work. A half-drunk wagoner ordered from me "a plate of soup, and quick," and when he noticed his error, he walked calmly away.

I have so much on my hands that I have not yet gone to the children's hospital. Now I am almost done with the visits and, again, one task is behind me.

By the way, we will still do something here for St. Nicolaas [on December 5] even though, from my side, it will not be with the usual silly poems, which are, in any event, already crazy. A while ago, I drank afternoon tea at Mary van Eeghen's.[262] She was very kind and lovely, and the children were also at home. What a sturdy girl Emily has become! Henkie was completely immersed in a little book and spoke very seriously, as children do.

Mama, who, as always during these times, has all of her memories about the last days of Cobatje[263] and of Papa, is now feeling twice as poorly

---

261 Agnes Elisabeth ter Meulen (1879–1951): married in 1905 to Daniel Cornelis van Eibergen-Santhagens (1874–1959), manager of *N.V. Mij. tot Exploitatie ter Suikerondernemingen,* which owned Karang Soewoeng, Adiwerna, and Djatibarang sugar factories, operating in the Dutch East Indies.

262 Maria (Mary) van Eeghen Boissevain and their children, Hendrik (1889–1928) and Emily Heloise (1890–1969).

263 Jacoba (Cobatje) Hermina de Vos (1874–1883): late sister of Wil.

since there was such bad news about Jo. While there is no danger, not only has the kidney been added [to her ailments], but it is also a fusion, so that she is now being treated for five different things. She wrote that it felt like she was being torn apart and that recently she all of a sudden burst into tears, for which Thure Brandt[264] reproached himself and calmed her down again. She is firstly treated by his assistant, a young girl, who massages her externally, including both her knees and thighs. This prepares her for the dreadful internal [massage]. She is very exausted afterwards and then takes a few days of rest; but when she ate at our friends' from the Finnish spa resort at one point, she must have been as if in a dream and felt very badly. Furthermore, she does nothing other than reading, writing and dozing, all on the couchette.

Now, I shall tell you something about Lady Angus. Mrs. Oyens,[265] who was in Montreal seven years ago, told me that she found that lady "so bourgeois." When the Oyens were there, the Anguses were also in the hotel while their lovely house was being built. Time and time again, crates arrived with all sorts of household goods from London, and Mrs. Oyens went to admire them. Among other things, there was a white, red and gold wash-set. Lady [Angus] was so enamoured with it that she put the chamber pot on the fireplace mantle and said that she could actually use it as an ornament. Typical, eh?

I am now playing an old French gavotte with Mrs. Bosmans, of which the composer is unknown. In about fourteen days, Mrs. Bosmans will play at the Concertgebouw. She and Kes[266] each will play a piano piece by Mozart. I would like to attend. Mama had wanted to come along to the rehearsal of the Cecilia Concert.[267] It was very beautiful, but I had heard [another concert] previously that spoke more to me. The symphony, *Auf de Campagne* by Strauss[268] (a young composer), has a very beautiful beginning; one could see the still plains. And the end was an allegro with "Funiculì, Funiculà" as the main theme — odd that the idea of a simple Italian [song] is so revered. The same day, but in the evening, of course, folks sang the same tune in *De Doofpot*, like the song "Diender, Diender,"[269] and so forth.

P.S. Here, at the beginning [of the letter], is also the end of my story. I want to thank you warmly once again for everything. A big kiss from

---

264 Major Marten Thure Emil Brandt (1819–1895): Swedish gymnast and developer of massage therapies, in particular for women.

265 Marie Cornelia Reijnvaan (1854–1926): married in 1879 to Hendrik Jan de Marez Oyens (1843–1911), banker.

266 Willem Kes (1856–1934): Dutch conductor and violinist.

267 Organization Caecilia, established 1841, held Caecilia Concerts to support aged or needy musicians and their widows and orphans.

268 This refers to Richard Strauss' 1886 symphony *Aus Italien*, the first movement of which is *Auf der Campagna*, incorporating the tune of "Funiculì, Funiculà," purporting it to be a Neapolitan folksong.

269 *De Doofpot* is the name of a revue by August Reyding (1863–1930), which includes the song "Diender, Diender," probably meaning "Officer, officer."

your loving Wil. Many greetings from Mama and Cor and also, of course, for Karel when you see him.

A32074000148-152 [Heleen to Wil]
Pincher Creek, November 27, 1891

Dear Wil,

Karel has little opportunity to write, but he experiences a lot, and if you promise me that you will not make a fuss about his adventurous existence, then I will write you regularly about all his heroic deeds. At about the time when you have read this letter, by the way, he is already on the way to safer areas.

Last Saturday [November 21], now a week ago, he came here to have a buggy repaired. The previous day, he had come, driving hastily, to the [La Grandeur] farm to see me [there, because I could not travel due to my hurt wrist], and then, something broke. He had taken the same path where I had tumbled twice, but he had said that his pony was very quiet and sure-footed. The river was almost completely frozen over so he could easily cross the small gully. During the night [of November 21], he stayed here in the hotel and the next day set out upon the return trip at 9:00 in the morning. It was a pity that he could not stay a little longer that Sunday, but it had snowed a lot in the evening and I was afraid that it would be more troublesome to find the way if it was left until late. In the meantime, the camp had moved. Therefore, he would have to go first to the old campsite near the farm and then try to find the trail from there. The weather was sunny and clear and, happily, it stayed that way the whole day. At 1:00 in the afternoon, he reached the old campsite after a very pleasurable trip without any adventures. I will just tell you the sequel in Karel's own words as he wrote to me about it the next day:

> I unsaddled my pony, brought him to the stall and later to the creek to drink. Coming back from there, he broke out of the halter that I had placed around his neck; he let me get close to him for a moment, and then, when I thought I had him in my grip, I held him too tightly and he knocked me to the ground with a sharp jerk, wonderfully rolling himself over a few times in the snow, and then slowly but surely he wandered back to the stable on his own. I had a lovely lunch at the farm: meat, carrots and potatoes and rice with milk and sugar.
>
> There was no day of rest at the farm. They had been catching some calves, and before the farmers could get their horses in the barn and have lunch, it had become late. I saddled my pony again and began to search for the trail, according to the directions given by the farmers who saw the camp being moved. It did not work and I returned to the farm to ask whether someone would be able to

accompany me for a little way down the road. Luckily one of them declared himself disposed to do that and, at the end, brought me finally all the way to the camp (on horseback). What a beautiful day it was on Sunday. Didn't you think it was a beautiful day to go riding?

So much from Karel. From the man who brought me the letter, I heard that Karel had not returned during the next days to the camp. He would have been riding from work to [the camp] on Mr. Hogg's horse, but the work had taken a long time. It was dark, neither sun nor stars; he had gone in the wrong direction and luckily landed at the farm where he stayed that night. The terrain here causes a lot of difficulties and the work often takes a long time, but the whole party mostly stays together and then they will find the camp, even though it may be a long search.

It astonishes and delights me every time that Karel can endure all those challenges so well and, despite them, become so positive and healthy. No trace of asthma or shortness of breath!

November 30: During these last days, it was beautiful mild weather. The snow is almost completely gone, and I think that Karel has also had a lot of enjoyment on his long trips. The sky was delightful, and the landscape looked so rich in the beaming sun. I did not see him on Sunday, but it did not surprise me because the camp is far away and the people and animals certainly need their day of rest. Karel had also dissuaded me from looking for him.

It is possible that I will not see him any more before the work is finished, and I am afraid that, during this time, regular updates from him will become sparse. But remember, no news is good news and all serious things will be telegraphed. For him, the first weeks will be almost the same as the last ones, only now it will become more enjoyable, since he has everything exactly the way that he wants it. Very high overshoes, enough blankets, etc., and the weather experts say that we will keep this beautiful weather until Christmas.

What a difficult sea crossing Jo had! Will you keep me up to date on how it is going with her? It will have done all of you some good to have seen her for a little while in Berlin. How is Willem Coster doing? Will he stay in the south for the winter?

Bye, dear Wil. Say hello to your mother and Cor, embrace them warmly, from your Heleen.

A28335001495=98 [Heleen to Mother]
Pincher Creek, December 2, 1891

Dear Mother,

Mail day today: I received a delightful shipment, as if it was my birthday, a letter from each one in the family, dated between November 7 and 13.

There are also five for Karel, among them the one from you and Papa dated November 10. Those, I will read later, only when he has first had them, and therefore I cannot yet answer them. I would love to answer each of the sisters, but I have only three-quarters of an hour, and therefore I write just to you now.

The mail here is so strange. It arrives on Wednesday evening and Thursday morning, and then it comes again, but not before Tuesday of the following week. It was lovely to feel like I was with everyone again. I read [the letters] at the home of Mrs. White Fraser, where her husband brought me the mail, and in those cozy surroundings, I could so easily think about home and imagine talking with everyone. At 6:00 p.m., I went to the hotel to get dressed, and coming outside, I suddenly realized again that I was so far from home. There is no street lighting, and between the houses, at every turn, are stretches of open prairie, and the ground is rough and bumpy. Even so, it is enjoyably invigorating, but cold weather.

It was a doubly good day today, because I also received news from Karel, a long letter from the camp. A lot more cheerful than previously. He now enjoys the beautiful mornings and the long treks. Seemingly, it does not tire him so much anymore. Two more workmen have arrived, so he will be relieved of the tedious chaining and will be able to concentrate more on the engineers' work. He started this life, in fact, only as a temporary health measure, but now he is starting to think about focusing further on it. The best workmen earn $40.00 per month, Brooks, an engineer, $100.00. With a little bit more practice, he could quickly do engineers' work. With numbers, he is quite ahead of everyone, even Mr. Hogg. I hope that I will soon speak with him once again.

Tomorrow, the camp will be moved again, and then it will perhaps be closer to the Garnetts'. I will be staying there tomorrow and then will try to find him on Sunday. One of the Garnetts will probably take me to the camp. During the last days, it was delightful — bright, clear weather — and now we are reading about the horrendous storms in the Channel and the North Sea, and we rejoice in our safe life here!

My wrist is getting much better. This afternoon, I played *quatre mains* with Mrs. White Fraser, mostly *trois mains*, but the left hand sometimes also took part. The sling and the bandage are gone. I can dress myself again and do my hair and hold light things. Only rotating the wrist is still impossible, as is bending the hand down, but that will all come out fine. I feel completely well and, today, I am in especially high spirits. The only thing that bothers me a bit is the uncertainty about the future. I do not know what you would think if I travelled by myself, on my own, back to Calgary and from there perhaps to Vancouver, etc. If you were here and could see how it is for women to travel alone, and how helpful and polite everyone is, you would think nothing of it.

I find it such a pity to not make use of the opportunity to see this part of the earth. In Montreal, I would rather not be without Karel for very long. I will get caught up in a cycle of entertainments that I do not find desirable for our frugal life, and it will not be much longer before I start working at the hospital there. I have written to Mr. Niblock about when I think that I will be taking the train again. Then I shall see him along the way, and he can advise me about my further plans. Do not worry at all, especially about my situation. I remain always surrounded by caring friends.

There was again a fine spectacle on the road, today. Two heavily loaded wagons, hitched to each other and harnessed with six horses, stood waiting unattended. The wind flapped a rope against one of the front horses, who then started jumping, immediately followed by his mates. All six of them jumped forward but got tangled up in the reins; they could not go straight forward and the whole outfit turned around in an unbelievably small circle. The pharmacist[270] (also a seller of writing paper, toys, etc.) quickly came out and grabbed the two front horses, and after a lot of jumping and turning, they were brought back to rest and the wagons that collided were put right.

Today, I also played piano downstairs in the hall to the left, with three fingers and with very limited strength, but the cowboys found it lovely!

Now it is nearing 11:00 p.m. and the man that sleeps [in this room] goes to bed at eleven, so my letter ends now.

Congratulate Thijs very much for his membership in the senate. It was an enjoyable letter from him, and I would very much love to answer him right away (also the others, mind you). Thank them all very much. I also received extremely enjoyable letters from Wil and Jeanne des Tombe.

Bye, dear Mother, much love to Papa and everyone, and an affectionate kiss from your loving Heleen.

---

270 Edward James Mitchell (1851–1910): druggist in Pincher Creek; married to Elizabeth Rueffer (1851–1922); later moved to Twin Butte, where he was postmaster. Their gravestone stands in the Pioneer Cemetery in Pincher Creek.

Chapter 6

Stake-Marker in the Crowsnest

Heleen moves in with the Garnetts on their farm, known as The Grange. She and Karel are still within reach of each other, weather permitting. With the new year fast approaching, and still awaiting news from Van Horne, Karel's work takes him further into the mountains. Heleen decides to leave the area and sets off for Calgary and further adventures.

394A28335001499–1500 [Heleen to Mother]
The Grange, December 4, 1891

Dear Mother,

It is a pleasure to be in a well-run and tidy house again. This morning I enjoyed my bath and plenty of water and towels, and now feel clean again! This house is quite roomy and cozy. The one part is for the married couple and a child, a jolly, amusing little boy, five years old; the other part is for the two brothers. There is a second floor where I have, among other things, a lovely, airy bedroom. When I know the house better, I will give you more details.
 Mrs. Garnett[271] is very friendly and agreeable, not as beautiful or stylish as Mrs. White Fraser, but I think that I will get along very well with her.

---

271 Alice Mary Leslie-Smith (1851–1926, Quamichan, B.C.), born in Macau, China, was married in England in 1885 to Louis Osmond Garnett (1850–1928, Quamichan, B.C.), who, along with his brother, had come from England to the Pincher district in 1879 to establish the Garnett Ranch (The Grange). It was situated fourteen miles southwest of Pincher Creek, on the south fork of the Oldman River. Louis appears on the 1881 Canada census with two brothers, Charles Arthur (1840–1919, Duncan, B.C.), a famous cricketer, and John (1848–1898, Yukon). Another brother, Walter Emilius (1842–1892, London, England), is registered on the 1891 census of Canada. Sources: Pincher Creek Historical Society; Royal B.C. Museum Archives; www.thepeerage.com/p55981; www.pioneersalberta.org/profiles/g.html.

[28] The Grange Ranch, west of Pincher Creek

I had planned to be here only about four days and wanted to leave my suitcase behind [at the hotel], but Mr. John Garnett, who came to pick me up, absolutely wanted me to bring it along. For that I am also pleased, because if the weather gets bad, then we could be locked up here for a while.

Tomorrow is a public fox hunt, or maybe wolves — that I have not yet understood. When the English talk to each other about hunting, they speak terribly indistinctly. All of Pincher Creek and the folks from the neighbourhood will be gathered there, and we too!

The departure from Mrs. White Fraser was affectionate. We promised to exchange portraits and letters. The injured arm is an expensive business, $30.00 for the doctor and $4.40 for the pharmacist!

Just before I left, a letter from the camp arrived. Yesterday, they moved to six miles from here. That is very close by. I will see Karel now, for sure, on Sunday. I sent him the letters from you and Papa, along with three others. We have not yet seen the mailing of the *Handelsblad*, but we have enjoyed a lot of the *Rotterdammer*. Nice that the ice-clearing was successful at the Provincial Council. Will there be a strong enforcing director in place of Oort?[272]

Mr. Garnett's father was a country squire in England and twelve years ago lost a great deal of his fortune. The boys, who had never before lifted a finger, came here to make a fortune, but that is going slowly.

---

272 Egbert Oort (1836–1891): dockmaster; member of council of Zeemanshuis; married to Gezina Oort (1852–1936).

The oldest one is now completely grey, with a long beard, and his name is Walter. He heads the table and speaks as little as possible. The youngest is Louis, married, who looks to be between thirty and forty years old. There are still various other brothers spread around the world. One is an officer and adjutant, or something like that, of the Queen.

Much love, from your Helena.

A29648000011-12 1501-2 [Heleen to Thijs]
The Grange, Alberta, Canada, December 4, 1891

Dear Thijs,

The Grange is the home of the Garnetts, twelve miles from Pincher Creek. I arrived here yesterday evening at 5:30, after an amusing ride of two hours. At the usual crossing point, the river was too dangerous because of the ice on both sides, and Mr. John Garnett, who had come to get me, had tried another road in the morning that appeared to be better. I had not yet ridden [in a carriage] since my unlucky trip, and at every steep hill or sharp turn I prepared myself to jump out (in my thoughts), but I made sure that my neighbour did not notice those moments of weakness. In the meantime, he told me very amusing stories about how they sometimes were busy for three days covering the same distance because of the carriage being stuck in the river or the snow being too slippery to drive up the hill.

Today the river was low and there was nearly zero chance of being damaged by the current, but it seemed to be tricky to guide the foursome straight down the bank toward the ice, over of all those broken stones. In the middle of the river, the horses stopped for a bit to drink. The bottom was full of large stones that I could see very well through the crystal-clear water. The longer we went, the closer we got to the mountains, which were beautifully coloured under the setting sun, and after the river, I forgot all of my jumping preparations in my increasing awe of the landscape. For a while, I even held the reins with my injured hand while, with the other, I helped Mr. Garnett with putting on his fur. (He had dressed very smartly to come pick me up, in a light overcoat with a nice handkerchief in the breast pocket, but with the sunset, it became too cold.)

I do not believe that you can get a clear image of a buckboard. It actually looks the most like a freight wagon, with high wheels and a wide coach box across it, with springs underneath. In the carriage, other than my suitcase, were valises, etc., and a large number of packages and crates, because Mr. Garnett had done some early shopping in Pincher Creek. It is very lucky that I arrived yesterday, because last night it snowed again, and more snow threatens from the heavily clouded sky, so they would not have dared to go today.

The house is the largest in the area, much higher ceilings than I have seen here, as yet, and very comfortable. It is lovely to be set free from the noisy hotel, and the breakfast and the family are very enjoyable.

This morning I went along to the stalls where the horses were brought to drink. I also saw a large number of calves that were greedily eating from a long hay rack that was separated from them by a fence.

A28335001501-02 [continues on]

Now you know where I am and I can tell you that I had a great deal of pleasure from your letter of November 12. I find it very nice that the three cousins are together in the senate, and do like the decision to hold the four-day party. I am convinced that you will get this decision through [the senate]. Nevertheless, it will take a lot of thought to make those four days twice as festive and enjoyable as that of seven days. I think that IJ or Amstel should support you and that Nereus[273] will have an active role in the festivities. If you folks hold an evening party on the water, the navy and merchant fleets will certainly, out of politeness, light up the area. With this, then, you will also gain, for sure, the goodwill of the citizens. It will be difficult to make it something particularly student-like. Make sure that you issue a rule that forbids unharmonious support from rattling steam whistles.

[The] Sociologische Club[274] (what is the name?) I am pleased to hear about, and Naber[275] will be better situated there than in *Propria Cures*. Is he satisfied with his involvement with 'Lloyd'? With interest, I also saw in one of the old newspapers the formation of a new *Algemeen Werklieden Vereniging*.[276] Do you sympathize with that, or have you heard little about it?

You shall for sure have a full, busy winter; I am pleased about that, but will you also take care of the shell that encloses your noble mind? In other words, do not forsake sport entirely, because it is such a wonderful thing to be very strong and very healthy (!), and would you also defend the position that every 'gentleman' must also learn a craft and then put it into practice? Did you know that, at one of the universities in England (I think Shrewsbury), it is mandatory to learn gardening and carpentry? There, they educate ministers, in particular. I also found it enjoyable to hear about Arti. How are things with your own painting lessons?

273   Nereus is the Amsterdam student rowing club, founded in 1885. "IJ" is the Koninklijke Nederlandsche Zeil en Roei Vereniging (est. 1847) and "Amstel" is De Amstel (est. 1874), two of the oldest rowing clubs in the Netherlands.

274   This is likely in reference to the first Social-Democratic Student Union of Amsterdam, the Sociaal-Democratische Studentenvereniging (1891–1893).

275   Henri Adrien Naber (1867–1944): physicist and teacher, who as a student wrote articles for *Propria Cures*, a weekly student paper first published in 1890 by the Amsterdam Student Corp. at the University of Amsterdam; married to Petronella Jacoba Boelen (1870–1953).

276   This may be in reference to the establishment in 1891 of a new Catholic workers' union under the umbrella of the existing federation of unions, the Algemeen Werklieden Verbond.

I read quite a good article about Rudyard Kipling and saw his portrait, a bit *sinjo*, *forsch*,[277] with a slightly dissatisfied expression. I received his verses about Simla[278] to read from Dr. Mead in [Pincher Creek]. They are mostly about the local situation [in India], which for us is not so enjoyable but in some respects is still interesting.

Bye, Thijs, many greetings back to Notje. He will be sorry that he cannot do everything at once, working hard and being senator. Nice that the first [team] has won, after all.

What is Robbie W.[279] doing? With a warm kiss, your Heleen.

P.S. Sunday evening, December 6: I had a visit from Karel. He is doing fine and looks more and more like Daan de Clercq. We have said goodbye until we see each other in Montreal. HB

KLAB09193000013 [Father to Karel]
Amsterdam, December 5, 1891

Dear Karel,

Since my last letter, I received yours from the camp after your first days of practical experience with 'roughing it'. I sympathize with you; it is quite a job to get used to such physical exertion, but I am very delighted with your initial success. After all of these experiences over the last months, it must be a gratifying feeling for you to keep up with the other young men. After having read about this way of working, in your letter as well as in *Fraser's Magazine*,[280] I can well imagine that American builders would find the surveying brigades [in the Dutch East Indies] extremely slow.

It was with a grateful feeling that Mama and I read your letter one more time this evening. Whatever outcome will be of this journey, with an eye on your career, it will have already proven to have served you well when you are feeling again courageous, high-spirited and resilient; and that is beginning to come, no? With profound affection, we think of you and of our courageous Heleentje, whose presence and caring for you is so valuable and gives us such peace of mind. How that child has had so many interesting encounters and introductions!

277 The portrait of Kipling appears to Heleen to be a strong character with Indian-European features: *sinjo*, an Indonesian word meaning of "mixed blood," and *forsch* from German, meaning "strong."

278 Simla (now Shimla) was a hill-station and the summer capital of British India.

279 This is likely Robert (Robbie) Leonard Wolterbeek (1869–1925, London, England), who moved to the USA in 1892; first marriage in 1894 in Long Island to Marguerite Seymour Mellen (1870–?); second marriage in 1905 to Annette Pauline Caroline Groenewald (1879–1967).

280 Jan is probably referring to *Fraser's Magazine*, a general-interest magazine published in London in the nineteenth century. It began in 1830 as *Fraser's Magazine for Town and Country*. In 1882 it was succeeded by *Longman's Magazine* (a literary magazine), which ceased publication in 1908.

Probably, you will receive this letter around the end of your surveying work. My hope is that then, through the mediation by the president, Mr. Van Horne, you will again get other work. If that does not work out, perhaps try on a ranch or with a breeder to get practical knowledge of that business, in order to find out if there is a living to be made from that. I would think that $10,000 or ƒ25,000 would be just about the maximum amount of what I would think is acceptable for me to invest in a Canadian agricultural business and would like to hear from you as to whether you could start something with that amount.

Today it is St. Nicolaas, but this year it just passed quietly for us. The remembrance of our happy holiday of last year made the contrast too great. Uncle Toon always came to us on this day, and it was an occasion in which he was normally very pleasant and easy to talk with. As soon as he was inside, out marched the lovely presents, and it always gave him a lot of pleasure watching the surprise and the enjoyment of the recipients.

Today I received two thousand guilders on your behalf as a bequest and will probably invest that in 4 percent gold bonds with the Illinois Central Railroad Company. In the case that you settle there, then the money will probably be very welcome.

As St. Nicolaas, I sent a small carved letter box to Wil, with the wish that she could save many of your letters therein, but also that a happy reunion, before it was completely full, would make that unnecessary. I hope to see her again soon. She is keeping herself well and, happily, there are better messages about Jo's health, so that Mrs. de Vos is also somewhat cheerful.

Many greetings, also from Mama, your loving Father.

A32005000394–395 [Father to Heleen]
Amsterdam, December 5, 1891

Dear Helena,

What lovely letters you have written to us. How we have followed you with suspense on your coach trips through the wilderness with the scout in front, and with your visits and acquainting yourself with camp life. Good that you are so well received everywhere and that you can be of so much use to Karel. Regarding the last news from the camp, after he had worked and had been on his legs for ten hours, I am very satisfied.

Things are going quite well here, but life is still not without incident. First, I was taken aback by the death of Captain T. Bakker, who passed away in London [on December 3] from pneumonia, just at the time that he would have sailed with the SS *Celebes* to Halifax, [Nova Scotia]. I was with him in London just three weeks ago to sign the charter. At that time, I spoke with him about his life and his family, etc. He was just as old as I am, very much respected and, in our company, mourned.

The second incident was the strange sort of indisposition suffered by Jan Kruseman.[281] He had been fretting over his assurance business, believing that he would not succeed, hankering once again toward more scientific work, and finally became so 'addled' that some advice was needed. Dr. Delprat approved of him going on a sea journey. Yesterday he took that advice and today he has already departed on the SS *Prins van Oranje* to Genoa, set to return by sea on another ship.

Of a more pleasant sort was my business with the provincial government, where, last Thursday, the subsidy for the ice-clearing was unanimously approved after I forcefully argued against the opponents, Coninck Westenberg[282] and Groen van Waarder.[283]

Today, I received the legacy from Uncle Toon for you, in the amount of ƒ2,000, which I shall invest for you.

I find it excellent that you are keeping in touch with Miss Van Horne and I hope that Karel will still be helped with a career through the influence of the Canadian Pacific after this 'probation period' is over. Dr. Delprat was very satisfied with the results of his physical exertion and only regrets that the work will be completed so soon.

It will be very strange to be missing you on St. Nicolaas, my birthday [December 12], the birthday [December 25] of my 'little Christmas child' [Heleen], and during these convivial days at the end of the year. I hope you both will be together for Christmas and will have faith in the future.

God bless you my darling, your loving Father.

A32074000159–160 [Heleen to Wil]
The Grange, Alberta, Canada, December 6 [1891]

Dear Wil,

It is Sunday and, after fourteen days, I have seen Karel again! He looked swell. His beard was ugly, his hands full of small cuts and scrapes (but remain whole, though quite weathered), and his eyes were so lively and clear that it was a pleasure to see him. I am here at the house of the Garnett brothers. Karel's camp is seven miles away and he rode here. The work still goes well. Two new workers had arrived but were dismissed again because they would not do the usual 'chaining'. Karel stayed for lunch and then rode back again.

Your letter from November 10 gave me a lot of pleasure. I received it three days ago in Pincher Creek. At that time, I had not seen Karel in

---

281 Jan Kruseman (1867–1949): lawyer, advocate for social housing, judge; married to Henriette Pauline Ankersmit (1870–1948).

282 Johannes Coninck Westenberg (1830–1907): a member of the Province of North Holland Legislature; married to Catharina Hermana Sluiter (1832–1916).

283 Herman Frederik Groen van Waarder (1846–1904): a member of the Province of the North Holland Legislature; unmarried.

many days and felt a bit lonely, so it did me a lot of good to read that you had thought about and sympathized with me.

I will stay here for a few days to help my hostess with sewing a dress. She has no clue and there is no seamstress here in the area. As such, all of her clothes are dated from the abundant-drapery period. I do not understand how she dares to be seen. She can neither cook nor sew and had an illness after the birth of her first child by which, as a result, she can walk little and barely bend over. Therefore, she also finds life very difficult and constantly complains about the cold and the wind. She now has two maids, and her husband and two brothers also do a lot of the housework. The good soul is now busy making a flannel shirt for her husband, and he must give her advice as to how she should cut it. All the men treat her with great condescension; all the time it goes "You goose!", "You duffer", etc. Only with me is she attentive and friendly. She loves to read and talks about it very enjoyably.

Yesterday, I had a lovely ride on a pony. Out of precaution, because of my swollen hand, which I cannot use very well yet, they firstly gave me the tamest pony, but he was so astonishingly lazy that I had to constantly hit him and, therefore, still had to use my left hand to hold the reins. Then I got another one, who ran like a greyhound without a crop, and it was lovely.

We rode to Mrs. Clarkson's,[284] the decent scatterbrain in the family — well over forty and not yet married one year to a man of thirty-five. She gave us lunch, but it was a very bad, uncooked beefsteak pie. Mr. Garnett and I are both sick from it today, but with no hard feelings. We had a wonderful trip back home, almost all at a gallop, except when it was steep going downwards. We are now amid the mountains, and the landscape is majestic.

Bye, dear Wil. Courage and strength. God's blessing for the new year. Yours, your warmly loving, Heleen.

A28335001503–1504 [Heleen to Father]
The Grange, December 8, 1891

Dear Father,

The mail has left, but I fear that it will arrive very late in Amsterdam, because it was not possible to cross the river during these last days, and so the people with the mail will come too late to Pincher Creek. I so hope that after the early days of agitation, a calmer frame of mind has followed, and you can patiently bear about fourteen days without tidings. I also do not expect any letters for the time being, because I had my

---

284 This is probably Nellie Humphrey (1853–1939): married to Robert Barton (Chappie) Clarkson (1858–1921), who had joined the NWMP and became a pioneer rancher in Pincher Creek in 1887. He was a noted horseman who played polo. Nellie is also reputed to be an excellent horsewoman.

mail sent to Calgary again, since I had expected to be there soon, and if my letters come here when I am already gone, they will certainly not catch up with me in the first weeks. But the last mail was so good that I can live on it for a little while.

I am now living the real ranch life here. It is very interesting to experience this once, in the harsh season, but I am not regretful that Karel finds little pleasure in it. It is a continuous battle against the elements and the rewards are few. Yesterday, the wind blew hard; snow blew up from the ground in clouds. Last night, a piece of the chimney tumbled down. The fence that enclosed the calves was knocked down and the calves fled to their mothers again.

After breakfast, the men looked out of the window with concern. (This is the double window where the snow had blown through.) I warmed myself by the heating stove. Suddenly, a cry of despair sounded from a man at the window. "Oh, Walter. The hay!" All the hay that they had harvested, with such hard work and diligence, was spread out by the wind for miles. Like a large dust cloud, it danced in the air around and over the house. The heavy poles that were to protect it lay flat. Immediately, they all ran outside to save what was remaining, but walking against the wind required all of their might and, time and time again, they had to stand still to catch their breath. A little bit later, one of the brothers came inside and remarked that the roof of the henhouse was blown away. There was no talk of restoring it in that weather. Soon, all three came inside and buried themselves in newspapers or books in order to try to forget the misery of the storm.

In the meantime, Mrs. Garnett appeared to be the most miserable of all of them. She complained about every new mishap *ad infinitum*. Moreover, she could not stand the noise of the wind and also said so with every fierce gust, which was about every half-minute. I was happy to have work to do, proposing to make a shirt from an old skirt, and I was glad to flee with my stuff to the dining room and immerse myself in the secrets of its cutting. I again ensconced myself there right away after lunch because I noticed that so long as the wind was blowing there was no chance for another 'stroll', but during the tea at 4:30 . . . [Ends abruptly].

A28335001505-6 [Heleen to Li],
date unknown, fragment

. . . (a raging storm broke out) I could immediately play and laugh about it and the blunders of the others. He thought I was very nice because I listened to one of his smart remarks. He has read a lot and when we are alone, we have pleasant conversations, and I have even heard him laugh joyfully a few times.

A moving force arrived yesterday in the form of the entertaining spirit of Jimmy Routledge. I believe that I have already written about him before, his wooden leg and his merry, infectious laugh. He is a giant like Gerrit den Tex,[285] but less portly. He has much more reason to be unhappy than the Garnetts. He must leave here (he cannot stay in England and does not know where he shall move to). Riding and hunting are all the world to him, but his wooden leg often makes it difficult. Yesterday, he was in the area to search for cattle and stayed here for the night. In the morning, he stayed inside and sang with a lovely but untrained voice, all sorts of songs, among which was "Wait 'Til the Clouds Roll By"! He also once again told beautiful stories of accidents and adventures which, at the same time, were very terrifying, but he told them in such a humorous way that we all, even the gloomy Garnetts, roared with laughter.

The wind was blowing quite stiffly again and the Garnetts were loath to go out riding, even though John had planned to go to the camp and I would gladly have sent my letters to Karel. In the afternoon, I went out by myself and found that the wind was not so terrible and was wonderfully invigorating. The sun was also delightful. I walked from the one hilltop to the other and enjoyed the lovely mountain landscape. I now know various mountains by name and they have become my friends. I sang my Dutch songs as loud as I could with the wind, in order to hear how they would sound in the mountains, and came home wonderfully refreshed. I would very much like to come back here in the summer. The outdoors is always lovely.

Many thanks for the *Liefdadigheid Circulaire*.[286] I am really pleased that you have accepted it. That can only go well if everyone who makes visits to the poor helps to improve the situation of the others. Perhaps it will also help you with your hospital work, but I can also understand that you could get awfully busy with it. It is good that you have taken up [learning] Norwegian in order to not completely drown [in your work] in the Jordaan[287] domain.

The people here regard me as a wonder because I can gobble up their words, imitate them with success, and they almost fall backwards when, after inquiring, they find out that it is not my 'only accomplishment'. Before I came here, folks had told Mrs. Garnett that I had two million, or would get that, and that I spoke eleven languages. How they got that, I do not know, because I always take the first opportunity to say that I have to be frugal and that Karel must earn his own living, and I never talk about a foreign language but chatter about 'stock' and 'colts' as if they were cats.

I shall just tell An about my pony adventures. Much love from your Heleen.

P.S. Just like you two in the past when the train came by, I also say "Bon voy-a-a-a-ge."

---

285 Jhr. Gerrit den Tex (1858–1889) was an engineer who died in Losarang, Java, now part of Indonesia.

286 The Liefdadigheid naar Vermogen (also L.N.V.) was a charitable organization established in 1871 that sent newsletters to its members, such as the *Liefdadigheid Circulaire.*

287 The Jordaan was once one of the poorest neighbourhoods in Amsterdam.

A32005000404-406 [Wil to Heleen]
Amsterdam, December 8, 1891

Dear Heleentje,

If I want to give you some sign of life on your birthday, then it is now high time that I start with my letter. Because of your moving back and forth, you will be so hard to reach and your letters are underway for less time than are ours. Still, it seems so strange to write so very long in advance of a birthday. The reality is diminished over such a distance. But I, who have so much to thank you for, along with all the others that love you, will be with you on the 25th. I hope so very much that you will begin a happy new year of life and, a few days later, enter a blessed 1892, and that you will find satisfaction during that year in your heart and mind. If anyone has earned this, it is you. And still, all of this perhaps pertains to the many mysteries that we really cannot solve, no matter what attempts we employ toward them. One small comfort for [you] on that day, now that you are so far away from all of us, is that, had everything gone differently, you would have been in Karlsruhe, [Germany], around that time and not at home, anyway.

How thankful I am for your last two letters, one right after the other, bringing such good news about my dear Karel. That he looked very good, his eyes also looking clearer again, etc., all of which makes us so happy. Only with the news that the work will perhaps be done so very soon do we feel sorry for him. It did him good, and after, what shall he do? After all, Montreal has not such a good climate, it is much more expensive to live there, and then he must again take that long journey by train that will make him short of breath. Also, for you, I find it very sad that you can see him so little and must travel all by yourself.

I see you now, every time, as a dark silhouette on a low beach, appearing against a mass of grey waves, with your clothing fluttering in the wind, standing firm and staring into the distance. How does this come to me? I do not know, but I find the journey alone in such a strange land so unsettling. You were right to say that it is good that I did not travel with Karel, because that would have meant that now it would still be very difficult to be so long without him. Being at such great distances, one knows well that you cannot travel together. One calmly accepts it and one is less afraid to just submit to their sorrow when it becomes too heavy.

Do you know how sweet Karel has been again? A while ago he wrote to Thijs to make sure that I would get a volume of verses by Sully Prudhomme[288] on St. Nicolaas day, with these words in [Karel's] own hand on the front page:

Le vrai de l'amitié, c'est de sentir ensemble, c'est fait ce qui nous reste à nous de notre amour. Canada-Amsterdam, 5 Dec 1891.

---

288 René François Armand (Sully) Prudhomme (1839–1907): French poet. Karel's sentence begins with the closing line of Prudhomme's poem "Aux amis inconnus" and ends with his own words. "*The core of friendship is to feel together, that is what we do with the remains of our love.*"

Melancholic words, aren't they? But still it did so much good, as proof of his love on that evening, even though the words were also deeply doleful. But he wrote them in Calgary when he did not feel well, even perhaps in a miserable mood. Poor, dear Karel. I was so glad to know from your letter that he has courage and spirit once again. A difficult moment. Before, everything was so normal. We had never celebrated St. Nicolaas together. And even though the day was, of course, not quite as good, once we were again going on as usual, everything seemed so natural; although, for me, the real joyfulness was missing.

But then, that parcel (!), and later came a box for letters from your parents, with a thoughtful verse from Papa saying that he hoped that the box would be filled with new letters before he came back, which was also so lovely. [Li] sent me correspondence cards, Miep, a basket with plants, and An, the same calendar that they use at 717, also mailed to Karel.

My own mama also spoiled me very much, also a box for letters, according to my wish list, and, among others, a lovely little desk lamp with a red shade. Cor gave me a frame with gilded clover leaves on the corner, for a portrait of Karel, and to go with it, Jo wrote a verse for her.

At the same time as my book from Karel was delivered, Cor received a parcel enclosing *cartes de correspondance*, small, pink and lovely. The friends were not allowed to say anything, because the deliverer, whom they were not allowed to name, had whispered mysteriously and forbade them to speak. On the inside of the paper in which the Prudhomme was wrapped, however, *Boissevain House* was written in pencil. Along with that, I had nevertheless figured out right away that it was Thijs who had arranged it, because, recently, he skipped over a long piece from a letter that he was reading aloud and instead said that Karel was somewhat melancholic. We thought at the time, of course, that Cor received those cards also from Karel, through Thijs, and found it so nice that he thought about it, that is, that we both got a parcel. Yesterday, in the evening, however, Thijs came to thank me for a book that I sent to him and, when Cor was out of the room (to get a doll that she had made that represented [an Indigenous woman]), Thijs said right away that the cards were from him. "The only impertinence that I have ever permitted from myself," he said. I was not allowed to tell her until he had already left. A silly boy, but still, so nice for him to think that she also should have something. He always perks me up so much by his jokes and funny stories.

Auntie van Rhemen[289] will be staying with us for a few days and, after that, shall witness the christening of her latest grandchild. My cousin, van der Hoop,[290] is doing better than expected. Her son was just born on November 14. On St. Nicolaas evening, although they now live in Kralingen, she was already with her husband and child at her parents-in-law's, who live in Rotterdam. Rather strange, isn't it, that she, who we

---

289 Caroline Cecilia Leembruggen (1846–1921): sister of Wil's mother; married to Alexander Baron van Rhemen (1839–1877).

290 Johanna Cecilia Elisabeth Baroness van Rhemen (1868–1909): married to Adriaan Cornelis van der Hoop (1858–1922), stockbroker.

never thought would do well with her first labour, now has her second baby already, and that our Jo, who, except for her throat, was always much healthier, has ailed so. Now, happily, she is much better. (A big relief for Mama, who made herself so anxious.)

[Jo] now hopes that she will not have to remain under treatment for too long and part of it is already sorted out. The loose kidney takes much longer, but for that, she must massage and take care of herself. I received a letter again from her this morning, saying that there were now a German and a Norwegian who attended her treatments in order to learn from Thure Brandt. Ladies were, however, allowed to choose. The kind-hearted Jo said that she had said "Yes" because she thought that, with a little bit more embarrassment, she could be of use to other people who could be helped because of it, later on. I think that it is very kind of her; how one changes through pain, fear and circumstances. I do not know whether I would be so unselfish.

Otto also wrote to me in response to a letter that I received from Mr. Delbet,[291] the doctor from Paris, with whom we cemented our friendship on the boat to the North Cape [Norway]. Otto wrote to perk me up and to encourage me, because to his great dismay, he had been told that Mr. Delbet, who upon hearing the question "*Quand vel se marie-t-elle?*", wrote first to [Mama], and later to me, in order to warn me about marrying when the health [of a partner] was not good, and so forth. He did it out of good intentions and out of friendship, but his view of it was too gloomy. Therefore, I wrote back, two or three times, to explain everything and ended by sending a portrait of the both of us. Then yesterday, a letter came to say that he always tells the truth to some clients and with others, lets them do as they choose, and did not want to count me among the latter and wished to be a friend. He felt sorry if he had caused me too much sadness. But [he asks], why had Karel not been drinking *des eaux du Mont d'Or*, since all asthma patients recovered with it? And, of the portrait, he must have seen that Karel had no aura of illness or weakness. Furthermore, he found us both very charming and Karel an open, good and intelligent figure with a distinguished look, etc. That is all true. Thus, he came, he saw, he conquered! In the meantime, I am glad that he is already less worried after hearing that Karel is already better (having seen his picture), because he is really a loyal friend to us and, on top of that, a capable doctor. But still, you do not know how much his letters with inherent warnings and French ideas about marriage bothered me, even though I had to acknowledge that he does it for my own good.

Now I am really going to stop. Apropos of nothing, Miss Janssen[292] is engaged to J. de Goeijen. On Saturday, Cor is going to a ball at Ankersmit's[293] and, this evening, I am going to the Concertgebouw to hear the concert, in order to raise money in support of the holiday camps

---

291 Dr. Pierre Delbet (1861–1957) was a French physician and surgeon.

292 Folmina Margaretha (Mien) Janssen (1866–1960): in May 1892, married Jan de Goeijen (1861–1945), an investor in the Kansas City Southern Railway.

293 This is probably the family of Henriëtte Pauline Ankersmit (1870–1948), who lived at Keizersgracht 126.

for schoolchildren, which was organized by [Coo] den Tex. On Thursday, perhaps I will go to a Mozart concert to hear Mrs. Bosmans play, she and Kes,[294] on two pianos.

And now many greetings from Mama and Cor, and a warm kiss from your loving Wil.

A32005000392–393 [Father to Heleen]
Amsterdam, December 11, 1891

Dear Helena,

What lovely letters have come from you this last week, but how I quaked yesterday about your story of your journey with Aunt Emily's [Irish] compatriot as the coach driver, over hill and dale, through frozen rivers and in the blizzard!

Before I gave them to Mama, I quickly telegraphed Hosmer about where you and Karel are and how you are doing, but when I came home, they knew all about it because of Karel's letter to Wil. Luckily, the same letter also announced his safe return to the camp after his visit with you. Mama held herself very bravely and spoke very sensibly about it.

We had Maria Blijdenstein[295] over for dinner. Li had much to say about the St. Nicolaas party held for the children, etc., and at about 8:00 p.m., just when Mama was to go to Grandmother's to find out how she is doing, we received the telegram reply from Hosmer saying that [you] are both doing well.

I think that you will be bothered by your sprained wrist for a long time. Ruys also injured his right hand, due to his fall on the Zeeland boat. He still cannot write and has much tingling, which is unpleasant for him and disturbs his sleep at night. But still, it is great luck that no worse injury has come to you. Child, child, do pay attention to your good health! Do you know that you wrote in your previous letter that I was to reassure Mama that you would not ride, other than with a government team and with trusted folks? And now you go out on the trail with such a wild Irish! That comes from women's emancipation! Now they pose as coach drivers and then throw you onto the side of the road!

I find it unbelievably lucky for you to meet such a sweet [woman as] Mrs. White Fraser in the snowy wilderness. In the far corners of our eastern agricultural provinces, you would have very little chance to meet a woman with so much refinement and multifaceted knowledge. It is, nevertheless, a surprising thing, this *franc-maçonnerie*, that feeling of being comfortable among people, of whatever nationality, who are at the

---

294   Willem Kes (1856–1934): violinist, pianist, conductor and composer, and the first chief-conductor of the Concertgebouw Orchestra in 1888 in Amsterdam; married to Bertha Auguste Elise Koch (1881–?).

295   Maria Catharina Johanna (Sissy) Blijdenstein (1876–1910): married in 1899 to Walrave Boissevain (1876–1944), brother of Heleen, city councillor in Amsterdam, member of Parliament, chief of freight for the SMN. Walrave remarried in 1913 to Romelia Abramina Kalff (1877–1968).

same level of refinement. A while ago, I read in a French book "*les gens de bonne compagnie ont un certain shibboleth auquel ils se reconnaissent immédiatement*"; it is also just as difficult to be so familiar with folks who are standing on a different level of refinement and who recognize right away that they cannot be so free and easy as with their equals. I also think that it is not as pleasant for Karel in the camp. I fear that the engineers look upon him as an intruder and an errand boy, and he is not the sort of man to easily rise above it, while I can imagine that the chain work (which is really labourer's work) would not be easy for him. Now, do not fret about it. Later on, it will make him, in comparison, more content with hardships in other jobs.

What shall he take on when he finishes with this survey work? Delprat, who is very satisfied by the way, was sorry to hear that Karel's work in the open air would be finished so soon. Would it be possible that he could be placed as a volunteer at a farm (to see the work and to participate in it) before he decides to make it his vocation, or will the Canadian Pacific find some more congenial work for him?

And what is he thinking about Wil? The poor child was completely frustrated over his St. Nicolaas present, wherein he alludes to a great love but jests about a French friendship [*un grand amour, mais se resiant sur son amitié française*] or something like it. I can very well understand that he wants to avoid the appearance of tying her to a possibility that one would blame him for, if afterwards, it is decided to not let the wedding go through. But this is, indeed, almost overdoing it. Luckily, the dear child is so trusting and accepting. But I do know that Mama, for example, who possesses so much abnegation, after all, in this case, would urge for commitment and ask, "What are you up to?" Watch what I have to say — we must not rush and [must] leave a lot to Karel himself, because he will not find peace until he has taken Wil into his trust.

It took me some effort to dig up 'Pa Quack', and I shall certainly quickly send the latest volume of *De Socialisten*[296] to you. To my disgrace, I must say that I have had it lying in front of me on the table now, already for four weeks, but have not as yet taken it in my hand. The same goes for the book from Meijboom,[297] which also came out as a series.

Welk een leven welk een leven
Toen Deel één verscheen in 't licht
Aan de beurs zelf werd geheven
Ja van al dat nieuwe licht
Was de effecten toch ontsticht,
Maar nu zij wij aan deel zeven
En is al wat hij verricht
Al vergeten en vergeven.

[Sully Prudhomme, translated from French into Dutch]

---

296   H.P.G. Quack, *De Socialisten: Personen en stelsels* (Amsterdam: P.N. van Kampen, 1875–1897, vol. 3 of 6).

297   Margaretha (Marg) Anna Sophia Meijboom (1856–1927), women's movement activist, publisher and translator.

By the way, there is also a study in it about Prudhomme that is supposed to be very good, and when I have some leisure time, I shall read it.

I am very busy at the present and that is good for me; on the whole, it is a pleasant busyness. Regarding the KPM, being a new business, things are already going very rosily. The traffic on the routes is very heavy and the opinion of the public in the [Dutch] East Indies about the business remains, altogether, favourable.

There are, however, unusual difficulties. For example, we are being threatened by a big movement initiated among discontented machinists. They were hired under advantageous conditions; however, they noticed that in [the Dutch East Indies] they have to hand over 2 percent of their pay for the benefit of patent taxes.[298] In the Indies, that is again being collected from the sailors — something that happens nowhere else. The Nederlandsch Indische Stoomvaart Maatschappij is paying the patent tax for its personnel. This is against all the rules and regulations and completely incorrect, but on the other hand, people who are employed by us did not know that they had to pay this expense. Therefore, we have found a way to compensate the present incumbents without going against the spirit of the law.

Another incident is that our agent on Lombok [Dutch East Indies], an Arab, was murdered, according to some — or lawfully crucified, according to others — because the Sultan suspected him of plots to dethrone him and to hand Lombok, which is still independent, over to the Dutch. All of our paperwork has been confiscated by the Sultan and it could be that we have not heard the last of it. But Tak, Cremer, van Dedem,[299] etc., do not want to know anything about a dispute with Lombok (which is inhabited by folk just as fierce as those on Bali), which is completely within its rights with wishing to remain independent.

Concerning the [SMN], we had quite an incident with the staff on board a homeward-bound steamship, which ended in the dismissal of almost all the machinists. *Le vin ou plein de genièvre* and the women played a role in it. It was a quite a tragedy. However, for the reputation of the company, we could not waver.

Furthermore, the correspondence with Holt will be continued and I think that we will soon have a meeting in London to determine the preliminaries for a contract. These are delicate transactions for me because those who are not part of the negotiations have big mouths, of course, so that one has little joy in his work in general, other than in the conviction that one has advanced the prosperity of his company.

In dealing with the estate of Uncle Toon, I also, of course, have some things to do, but Uncle Menso does much more work on it, after all; he keeps the 'cashbox' and writes most of the letters. A while ago, we brought the largest part of the monies to the Nederlandse Bank, where it

---

298   This is a form of tax that applied to those with certain professions or trades, the amount being set by a tariff schedule.

299   Willem Karel Baron van Dedem (1839–1895): lawyer and Minister of Colonies; unmarried.

will stay in order to make the annual legacy payments from the revenue to Uncle Sebald and [Toon's] assistant, Suwerkrop. In the end, Mama will eventually inherit something from him, but since the 'Toon-Nella trust' is to be liquidated at the same time, the personal tax must be paid on it. Therefore, no significant increase in the household funds will follow from it. Later on, after the beneficiaries have passed away, perhaps the capital could still go to the benfit of my then-living children.

Your good wishes for my birthday, I really appreciate. But, like the commander of a fort who is always thinking about a threatened point — just like a mother is with her sick child — I am always preoccupied for the future of the oldest son, from whom I had expected so much, who has excellent gifts of intellect and heart, and who landed in life-circumstances from which he could have made such a wonderful career. What is his future? What will he make of his life? In Canada, he can become happy, but then he must totally assimilate in the same way as, for example, Ramann[300] has done in Holland. There, just like *The Virginians*,[301] he can become the head of the American branch [of our family] and then his children, like 'chips off the old block', will come to visit in order to be amazed by the Dutch peculiarities about which they have heard their parents speak.

Yesterday, we had the captain of the icebreaker *Berlin*[302] (whom Karel saw in Stettin) with us at the [NSM]. He breakfasted with the complete board of the Vereeniging [voor Algemeene] Scheepvaart Belangen[303] and told us a lot about his vessel.

I count on other correspondents to inform you about Aunt Su having been run over, which turned out all right; about dinner at [Coo] den Tex's and the changes within his office; the death of Jacob Fock,[304] father of David[305] (should you also send him a card?); the appointment of Louis van Heukelom as director of the [Nederlandse Bank], which gives me a lot of satisfaction; I will now tell both of you that Jan Kruseman has already written to me from Southampton that the sea journey had a favourable influence on his depressive mood.

Today, I bought a lovely etching, portraying our young queen to the core. That is a birthday present to myself. Don't you find that clever?

Warm greetings from your loving father. Kind love to Karel; I shall write to him soon.

300   Christian Wilhelm Justius Ramann (born Germany 1833–1907, died Amsterdam) was a broker in coffee and a ship owner; first marriage to Susanne Mariane Stants (1833–1861); second marriage to Rebecca da Costa (1832–1905).

301   This likely in reference to *The Virginians* by William Makepeace Thackeray, English author (1811–1863), published first as a serial, then as a book in 1859.

302   The *Berlin* was built in 1889 by the Stettiner Maschinenbau AG Vulcan in Stettin, then Germany, now Poland.

303   Association of Shipping Interests, regarding shipping routes in and around Amsterdam and the North Sea Canal.

304   Jacob Fock (1817–1891): merchant; first married to Cecile Dorothé de Kock (1813–1844); second marriage in 1847 to her sister, Sara Adriana Dorothéa de Kock (1816–1888).

305   David Abraham Fock (1857–1902): banker; unmarried.

```
A28335000714-719 [Karel to parents]
In camp, Crowsnest Pass, December 11, 1891
```

Dearest parents,

After lying for an hour to rest in the tent, warmed up by the roaring stove, I feel so refreshed that I feel up to writing a weekly letter. Tomorrow is Sunday and, therefore, I do not have to go to bed early; it is better to say "in bed" because I already lie ["on" the bed] "on" my belly with a writing folder in front of me. Indeed, since all of the room is taken up, day and night, by the made-up beds and the stove, it is difficult to write anywhere else.

Yes, today was a busy day. Now that we have arrived in the mountains, work will become gradually more difficult. For our railway, they always look, of course, for the lowest land, to minimize elevations and steep rises for the track. Of course, we find the lowest land along the riverbanks, and these are, in particular, difficult to traverse. On top of that, the river winds in the most crazy and unexpected curves, so that we must cross it quite often, since a small bridge is cheaper than a long detour. Should the rivers be fully iced over, then the crossing would be easy. Also, without ice, the rivers would be accessible for the horses and wagons and, in this manner, we could get across with dry feet. But unluckily, there will be a few metres of ice all over, and then a couple of metres of open water, and then ice again. For example, on the profile below, the river would be passable for a team of horses, but the plunge through the ice into the water hinders the crossing. If the team has to cross, then we hack away the ice at that spot; but, if we can do without the team of horses, then we cross the river on foot. Then we search as long as it takes, upstream and downstream, until we have found a place where we can jump across the gully, or where the river is completely frozen. Of course, with the variable freezing and thawing of this season (the real winter will start in the new year), there is no shortage of ice floes and thawing ice, such that all of these crossings can sometimes be quite dangerous. And then, there is the surveying of the line along

[29] Diagram by Karel of Oldman River with wagon

ravines. The engineers stand on both sides with their instruments and take the 'direction' over the ravine, but we poor 'chainers' must go through the ravine with the chain. It takes your hands and feet straight through the undergrowth, meanwhile chopping trees that are in the way — it is rough work!

Today, I was so careless as to work downward along an aiguille, where the wall of the hill was too steep to descend below. Hanging onto a tree root, I could not get up, nor could I slide down, since the hill ended in the river, which was five or six feet deep there. I was saved by one of the other crewmen, who, upon seeing me, crossed the river, climbed above, and reached out a hand for me so that I could haul myself up. At the same time, Brooks sank through the ice and went up to his shoulders in the water. When we came into the camp, we had all, at least once today, fallen through the ice.

I am not patting myself on the back about making a reputation in Canada with this sort of work; I fear that neither education nor aptitude made me suitable for it. Little muscle-power, weak eyesight, not very handy — enough reason to take a back seat to this bunch of robust Canadians.

Last week, I wrote to Van Horne that camp life suits me very well and that I have developed a strong interest in the railroad business; that the only business in which I had any previous experience was steamship operation; that cattle ranching was not my cup of tea, but in the event that it was my only option, I would concentrate on that business; but started by telling him that I really like the climate and that I wish to settle in Canada. He has yet to reply, and I am very anxious to hear from him that he sees a chance to train me in a CPR office so that I may become a Canadian railway man. He will most likely write or telegraph for me to come to Montreal, and then we shall talk about the matter.

These Canadians (and especially him) take distances of a few days on a train very lightly, and most likely, the sort of work that I did this winter will no longer be available; if they want more practical experience, it will have to wait until the spring.

Helena is still staying at the Garnetts'. It is somewhat troublesome to visit her every Sunday, since I need that day for washing and for mending. You understand what our footwear must endure on the rocks and in all of that ice and snow. Last week, a fierce storm raged. We had gone out to work but had to come back. We had difficulty staying upright. Coming back and preparing ourselves for a day of rest in the tents, it turned out that our campsite was too exposed and that all of the tents were starting to tear apart. One was torn straight through the middle. Hastily, everything was taken down and we moved camp a bit lower, into the bushy riverbanks. There was a lot to chop down and to haul before we had a 'roof' over our heads again. Luckily, the snow had waited to fall until we had reached that point. Since then, we have been very comfortable in the tents.

My health is still very good in these circumstances; last week, a foreboding of asthma, or at least a stuffed nose. But it did not hinder my sleep nor my work.

By the time that you have received this letter, I will have started the new year very hopefully. Do the same thing for yourselves. Greet everyone at home, also Grandmama and the by-now completely recuperated Uncle Toon, and all of our other friends. From your loving son, Karel.

Sunday morning [December 13]: At the house of the Garnetts, where I came to celebrate Father's birthday with Heleen. I thought that it was the 12th today; dates fade a bit in camp life. Tomorrow, she will return to the civilized world and will most likely visit the western cities Banff and Vancouver. She looks very good but did not have a very cheerful time last week. Barely reasonable weather in a house where the mood is not very pleasant; quite decent, but bad-humoured. My job will keep me busy, most likely, until mid-January.

Letters received up to and including November 20. Many thanks to Mama for hers of the 8th, and the one from Papa of the 10th. My letters are still in Pincher Creek, but I read those of Heleen.

I am very much struck by the passing of Uncle Toon. What a sad time that you folks have had there. Heleen was also very much affected [by the news]. She loved him and she knew that he loved her. She finds it very horrible to think that she had written to him when he had already passed away. That would not sit well with me either. Still, I think that it is a good thing that she did not telegraph, and so, therefore, we were spared the suspense [of waiting for a] telegram during the time between that and your letter.

But now I will finish. The few moments with Leentje are too valuable to spend too much time writing long letters. Keep yourself well, dear Mother. Write to me as often as your heart tells you to. I read your letters with due regard to what you have asked of me and find it lovely to get a short letter now and then. I part now from Helena and will be pleased to receive special messages.

Once again, warm greetings from Helena, who encloses a kiss, and I, something like that, your loving Karolus.

A29662000037–38 [Heleen to An]
The Grange, December 13, 1891

Dear An,

Yesterday was Papa's birthday and I have not the faintest idea of how things went at home. It feels so far away. I hope that everyone is at home together, Mama only a little bit subdued but strong in the arms of her family. I also hope that you folks now have the good news from Macleod, but it could have been quite different, so I do not dare to think about it.

An, I wish that I had a bit of your horse-riding verve. A few days ago, I took such a lovely trip through the mountains, but my pony fell in a hole and I became really frightened and did not want to go on.

The previous day, I had also ridden with much pleasure (and some fear); galloping over the wide spaces is fantastic when there is not too much snow, but my pony is a well-known stumbler and when the snow becomes suddenly deeper, he gets scared and likes to go down on his knees. Now, that is mostly not the case if I recognize the deep snow and stop him. Traversing the descent of the steep hills was also, in the beginning, a scary feeling, especially because the snow there is often very deep, but what I found the most dangerous is that often, underneath the snow, there is a layer of ice from old snow that had once thawed and then refroze. Of course, one can see nothing of this, and the pony always finds this very scary and then stumbles on purpose. Slowly, I have gotten used to all of these frightening situations and can now fully enjoy the beautiful landscape.

We descended into a welcoming valley with velvet, dark pine bushes against the snowy slopes, and again and always with renewed pleasure, we saw the mighty mountains, the tones of the colours constantly changing, as if they were wearing a new coat around the unchanging forms. Large herds of horses in their warm, red-brown winter coats were playing with each other and then suddenly stood still to look at us. Sometimes a prowling 'coyote', the small wolf of the prairie. I lost my lorgnette during my first accident and had not yet seen them up close enough to decide if we would call it a 'jackal'. Karel saw many of them and, just now, one was shot close to the house here, by a group of hunters.

If I were to be staying here longer, Mr. John would have caught a horse for me that now runs loose about twenty miles from here. Yesterday, I saw a couple of horses being caught close by. The whole herd is driven into the 'corral', that is, [surrounded by] a wooden fence. Then the man enters on foot with a large rope and, very slowly and quietly, the chosen horse is approached — talked to in a friendly way and softly pushed against the railing. Often, the horse jumps away again and runs around with the others in a circle.

A296620000055–56 [continues on]

When it is calm again, one tries once more to push it into a corner and very calmly works a rope over its neck and ties it up. If that does not work and the animal is still wild, then they take a lasso and throw it from a distance over its head.

The horses are never bad-tempered if they are running free, and sometimes are so tame that they will not move at all out of the way when we pass them. But the cows always come toward the women, and I have heard many stories of men who were pushed to the ground by them. Until now, they have always taken flight from me.

I am reading, with much pleasure, the stories of Rudyard Kipling. I am glad that I have read *The Light That Failed*. He is well known here and is much talked about. "Wee Willie Winkie," among others, is sweet.

An, do you know whether Gi den Tex got my letter? I wrote him in the beginning, together with a birthday letter to Aunt Hes, and, from either of them, I have not yet heard if the [letters] have arrived.

Tomorrow, Monday, I will take the way back to Calgary. I received a telegram from Mr. Niblock, who is to meet me along the way and help me further.

The bishop[306] is in Pincher Creek today and will most likely travel with me to Dunmore.

Bye, An, a warm kiss from Heleen.

A32074000161-64 [Heleen to Wil]
Macleod, Canada, NWT, December 15, 1891, Tuesday evening

Dear Wil,

Now I have truly parted from Karel for a longer time but, in the end, I still had a most pleasant Sunday with him. I had not counted on it because, on the previous Sunday, I had noticed that all of the other folks in the camp very much needed the Sunday to rest and to patch up their stuff. So, it was tough for me to know that Karel had to ride so much again on the only rest day in order to visit me. We got relatively little enjoyment out of it, since we were always surrounded by the Garnetts and, therefore, could not even talk easily. Earlier, I had advised him to stay in camp with the others, yet for me, it was a lovely surprise when I heard his well-known "*Hop hop!*" at around noon. Beforehand, he had washed his own clothes, which he had found very difficult to do, but nice work with which to clean his hands, and then he had ridden to me at full speed. His overshoes were severely damaged and it was necessary to mend them. That we did together, while we read and talked about the letters from home.

The death of my faithful Uncle Toon has struck me very hard, and it was lovely to be able to talk it over for a little while. In the meantime, the letters from Li and An about the funeral had arrived, so that we could now come to terms with it together.

Karel himself was the very image of good health. In the last days, he had climbed many steep areas, whereas in Holland, he would go nowhere near them. Mrs. Garnett noticed now, for the first time, that he wheezed while breathing, but he was not bothered by it.

The [crew] also had to deal with a storm, again. While all the men here stayed in the house, there they went out anyway, and after a desperate fight against the wind, they tried in vain to hold their instruments in place. Everything was swept away, and for the first time, they had to return to camp without having completed the work. There, a new task awaited. They were blown away. Bedding, clothing, etc., was flying through

---

306 Bishop William Cyprian Pinkham (1844–1928), who later became the first Anglican bishop of the new Calgary diocese in 1903, was married to Jean Anne Drever (1849–1940).

the air or lay scattered here and there in the thicket. They were busy until the evening, rebuilding the tents quite a bit further into the thicket, and over the next days, they found various items here and there. Karel's fur hat was among them, a long way from the old camp. This week, the camp will again be moved a long distance. It will be in the midst of the mountains and difficult for me to reach it. So, we said goodbye, and the following day, one of the Garnett gentlemen took me back to Pincher Creek. The river was very safe. The ice was broken and the water not very deep.

I began once again to get over my fright, and after a noisy night in the hotel, I let myself bounce around with the most equanimity, in the most ramshackle of all of the old worn-out 'coaches', for five and a half hours in one stretch to Macleod. I had great company in the form of Mr. Jonas Jones,[307] a gentleman, prosperous rancher and well-known comic from Pincher Creek. We were both sitting on top, and he was a very amusing travel companion. What was less enjoyable for me than for the driver was that, after the first half-hour, [Jones] produced a bottle of whiskey and claimed that the coachman would drive so much better were he more or less drunk. It was not cold and the wind was quite bearable, but for the first time here in Canada, the sun was completely obscured. We left the mountains behind us and, in the fading light, saw nothing other than the monotone prairie.

[30] Jonas Jones

A little bit beyond halfway, I had had enough of it and went to sit inside. There, I found Mr. Ashley Elton,[308] a very notable English rancher who was taking his sister to England.

The sister was more or less troubled. She sat very still in the coach and scribbled constantly with a pencil on a piece of paper. She did not speak unintelligibly, but her memory was evidently quite impaired. As soon as she needed to say a name, she became bewildered. Tomorrow, they also go on to Lethbridge. It is nice not to have to do the long journey alone.

307 Jonas Jones (1859–1905) was a part-owner of the North Fork Ranch, near Fort Macleod, and a president of the South-Western Stock Association, established in Fort MacLeod in April 1883. He was married to Annie Machin Berney (1873–1927).

308 Edmund Ashley Elton (1865, India–1933) came with his father and two brothers to settle in the Pincher Creek area in 1886 and, in 1899, married Elizabeth F.M. Reid (1875–1955). Ashley's sister, Maude (1871–1962), arrived in Lethbridge with her mother (Ada Bagshaw Elton) in 1889. In 1898, Maude married John Henry William Shore Kemmis (1867, India–1942, Alberta), a rancher at Pincher Creek and member of the Alberta legislature, 1911–1921.

Here in Macleod, I went right away to visit all my friends, all of whom greeted me very warmly. The parlour of the hotel with the bedroom beside it is now occupied by an ill man who had typhoid fever and now is still very weak. The poor soul, to be so sick in a hotel. This evening, I sat with him for a little while, but he did get a lot of visitors, and now, I just write this in my bedroom, on the wash-table by candlelight. The wash-table has drawers, so it is not comfortable to sit at. Therefore, I shall just sign off.

A lot of love from Karel. Oh, yes, and he got a letter from your cousin Pompe.[309] Would you like to tell him that Karel has received it, but is in no position to write back? He hopes that your cousin's ailments do not any longer embitter him and thanks him kindly for the sympathy which made him write the letter. Cor's lovely letter gave both of us a lot of pleasure. Will you warmly greet her and your mother for your loving Heleen?

[31] Maude Elton

P.S. Oh, and Wil, while I was staying at the Garnetts', from Monday to Saturday, I made a bodice from an old black skirt that I had to first take apart and iron. I sewed every stitch myself and, on Saturday, it was finished, and it fitted smartly. I just went about as if I found it very normal, but I was really very proud of myself about it.

A32005000402–403 [Father to Heleen]
Amsterdam, Dec. 15, 1891

Dear Helena,

After many storms and rainy days, I see the sun again for the first time and, therefore, I wish to try to put some sun into my soul. I am very pleased with the telegram that was sent to me through London on December

---

309 Adriaan Anne Pompe (1865–1949): physician, who as a young man lived in Hudsonville, Michigan, not far from Grand Rapids; married to Belle Maud Hudson (1869–1940).

12, from which I read that you were both doing well and were thinking that you would soon arrive in Calgary. I long for you both to come back again to the civilized world now that the season has become longer and harder.

My birthday turned out to be better than expected. The breakfast was enjoyable. Mama honoured me with a lovely vase that now adorns the bookcase as a companion to the bust on the other [bookcase]. At the office, it was apparent that I must go immediately to The Hague, where I spent the afternoon in meetings with Mr. Hofstede[310] [and] Mr. van Dedem, with whom I once again recalled memories of Zeeland, but who was so busy with the Billiton[311] contract that no sooner than after Christmastime will he start on the post contract.[312] On the train, I travelled with W. van der Vliet[313]; Enschedé,[314] editor of the *Haarlemmer Courant*; de Bruijn,[315] chief engineer of the [Hollandsche Ijzeren Spoorweg Maatschappij (HSM)]; and the father of Aki,[316] who wrote a piece in the *Java-Bode*[317] about Karel, which meant that I could not even make an attempt at reading the *Fairplay* that I had taken with me.

I have still forgotten to mention to you that I also had a very pleasant discussion with Minister Tak. Both van Dedem and Tak requested that I send you their greetings.

In the morning, I exchanged our congratulations with A.C. [Wertheim]. Enclosed is a picture of the vases and an accompanying letter that I sent to him, and his answer.

We had Uncle and Aunt Niek and the Piersons for dinner, along with Wil, who wore a lovely dress and was very amiable. You can understand that there was much to talk about with the Piersons. He is very positive, finds his new position highly interesting and is very busy with his plans for reform. But I believe there are still many deceptions waiting for him, because when he touches the wallets of the well-to-do, all of the objections against reorganization will be broadly disseminated.

Furthermore, Mama and I are making ourselves useful by dropping by those who had given their condolences about Uncle Toon's passing. Sunday,

---

310 Joan Pieter Hofstede (1861–1930): Chief Director of the Ministry of Transport and Public Works, Trade and Industry; married to Aurelia Joukina Reeling Brouwer (1866–1961).

311 Billiton (1852–1942): originally a tin mining company; taken over by Royal Dutch Shell in 1958.

312 This refers to the proposed contract between the SMN and the government for shipping mail.

313 Willem van der Vliet (1820–1902): lawyer; married to Louisa Catharina Elisabeth von Hemert (1826–1896).

314 Jan is probably referring to Johan Enschedé (1851–1911): owner of the firm Joh. Enschedé en Zoon in Haarlem, printers of, among other things, the *Opregte Haarlemsche Courant*; married to Henriette Francina Krantz (1855–1921).

315 Cornelio de Bruijn (1846–1905): chief engineer of the railway company HSM; married in 1871 to Cornelia Wilhelmina van Blommenstein (1845–1880); second marriage in 1884 to Johanna Antonetta de Kantor (1858–1919).

316 Isaac (Aki) de Bruijn (1872–1953): banker, art collector; married Johanna Geertruida van der Leeuw (1877–1960).

317 The *Java-Bode* is a newspaper published in Batavia, Dutch East Indies, 1852–1957.

we found many of them at home, so that instead of forty, we could only visit twenty. At this rate, we will not be finished before Christmas. With Uncle Menso there is a constant exchange of letters about the details of managing the estate. About essentials, luckily we do agree, but there are all kinds of things to decide. He works very quickly and well, but wants to discuss or record everything, while I would be completely satisfied if he would arrange things according to his own discretion.

Along with Wallie, I visited the SS *Prins Alexander*, which had received damage during a collision with an English sailing ship but now is safely moored at the Handelskade. It appears that Wallie is behaving very well at the Handelsschool.[318] He finds it much better than at Swildens.[319] Mia is making big strides in French and German. She comes to consult me often about such horrendous themes — the curse of school for all youth. She has now started to paint enamels and has made a lovely ashtray for me.

Mrs. Wilkens[320] (having a lot interest) asked me about the chances in Canada with respect to her son, who also would prefer to enter into agriculture in the open air. I shall let her know something or other as soon as I am informed about it.

Now darling, all the best for you, and a warm kiss from your loving Father.

A28335001507-10 [Heleen to Mother]
Lethbridge, December 16, 1891

Dear Mother,

My last coach ride has been joyfully completed. Soon I will be again on the train and I find it almost a pity to leave the old way of travelling. It was lovely warm weather and I enjoyed being on top of the coach, safely nestled between a pleasant French-Canadian coach driver and a jolly small grocery store owner who has been here for twelve years and was going to visit his family. This man drove much better than the one from yesterday, who constantly fell half-asleep and from time to time had to stop to change something on the harness. We also had to stop halfway to have lunch and to change horses.

Mr. and Miss Elton travelled together with me to Dunmore. She is more or less troubled due to being overworked. She is weak, quiet and often does not understand what people are saying, but she speaks normally. I made her a little bit comfortable here so that she can get some rest and get into bed; she is very thankful for every small attention.

318   The Handelsschool in Amsterdam (1867) was the first public high school there that focused its curriculum on trade and commerce.

319   Instituut Jelgerhuis Swildens, Amsterdam: private school started in 1874.

320   This is probably Jeanne Theodora Bosch Reitz Wilkens (1835–1911), regarding her eldest son, Unico Hendrik Wilkens (1867–1898).

Her brother is a very nice travel companion, looks a bit Norwegian, so blond-blond and such blue-blue eyes. He is interested in many things other than Canada and horses. He has very agreeable and sophisticated manners and is *aux petite soins* for his unhappy sister, whom he is taking to England for her recuperation and health. From Macleod, he also wired for couchettes for them on the night train to Dunmore. On that annoying coal route, it is pleasant to have company (which I would not have been without, by the way). An agent of the CPR was waiting for me here with a telegram from Mr. Niblock. He had taken care of everything and told me that someone else from the CPR was to travel with me to Dunmore. There again, another functionary awaited my orders.

I was barely in the hotel when there was a gentleman with a telegram from Mr. Van Horne again. I had wired him that I was on my way to Calgary and Vancouver, and he answered me at great length that he was sending his letters of introduction to the gentlemen Browning[321] and Angus[322] in Vancouver. Mr. Niblock will probably let me travel in his own rail carriage. Now, he is again on one of his inspection tours, but in the next week, he will come and pick me up in Calgary.

It was lovely in the coach, yesterday and today, to feel that my fear had once more gone away. Since my fall, I have still been a little bit jittery in a coach and on horseback, but now that is completely gone. I am now in charge of myself again and can freely enjoy all that is new and curious while travelling. The sunsets here are indescribably magnificent. In Macleod, all of my lady friends found that I looked so much better; Miss Elton [said] she could see clearly from my face that I was never ill (!), asked whether I took good care of myself and remarked on what this lovely air can bring about!

I still have so much to say about all those messages from home, but never get around to it because there is so much to say about ourselves.

The fainting of Wallie at the funeral is not at all pleasant and I am glad that Delprat has taken things in hand. Even if it was something serious, at least nowadays there is much that can be done about it. I am very curious about what he has to say about it.

Then the house construction — I have received so many opposing reports, but I understand that they wavered about it for a long time until the completed plan was in the bag. Now, to make plans can never hurt. If everyone at home [717 Keizersgracht] has had the same appreciation for it, then there has been so much gained.

I thought it was a very nice plan of Papa's to send Mr. Hosmer a Christmas present. He remains very considerate of us and wires once or twice each week. Did I write to you a while ago that there is a Mrs. Hosmer? That, we just realized on the last day in Montreal. At that time,

---

321 John M. Browning (1826–1906): Vancouver city councillor; land commissioner of the CPR; lived at the corner of Burrard and Georgia; a trusted friend of Van Horne; married to Magdelena Howden Norval (1833–1914).

322 James Alexander Angus (1833–1903): wine merchant; married to Mary Fairweather (1838–1925); father of Richard (1870–1950), who worked as a clerk for the CPR at the time.

Mr. Hosmer told us that his wife would come for a visit. I would not have been home and therefore could not have seen her, but it seemed to us that Hosmer had already thought about that and that he did not want to present her straight away. We also did not find out what his address is.

Dr. Black mailed two catalogues about medical books from New York, along with the addresses of the booksellers, but for now, I shall have little time for study and therefore will not yet be ordering books. They all looked very expensive to me.

I wrote to Papa that I would send a newspaper with the description of the storm, but I could not obtain one. They all say that it was the worst storm that had ever raged. The church in Macleod had been shoved along the ground quite a bit. (That happens often here with houses!) A man was blown off the bridge, with horse and all. About one new house, of which the interior was still to be constructed, the whole roof, with various rafters attached, was blown fifty feet over an even higher house!

During the last days, I have read no newspapers at all. In the hotels, I do not dare to go into the smoke-filled rooms where they are. My coach driver told me today that there had been fighting between the English and the Russians in Asia, and that five Englishmen were killed. If that is true, it could have horrible consequences, but I would rather not believe it before I hear more about it. It is otherwise very nice to see how very dedicated the ranchers are to reading their newspapers and magazines. [Chappie] Clarkson had read a very interesting article in the *National Review*[323] about a possible European war, in which the Dutch army was spoken of in very commendable terms!

Bye, Mummie, with a big kiss, your loving Helena.

---

323   *National Review* (London): a conservative newspaper established in 1883.

Chapter 7

Forty Miles through the Snow

Heleen rings in the new year in Calgary, and Karel with the survey crew in the Crowsnest Pass. Heleen begins to tire of the 'city-folk' in Calgary and is missing her friends, in particular the White Frasers. Karel still struggles with the lack of mail service and wonders what future work prospects there may be down the line.

A29670000018-21 [Heleen to Li]
Calgary, December 18, 1891

Dear Li,

Travelling through rugged mountainous country in deep snow, over and through half-frozen rivers, in blizzards and storms, on or in a creaky and an almost-crumbling coach, is very adventurous and interesting. But travelling in your own comfortable salon and sleeping car, which one can rest in at any time and where one can order the finest dinners and *soupers*, is not to be sneezed at. I have learned that for an 'unprotected female', tired of all the bouncing about, the latter way of travelling is extremely refreshing.

   At 3:00 p.m., my royal carriage arrived in Dunmore and, since I had absolutely no desire to stay there longer, we departed immediately toward Medicine Hat, a half-hour's distance. This is where Mr. Niblock lives and, as such, deserves a closer look.

The adjutant of 'her highness',[324] at the same time steward, cook, cook's aid, *valet de chambre* and 'lady-in-waiting', escorted me on my walk through the city. First, we were introduced to the famous bear and two new young bears, in chains behind a wooden fence. There was a signboard with a touching story about how the bear sacrificed his freedom for the [sake of the] new hospital and was pleading for the public to help [support the cause]. The connection was not all that evident, but the [collection] box made the goal clear. The 'Princess Badroulbadour' immediately brought out her well-filled gold wallet, but because the opening of the box was too small, she spoke with equanimity — "See, here is a tenth of the amount" — and the precious metal clinked into the empty box.

The adjutant expressed his thanks in Sioux, since he spoke the language, and since the princess had let her wish to visit the hospital be known, they both directed their footsteps toward it. The visiting hours of the hospital were already long past, but the distinguished stranger and her lackey were, nevertheless, allowed to go in. The princess clearly let her satisfaction with the high, light wards, the good beds and the practical design of the building be known. She conducted herself amiably with a few patients, a boy who had broken his ankle and a crippled old man. The adjutant followed discreetly, but the strange odours of the hospital air were not very much to his liking, as he later mentioned to the princess.

The two gas wells and the lovely railway bridge were also honoured with a visit. Afterwards, the distinguished guest turned back to the railway car. There, she received Mr. Niblock, who was on his way with a couple hundred tough-looking guys from his division who, while passing Medicine Hat, had waited for her [and her adjutant]. [Mr. N.] inquired as to whether the princess was satisfied and wished to renew her orders, should she want to use the carriage again. Her highness let him know her intention to spend the Christmas holidays in Calgary and, with that, she would begin her trip through the mountains with her carriage. With this, Mr. N. took his leave.

In the meantime, a lovely *souper* was prepared and the princess ate with relish. The adjutant appeared to be just as handy a waiter as a competent cook.

A29670000021 [continues on]

Her Highness poured over *Ravenshoe* by Henry Kingsley, loaned to her by Mrs. Garnett. A bit later, the adjutant proposed a game of checkers and, since the princess was too sleepy to read pleasurably and the conversation of her lackey was also none too brilliant, she agreed. The board and the pieces came out of a cupboard and the game began. The critical moment, when one party had more checkers, had come when, Swoop! Boom! Ta Daaa!

324   In her story about her trip to Medicine Hat, Heleen cheekily refers to herself as "her highness" and as the fictitious Princess Badroulbadour, who married Aladdin in *The Story of Aladdin; or, the Wonderful Lamp*.

The board and all the pieces flew into the air and the players jumped up. The night wagons that were to pull her along had been attached! Now came a new aspect to the game, because the jolting kept repeating itself and more measures for the game itself were then necessary to keep the board in balance in case of unexpected shocks. Soon, they went on.

Checkers was not a strong point for the adjutant, and her highness taught him *Qui perd-gagne*.[325] He found it an extremely hilarious joke and laughed exuberantly with quick moves. So the evening continued until the princess had had enough of it. She began to read the paper that was brought to her and, after that, again her book. At 10:00 p.m. she wanted to embark upon her rest for the night. Upon this, the adjutant told her that he was to visit the machinist. He stepped over the balcony and she had the realm to herself.

An episode that I have yet forgotten to mention: While passing the railway bridge, I was invited to look out from the last balcony [at the back of the wagon]. I went and looked straight into the gigantic fiery eye of the trailing locomotive, which seemed to want to devour me. That was not the real reason; it was really for the view of the frozen river that meandered through the dark hills, spectacularly lit by the huge, low moon, lightly shrouded by a small streak of cloud. On our way we stopped often, but I still slept very well, certain in the prospect of being able to lie there as long as I wanted to — not like the regular passengers, who had to get off the train at 2:00 a.m. in Calgary.

At 8:00 a.m., I was fully awake. By then, we had arrived. The steward stoked the heaters and prepared my breakfast. Then he went for a walk while I got up. The carriage consisted of a salon with canapé, easy chairs and a table, separated by a door from the bedroom, which has four berths, a little washroom and a cloakroom with many clothing racks, then through another door, the kitchen with a berth for the cook. The boy was a unique specimen and reminded me of Cornelis from Papa's office. Cooking was his hobby and his ambition was to become a cook of a dining car. He was not shy and was very refined in his manners. After breakfast, he brought my mail to me. Eleven letters for me! *Rotterdammers*, *Propria Cures*, etc., etc. I kept reading until coffee time, wired Hosmer and received an answer that he had wired to home, as I had hoped.

Now you folks know that I am out of danger from running horses and wolves. To the Alberta Hotel for lunch: 'shake hands with the proprietor'; nice, tidy room, prettier than the previous one; to the post office; shopping for Mrs. Garnett; visit to Mrs. Lougheed, who invited me . . .

A28335001479-80 [continues on]

. . . to stay. Her house is now almost finished, only the sidewalk is absent and one makes do with a few crates and planks in order to reach

---

325   This is probably a version of 'suicide checkers', or 'who loses, wins'.

[32] Lougheed Mansion

the high door.[326] She received me in a spacious, elegant salon. It is almost a shame to have to leave this comfortable hotel. There are almost no guests and my room is very comfortable, but being alone will bore me quickly enough and it is difficult for me to refuse. Mrs. Lougheed is a little bit 'mixed-blood'; up until now, she has only talked about her boys [pronounced "booies"]. The children look quite amusing.

And now, all those letters! It was wonderful. Today, I am living completely in Holland. Your experience with how the police dealt with the insane young woman, I found most interesting. It is sad when so much effort is expended without any result. I hope that you are more successful later. It is a disastrous situation. My experience with the mentally ill [Maude] Elton, the day before yesterday, although of a different sort, helped me to understand this more clearly. It was quite moving the way that she told me she was not allowed to take that medicine. Someone had told her that she would then bleed to death, but she could not explain

---

326 The house, a mansion, then called Beaulieu (now Lougheed House), is now a museum and located at 707 Thirteenth Ave. SW, Calgary. Heleen would not have known that she was to be a guest on traditional Blackfoot territory (now acknowledged as Treaty 7 land). It is near the confluence of the Bow and Elbow Rivers (along which Heleen loved to walk); this territory is acknowledged as the home of the Métis Nation (Region 3). Treaty 7 was signed in 1877 by representatives of the Queen and members of the Blackfoot Confederacy. Among the numerous signatories to it was James F. Macleod, as well as Mary J. Macleod and Belle's aunt, Eliza Hardisty, two of the six women who signed as witnesses. See: https://hcmc.uvic.ca/confederation/en/treaty_07.html. The personal views that Heleen expressed about Belle, especially her assumptions about mixed-blood persons, were certainly of the time. Source: https://www.communitystories.ca/v2/conflicting-loyalties_allegeances-contradictoires/story/land-acknowledgement/

this to her brother. She was touchingly thankful to me, even though I helped her brother, and she was willing to allow me to lead her in everything else.

These men in the west, who you thought that I would nurse (it only happened a few times, but I always had to move on again, so soon), are peculiar creatures. They were always very reliable and companionable, and absolutely did not flirt. But when I left, some of them were just like *Appelmoes*.[327] Like John Garnett, among others, who brought me to Pincher Creek and there, out of kindness, stayed until I went on. He was painfully shy, and quite happy when he could tell someone else, while I was sitting beside him, that it was so unpleasant to be alone and to have no one who cared about him, etc. Routledge, the giant with the wooden leg, was also very warm and 'manly'. I have never seen anyone with such a very sorrowful face at rest and such a hearty, jolly laugh.

I don't care if you call me Heleentje, so long as you keep the 'He'.
Bye, Heleen

KLAB09193000020 [Father to Karel]
Amsterdam, December 19, 1891

Dear Karel,

Many thanks for your letter from the end of November, about your first Sunday in camp.

Very thankful and happy about your strong views and courageous resolutions; I will face the new year with a calm feeling. You can be assured of my support. I am often with you in my thoughts and wish perserverence and spirit for you in these difficult times.

I have only five minutes before the mail closes; I just came back from IJmuiden, where I escorted [Thomas] Wallis with the SS *Prins Hendrik*. Soon I will write extensively to you about all the goings-on.

We are doing well. Yesterday, we had an enjoyable dinner with Wallis and Wil, who is doing fine.

God bless you, your loving Father

KLAB04554000201 [Karel to Wil]
In camp, December 20, 1891

Dear Wil,

Since I last wrote to you, my life has plodded along in the same way that it has done since November 11. The discomfort and the effects of my unfamiliarity with camp life have slowly given way and work has become more difficult, more enjoyable and more varied the closer we come to the

---

327   *Appelmoes*, literally "applesauce," refers to being soft and mushy, and is often used as a term of endearment.

mountains. Such a curious month of December, this time!! It is beautiful weather every day. One moment there is a stiff, warm breeze that does not melt the snow but rather evaporates it, then a day of sharp frost that one does not feel because the air is completely still. Especially on those days, working, and particularly physical work, is a pleasure. Then, I forget my sorrows and my longing, and I feel younger and sillier than in my youngest and silliest period, long before I sought your hand. I join the boys when they are throwing snowballs and horsing around with the dogs or crisscrossing over the water of the Oldman River or throwing large pieces of rock from twenty feet to tumble down into the rapids of the mountain stream. Then I fully feel the zest of life!

Also, it is a completely unique pleasure to be in beautiful, extremely beautiful, nature, not just being there because you must, but because you wish to be. I assume that I am not making myself clear here. I mean that one normally goes outside, searching for picturesque places in order to linger there for a while, with the feeling that it is then your duty to find it beautiful. Here, on the other hand, it is wholly by chance; the beauty of nature is an incidental circumstance. Even in the absence of that, I would still work here. Later on, because I must give up my place at the table to Brooks, I will try to describe the beautiful sunrise which I, for sure, would not enjoy so much if I were to see it from the top of the Rigi-Kulm,[328] surrounded by a gathering of hotel guests and waiters.

A premiere, in the early hours of a winter morning. A premiere for which the elite of the chic, but also the large masses, have eagerly longed. A colossal amphitheatre with purple covered benches that extend to both sides. In front, trumpets and trombones, shining golden on the outside and with golden tones on the inside — a painting of gold. Then rows of pink girls, blushing from delight and longing, yearning for her arrival, the appearance of the *belle du jour*, who shall do an improvisation, about what, one does not yet know. But it will be beautiful — like one has read about in black and white in *De Morgenster!*[329] — and blushing blond girls nod their heads to each other and move closer together to make room for more pink gowns and more purple crowns. They slowly advance though the tightly gathered crowd of the rabble (that stands in front of the doors of the theatre, as they could not purchase entrance tickets) and through the rows of distinguished gentlemen dolled up in dark clothing, blushing from enjoyment as they receive a nod or a smile from the beauties that pass them. All the while the pushing continues and the golden sound of music peals through the pure, silent morning sky. Look. There. She appears — the star on the literary heaven, as *De Morgenster* has called her, metaphorically and in a circumlocutory way. She appears on the stage with quiet steps, because it is in her conviction that she does good work and the light that she spreads will be a blessing for thousands.

328 The Rigi, or Mount Rigi, is in central Switzerland.
329 *De Morgenster* (the *Morningstar*) was a Christian magazine of the mid to late nineteenth century.

But what is that? Why do the pink girls and the darkly clothed men blanch? Why do they leave their seats hastily and rush to the exits? Why do the dark men and grey masses and rabble push forward to chase that woman away? Is their vanity offended that she is more lovely than their wives, as well as their daughters, who, just before, were seated in their purple chairs but are now made invisible by this stream of grey and black? Or was the light of truth that she shone in this gathering too bright for the blushing swell of ignorance that her public was comprised of? Or is it the slogan "Crucify her, crucify her!" that overpowers the trumpets and silences the trombones? I do not know. One will be suppressed, darkened by that cloud of ignorance that calls her 'Volksfeind'[330] (you read Ibsen's lovely drama?) and which buries her under slander.

For a long time, she vanished from sight, her beautiful voice brought to silence, her brilliant eye darkened, but still, splendid Triumph! Her work lives on. The light she ignited could not be extinguished; even though the Sun has gone, it is Day!

This is one of the dozens of very lovely spots that I have enjoyed during our rides, or our walks, toward the place for our surveying, each place quite different but all splendidly beautiful. To keep up the comparison, I have been able to see everything that happened there, on the southwestern horizon above the prairie, but also in the west, where the steep hills of the Livingstone Range form the horizon. It was a beautiful scene because the red in the east reflects off the snow white in the west and colours it with muted tones of its own glow! Oh Wim, it is lovely while it is happening; it fills your entire realm of thoughts, except the one that never leaves. Oh, that you were with me; there is no room for anyone else, for example, those who [complain about] how hard the bench is and how terribly the carriage bounces over the bumps and the potholes of the prairie.

The two-horse team is otherwise driven very well by Jack MacKenzie, "the most reckless teamster I ever came across," as our chief has attested to. He does not shrink from the worst slopes and most perilous river crossings, and keeps his mad joviality wrapped in a language peppered with the most unimaginable profanities and curses toward his brave horses, Frank and Queen, and it is only because of this that one would forget one's fear that the carriage could roll over at any moment.

If the job is not too far from the camp, Spot and Joker, both camp dogs, come with us, Spot [walking] under the shaft of the wagon in between the two horses — but he leaves this location when his presence is demanded elsewhere. He is very observant and not a hare nor chicken in the area escapes his keen nose, upon which he races over the snow-covered prairie toward a small brush thicket and chases an innocent hare, or stays and keeps on barking in front of a pile of rocks, under which a small weasel is hiding, until his last breath (or until he is

---

330   A translation into German from the original Norwegian title, *En Folkefiende* (*An Enemy of the People*), an 1882 play by Henrik Ibsen in which the title character fights against hypocrisy and ignorance.

called back from the wagon). Once, I even saw him chase two coyotes who fled from the wagons and from the brave, lame Spot, who would certainly have been shredded to pieces by them if it had come to a fight. One of our back-picketers never goes out without his revolver and, now and then, shoots at a coyote (a kind of small wolf) who passes by at about 100 to 200 yards, never hitting the mark, of course.

Yes, Spottie is lame, and his left hind foot was once wedged between a horse's hoof and a stone, and since then, it has remained a little stiff. At any rate, he limps on a hard road, but in the soft snow, setting down his feet doesn't hurt him and he is infinitely faster on it than Joker, a black, long-haired dog. [Joker] is much less well-bred but, on the other hand, is more amusing. He can jump a few feet high over obstacles and can successfully rip one item or another off the head of Willem Coster. He catches everything in his mouth that you can throw at him (even horse droppings if there is nothing else — dry and frozen, of course), and now and then he makes up his own jokes and parodies his friend, Spot. When Spot has difficulty walking on a rocky road, he goes beside him and walks with a limp. Perhaps it is sympathy, like sensitivity, that inspires him to act like this, but Spot doesn't interpret it that way and furiously goes for him (deems it worthy of a better cause) and the poor Joker, whose teeth have been blunted by catching too many stones, mostly gets the worst of it.

The prairie work is now behind us and we are working forward through steep, bare rocks or thick forest. Beautiful pines in this area and lots of shrubby undergrowth. A few years ago, an enormous forest fire ravaged an extensive area. Yesterday, we worked miles away in a forest where the light green of the unbranched young pines overshadowed the dead forest giants, who were killed by the fire before the birth of the [young pines]. [The giants] lay haphazardly, crisscrossing each other in a jumble, some now charred, but most of them evidently having been fatally singed or damaged to the roots, [thereby] succumbing to an internal sickness, just like our dear Uncle Toon, the first of the many friends who I may never see again.

I thank you very much for your November 15 letter wherein you gave your condolences about his passing. I enclosed your letter to Helena in one of my own to her, because since [last] Sunday, we are no longer neighbours. She is again back to the civilized world and shall travel alone through Canada. Indeed, a "daring undertaking" (Tollens[331]), but we must draw courage from the friendly treatment that, up to now, has been conferred upon us by the Canadians. Her stay was very beneficial and enjoyable for me; our last Sunday afternoon together was especially very pleasant and we had a lot of things to talk about. It was somewhat impolite to take so little notice of the host and hostess, because we

---

331 Hendrik Tollens (1780–1856), a Dutch poet, author of *The Hollanders in Nova Zembla – 1596–1597 – An Arctic Poem*, wrote about this "daring undertaking" ("*een stout bedrijf*") in search of a route to the Dutch East Indies, which ended prematurely with the explorers becoming stranded on the island of Nova Zembla in the Russian north.

spoke in Dutch with each other in a corner. But they understood that our moments in each other's company were valuable and indicated to us that it was not such a bad thing to be on our own.

Eh, dear child, it is, for once, so comfy to talk with you, uninterrupted, for an hour. Clarke and Hogg really want to come and sit at the table. For now, enough; perhaps tonight, another few words. Bye-bye, Your Karel.

KLAB04554000207 [continues on]

December 20, 1891: Yes, darling, yet another hour for you on this Sunday. I still have so immeasurably much to say to you, except what I am not allowed to say — but I still have to answer not only the already-mentioned letter but also your letter of November 6, which I received in good health and wrote about to 717.

It appears that all of you got nothing out of your trip to Berlin. In the next letter, I hope to receive your message about Jo's well-being. Hopefully this doctor finally knows what to do about her illness! Many thanks for your report about the prospects and on the well-being of Papa and Mama. Please keep me informed about it.

About the difficult times of [Willem] Coster, I am very sad. Also, I love him; he would have been a friend to both of us, if — oh, well — if our beautiful dream were to become a reality.

And are you still so busy? Well, when I read the message, I didn't laugh. In your previous life, I thought that 'no time' and 'too busy' were unbelievable expressions, but now, the way you have planned it, you will have to juggle just to fit it all into a 24-hour day.

Thanks also for copying the fairy tale from *Elsevier's* monthly magazine. I find it so-so. A lovely idea in a poorly developed format. Do you know that we also had those ideas and had shared them with each other? But that is, of course, exactly what appealed to you about it, and also to me. "Precisely my idea" and usually great praise, but the format is inadequate; grant me that. The writer chose a difficult genre, and everything that is not of high quality is of very low quality. Multatuli had great success using this idea in his "Japanese Stonecutter,"[332] but few are gifted in writing this way.

I think that it is very nice that your style has improved with writing to Canada. You have no idea how Mama was often annoyed about her own 'kitchen maid' notes (between you and me) and her unfamiliarity with some of the rules of the Dutch language. She writes French more accurately than Dutch! Now that I am on this subject, I ask your leave for an innocent, critical remark about a *lapsus linguae* that appears frequently in your letters, namely, about the conjunction *that*. ("Dr. J. says I look good now." "Mama finds I ride horses . . .", etc.) Do you know (that) you do that and (that) experts would call this a horrific Germanism?

332 This parable, "Japanese Stonecutter" by Wolter Robert Baron van Hoëvell, was later used by Multatuli in his novel *Max Havelaar*.

You also advised me to take a firearm along to these remote areas. Well then, I have my gun with me and have already used it to shoot a partridge. Now that we have arrived in the mountains and the woods, I carry it with me daily. But there is, of course, small chance to meet wildlife and to get a shot off in such a large and animated group, as our outfit is, because one constantly hears shouting from one end of the line to the other: "Charley, put your rod up," "Boosie (that is me), have you enough stakes until the next hub?," "Chain ahead," "Out of the line there, you potato-trap" and a couple of swear words, etc., etc., etc. (the last of which are not meant for me).

Finally, I congratulate you on reaching the age of majority, and it is not completely coincidental that these wishes appear on the last pages of this letter, because they are difficult to formulate. I could not have done so had you eased your future away from mine and our ways had separated. Still, if my hope of recovery turns out to be in vain, if my certificate of incompetence is not revoked, then I would know what I must wish for you, even with a bleeding heart. But, since you remain for the invalid drifter what you were for the 'world-conquering' man, I have no ability now, at the ending of your age of minority, to wish you anything in particular for the future.

Even so, this legal process will not make much difference to your civil rights. That is, signing a pair of signatures with a straight face (as your mother and her lawyer advise you) regarding the significant business concerning your share of your father's estate and all that will be for the time being. Still, it is a date for internal contemplation and the least that I can wish for you, in your future life, is that you can always live with as much self-fulfillment as you do at the present, now that you have bravely accepted a difficult, very heavy task, and are so energetically carrying it out. My darling, you will be in my thoughts on that day and I will bless you more solemnly than I do every day.

"*Pour la clôture définitive et sans remise*," as Grandmother Boissevain used to say, I shall once again recommence with this letter. I was rudely interrupted and now I sit on my bed writing by the light of a pretty good wax candle fixed upon my *toilet-necessaire*, which in turn rests upon the case for my revolver. I still wanted to ask you, in my name, to thank Uncle Jan and your cousin Pompe very much for their letters. Uncle Jan relieved me (with his usual amiability and unwavering courtesy) of the task of replying. Let him know that I temporarily accept this release and that I am very touched by his compassion; also write to me particularly about the fate of the automatic salt-drying scale, I am very interested in that.

I compliment you folks on your interpretation of the old Hebrew view of the power of the family bond. Really, if one is already being encumbered by boils, being pestered by an aunt and two cousins is not going to be conferred upon everyone.

You also asked in your letter about a description of the "work" that I carry out in my "job"! Dear child, my work is 'to become healthy' and I do not consider this a 'job'. The idea was for it to be a cheap spa-cure, if

I may call it so. And that idea has, in the execution, completely fulfilled my expectations. The following should still give you an idea about our work today: This survey is the preliminary survey,[333] the first step toward the construction of a railway and the exploration of the country. After this survey, a global calculation of the costs will be made, which makes it possible for the contractors to tender for the construction project. The chief engineer leads on horseback and determines the best route for the eventual rail lines.

This is naturally very easy on horizontal prairie terrain, where the rule is "a straight line is the shortest distance between two points," but in mountainous and river-crossed terrain, it is very difficult. Anyway, for the best-looking route, he turns to his engineers, two in number. The first observes which direction the line takes and has an instrument for that, a compass on a tripod with a telescope on top of it that ensures precision over far distances; for example, like the little sketch depicting the terrain with a hill and a river, in between which the line must span. Then the engineer installs his instrument in turns at *a*, *b*, *c*, *d*, *e*, etc.

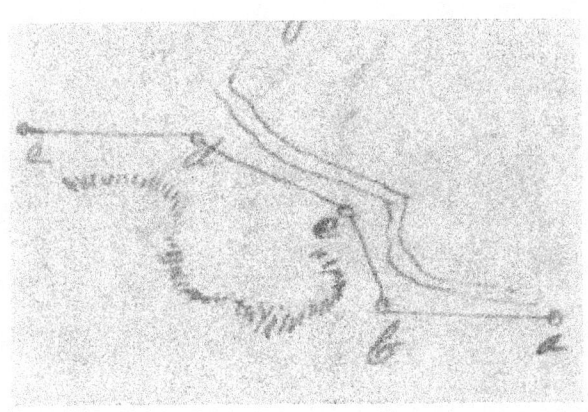

[33] Karel's diagram of the distances measured following the river

A man with a wooden stick about seven feet long, with an iron point on the bottom and a small red flag on the top, follows [the engineer] and then goes ahead of him, so that if [the man with the flag] is at *b*, the front-picketer is at *c* and the rear-picketer is at *a*. Those points, *a*, *b*, *c*, *d*, etc., are called 'hubs'. The distance in between them is measured very precisely with a measuring chain that is 100 feet long. For example, on the drawing the distance *a–b* is 1,560 feet, and *b–c* is 1,133.7 feet, etc., exactly in tenths of feet. The second engineer also has a telescope on a tripod and is assisted by a 'rodman', who is equipped with a wooden pole that is telescopic to a height of twenty feet and marked with clear numbers in feet and inches. He places this rod every hundred feet by each stake that the chainers have set and firmly driven into the ground, and the second engineer reads through his telescope how much higher or lower that point of the line is than his instrument, the elevation of which he has already ascertained by the same method.

333 Karel describes the process of a preliminary survey, an instrumental survey of the selected route in order to determine distances, directions and altitudes. He mentions technical items such as the theodolite and the 100-foot measuring chain, as well as the crew members of a typical survey party, which can include a chief surveyor, transitman, leveller, rodmen, chainmen, topographer, draughtsman, a cook and packers.

I am entrusted with the making and marking of the stakes or poles. In order to do this, I chop a not-too-thick tree or large branch, cut it into pieces of the required length and thickness, cut a point at one end, and on the other side, by cutting through the bark, making a flat place upon which I can write. On there, a sequence number will be marked, showing how far we have gone. Every hundred feet is one mark. We have now reached no. 2,670; that is, therefore, 267,000 feet, and since a mile is 5,280 feet, we have already chained more than fifty miles. There are days that we progress five to six miles, that is, therefore, 250 to 300 poles to make, but then I am assisted by the teamster or one of the chainmen. Each time, the second engineer records in his book what he has read from the rod and, therefore, we know each time how much the line rises or lowers. Then he is in the position (in the evening in the tent, on paper especially designed for this) to make a sketch of the line. For example, so:

Along with that are indicated the type of soil and other particulars, and from this drawing, one can see how many ravines have to be filled in, hills tunnelled or rivers bridged; then the cost estimation can be calculated. So, you can see it is very interesting work, but my contribution to it is very modest. Every manual worker would be able to learn it in a short time, even though making the pointed stakes quickly and well was not as easy as I had thought.

[34] Karel's sketch of line elevation

Of course, I did not have to do this work and, as a tourist, could have followed the movements of the troop if I had wanted to. But I wanted to show those guys in Montreal who sent me here that I am not afraid to use my hands and, when they give me the opportunity to work, that there is no absence of goodwill. That is why I accepted this day-labourer work and hope to accomplish it fully and to the best of my ability.

Recently, we have hired yet two more men as axe-men, who must make room for the chain and the instruments, because now the line often goes through thick woods. The river must still be crossed repeatedly. However, while this was previously done easily with the help of the teams, due to lower banks, now the steep, thickly overgrown banks are often impassable for the horses and the wagon. Then we wade across the river with neither shoes nor socks (!) (that is a cold expedition over the ice and the snow and through the water!) Or [we cross] with the aid of a tree standing close to the banks, which we cut down so that it falls onto the other bank. But then, walking on a wobbly tree trunk is not pleasant work. It is an amusing thing to have done so, and then to stand on the other bank laughing at the crazy movements that the ones who come after must use in order to keep their balance, and even crazier when they lose it and, with a loud splash, fall into the water that is almost nowhere (unless it is near the steep rock cliffs) more than five feet deep.

I spend evenings with the drying and repairing of wet and torn clothing, doing a bit of correspondence and some reading. I have read, with much pleasure, a few of Ibsen's dramas, *Ein Volksfeind* and *Der Bund der Jugend*, as well as *Die Stützen der Gesellschaft*, which very much captivated me. They are evocative. He is a powerful writer. You can read them in the original, certainly with more pleasure. Write to me about what *Ein Volksfeind* is called in Norwegian.

For your birthday, I will not send a present that has been chosen and given to you by someone else. That will have little value to you anyway; let this letter serve in place of it. This is my own fancy handwork, just like your birthday present for me was.

Bye, darling, I think that I will celebrate your birthday with Helena and together we will think about you, out loud, and then you can hear it, perhaps? Your deeply loving, Karel.

P.S. I have not read my letter over because I am so sleepy. That is always the case after supper now, just like a marmot.

A32005000388-391 [Wil to Heleen]
Amsterdam, December 21, 1891

Dear Heleen!

Already a lovely letter again from you to be answered, and almost at the same time as one from Karel, which I answered yesterday. In the letter, he told me about the accident that happened to you and now I realize that I have not even talked to you about it yet. But you will most likely get this one when your wrist is already better. How nasty a thing distance is when specific things are happening. Such as now, with the passing away of Uncle Toon. Your mother just received letters from both of you in which you spoke of his recovery and about the sorrow that she must have had from his illness, and then, how you would have hardly expected such a sad outcome.

But with respect to yourself, I am so thankful that it is once again going so much better. It was, in all likelihood, a big shock. First the runaway and then, when you were conscious again, to notice that you were really hurt. And then in a country where there are so few services. How did you manage dressing and fixing your hair? We heard of it first from Karel's letter and I was so glad that your mother could tell me that (even with the accident) you were doing fine. How lovely that the people are so caring. The Garnetts, whom you described to Li, also seem nice, at least, one of them.

And how divine that Karel feels so well. He wrote to me: "The way I have it now, I have never had in my whole life, as yet." And then, that the work has suited him, and he noticed that he was of good use to them.

On Papa's birthday, I was there for dinner, along with Uncle and Aunt Hes and Gi, and Mr. and Mrs. Pierson. Mr. [Pierson] toasted the "birthday boy" and the "two who were far away." Papa answered so adorably and proposed a toast for my happiness in the future. It was a mixed feeling of both thankfulness and sadness for me, but you do not know how lovely it is that your parents are so sweet to me.

Yesterday morning, I was also there to exchange letters and then also saw Karel's Atjeh Cross and the diploma. There was also the album page (that your father had made for the [van] Tienhovens), which is a sketch of one of the receptions, to remind one of all of the visiting ladies and gentlemen and the recitation by [Mrs. van Tienhoven] for an intimate circle. That will certainly please them, because it will be something completely different than what most of the others would give. You have no idea how uplifting that short visit was, all those good things and the renewed hope and courage in Karel's letter.

Cold weather, 3.5° *Réaumur* below zero. For you 'Canadians', a laughable freezing point, but for us, it's cold enough. However, I must confess that I absolutely did not get a frozen nose or ears, because there was no wind.

Oh, Heleentje, we received such wonderful news from Jo! Just think, she has recovered! Thure Brandt was himself astonished about it, that at the end, it passed so quickly and that she is now already in Berlin on her way home; Mama waits for a letter from her in order to go receive her there once again, this time all by herself. You can understand how thankful [Jo] is. And Brandt must have also strengthened her morale. She sent us his portrait so that we could see what he looks like, and he had written a few Swedish words on the back and signed it "*gamle vännen* Thure Brandt 1819."[334] That such an old man still has such a steady hand. He has a good, old Swedish face, distinguished and pleasant. [Jo] found the parting very sad. She had also been four times to the hypnotist, Wetterstrand,[335] for her headaches and sleeplessness. (Otto was also there for the first time.) But, despite the few times she had seen him, Jo was one of his most receptive patients. She had to put up one hand and move the other back and forth and she did not feel tired in the least.

Also, her sleep was much better after the treatment; the proof that it was not an unnatural sleep was that she woke up one morning because of the creaking boots of the neighbour in the room beside her. Wetterstrand gave her his portrait, so that by looking at it, she could always go to sleep again. Another patient, a woman who suffered with her throat, had

---

334   Translation: "old friend Thure Brandt 1819."
335   Otto George Wetterstrand (1845–1907): Swedish physician and psychotherapist.

to grab Jo's hand and to tell [Jo], while she was under hypnosis, what Jo had to do to [later] hypnotize herself by using the portrait. After that, they tested it, that is, "Jo should sleep for fifteen minutes." [The other patient] and Otto took out their watches, Jo looked at the portrait and said that she wanted to sleep for fifteen minutes. Almost immediately after that, she went to sleep and woke up exactly after fifteen minutes. Do you not think this is remarkable? Nevertheless, I would not find it very pleasant. She therefore saved the portrait very carefully. Dr. Voûte[336] says that one always hypnotizes oneself and, the next time, he will explain it to me.

He came for Mama's knee, in which she has rheumatism. She was limping and in a lot of pain. It had gone on already for fourteen days and, when she went for a constitutional in the city with Cor, the burden was too heavy and she had the greatest difficulty with coming home. It is now much better, however, and she can travel to Berlin. Your mother, who was just here, promised to send overshoes to Mama for the journey. We find that lovely, because Mama is, of course, quite susceptible from sitting around at home. I immediately asked Voûte, once again, about the pain that I have in my shoulders and neck and he said that it was caused from the time that I had strained [myself] while at the Kindervoeding. I thought that I had rheumatism in my neck, but he says that by rubbing, I have made my muscles more sensitive. He said that I should not use my left arm too much, but that is difficult when is one is left-handed. He will send me a liver-oil preparation because he thinks that I am too thin. A beautiful expression! I think that he means that the hinges must be lubricated, somewhat.

A while ago, a book was sent to us on recommendation by van Heteren.[337] It was a Norwegian book about Holland by a certain Ipsen.[338] He discusses various cities, particularly a lot about Amsterdam. He provides photographs from everywhere and portrayals of, amongst others, Beets,[339] Busken Huet,[340] Multatuli and a few scholars. Also, [Ipsen] had been to van Eeden's[341] in Bussum and was very enthusiastic about him and the interior of his house, the children, the Norwegian books; everything was brought up. Herman Gorter,[342] van Eeden, and Ipsen walked together toward Muiden and they

---

336   Alexander Voûte (1847–1922): medical doctor; married to Sophia Eliza Kruseman (1862–1915).

337   J.H. & G. van Heteren: bookstore in Amsterdam.

338   Peter Alfred Buntzen Ipsen (1852–1922) is a Danish author, whose book *Holland* was published in 1891.

339   Nicolaas Beets, pseudonym Hildebrand (1814–1903): author, poet, pastor and professor in Utrecht; married to Jkvr. Alida van Foreest (1818–1856).

340   Conrad Busken Huet (1826–1886): Dutch literary critic and pastor of the Walloon Chapel in Haarlem; married in 1859 to Anne Dorothee van der Tholl (1827–1898).

341   Frederik Willem van Eeden (1860–1932): psychiatrist and writer; married to Martha van Vloten (1856–1943), translator of children's literature.

342   Herman Gorter (1864–1927): Dutch poet; married to Catharine Wies Cnoop Koopmans (1865–1916).

told him about the Spanish.[343] [Ipsen] said something like, "Hey, then it was less quiet to live here," and van Eeden answered, "Yes, but not so boring". In the evening, van Eeden had also read out of *Ellen*[344] for them. Ipsen was terribly thrilled with it and used long excerpts from it, among others, about the farmland, the forest, and I also believe [this line from Ellen], "Why do you love the Dead so much, my love?" I am very anxious to know what the Norwegians will think of the book. His critique about Amsterdam, I found not always correct. He did not do justice to the lovely bend of the Herengracht. He found the street along the canal (and also the houses) too narrow, paying no attention to the trees, the fact that only one family lives in a house, and that they are very tall.

Last Friday, your parents also asked me to come to dine, in order to meet Mr. Wallis. What an original talker he is. There was funny incident at the table. Mama knocked against a glass before the Grace, and Mr. [Wallis], who thought that it was a sign for a toast, let out a cry of joy and when he saw our bowed heads, stopped all of a sudden. For us it was very difficult not to laugh, and, because of this, the prayer was not so solemn. Papa told Mia to go to the corner and I also applied for a place there; everyone giggled for a very long time after that. Mr. Wallis also made us laugh about his indignation with his son-in-law and found it also, I believe, very awful that I would ever go to Canada. His credo was, however, that a son gives a daughter, but a son-in-law takes away a daughter. The receipt of a son-in-law seemed to have no value for him.

Willem Coster is on his way home, via Lisbon, to Paris. All we know is that there was a telegram (I believe to Liefdadigheid) [which said] that the crossing from Madeira to Lisbon had been terribly stormy and we do not know the date of his arrival. Delprat must have quite recently said that he does not appear to be in the final stage. I hope so. We so much wished to put some roses or other flowers in his room for when he comes home, and now find it so unsettling to know nothing for certain.

What do you think about the journey of Jan Kruseman? This will certainly agitate Willem, that office life falls short for Jan. At first, I was so afraid that it was still about the unpleasant history, but now I know that that is not the reason. It would have been a long time after that, anyway.

A while ago, we received a letter at the Kindervoeding from a woman, Liedermooy,[345] requesting benefits; [there was also] a little child, Gerritsen,[346] who walked with her bare head in the rain and was very

---

343 This is in reference to the Dutch War of Independence, a.k.a. the Eighty Years' War (1568–1648), against the occupation of the Netherlands, Belgium and Luxembourg by the Spanish.

344 Frederik van Eeden is the author of *Ellen: Een Lied van de Smart* (Amsterdam: W. Versluys, 1891), a book of poems about sorrow.

345 Catharine Liedermooy (née de Vries) (1865-?): lived at Binnen Oranjestraat 16; married in 1884 to Christiaan Liedermooy (1861–?).

346 This is likely one child of the family of Henricus Gerritsen (1858–?) and his wife Anna Betje Kuiper (1852–?), who lived at Bloemstraat 196, Amsterdam.

thinly dressed. I wanted to give the latter a warm hat, and about the former, I wrote to the Liefdadigheid. Miss Bundten[347] had already once given them a voucher from the Liefdadigheid. Mr. Kalff[348] answered right away that even though the woman, thirty, and the man, twenty-nine, were still somewhat young, they were honest. Last Thursday, Cor and I went first to Mrs. Liedermooy, who lives in the Binnen Oranjestraat (a side street of the Haarlemmerdijk in an alley) and works for an elderly lady who lives next door. There were two big cupboards and two proper chairs. She told us that her husband had no work and that they had no food. The little boy that comes to eat at the pension was the oldest of their three children. (Number four was expected.) We gave her some of the coupons for coal, beans and a loaf of bread.

After that, we bought one warm hat and then went to look for the Gerritsens. I had not remembered very well whether it was the Rozenstraat or the Bloemstraat 93, but was almost sure it was the Rozenstraat. There we landed in a barbershop where a decent fellow was getting a haircut (after having asked [the way] in vain at a bakery). They advised us to knock on the door at 193. This was a small store with a stairway on the side and an alley beside it, from where the noise of an intense fight came. This was also not the right place. I would have preferred to go home and ask again correctly, but Cor was strong and therefore we went to the Bloemstraat and found them at the end of a narrow alley in a room with a shed in the back. The mother and a girl were at home. There must have been ten of them there. The woman suited us fine, but today she came with Rilletje, the child of the barber, to ask for some more of the coupons, since they had no food during Christmas. The husband was sick and had jaundice. Mama did give money this time but said that it should not become a habit. She finds it quite coincidental that the man had become sick now. I do not know, perhaps true, but nevertheless, I find it too bad that they came asking again right away.

And now, dear Heleentje, I will finish. Many greetings from Mama and Cor, and a warm kiss from one who loves you, Wil.

A28335001511-16 [Heleen to Mother]
Calgary, December 22, 1891

Dear Mother,

Many thanks for your lovely letter from the beginning of December. I received (along with a mass of newspapers) a very enjoyable letter from An, for which I also say thank you — and the telegram of December 11,

---

347 Jeannette Geertruida Bundten (1840–1909): secretary of the women's committee of the board of the Kindervoeding.

348 J.H.A.A. Kalff (1846–1910): banker and chairman of the L.N.V.; married to Ellegonda Duranda Rutgers van der Loeff (1850–1935).

which arrived in Pincher Creek when I had just left there. Wonderful, isn't it, to receive such a quick message? I hope that the telegrams of Mr. Hosmer have satisfied you. I can understand that you wish to know exactly where and how we are as you read about all of the touring and travelling. I have heard nothing yet about the chest. It is a lovely thought that there are Dutch books and sweets on the way; unwrapping them will be a great pleasure, but it shall definitely take a long time. First, I will go through the mountains for a couple days and then when I come back, I may perhaps go to Vancouver.

I received my letter of introduction.

The people in Calgary are not yet so dear to me that I have a yearning to stay here for a long time, and so long as Karel's future is as yet undecided, it seems to me that it would be good to get to know as many places and situations as possible. Now I am helping here with decorating the church. I am keeping myself very busy and it is a good opportunity to get to know people. There is little enthusiasm for this work. Yesterday, the fat (à la Marianne Wolterbeek[349]) wife of the colonel of the police took the lead and asked me to take care of the pulpit. "Just go ahead." Most came only in the evenings to flirt with it and pleaded with me to come tomorrow evening; then, there will be a kind of general reunion. If it is not too windy, I might as well go.

It is quite amusing to get an impression of the 'man's world' here. It is quite strange that I am considered to be a citizen right away, while I, myself, feel completely like a traveller, observing the people and the things as if it were a comedy that played only for me. This creates a good opportunity for me to make judgments. Most of the people have been here only for a short time. (The city is only seven years old.) But it is funny how eminent the first citizens consider themselves.

Today, I walked home with a young lady [Kathleen Wilkins] whom I was really drawn to. She looks like Anna Janssen-Rehbock,[350] and three months ago was married to an English gentleman, Mr. Wilkins. He is the administrative assistant of the post office and has a small ranch. [He] must travel three days every week with the rail service and is now away for ten days. She is very alone in her little house, where she does all the work herself, and feels very lonely. She comes from Ottawa and had never cooked before she came here. She is full of admiration for her husband: His musical talent. How he reads aloud. His England. Everything! The ladies that have already been here a little longer, and who always do the work for a large family, are in no hurry to give her any help with her difficulties and only tell her about their acts of domestic heroism. She lives nearby. I shall most likely see her once again.

---

349 Marianne Antoinette Wolterbeek (1838–1898): owner of Villa Maris in Zandvoort, a pension for poor Amsterdam women and children.

350 Susanna Dorothea Anna Rehbock (1862–1933): married to Christian Wilhelm Janssen (1860–1927), director of the Senembah [Tobacco] Company, plantations and trading.

[35] Kathleen Hollingsworth Wilkins, c. 1920

[36] Ernest Drummond Hay Wilkins, c. 1920

I enjoy being busy. The doctor came to see Mrs. Lougheed's maid and said that her ankle was bruised and torn. [He] praised my bandage and put a plaster cast over it. She may try to walk tomorrow. Today I helped with the housework, sweeping carpets, dusting, making beds. I saw that the kneaded bread was shoved into the oven!

December 23: Yesterday evening: Christmas shopping with Mr. and Mrs. Lougheed in a thick, soft snowfall. It is very pleasant to be part of the Christmas bustle, and the children believe very much about 'Santa Claus' in the chimney. Here, he rides in a sled with six [sic] reindeer, is a little man and lives in a hut in the mountains where he makes toys.

The Hudson's Bay Company, one of the stores, had a lovely collection of books, Christmas magazines, all the small books by Nesbit[351] and so forth. Enjoyable to browse around, but everything is horribly expensive. I bought a book for each of the [Lougheed] boys. Clarence, six years, can already read, but there are no children's books in the house. The children are left completely to themselves, traipsing throughout the entire house, and when they hurt themselves or break something, they get harshly scolded or receive a 'whipping'.

Yesterday, Clarence left at 2:00 p.m. and came home at 6:00 p.m., completely numb and exhausted from a toothache that was left unnoticed.

---

351   Edith Nesbit (1858–1924): English author and poet.

In the evening, when we came home, he was already in bed crying, still wearing his clothes and all. A lot of muttering and a couple of slaps followed — undressed and back in bed, again, under increasing screams of the patient, who seemed to be busy working himself into a nervous fit. Lights out and Mrs. went downstairs to the furnace that did not want to burn, the consequence of which was that the house was cold. In the meantime, the boy yelled. The longer. The louder. Mrs. had once told me that [Clarence] was very nervous and the doctor had warned about not getting him wound up. I went to him and turned on the light; the child appeared fiery red from yelling and screamed, "Go away, go away." A few softly spoken words and a glass of water quickly got him to calm down, and when Mother came upstairs, he was quietly sleeping on his side.

[37] Isabella (Belle) Lougheed and son Clarence

Mrs. [Lougheed] is a bit mixed-blood and putters about in the kitchen and thinks as little as possible. She is very happy with her beautiful house but neither she nor her husband, a common parvenu, feel at home there. It is funny to see his face when he wants to read the paper in the drawing room and does not dare to sit down on one of the light silk uncomfortable chairs and, finally, carefully sits down on a corner of a chair in the middle of the room under an electric lamp. After every sentence, he hesitantly says, "Miss . . . Boissevain" because the name is so difficult. Also, after every sentence to his children, "Hey, son." That gives me the impression of one our servants saying [the formal *you*] to the children. He has never been on the coast and thought that Italy and the Netherlands bordered each other.

With many greetings to everyone, your Helena.

A28335001515-16 [Heleen to Mother, no date, fragment]

I know all her girlie tribulations by heart, her complete course of life, that of her brothers, sisters, mother, etc., etc., all of her comments about everyone in Calgary, and now I cannot possibly hear it anymore. My thoughts are somewhere else, and I must also be an unpleasant guest for her.

Mr. [Lougheed] is afraid of me and I am not inclined to make him comfortable because his casual manner with other ladies is, to me, indescribably childish. On top of that, he is churlish to his wife and has had no conversation with her other than when he hosted many New Year's visits.

The visits really were quite amusing and made me think about the coffee time of the office workers at the Herengracht. They came in parties of three to six, at the same time showing off while sitting on the light chairs of the drawing room, and then they were led to the dining room for whiskey or coffee.

Would you please thank Mr. Quack very much for his *Socialisten*, also Papa and Li for their letters?

In a hurry, with sincerest love, your Helena

KLAB09193000020 [Father to Karel]
Amsterdam, December 22, 1891

Dear Karel,

A few days ago, I received a letter from the Minister of the Navy with the service cross and diploma for you regarding Atjeh. I put them into the safe after having pleased Wil, as well as the family, by showing them. I thanked the minister in your name. It is a nice souvenir of your active service. Would you like me to pack them into the next crate and send them to you?

A less pleasant surprise from The Hague was the voting down of the request to the Minister of Transport, Trade and Industry[352] for ƒ12,000 per year for the ice-clearing. The request (that was contested by the Commission of Reporters of the Parliament, and by van Gijn[353] from Dordrecht, and by Conrad,[354] the former Inspector of Waterworks) was strongly defended by Minister Lely [as well as by the parliamentarians] Rutgers,[355] Perk[356] and others. It still fell, however, with a vote of fifty-five against forty-four. After the release of the unfavourable report, I had only two days' time and moved heaven and earth in those two days. I wrote and telegraphed all the members of the Parliament that I knew and

---

352   Dr. Cornelis Lely (1854–1929): engineer, Minister of Transport, Trade and Industry (1891–1894); married to Gerarda Jacoba (Mies) van Rinsum (1862–1914).

353   Simon Marius Hugo (Hugo) van Gijn (1848–1937): lumber merchant, member of Parliament, philanthropist; married to Johanna Heilina Roodenburg (1849–1925).

354   Jan Frederik Willem Conrad (1825–1902): engineer, member of Parliament; Chief Inspector of Public Works; married to Sara Antonia van Kerkwijk (1825–1889).

355   Jhr. J.W.H. Rutgers van Rozenburg (1830–1902): lawyer, member of Parliament; married to Hilletje Tinholt (1829–1878).

356   Cornelis Egbertus Perk (1843–1893): Mayor of Anna Paulowna, member of Parliament; married to Jkvr. Detje Cecilia Agatha Strick van Lindschoten (1868–1893).

encouraged my fellow members [of the Provincial Council] to do the same. I conferred with Secretary Dirksen,[357] who was, in The Hague, in cons-tant contact with the minister, with Rutgers, etc.; however, to no avail.

Now the commission claims that a separate proposal, a sort of legislative proposal, should have been made. However, during the budgeting, they certainly put forward all sorts of doubts about the success and objections to the money that it would cost. Therefore, I fear that the minister will not willingly expose himself to a second failure. Tomorrow, I will go to him and I shall hear whether there is still any chance. If it ever comes to fruition, you will have to admit that I have shown that my patience is as tough as molasses. It was entertaining to see how infuriated everyone was with Conrad. I wrote him a letter in which I told him that I found him too respectable a man to be satisfied with a negative triumph and asked of him if it was possible to tell me what has to be done now. You should also be aware that I have already dealt with him about the whole matter (from the first use of an icebreaker on) and that I have never had any indication that he would not support our way of working. I do not as yet have an answer.

Jan Kruseman has arrived in Genoa on the SS *Prins van Oranje* and says that he has completely recuperated and hopes to face life again with full courage. On the SS *Koningin Emma*, which [also] passed through at that time, only one hypochondriacal passenger for Holland remained on board, so Jan will stay a few days in Genoa and will come home overland.

Tonight we shall talk to Insinger,[358] and I hope to get some insight from him about the pros and cons of his business. I have not yet met him, since we were not home when he came to our door.

Our neighbour [from Vogelenzang], Mr. Willink van Bennebroek,[359] has passed away at the age of forty-seven. I believe that consequently, his family (that played a huge role in the history of Amsterdam trade) has died out.

We had a few pleasant days with Wallis, who had come over for a conference with Ruys and us about the Holt matter and who returned with the SS *Prins Hendrik*. It shall surprise me if we find an agreement with Holt. He is difficult to read and must, perhaps, still lose some more money before he comes to his senses.

Yesterday, a pleasant telegram arrived from Daniel Adolf [Boissevain][360] out of London (young Adolf because Senior is in America), who let us know

357 Jan Cornelis Dirksen (1858–1913): engineer; secretary of the Society for General Shipping Interests; married in 1892 to Jacoba (Coba) Hermina van Eeghen (1868–1945).

358 Frederik Robbert Insinger (1862–1946) was born in Amsterdam. He ranched twenty-two kilometres west of Yorkton, Saskatchewan, and is for whom Insinger, Saskatchewan, is named. He was elected in 1892 as a member of the North-West Legislative Assembly, representing the riding of Wallace, 1892–1894, and from 1894 to 1897 the riding of Yorkton. He later became a banker in Spokane, Washington, USA, and was married to Julia Nettleton (1868–1944).

359 David Arnoud Willink, Heer van Bennebroek (1844–1891): lawyer; married to Frédérique Leonie Marie Olga Elise Schuijt, Vrouwe van Bennebroek (1843–1872).

360 Daniel (Do) Adolphe Boissevain (1866–1916): banker; (son of Count Adolphe); married to Anna Slotthoff Magee (1866–1894) and later to Countess Madeleine Antoinette Valerie Marie Ghislaine van Renesse (1862–1923).

that Hosmer has also telegraphed it to both of you, to Helena in Calgary and to you in Pincher Creek.

It is beginning to freeze a bit here, therefore, Nella and Mia have already been skating. Our chartered Rotterdam ship, *De Ijsploeg*,[361] owned by the shipping company Blauwe Ster, has not yet had to do any work.

Enclosed are a few photos of Amsterdam that you can show to your Canadian friends in case they want to know what your hometown looks like.

Many greetings, from your loving Father.

A32074000165-67 [Heleen to Wil]
Calgary, December 25, 1891

Dear Wil,

Many thanks for your letter dated November 15. It took a bit long coming because it first went to Karel and then was sent again by him to Calgary.

Karel also got a letter from Jo from Stockholm, as always, brave and positive. It is most admirable to remain so cheerful with all those ailments and pain. I have sent an answer to her in Stockholm, but could you also give me her address in Russia?

Things are going the same with me as with you. The days are flying by; I have no time for my correspondence, but it seems like a very, very long time since I left Holland.

The people in Calgary do not appeal to me as much as those in Pincher Creek. They would rather behave as if they were 'city folks', but they don't know how and lack the natural ease of the ranchers. They fret about the work that they have to do themselves and when they do have a maid, they do not know how to direct her work. They all are completely focused on keeping house. Wil, if you ever come here to live, make sure that you can cook and bake bread and iron (!), and to work in such a way that, from time to time, fifteen minutes is left for reading. I do not yet know whether I will do my own housekeeping anywhere and look ahead with some concern about my own cooked meals, and think that, then, not much will come of writing letters. Anyway, it will sort itself out at the time.

It is a funny contrast between Mrs. White Fraser and Mrs. Lougheed. The one who made a teensy-weensy house cozy by the simplest means, and even gave it refinement, and the other who, with all her pomp, keeps her house uninhabitable, like a furniture exhibition. Mr. Lougheed is, for me, a particularly childish sort of creature. He is a lawyer, but by no means smart. Absolutely no upbringing or manners, bossy with his wife and is terribly taken with himself. There is an inkwell in the house that was given to me since it has never been used. He pretends to study the law in the evening, but I saw his book, *Anecdotes*, which instructs him on how one could make a lot of money as a lawyer with little effort! The other books in his rooms are Scottish and Irish anecdotes and jokes!

---

361 *De Ijsploeg* is a screw steamer used as an icebreaker, owned by the shipping company De Blauwe Ster, Rotterdam.

December 26: The mail has come and with it, your letter of December 8. Lovely, in time for Boxing Day, all my birthday letters. I hope that Karel's *Citations*, by Prudhomme, did not make you sad. He is now much pluckier than when he wrote it.

I can understand that Dr. Delbet (with his well-intentioned advice) had terribly frustrated you and I am very glad that the portrait converted him. How all those questions took on another aspect when they were brought so close to you.

Autrefois ces questions in ma raison s'enfonce	Once these questions sink into my mind,
Ne semblait pas m'atteindre assez pour m'offenser;	Didn't seem to reach me enough to offend me
J'interrogeais de loin, sans craindre la réponse,	I questioned from afar, not fearing the answer
Maintenant je tiens plus à savoir qu'à penser![362]	Now I want to know more than to think!

So much of real life, you will now understand more, and it will be difficult for you not to be able to go to Karel with all your difficulties, but if it will help you, then do write down your thoughts. I would very much like to talk to you often, but perhaps I can sometimes help you by letter.

I remain very well informed about how Karel is faring. Often with pencil, but he always finds the opportunity to send me a sign of life. They are now higher in the mountains, where the rivers are not so deep, and they can walk through it without shoes and socks — sometimes three times a day!

I have received so many lovely letters. I follow all of what is happening in Holland and that fills my thoughts with so much that there is little time remaining to feel lonely.

Bye, darling, with a warm kiss, your Heleen.

A29648000019-20 [Heleen to Thijs]
Calgary, December 27, 1891

Dear Thijs,

Your letter of December 7, with your kind birthday wishes, arrived here on Boxing Day! That was lovely. I also got a mass of other letters, among which was a most enjoyable and very friendly letter from Count Adolphe, and that gave me a lot of pleasure.

But now, I am reading your letter and therefore I wanted to thank you very much. It is quite nice, after all, to be missed a little bit, but you should not think that I did not appreciate my happy home or consider myself excess baggage, in particular. It was more the contrast between our own warm, rich happiness and all that struggle and misery outside,

---

362 This is a partial excerpt from Prudhomme's *Les vaines tendresses*, 1875. Heleen started with her own words "*Autrefois ces questions in ma raison s'enfonce*" but the original first line of the third stanza in Chapter 4 is "*Naguère ce problème où mon doute s'enfonce.*"

and my inability to contribute to the 'change for the better', that sent me away.

I find Tideman[363] tiresome with his turn-of-phrase exercises. Is he really thinking that he will become a literary talent? I thought that "Swijght Utrecht"[364] was very good and amusing, but I do not see many promising new colleagues as yet, whom you shall soon need.

I am sorry that Gijs [van Tienhoven] fails to appreciate Frederik van Eeden. Whatever van Eeden may be, he is certainly never narrow-minded.

How is it with *De Nieuwe Gids*?[365] Send them also on a little journey to me. I would love to read something by Kloos[366] once again.

But now for something out of another 'tap of beer'. Eh, eh, Missy? I have heard that you have started once again with your old habit of sending secret parcels to young girls. Phooey — and then, to turn the heads of four quite young ladies at the same time with such unexpected visits! It is going too far.

Do you know the address of Lilly Bicker?[367] If I return via New York, perhaps I will see her at Niagara.

When I experience something exciting again, I shall write something more about myself. These last days, I have done nothing other than read letters and newspapers. Conversation is not possible with my hosts. 'Madam' (mixed-blood in eighth degree) has no other thoughts than that it is difficult to have maids, and those of Mr. Lougheed I would rather not know. Tomorrow, I will have dinner at [Kathleen] Wilkins', in order to get acquainted with her husband.

Much love also from Karel, for whom you did a lot of good with your letter about Uncle Toon. Your sincerely loving sister, Heleen.

A32074000168-69 [Heleen to Wil]
Calgary, December 30, 1891

Dear Wil,

I am sorry that I did not mention your birthday in my last letter, but Karel has written to you and that is still the most important thing. Perhaps on January 14, Karel and I will be together again and, in our thoughts, will go to the Keizersgracht.

363 Peter (Pet) Tideman (1871–1943): Amsterdam author, lawyer, fellow student of Thijs; married to Anna Elizabeth Eman (1874–1942). At this time, Tideman was the editor of *Propria Cures*.

364 "Swijght Utrecht" is the name of a satirical piece in *Propria Cures*, probably referring to a tower that was part of the old city wall of Amsterdam and that was taken down around 1882. It was located at the corner of Nieuwe Doelenstraat en Kloveniersburgwal.

365 *De Nieuwe Gids*: Dutch illustrated literary periodical published 1885–1943.

366 Willem Kloos (1859–1938): poet; married to Jeanne Henriette Reine Reyneke van Stuwe (1874–1951), author.

367 Jkvr. Daniëlle Augusta Bicker (1871–1915): married in 1899 with Joan Marie Dutilh (1860–1941), medical doctor.

When you look back over the last year (that quite eventful year that gave you such great happiness and so much disappointment), it shall still be with thankfulness and faith that the happiness shall remain and grow, notwithstanding parting and sadness. I heartily hope, dear Wil, that it will be so, that you will look back on many happy birthdays without regret and will be able to say from the bottom of your heart that "God knew the best."

About me, there is now little to tell. The days pass quickly; I count them as 'mail days' and 'non-mail days' and of the latter, no memory remains. Yesterday, I ate at Mrs. Wilkins', twenty-four years old and married for two months. She was engaged for two years without seeing him and knew him for only three months before that. It is an amusing little 'doll household'. She still finds it very difficult to cook and he is not yet very handy in table service. But they have fun with all their little mistakes and are hospitable, as very few are. All of a sudden, the electric light did not want to shine. Lucky enough, there was still a petroleum lamp that was lit. But soon, it appeared that the oil had run out. "That is nothing," said Mrs. Wilkins, "I have a tall candle that will, for sure, last the whole evening." She went and came back roaring with laughter with an almost invisible end of a red candle in a pretty candle holder. In the meantime, [Mr. Wilkins] had found a can of petroleum and diligently went to fill the lamp. The little house is even smaller than that of Mrs. White Fraser in Pincher Creek and it does not have a double door. One steps right away into the salon. There were also two other guests, a good-natured old bachelor and a young doctor who loved music very much and held the lamp on his knee in order to have light near the piano. It remains cold here — the thermometer remains under zero Fahrenheit — but in the house, it is now cozy and warm.

With a warm kiss, your Heleen.

A32005000408-41 [Father to Karel and Heleen]
Amsterdam, January 1, 1892

Dear children,

The telegraph has served us well with the changing of the year, by sending over the ocean a thought, an expression of love and trust. Our telegram, composed along with [Coo] den Tex on Christmas Day, worked well, and yours from 'Hel Ka' arrived on December 30 and was translated by me as follows:

    Diminuo: Happy New Year to all
    Robora: Telegram received
    Salignus: Accept our best thanks

Corinthians II 5
> v. 6: Therefore we are always confident, knowing that, whilst we are at home in the body, we are absent from the Lord.

3rd Epistle of John
> v. 2: Beloved, I wish above all things that thou mayest prosper and be in health, even as thy soul prospereth.
> v. 14: Peace be to thee. Our friends salute thee. Greet the friends by name.

This translation was circulated among friends. Mama and I had also a separate discussion about the possibility that 13:4, following Corinthians II, 5:6, also had a special meaning; however, we kept it to ourselves. However it may be, with this telegram, you have given us a lot of pleasure and have made the changing of the years more relaxed.

We all went to church. I joined the congregation at the Remonstrantse Kerk, where Rev. de Vries[368] gave a beautiful, poetic sermon about commonplace things. It was striking, the impression that he gave me, by how he touched upon the lack of depth and conviction of the tragic seriousness of life. He said very lovely things about "the smile" and "the tear"; that one still must spare a smile for the lucky, even though a tear flows for oneself, etc., but *la grande voie de l'Evangile* was barely heard.

Aunt Hes was also in the church and I walked with her for a short while. She had good news from [her son] Kees. She had Karel and Paul[369] over and was very cheerful. We made an evening visit to Mama Brugmans, where Uncle Sebald was also present. The atmosphere was very good there. Later, at home, we had a joyful evening with a game of cards and a few oysters.

Today, there was a tremendous amount of rain. I stayed home this morning and was visited by the young ones. This afternoon, I went to the office for a little while, then to the sisters', and then visited Aunt Henriette Boissevain. Our family dinner was also very enjoyable. Wil came right away after the coffee and we had a very pleasant half-hour with her. I think that she is looking well, but her mother is very heedful of her and seems to think that she is somewhat despondent.

Uncle Jacob Pieter [Ko Boissevain] has become an associate with the firm Reiss & Co., where he has already worked for years. I am very happy for him, since it is in all respects a promotion for him and makes his position much more solid. He also really earned it, because he always works very hard and with much competence in the interests of the firm.

Tomorrow, I have to go to the Ministry of Foreign Affairs in The Hague for a conference about the quarantines.

Did I already tell you that I had written an album page [in the friendship book] for Mrs. Tienhoven? I gave an account of a 'soirée' at

---

368 Willem Marie de Vries (1840–1900): minister; married to Engelina Schröder (1837–1919).
369 Karel den Tex (1868–1930) and Paul den Tex (1871–1958): also sons of Aunt Hester.

which one does not get bored (namely, a reception of the mayor), and which had these lines [from "Op een vervelend Soirée"] by de Génestet as a motto:

Wie, Jonkers! zal ons met een lied van Hooft verrassen?
Wie, Dames, wie van u zou Tessels muiltje passen?

Everything was interwoven with remembrances of Antoinette Fruin,[370] Cateau den Tex, Philips,[371] Toon Brugmans, etc.

Just before the end of the year, I received a very peaceful letter from [Alfred Holt]. I had written to Crompton,[372] the manager, with a kind of ultimatum; however, I had told him that I would like to hear a personal opinion from [Holt], because I found that his general insights quite agreed with my own. Now the opinion has come and it is of such a kind that I believe that an arrangement can be made, maintaining mutual independence.

To me, Matthijs seems to have a lot of fun in his life and, I think, is popular with the young folks. Also, we often have pleasant, lively conversations here, at or after dinner. I have encouraged him to work every morning at least for two hours, from 10:00 a.m. to noon. That appears to be little, but it will advance him enormously while it disciplines his mind.

Our SS *Voorwaarts* will soon sail from Batavia via the Cape [of Good Hope] to Holland. She must call at Liberia to disembark the negroes[373] who were sent back to their land again.

Today, Uncle Karel conveyed to us all sorts of news about Alfred and Robert.[374] Alfred almost never writes, but Robert is beginning (as well in style as in content) to become a good correspondent. They are still cruising in the West Indies and have visited a number of the islands where Karel has also been.

These days I am reading:

1. *Le courrier de Chine*, an amusing description of life on board a French mail ship by the doctor of that company.
2. The first report of General Book, *In Darkest London*, by my friend James Bain,[375] speedily mailed to me. It is full of interesting

---

370 Elizabeth Anna (Antoinette) Fruin (1821–1891): married to Quirinis Johannes Goddard (1816–1906); medical doctor.

371 August Philips (1823–1891): lawyer, politician; married to Madelon Sophia Elisabeth Vermeulen (1825–1904).

372 Albert Crompton (1843–1908): manager of the Ocean Steam Ship Company from 1882–1901; married to Elinor Elizabeth Aikin (1849–1885).

373 This refers to African soldiers that served in the Dutch East Indies for the Dutch government.

374 Alfred Gideon Boissevain (1870–1922) and Robert Walrave Boissevain (1872–1938): sons of Charles (Karel) and Emily Boissevain.

375 James Bain (booksellers), 1 Haymarket, London SW, England.

particulars, but my overall impression about the realization of the plan is still a big '?'.
3. *Three Months with the Factory Workers*[376]: the personal experiences of a candidate in theology who lived among them. Full of important facts but in an impossible, overly sentimental style.

So, now and then you will receive an *Amsterdammer* from me, if I purchase one on Sundays. If that interests you, then I can certainly get a subscription.

This evening, we played whist with Wallie and Nel, who both have quite the *esprit de jeu* and were really jolly.

Today I was immersed in the catalogue of Uncle Toon's library, which is bequeathed to the city. There are interesting works about old law and about Amsterdam seals and topography; however, for all practical purposes, I find it very prudent that he bequested it to the state, because I would not know which of the beneficiaries would have had room enough to store it. Matthijs can choose from it, up to a value of ƒ100, however he has not yet made a specific selection.

I still have some hope that the [discussion about the] ice-clearing business is not closed forever. The minister is now preparing for a separate proposal and the city council will soon debate a plan whereby the City will commit to their contribution, if the state also commits to it. I corresponded with Conrad about the matter, but his answer did not amount to much. He evidently did not have the courage to defend an unpopular recommendation to the new members [of his own party].

Where is Dr. Black? We would have had a party to honour him in Amsterdam! *Enfin*, that might still come about.

Now dear children, keep well, and may the next Sylvester evening give us thankfulness about the new life that will smile upon Karel after the crown of suffering, worries and hardships.

Your loving Father.

A32005000412–417 [Karel to Heleen]
In camp, a couple of miles from Crowsnest Lake, January 2, 1892

Dearest, good, sweet Leentjesteentje,

Welcome to 1892! May it be a happy new year for you.
Contrary to my previous message, I hereby request that you not count on seeing me in the country before February. The work goes unbelievably slowly, 0.75 miles per day, continuously breaking trails through thick undergrowth of green and grey willow and heavy fir woods. Since December 22, the winter snow has set like a solid whole with a thick underlayer,

---

376 Paul Göhre, *Drei Monate Fabrikarbeiter und Handwerksbursche: Eine praktische Studie* (Leipzig: Grunow Verlag, 1891).

except upon a few hilltops which are still being blown clear; for now, the snow will not yield anymore until mid-April.

My luggage, as you know, once having been split among Montreal, Calgary and Macleod, now lies in parts between two boulders, about two miles from here. There is no way that two normally loaded wagons with two horses could follow the trail. The snow is way too high for that. Moving, therefore, has its own drawbacks. Two days ago, a double team with a wagon was sent ahead with stuff that was not required every day, including my suitcase. The wagon was unloaded somewhere (at an 'easy-to-find' place) and came back afterwards.

On New Year's Day, we moved our camp to 'The Lake', nine miles away, with one wagon, pretty full with a double team, and a wagon with the two weakest horses, lightly loaded. Even the pony had to pull a loaded buckboard this time. The remaining stuff was left behind, among which was the cook's tent and a collection of utensils. One hill was so steep that we, after removing two or three feet of deep snow with shovels (a lot of work), hitched up the three teams to the wagons and then we went, thrashing and heaving, the harder the better, until all of [the animals] and the two-legged ones (not without gasping for air) arrived on the top of the hill.

At four o'clock, we had made about six miles and set up our camp in the woods. The cook managed for the time being with a small, useless tent, and we ate our lunch standing. Today it snowed dreadfully, and in the afternoon a harsh wind came up so that it chased the loose snow across the prairie with an unbelievable speed. We mostly worked in the woods and were somewhat sheltered, but the walk toward home took us an hour on the flat prairie. A foot of snow on the ground becomes drifting snow! How welcome the camp then becomes, with a blazing fire and bowl of lovely fresh water and a warm supper. We lived on bacon and beans for a few days. Now, [we have] again meat, potatoes, and dried apples for pie, and butter, so we happily tuck in.

It is a mystery to me that this snow was not anticipated and that there was nothing arranged for sleds, snowshoes, etc. Besides all the discomfort, even the chance of being snowed in is not to be scoffed at; that would have been the decisive factor in being prepared.

Today the remaining stuff was collected with the double teams. Tomorrow is Sunday, I think. The cook's tent will be erected. Monday, our baggage will be picked up from the rocks and perhaps on Tuesday, in a similar way, we will move toward the lake. If it is frozen solid, then we can cross it. Otherwise, it will be a long way by the trail, and we will have to make sleds and go through it without teams; in other words, you pick up your bedding and walk. Finally, there are still very interesting experiences for me to come.

One section of the line will be 'located'. That is the future track, a section that has been definitively laid out and then marked with the poles, and so forth. That is the shrewdness of the CPR; it gives a kind of certainty to the work. A line that is 'partly located' exists already (in a manner of speaking 'is born', a *fait accompli*), while a 'preliminary survey' binds no one and then also no one is held back. I get a great deal of pleasure from learning this type of work, even though it takes yet more time.

There are rumours circling that this outfit will not be disbanded at the end of this job. It looks like there is something south of Macleod to be surveyed. I suspect, however, that in Macleod I will ask for my dismissal as a stake-marker in relation to Van Horne's answer to my letter (which I will have received by then). It will be just the same work as here, but somewhat more uncomfortable and considerably less enjoyable because it is open prairie where they shall be working.

On Boxing Day, I received your letter from Macleod, the only mail in ten days that was delivered for the whole outfit. Our letters seem to get stuck somewhere. I see that you did not get my telegram-letter in Macleod, but Hosmer will have noticed that from your own telegram.

What do you say about the enclosed 'literary work of art' cut out of the *Winnipeg* [*Free Press*]? The writer had evidently never been to Van Horne's home and twaddled on, nineteen to the dozen.

My ink is done! And I can not get another one here. Therefore, perhaps you will get no more than pencil-scratches in the meantime. By the way, our outgoing mail will soon be scarce and far between.

Keep strong, dear girl. Greet everyone at home, heartily. Always your very loving, Karel

P.S. Now that I have reread it, I find the piece about Van Horne not so silly, after all. You do read the Canadian newspapers, of course, if you can get a hold of them? Hosmer will certainly ask your opinion of the northwest country, and about British Columbia. Make sure that you are informed about it. For three weeks we had no mail and I will be going on horseback to [Pincher Creek] to pick up the mail, forty miles through the snow. How will I pull this off?

January 4, 1892: I have just managed to get some watered-down ink on the promise that I will bring back a bottle of good ink from [Pincher Creek].

Hey Leentje, do you have a good idea about English measures and weights? So, see here some numbers that will be handy for you in the appreciation of the communications from your precise friends.

```
1 inch = 2.5 cm
1 foot = 3 dm
1 metre = 3'3" (3 feet, 3 inches)
1 yard = 3 feet = 9 dm
1 mile = 5280 feet = 1584 metres
1 lb. = 0.5 kilos
1 litre = 0.2 gallons = 0.9 quarts
1 square mile = 259 hectares
1 hectare is a little more than 2 acres, hence 9 hectares = 22 acres
1 bushel = 35 litres
```

Do you think that I am pedantic? Good night, child. I will collect the mail and make preparations for my two-day trip. Ta Ta. Your Karel.

January 6: Pincher Creek, in the small salon with the old English naval officer (what is his name again Jacob — *Nelson*? [Augustus Jacob]) and my ex-comrade, Taylor, by the fire reading their mail. My expectation of a lovely evening, reading a bunch of letters and answering them, was clearly disappointed. Not a snip of mail for the whole camp!

From you, I received the German magazine with the translation of the Saloniki article. The address is postmarked "Calgary, December 30," and there you have celebrated New Year's and most likely your birthday, also in Calgary? In short, no news is good news and, the next time, I will for sure find a letter here from you.

I had a very pleasant journey on the way here. Beautiful weather with a stiff west wind at my back (that I hope will subside tonight and stay away). Up at 5:30 a.m. and before 7:00 a.m. on the way, first to the Gap, which you had also marked on the map that you made for me. At the Gap, the sun had just come up and it was a glitter of gold, more and more intense the closer it came, and where the clouds were, they became all pink and purple and gold. Oh, Leentje, it was so beautiful. My portrayal gives only a vague reflection of it!

At 9:00 a.m., I arrived at the Gap, where the Sulphur Springs are, as well as a hotel under construction and an annex building of 'Old Man Lee's'.[377] Cinched the saddle tighter and shored up the luggage. Letters for us? No! Oh, what a beautiful trail to do on horseback, with nothing to do but to look around and to appreciate it. At quarter to twelve, I arrived at Old Man Lee's; [he] is married to a Native woman and has six or seven children. A substantial homestead. He was busy building a sled, but stopped working in order to keep me company. The horse was well cared for. Twenty miles behind me! There, I found a mailed newspaper from December 4 (the letters were no more recent than November 17) and a *Java-Bode* with a positive and approving critique of the Saloniki article. More than that, very flattering about my piece. A nice warm lunch and, at 1:15 p.m., on my way again. A one-and-a-half-hour layover is unpermittably long, but the lunch was not ready sooner.

Along a fairly good, clean, thickly snow-covered trail through a treed area, à la 'de Vogelenzang', along the homestead of Mrs. Mills,[378] and from Eddy's[379] toward the Garnetts'. Mrs. Garnett paced like a polar bear on the veranda, again just as muffled up as the *femme de chambre* of *Bleak House*. I stayed on my horse. "Letters for us?" No. But folks had appreciated your cards.

377   William Samuel Lee (c.1835–1896): a pioneer; was married in 1871 to Gutosi k ake (Rosa Good-Striker Bullhead) (1857–1945) of the Kainai Nation. They lived at Rock Creek, north of Burmis. After he died of pneumonia, despite Dr. Mead's interventions, Lee's son-in-law, Jack Willoughby, brought his body to Pincher Creek, where he was buried.

378   This is the homestead of ranchers George Ashby Mills (1853–1929) and Caroline Emily Mills (1846–1943), near Cowley, Alberta.

379   Wallace Thurston Eddy (1862–1956): rancher in the Cowley region; married to Emma Clark (1866–1950).

A28335001533-34 [Fragment of letter]

Quarter to two, I think. Still fifteen miles! Hurry up, Mister!
  "What is the way to Pincher Creek?" I ask Garnett.
  "Well, well! Don't you know it?"
  "No, fool. Otherwise, I wouldn't have asked."
  "Well, Pincher lies in that direction." With a vague wave of his arm. "There is the moon. It is right in the direction of the moon."
  "I suppose there must be a well-beaten trail leading up there?"
  "Well, there are too many trails. Go as I tell you. You can cross the river nearly everywhere!"
  What a guy, eh? So, I quickly found a beautiful trail that, indeed, went straight toward the moon and crossed over the river, where sand was thrown like a complete road over the ice. Took that one, not knowing if my horse would have dared to cross the river somewhere else, and arrived here at 4:00 p.m., two hours earlier than I had expected when I rode out this morning. No snow at all on the last stretch. The pony proved to be tougher than tough. I practised a lesson that I received from the piqueur of the Hollandsche Manege,[380] namely that in order to save the horse on long rides, as soon as it starts to prance or rear, only then do you use your reins.
  The mail had just arrived here and the store was full of folks waiting for it to be distributed. I did my shopping, reserved a room, saw [Mrs.] White Fraser for a moment (she was unwell), and went to the post office. Letters? No, Leen!
  It is still quite disappointing to make such a journey in vain, and unpleasant to have the prospect of being the source of disappointment for the others. At 'the Old Man Lee' I also got a telegram of December 26, saying: [Ends here]

---

380   The Hollandsche Manege in Amsterdam is the oldest riding school in the Netherlands, dating back to 1744. The present building was constructed in 1882.

Chapter 8

Our Plan in Disarray!

The new year has, in fact, not brought any resolution to the uncertainty of Karel's stay with the survey crew, whose work contract has just been extended through April. Long-distance correspondence is beginning to lose its charms, and for Heleen, Karel feels further from her reach than her family and Wil in Amsterdam. With no news from Van Horne, Karel settles in for the long haul and Heleen begins to form a friendship with Kathleen Wilkins in Calgary.

```
A29670000042-47 [Heleen to Li]
[Toward the Hector station between Lake Louise and Field, B.C.] January 5, 1892
```

Dear Li,

Again, just like the last time, I'm in Mr. Niblock's [train] carriage, but now with company. Mrs. Lougheed and her friend decided at the last minute not to come along after all, but the sister of the girlfriend[381] [Mary Louise Wardlow], a sort of Lou Biben,[382] did go along. The beginning was just as crazy as the continuous procrastination. The carriage was to be attached at night to the freight train, and at about 10:00 p.m., we went down [to the station] and into the couchettes. Both of us, healthy, slept the sleep of the righteous, but as we awoke, our astonishment was unparalleled. We were still in Calgary. Due to delayed telegrams or some

---

381   Mary Louise Wardlow (1856–1927) is the sister of Elizabeth Trott (Wardlow).

382   Angelique Charlotte (Lou) Biben (1864–1936): married in 1894 in Smyrna, Turkey, to Christoff Da Ponte, a rug merchant.

other mistake, the train had left without us. We had to wait until the next evening; no use lamenting it, so I continued to write letters in the wagon and later on, my travel companion [Miss Wardlow] came to pick me up to go together to Mrs. Lougheed's, because I thought it was my duty to see her again and I also thought that she would give me something to eat. The reception was very good. She laughed about our adventure but did not invite us to eat, even though we told her that we had said to the young cook in the carriage that we would not be back until the evening. Also, the sister of my travel companion was at the Lougheeds' and had locked up her own house.

Enfin! At 6:00 p.m., on the go again and to the hotel, philosophizing about the irresponsibility of mixed-bloods. We waited in the salon of the hotel until the gentlemen guests were gone, dined well and then, in the evening, went back to the carriage. The next morning, we were still in Calgary, since the freight train arrived too late, but at 9:00 a.m. we departed with Mr. Niblock. I was glad that he came along, because since Mama's letter, I have had no peace at all with my travel plans and continuously expect a terrible accident. Say nothing about this to Mama if you think that she will find it unpleasant.

We went to Banff yesterday and, after all the remarkable things that were told to me about it, it did not disappoint. The photographs of Mr. [Jan] van Eeghen have given you folks an idea of it and I shall not dare to describe it. We had, and have, beautiful weather, cold but still, and a glorious sun in pure, clean air.

But for me, the glittering, snowy hulks were more frightening than beautiful. When we drew near the mountains, we went into the 'caboose' (the conductors' wagon with the lanterns) and climbed up to where, through the windows, we had a free and clear view toward the front over the whole train. It was quite a strange feeling to become absorbed into the mountains. The locomotive was far ahead and, in the snow, everything was so quiet. I did not sense the power that pulled us; it seemed that the power emanated from the mountains and we were irresistibly lured through the curving halls of a magic palace.

Calgary, January 7: Safely back without an accident!! Mr. Niblock found it blasphemous in the mountains to do anything other than to look out [the windows] and, so, I did not continue writing my letter. The first day we went to Banff, where we arrived at about 4:30 p.m. A sleigh with two fiery horses was waiting for us at the station and took us along abysses that made me dizzy. But slowly I became more familiar with all the mightiness, especially when evening fell and caused the mountainsides to broaden. A little bit later, I was completely bewitched away from the fear and worry (when a softly murmuring waterfall, magically lit by the half-moon, gave life to the silent grandeur) and wished to be all eyes and ears to absorb all of that beauty.

We also visited the hot sulphur springs and lakes, a big steaming bath, among others, in a deep grotto that we approached through a narrow passageway from the catacombs. Mr. Niblock strongly encouraged us to take a bath, but I did not let myself be persuaded. It was quite cold outside and the coming out of a warm bath into a sled driving home, I could not square with my Dutch notions of hygiene. We toured the CPR hotel, where two little old men with large grey beards and lanterns showed us the way. It was just like a fairy tale; indeed, it is a colossal hotel. This summer there were more than 600 guests.

We slept in the carriage (Mr. Niblock in another one, I believe) and the next day we went on to Dunmore, the end of Mr. Niblock's division. My first plan had been to return from Banff, but Mr. Niblock had to go to Dunmore and I felt safer so long as he was on the train; and, now that I was so far, I wanted to see more of the mountains to get over my fearful feelings. I believe that if Mama hears the circumstances, she will approve of my journey. I would never dare to admit to Mr. Van Horne that I was afraid to travel on his railway, and I would then have to explain to everyone in Montreal why I had not gone to Banff.

Therefore, we went further on, in the most beautiful weather you can imagine, but it still cost me a lot of effort in order to assuage my vague fears and to process all of the wonder that I saw. Again and again, the mountains took on the appearance of threatening shapes; then they looked like tents of an army of giants who were ready to crush their opponents on the other side of the ravine. "Excelsior"[383] also came into my thoughts again and again: "so cold and grey, lifeless and beautiful"; the plea of Sully Prudhomme about Truth seemed to be fulfilled, it is "*à vu la splendeur fût-elle meurtrière, dût-elle nous bruler les yeux.*"

Mr. Niblock was tireless in pointing out the highest peaks and curious places, and our reticence disappointed him. He told us of other ladies who he had accompanied through the mountains, among others, a "gushing" American woman who, out of pure enthusiasm, almost jumped out of the wagon. But Miss Wardlow was just like me, impressed, and could also find no words for the multitude of impressions.

Mr. Niblock is a good-hearted Methodist who told us his whole life history. How, as a youngster of eleven, he had run away and, since then, had worked and slaved a lot, such as a house servant on a ranch, a shoemaker, clerk, travelling salesman, switchman, conductor and, for the last eight years, superintendent for the CPR. [He spoke] of his repentance, curious redemption from multifarious sins; his deceased wife, who he had placed on a pedestal, and his plan to marry a very young girl; the education of his children; and so forth. Miss Wardlow turned out to be all right. She was a good partner in conversation and we had an enjoyable little time with the three of us. I enjoyed the sunsets and the night the most. The lamps were all lit for the dinner. Before that, and afterwards until a late hour, we sat in the dark rail carriage looking out at the yielding sun, or into the moon and starlit night. Especially during the return, which I enjoyed more and more; and even though I was lightened by the feeling of being back safely, I felt sorry for not having understood the proud, silent language of the mountains.

383   Probably taken from "Excelsior," by Longfellow.

Now, I am back, and have taken my room in the hotel. I have picked up my baggage from Mrs. Lougheed. She was very friendly, apparently not aware that she had been churlish; I was also benevolent, so that we parted cordially, in peace. I hope that I now have the opportunity to do something with my correspondence. Mountains of letters wait to be answered. On the train to Dunmore, I got the one from Aunt Gerarda. Please thank her very much for that. I wanted to congratulate Jo for her birthday, but now it is too late for that.

Underway, I received a precious letter from Mrs. Elton, the mother of the mentally ill girl that I had travelled with. She sent me an introduction for Victoria [B.C.] that I shall not use now, and gave me an open invitation to make her house my own, should I be in the area. Your own letter of December 13, I have not yet answered, and it was really so lovely and there were so many important things to be informed of: Evy's[384] marriage, the Cootjes, everyone's winter clothing and so forth. All the same questions from my new acquaintances are also beginning to irritate me: "How long will you be in Canada?" "Do you like the Northwest?" "How long in Calgary?" "What's next?" I would especially like to know the last one, in other words, "What a poor soul."

I hope that your visit to Jet [Versteeg][385] will cheer her up. I really feel for her. I hope that she will come through it and have a little easier life. For you, it would be a difficult task to have a few foster children so far away.

Ask Cor, sometime, how Cateau Tilanus likes being in Utrecht. From this letter, you could perhaps send some of it to Antoinette and Tol.

Much love to everyone at home, from your Heleen.

A32005000347-350 [Wil to Heleen]
Amsterdam, January 5, 1892

Dear Heleentje!

I think that it is very kind of you to so loyally keep me up to date about Karel's comings and goings, and to still write to me after the tiring days in the bouncing coach. I was just longing to see a letter from Canada. Actually, I was hoping for one from Karel, and then the one from you came as a consolation. By the way, I also learned from it that he is writing very seldom and hope that, after his journey, he will first write to your mother and grandmother to say how you feel for them with the loss of your uncle. Yes, I do understand how the first sad news in a foreign country affected you, particularly in a social environment that does not appeal that much to you and with those who could not know what you had

---

384 Eveline (Evy *or* Eefje) Biben (1867–1907): sister of Lou; married in Vienna in December 1891 to Mentor C. Da Ponte of Smyrna, Turkey, a rug merchant.

385 Henrietta (Jet) des Amorie van der Hoeven (1864–1933): married to Dr. Jacobus Versteeg (1862–1938), medical doctor in Heerde.

lost. What you must have felt by hearing about the sorrow of your mother, without being there with her. Oh, those awful distances that keep us so cruelly apart, when we would gladly wish to only exchange a single word. During those days, you will probably have often had the same thoughts.

And so, in that way, we have now arrived in the new year. [Last year] ended in misery and [this one] started in sadness. No, that I am not allowed to say, but oh, Heleentje, they were such difficult days for me. Not only because of the melancholic thoughts of how it would have been different, but I want to let you know that I have longed and expected to receive a word from Karel during the transition to the new year, when so much has happened to us. [On] Thursday, I thought that it would be Saturday and that helped me through New Year's Day, and Saturday, the mail still had not yet arrived. Sunday morning, "a letter." It was from you. It did me a lot of good, but all the more a disappointment because, to me, it appeared that I would have nothing to expect today, and that was indeed the case.

And then, although looking very tearful, I went to your parents in order to ask An about letting me read your letter and then, look, there Papa came with letters from Karel and yourself, which he read to us. Nice of him. In the one from Karel, written on a Saturday evening, was a sentence, "the weekly letter," and in another one, "and so you will be already in the new year when you receive this one." And then, I was really jealous. Every week a letter! No. I know very well that he is only allowed to write to me every four weeks, but the last one that I received from him had started November 7 and ended November 21; and then, a few lines from his hand really did me so much good.

It looks as if I complain about him a lot, but I did not want to do that. You are also no ordinary sister for him and no ordinary future sister-in-law for me; you know him better than I do. When you speak to him once again, make him understand that it would be so much easier to go through these times, and to go through them well, if he would not be so strict about writing exactly each month. And then, I so much value the special days of remembrance. Oh Heleentje, I would so love to be stronger and braver, and the folks do think and say that I am. Sometimes I manage, but still, I was already somewhat down those days and then the bravery and the strength disappeared.

How does it help if I faithfully swallow my liver oil and eat a lot, because Dr. Voûte thinks I am feeble (!), when my nerves muddle me again and the only remedy to keep them in order is evidence of Karel's love? No, I do not doubt his attachment, not for a moment, but life is so completely different there and what for him is properly curative is, for me, exactly the opposite. I do not mean that he does not think about me all the time. Oh, as long as he still thinks of me from time to time. I so much want to be healthy and strong when he comes back, and I am now so overly sensitive. When I walk quickly upstairs or downstairs, or move a little bit too much, then right away I feel everything pounding and I lose my breath. Mama says that that is nerves. Always those nasty nerves. One of our friends has influenza, poor lady. She was just engaged and cannot see him when he is away every six weeks. Also, I want to help Lina[386] with ironing, but it is not allowed because I have a cold and it is so tiring and is such a great change from hot to cold. Isn't that tedious? I find it awful to be tired after feeding the children and to be sleepy all the time, etc.

What a carping letter, eh? It seems so egotistical and so devoid of cheerfulness to give it to you now. But I am also so low-spirited. Your father did see that there was something, and I told Mama that I was a little sad because I had not heard anything from Karel; they said that they wanted to tell him so. That I do not like, because Karel will think that I am complaining about him.

Papa took me with him for a walk. It was Sunday and I always find that a difficult day, with memories and no normal work. We first went to your grandmother's for a short while. She was very well. Miss Lanting had influenza and Lies Pijnappel[387] was keeping her company. We walked along the Westerdoksdijk and the fresh air did me good. But it was very windy and now I have a cold. Lovely of Papa to come and get me. We also talked a bit about the future. It is so difficult to sort it out for oneself. Mama stays hopeful that it will not be necessary that I should have to go there. I, who had imagined that it would be about four, five or six years, begin to worry that it may be forever. I will do it, without hesitation, but it is difficult; I know that it will cause grief for Mama and then, I sometimes wonder whether I am doing the right thing. But it cannot be otherwise anyway. I love him so much and it would be terrible if he were to become less healthy because of me. Maybe I must not send you these letters and rather keep them for myself. It is still a great relief to pour my heart out. However, who knows whether it would go the same way if I wrote a letter to Karel? And this is all right with you, isn't it?

Just imagine that we are once again sitting on the canapé in your room, like the day of our parting. You said a lot then that did not get through to me because I was overly stressed, but afterwards, the words and thoughts came back. I shall now probably receive a letter from him this coming Tuesday. Perhaps he found it odd to write to me for my birthday and thought that two letters so close to each other would not be approved by Delprat.

Now, no more about myself, but it will also not be pleasant. Willem Coster is back; Sunday before Christmas he arrived, but Cor just heard about it from Mrs. v. d. Berg[388] on Thursday. We went there right away. He had arrived incognito because visiting tires him too much and Klaartje,[389] his house caretaker, let us inside after having promised to keep our

---

386 Helena (Lina) van Eijken (1865–1952): housekeeper; married to Engbert Kruidhof (1869–1957).

387 Elisabeth Antonia (Lies) Pijnappel (1871–1971): unmarried daughter of Menso Pijnappel.

388 Cardina Frederika Holle van den Berg (1840–1909): married to Norbertus Petrus van den Berg (1831–1917), president-director of Javasche Bank, 1873–1889.

389 This is likely Clasine (Klaartje) Elisabeth Meijer (1863–?).

visit short and that we would not be shocked by [how he looks]. Poor dear Willem, he looked so deathly ill, so shrunken, with a completely different face and another voice that sounded so hollow. He did not cough that much, but he does during the night and is also short of breath. Delprat has allowed him to go to the office, and he also went a few times on foot. From the Singel, past the Leliestraat to the Wolvenstraat, took him a good fifteen minutes. He wants to move by February and have the office at home. The work does him good and, according to him, Deprat had also said that the travelling did not do him any good, and that he would never advise a journey again. So melancholic, the way he is now. His sister came over, but he did not want her to stay. The ordeal with [Jan] Kruseman has also given him many regrets. Dr. Voûte, who is a cousin of his wife, spoke with Mama about it in order to understand how things were going at the office. He said that [Kruseman] had also had [this illness] once in his student years. This would reassure me, because I had once made myself so fearful that that conflict had something to do with our engagement and not only work at the office.

How many nasty things there are in life anyway, and how rarely one is thoughtful and thankful enough when one is happy.

Bye, dear sister. I hope to write something more cheerful soon. It is only a sombre mood. Not nice of me to choose you in particular to receive the airing of this.

Thursday, the cooking school begins. Hurrah! A new phase. I have remodelled a dress again. A four-year-old skirt altered into a dress for the Kindervoeding. It is now quite proper. And now I have started to make a new dress from the pieces that came out of my black skirt. It should become a fantastic outfit. Soon you will also get a portrait of me (taken by Cor) to show Karel what the self-made skirt with the same blouse looks like. But he should have the first one and I cannot write to him now, since I already wrote to him on the 20th.

Now, adieu, dear Heleentje. Many greetings from Mother and Cor, and a warm kiss from your loving Wil.

P.S. Happy that your hand is doing much better. I can understand that you do not yet have the same zeal for riding.

A32005000345-346 [Mother to Heleen, fragment]
Amsterdam, January 5, 1892

Dearest Helena,

I am sitting here in this quiet evening hour, at about 11:30, trying to use a steel pen in Papa's room. Elisabeth has left for Heerde, Anna is in bed with influenza. Nella is at a dance and Mieps is also in bed, so, therefore, I went downstairs to look for someplace cozy.

Today, Papa brought me the good news that he had increased the money that the widow van der Weijde receives for doing the washing; instead of five cents, she will now get ten cents for her kitbags and, for the pillowcases, three cents instead of two. I sent her a large washer-wringing machine that turns easily (just like a [double-roll hand-wringer]) and presses all the water out. She is very delighted with this — she got it in the morning at ten o'clock, and by noon I had already received an overjoyed letter because the bags now dry much faster and she does not have to stoke up the fire so much.

Today I visited cousin Noordhoorn[390] and shared your greeting by telegram, taken out of [the book of] John, about which she was delighted, and also considered it a personal greeting to her. And she then also specifically asked me to greet you heartily and specially, and afterwards, declared that you both are dear people.

Up until now, we have all stayed healthy, and Anna is getting better but is forbidden to get up and she is coughing quite a lot. Nel just received a letter from Gie Kruseman[391] with a request to cheer his mother up, because a visit from Nel would help more than a bunch of medicinal drinks. However, I cannot afford to lose her now because Miss Lanting is also ill, but if everything goes well, she can go from Friday until Sunday afternoon.

Last week, Matthijs, Anna, Betsy Röell[392] and I visited the Salvation Army, or rather the institution for the homeless. It was very interesting and what especially struck me was the effort and the cheerfulness with which one worked there, and the gratified faces of the sympathetic officers.

Today, we went to Rapenburg, where the big building for gatherings is, and the Ark des Vredes,[393] where, for forty cents, a young man can find every-thing that he could wish for. There, I sat talking for half an hour with a [Salvation Army] officer. You cannot imagine the tenderness and kind-heartedness with which he spoke about all of those "drowning" people, while one saw how happy he felt in his work and how he found it lovely to be able to bring sunshine and light where there is so much suffering. He promised me he would visit [the Kremer household], and already the same evening he called on them, to the great shock of [the Kremers], who thought that it was someone from the police. If it will help, I do not yet know.

With Aunt Martine,[394] it is once again a poor situation. She sold off a linen cabinet to cousin [Cornelis] Felix and asked me to buy a set of

---

390   Agnes Catherina Angelique van Maanen (1803–1896): married to Jacob Noordhoorn (1797–1872), commodity broker.

391   Gideon Kruseman (1866–1943): farmer; brother of Suze Kruseman Gruijs; married to Johanna Bosch (1867–1961).

392   Jkvr. Elisabeth (Betsy) Röell (1871–1937): married in 1895 to Jhr. Eric Willem von Wrangel auf Lindenberg (1864–1945), cavalry captain with the Huzars of Boreel.

393   Vrede-Ark, on the Rapenburg street in Amsterdam, was a shelter for homeless men.

394   Martine Margaretha Jacoba van Maanen (1831–1904): married in 1875 to Jan Bartholomeus Snellen (1830–1910).

table linens for her. Do you not think that it is sad, to have to struggle in one's old age?

The things that I find so lovely about your letters are the descriptions of all the people that you meet along the way, and therefore we understand your life so much better. How much sympathy I have for Mrs. Garnett. Have you still had the opportunity to give her, here and there, a gentle hint about how she could make the life of the three brothers happier, or have you not become so intimate? I can understand that Garnett and 'wooden leg' were full of sadness in watching you leave – they really thought . . . [Ends here]

A29662000039-40 [Heleen to An]
Calgary, January 7, 1892

Dear An,

I do think that you deserve a New Year's letter, but I fear, nevertheless, that you will have to do without, because this probably will arrive too late and I have no birthday wishes ready to write up. Twenty years! Do you also find that much older than nineteen? I found that when I myself was twenty, but now I find it very young. I understand from some of your claims in your last letter (November 27) that you sometimes feel as if you have experienced quite a lot, but don't get flustered by it, because life is richer and fuller than what you have seen of it yourself; and I really hope that you also will experience more of that this year.

I am so happy that you are now getting along so well with Aunt Hes and, about your walks with Thijs, I can assure you with full conviction that you are no exception regarding his reluctance. On the contrary, I have always heard the same from all the sisters. Even our brother [Gideon] always had objections to going out with Li. But another thing is that when he suggests it to you, you should not back off due to memories of previous peevishness and, one day or another, it could become very enjoyable and that would be so good for both of you.

Thijs may sometimes also have a reason for his moodiness that you do not know. Try a little harder to get along with him and to not let your own opinons and way of behaving prevail in your thoughts too much. I do not know if I am making myself clear, but I think that after all that we have talked about together, you will know that I do not intend anything unpleasant, but only kindness, and that I also do know that many things that we want are not always possible.

Good gracious! I wish that old lady would keep her mouth shut! Here, in the room, is a recuperating spinster who has not seen anyone for two months and now wants to talk with me. First, I wanted to read (Quack's *Socialisten*), but that did not help. Then, I thought that I could get her to be still with the newspaper (the one that is always brought to my room), but she claims that she cannot read the faded print.

I definitely have enough friends! For three hours today, I was busy again with explaining to a grieving little lady [Mrs. Elizabeth Trott[395]], who was again on her way to a nervous breakdown, that it is very enjoyable to be released from a man, that inferior sort of specimen, a baby and a difficult loudmouth, and that when that malicious family wants to take away her dead husband's property, she should be very happy to be released from her burden of that worthless scum of the earth. I was, myself, not completely convinced, but spoke all the more with passion so that she had nothing to say in opposition and, then, remarkably refreshed, [I] visited a friend who is still being put to the test by her husband and child!

Yesterday, I again received a lovely letter from Addie Van Horne, as well as a telegram from her father about return tickets, and one from Hosmer out of courtesy. I feel wonderfully free to be in the [Alberta Hotel] again, where everyone runs for me.

Ta ta, and a warm kiss from your loving Heleen.

P.S. Would you please give the enclosed letter to Papa? You may also read it.

[38] View of Calgary, c. 1890

395   Elisabeth Jane (Wardlow) Trott (1852–1921): married in 1888 to Samuel William Trott (1847–1891), pharmacist. Their baby son, Bruce Wardlow Trott, was born on April 5, 1891 and died on August 31, 1891. He is memorialized with his father in the Union Cemetery of Calgary.

394-A32005000418-421 [Father to Heleen]
Amsterdam, January 7, 1892

Dear Helena,

Now, just a word about your letters to me of 8 and 10 December and about the other letters regarding your arrival in Calgary, which are, as a cornucopia, spread out from the postbox among the members of the family and Wil. What a diverse bunch of characters and situations that you have come to experience!

The day of the storm at the Grange sounds dreadful. You have described it very well. It is as if I were there, but how discouraging it must be for the pioneers to see all of their hard work, done with their 'bare' hands, be destroyed in one day. The impossibility of walking against the wind reminded me of the Pentecost storm at Duinvliet,[396] when the wind made a hole in the roof of the hayloft and all of us had to work with all of our might to fill the hole, or otherwise the whole of the roof would have been blown away.

The Garnett family was no exhilarating company for you, but I think that the inept wife should have certainly appreciated your presence there. Was she of the same social standing as the Garnetts, and also English, or did he get to know her in Canada? I do think the former, but then she would not have been suitable to 'rough it in the bush' anyway.

What a lovely diversion you gave us with your description of the triumphant trip of Princess Badroulbadour, with her retinue in the salon car of the Canadian Pacific Railway and her game of checkers with the factotum!

It is very good for you to be able to cope in strained circumstances, but there is still something so pleasurable about comfortably staying in well-appointed places, so that you won't have regretted your return to civilization. Through your letters, our friends can now also imagine a vivid picture of life in Canada, and we even have to be careful that they are not being shared with people who have had nothing to do with it, because you are getting a certain reputation, and in 'Society', therefore everyone wants to know something about it.

Yesterday, Wil was with us. We were in *petite comité,* since Li was in Heerde, Thijs out for dinner and An in bed. The conversation was very enjoyable and [we] finished the evening playing whist with a 'dummy'. Nel was visiting the van Nottens. An has a touch of influenza, but she is well on the way to recovery.

Wil's birthday is the 14th. I hope that, for a lovely present, she will receive, then or before, a letter from Karel, because, like many dear people (Cateau den Tex, among others), she is very attached to birthdays and now is already so saddened because she has heard nothing with the new

---

396 Duinvliet was a country house in Overveen, Bloemendaal, once owned by the parents of Jan Boissevain and taken down in 1878.

year. I can understand very well why he writes little, but he must pay attention to those special days. This morning, Mia came back from school *en pleur et en larme*, because Miss Mingelen,[397] who had been sick for some days, had passed away. As you know, she was a very good teacher. I have encouraged Mia, along with some of her friends, to place a wreath on her grave. She died in The Hague.

This afternoon at Mama's house, the notary Pollones[398] will handle the distribution of the estate of Uncle Toon. Mama will get shares and some of the furniture, etc. However, the proceeds [of the shares] will be spent, for the most part, on the annuity to be given to Uncle Sebald and Suwerkrop, and on the allowance for Grandmother (who was receiving that from Uncle Toon), which she cannot do without. Grandmother gets the house on the Leidschegracht and some shares and also a part of the household effects.

I am deeply thankful that I do not need any inheritance in order to live to my own tastes and to not have to be 'grasping' in these kinds of affairs. By the way, it is, once again, a harmonious apportionment. Uncle Pijnappel is impartiality personified.

Yesterday, the Gie Mietjes[399] came here for dinner. (Very jovial — the gentlemen went to the Grondwet[400] that evening.) Uncle Ko and Aunt Gerarda were also to come, but he had a stiff neck. This was very sad because we see each other so seldom, and when we do, it is with pleasure. He followed the treatment of the German pastor, tub bath without drying, and I think that he developed rheumatism. In the beginning, he found it lovely and had never felt so good. He just became an associate at the firm Reiss & Co. and has, therefore, finally reached the position that I had wished for him for a long time.

This morning, it looked as if we were in Canada. The thick snow carpet lay over the earth; everything was still, white. There was, however, little frost.

A postcard from Karel, sent from the camp, [dated] December 16, brought me, among other things, welcome news that he will not forget to write to Wil before her birthday, so that what I wrote in the previous pages no longer applies.

Li's stay in Heerde came to a speedy end. It seems that she had arrived there with a bad cold and therefore returned home yesterday, much earlier than she had planned. Now she is lying in bed, most likely also with a bit of influenza, but without fever.

397 Geverdina Johanna Mingelen (1848–1892): teacher (Special) Secondary School for Girls, Amsterdam.

398 Jean Charles Gerard Pollones (1838–1909): solicitor in Amsterdam; married to Johanna Frederike Wilhelmina Diest (1857–1933).

399 Gideon Maria (Gie Mie *or* Uncle Gi) Boissevain (1837–1925): banker and economist; brother of Count Adolphe; married to Louise (Aunt Lu) Caroline Toe Laer (1837–1915); likely visited along with their daughter Caroline Augusta Antoinette Sophie Boissevain (1868–1945) and her husband Gideon Stephanus de Clerq (1862–1942), editor of the *Algemeen Handelsblad*.

400 De Grondwet is an electors' association in Amsterdam that was named after the constitution of the Netherlands, titled De Grondwet.

The 'official notice of marriage' party for Wolterbeek–van Eeghen[401] was yesterday. Uncle Niek and Aunt Hes assisted her and were very satisfied. It was a lovely party and the girls, with Cateautje[402] at the head, played beautifully, *Zehn Mädchen und kein Mann*.[403]

A new novella by Couperus called *Extaze* is in [*De Nieuwe Gids*] from January. It sketches the attraction (which was a slow rise to a passionate love) between a married woman and the friend of her husband, which came to an end because the friend left her just in time. We have had philosophical discussions about it and came to the conclusion that it is also a very disquieting read. But the style and the phrasing are very nice!

Finally, I have come to the end of the *Drei Monate unter Fabrik Arbeiter*, by the German theologian. It is a serious book and the man does his utmost to genuinely convey his experiences. However, he has such a heavy style and ties to every statement such irritating moralizations that it is almost unreadable. Thijs will write a piece about it for *Propria Cures*.

Our doorkeeper at the Nederland [NSM], about whom I believe I have told you before, was associated with a woman who was hopelessly alcoholic and spent all the household money. Yesterday, [he] found her dead in bed. It was, at first, quite a consternation, but he now recognizes that it is a true salvation.

Christine[404] departed this morning in tears toward Friesland, where her mother has become ill and was taken to the hospital. Mama believes that it is not *periculum in mora*, but once the panic sets in, there is nothing that can be done about it.

The first party at the Royal Court, a reception, went very well. Mr. Cremer, with whom I spoke the following day, was full of praise for Queen Emma,[405] who paid homage to her guests. Everything must have been perfect.

The Röells[406] became commissionaires of Het Casino.[407] I am curious as to whether one of our girls will end up going there.

---

401 Petronella Clasina (Nel) van Eeghen (1870–1954): married to Jacob Cornelis Wolterbeek (1863–1939), tobacco broker.

402 This is likely Louise Catharine (Cateau or Loukie) Antoinette van Eeghen (1884–1979): feminist and peace activist.

403 This is one number from the 1862 opera of the same name, by Franz von Suppé (1819–1895), an Austrian composer of light opera and other theatre music.

404 Anna Christina van Veen (1863–1949): servant; married in 1903 to Jan Roos (c.1876–1939).

405 Queen Wilhelmina (1880–1962) became Queen of the Netherlands in 1890 at ten years old but was not formally crowned until 1898. Her mother, Emma, was Queen Regent during this time. In 1901, Queen Wilhelmina married Duke Heinrich Wladimir Albrecht Ernst of Mecklenburg-Schwerin (1876–1934).

406 Jhr. Cornelis Röell (1867–1907): mayor of Eemnes; married to Jkvr. Maria Henriette Rutgers van Rozenburg (1872–1923); brother of Willem Frederik (1870–1942), banker and politician, married to Catharina Elisabeth Boudewina Baroness Stoet van Oldruitenborgh (1871–1941).

407 Sociëteit Het Casino (1816–1934): the chicest private club in Amsterdam, where many of the members were of the nobility.

Farewell Badroulbadour, I wish you well. Many greetings from your loving Father.

A28335001517-18 [Heleen to Father]
Calgary, January 8, 1892

Dear Father,

I do not have much to say but I must thank you very much for your letter of December 15, with the verses, and the answer of December 12. You were the first again this year and had, again, chosen your words very well. I do not remember you ever reading that aloud. Is it an old favourite or have you just recently found it?

A.C. [Wertheim]'s affectionate answer, nicely expressed and beautifully phrased as always, seems to me to be somewhat more melancholic and concerned than before. I fear that since his illness he does not feel like his old self again. Do you want his letter back? If so, I will send it to you. I shall save it for him, with your verse, anyhow.

I am also extremely flattered by the greeting from our friends Tak and van Dedem. Here, where they put so much importance on being acquainted with the powerful, I have started to feel quite important with so many prominent friends. Again, I have read, with much pleasure, a thick *Rotterdammer* (eighty pages). It gives an overview of the [government] budget, and it seems to me that everything is being handled faster and more vigorously than before, most likely because some of those responsible for the budget are my friends. There was also a lovely piece of history about Norway and Sweden and the situation in Germany, also so very clearly explained.

It is nice to be so up to date, but it is rather strange to not talk about it with anyone. In the mountains, we became acquainted with a Swedish road inspector, a very pleasant man with broad knowledge, who, among other things, knew a lot about Holland's waterworks and dykes. Mr. Niblock listened with attention. He knows very little, but I have seldom seen anyone of his age and position so easily acknowledge this and be so eager to learn, also from his subordinates. His relationship with Percy, the cook, was noteworthy. It seemed more like that of the *confidante* in French tragedies. Percy always has a ready answer, often a disapproving judgment about the dealings of his boss, and if there was a reason, teased him about breaking a stool or a glass. Mr. Niblock found everything just fine and gave him his ticket for the Charity Ball on Wednesday. [Niblock] is also always good-natured, sometimes funny and very helpful.

From Karel, I received good news last week. He is high up in the mountains and in deep snow. He crosses rivers and balances on tree trunks and does more of those sorts of playful things. Soon his work will end. I await him here. Other than that, nothing serious.

Much love from your Heleen.

P.S. I still forgot to thank you for the *Amsterdammer* with the humorous piece about the fun of paying wealth tax and how to digest it well. Will it be implemented in Amsterdam? I find it quite reasonable (I do not know exactly why) and also received with thanks the report about Kindervoeding. Has An protested against the muddle about her and Jo's names? HB

A32005000351–52 [Karel to Heleen]
In camp, Crowsnest Lake, January 8, 1891

Dear Leentje,

Good gracious! Our plan is in disarray! [James Ross] sent orders to 'locate' the line back from the summit, a job that will need all hands until the middle of April. I expect that [Hosmer and Van Horne] will not demand from me that I keep doing this 'stake-marker' job, but find it difficult to give my resignation without them asking for it. This is why I will keep watching the developments here and will not yet talk of quitting. So long as we work in the bush, my departure would not displease the chief too much, and before he is again on the prairie, he has plenty of opportunities to replace me. [Hosmer and Van Horne] received my letters on December 26. I count on an answer at the end of this month, and that this answer releases me from my current job. In case you agree with me about this, you can therefore count on it that I will rejoin you somewhere after the middle of February, but of course, I cannot assess this and, so, await more details from you.

Our mail supposedly has been lying around for three weeks in Fort Macleod and is being held by mistake. Only what you send addressed to [Pincher Creek] comes through to me, but everything that comes from Hosmer stays behind. The team that is delivering this letter [to you] picks up paperwork once each month. Most likely, for the time being, there will be no more communications with the outside world.

I find that I am compelled to spend more than ten dollars on clothing and shoes; I have ordered mitts, shoepacks, overalls and German stockings. Do you know what all these things are? Probably there is nothing in stock in Pincher Creek and, therefore, I shall linger on in my worn-out overshoes. Today, I had to wear an overcoat during work. It was that bitterly cold. The scenery is overwhelming. The lake shore is 'easy as pie'. We chained over the two-foot-thick ice.

My return journey from Pincher Creek took place during a snowstorm. I lost the trail a few times but found it again every time. Once, after an hour of searching when I got tangled in the underbrush, I almost sank through the ice, my horse fell on the ice, etc., etc. I came by a camp of Indians, with seven tents made of cowhide, and women and children. Men were hunting. I met one walking on snowshoes.

Upon my return, as I had expected, the camp had moved, and I followed their trail and, at 5:30 p.m., I arrived in camp. The horse, honestly tired. The rider, ditto; but at the moment, not too stiff and no scrapes . . . (I say, without blushing).

Last night, I was quite short of breath and this morning it was off to work with wet shoes. Overcome by the cold, things were a little difficult. Back to camp, good and warm, dry shoes and doses of bicarbonate (as a refreshment because my digestion is very good). Lunch in camp and after that, at work again. Now, Friday evening, I'm as healthy as a fish.

Bye, bye, warmest greetings, your loving, Karel.

A28335001519-23 [Heleen to Mother, fragment]
Alberta Hotel, Calgary, January 10–12, 1892

Dear Mother,

I am enjoying my freedom in the hotel. My trip through the mountains has also refreshed me very much. I see everything differently than from within the oppressive atmosphere of Mrs. Lougheed's house. The first day, I stayed incognito in the city. Wrote letters and began to repair my togs because everything wears terribly here. I put new lining in sleeves and hems in skirts.

Yesterday, I went again to visit Mrs. Wilkins. She was alone once more and felt miserable. While I was travelling, she had had a flood due to a burst water pipe. She rushed to the plumber, who was not home, and asked for help from a strange passer-by, who turned off the pipe for her. After that, she scooped all of the water out of the cellar herself. She has a cold now, but her real reason for feeling sick is something that has been coming on for months until it reached a crisis. Yesterday, she was busy ironing shirts. I helped her with the other housework and towed her along with me to the hotel for dinner. We sat very comfortably at an empty table in a corner with our backs facing the other guests. Since I know so many gentlemen, it is difficult to look in their direction.

After dinner, we went to the parlour, where we had the place all to ourselves until the room servant brought two calling cards: from Dr. Fraser[408] and another from someone we did not know. "Let them come in." The other was a pleasant English rancher from Macleod. It was nice to hear again about my friends there. Cheerful general conversation and at 9:00 p.m. they left again. Yet another hour of chatting with Kathleen Wilkins and then the question arose about going home. I had already thought about that. I rang and told the servant that I was to take Mrs. Wilkins home and requested an adjutant from the hotel. The man readied himself immediately but came a moment later to let us know that his boss

---

[408] Samuel Martin Fraser, Lieutenant Colonel, NWMP (1868–1935): medical doctor; married to Noemie Paré (1876–1959).

would do the honours. It was a beautiful clear night, but sharply cold. (It had been eighteen degrees below Fahrenheit during the day.)

Today, Sunday, I will be going to the McCauls'. This morning, I poured over *De Socialisten*. Papa wrote about Prudhomme, but that part does not appear in my volume and from the text it seems that the last piece was from the previous volume!

January 12: Dearest Mother, just now I received your letter of December 21, and it is my great pleasure to immediately answer your questions.

In Pincher Creek, I usually breakfasted downstairs. There were two tables, far away from each other, each for six people. After I had hurt my wrist, I always came late; if there were still a few men, then I usually sat alone at a table. A few times, I took breakfast upstairs, but early in the morning — it was often so cold there, and the plates, etc., were left for so long that it afterwards became unpleasant.

Maud, the maid, helped me get dressed and do my hair, but she often forgot about me and I would have to wait until I heard her heavy step and then call loudly. That was always after her breakfast and that of the guests and, therefore, quite late. She was abominably clumsy, indescribably sloppy and always had dirty hands. The little room was terribly stuffy at night, since I had to keep the doors closed due to the drunken cowboys who often mistook their own doors; and the window was close to my head so, during the continuous cold storms, I did not dare to keep it open. In the beginning, if I was downstairs early for breakfast, it was oddly 'gloomy' because then there was no daylight yet, and the large, hollow room was lit with petroleum lamps on the wall at a great distance from the tables.

My wrist is back to normal again. It was only a bad wrench, or in other words, 'sprain'. One muscle is not yet completely normal, but I only notice it with unusual movements. I pound again on the piano as I used to.

I thought that I had written about 'Old Auntie' the washerwoman,[409] but perhaps that was to Tol Waller. She is a negress who always smokes a pipe and wears a Jacobian hat, is stiff with rheumatism, not averse to whiskey, very good-hearted and talkative. She has functioned as a midwife and dry nurse for all of the children in the surrounding area for the last twelve years and has portraits of all the babies, which she showed to me. She washes and irons very properly for a dollar a dozen, the normal price everywhere here! Karel saw her last week in Pincher Creek and she sent her greetings.

About my journey to Vancouver, you will already be informed by the time you get this letter. By the way, I am never lost or lonely here in Canada.

---

409   This is undoubtably "Auntie" Annie Saunders, an Alberta pioneer and former slave, having travelled up the Missouri River from Fort Benton, Montana. The 1891 Canada census lists her as being forty-five years old. She worked first for the Macleods, then started her own laundry business, a restaurant and a boarding home: "Good accommodation for ladies." She remained close to the Macleod family, even after their move to Calgary. She died in Pincher Creek, July 27, 1898.

[39] "Old Auntie" Annie Saunders, Pincher Creek

I am more concerned about all my time being caught up with new friends. Mr. Van Horne provided an introduction [letter] for me in Vancouver and, also from others, I received letters for Victoria.

You should not expect too much about Karel's calculation wonders. He knew that he could do it faster and better than the others, but he held himself back from showing them. Once he made a discreet remark, but they were not impressed by it. Yesterday, I got a long letter from Karel, of which I include a part. Do realize that we are, in practical terms, further from each other than Amsterdam is from Montreal? At the fastest, his letters to me travel eight or nine days, and mine seem to not reach him at all. I have written to him three times each week since I last saw him and all those letters have not yet arrived in Pincher Creek. I think that they are stuck in Lethbridge. The mail administration there must be very bad. From Karel's letter, you will read that the work will take considerably longer than we thought. That should be good for his health, but the high mountain air seems to be less good for his asthma. I am disappointed that the decision about the future will be postponed again, and it is an unpleasant feeling that he is so completely out of my reach. [Ends here]

A29670000048-49 [Heleen to Li]
Calgary, January 12, 1892

Dear Li,

I have finished my letter to Mama and see that I have left one question still unanswered, that is, whether I had books to take to Pincher Creek. I had my French poets, the Dante, and the nursing book from Dr. Black that I diligently studied over fourteen days. The White Frasers loaned me a very interesting book about the Indians, and Dr. Mead gave me a few enjoyable, fun novels. I also sometimes looked through a grammar book about the Blackfoot language, but it was too difficult to learn it that way. I thought that I had written everything, but perhaps Mama had not read it during a moment when she was fretting about it.

Yesterday, I received a very nice letter from Mrs. White Fraser, which I hereby enclose. I had mentioned that I would perhaps come back in the spring, in answer to all the lamenting that I would not see their beloved land in the summer. I would also find it enjoyable if there was a chance [to visit], and since I absolutely do not know what the spring will bring, I could just as well say that as anything else.

Yesterday, I ate at Mrs. Wilkins' again and played *quatre mains* with her husband. They would like to have me about the house all day, but I think that for the few days that they are together, they should be allowed to enjoy some time alone together undisturbed and shall therefore stay away today. Making music with him gives me a bit of an unpleasant feeling while she is busy in the kitchen, and he is constantly scoffing about her minimal musicality. He also wanted to sing with me, which he does very badly, and never wanted to do with her.

In the evening, Mr. McCaul came to take me home. He and his wife were to go to the McCarthys'[410] to practise a dance and they were to take me along, but Mr. McCarthy has influenza and they did not go. It was extremely kind of him to come anyway. I get along very well with him. He would also be a very pleasant guest in Holland. They have all done their very best to get me to the ball again tomorrow evening, but I flatly refused. I do not trust the 'gentlemen' enough. Here, they are astonishingly and easily enthralled and they hang on to my every word. According to me, none of the women are savvy enough to be an effective chaperone and, for myself, I am especially afraid to become flirtatious. Perhaps I am too scrupulous about it, but I must still stay here for a month and I do not want to have any unpleasantries, especially now that I am staying in the hotel.

Mama also asked about bears and wolves. Karel sees a lot of coyotes, which are small wolves, and I saw one myself while riding with one of the Garnetts, but so far away that without my lorgnette I could hardly see it.

What a pity that the money for the ice-clearing has been voted down. You would just wish to take one or another of them and box their ears. It was lovely to see Karel's Atjeh Cross arrive.

Sorry for the [ink smudge]. My inkwell sprung open in the box and a terrible ink mess was the result. Ta ta, and much love, Heleen.

A32074000246–47 [Heleen to Wil]
Calgary, January 12, 1892

Dearest Wil,

Many thanks for your letter of December 21 and, also, much happiness with Jo's recovery. That is a great delight for all of you and I also had not expected it so soon. She shall now move into the new house with more

---

410 Peter McCarthy (1839–1901) worked for Herald Publishing Co. and in 1888 became a partner at the Lougheed McCarthy law firm. His first marriage was with Carrie Kemp (1840–1873), and his second marriage was to Jane Kemp (1844–1932).

cheerfulness than ever, and I hope that it will be a happy year for her. Is she now actually completely healed, and can she walk and ride again if she wants to?

That Norwegian book by Ipsen seems also very interesting to me. If he portrays van Eeden and Gorter as typical Hollanders, then his judgment will be much more flattering than we deserve. It is not the great 'Ibsen' is it? If so, van Eeden would have spoken to us about him. I am curious about Thijs' and An's visit to Bussum. Strange that that becomes a kind of familiar thing to do.

Wil, I believe that I have badly answered many things from your letters, among other things, you were so kind to suggest sending me a monthly magazine about nursing or something else and I have replied nothing about it. Every time that I wrote to you, there were so many other things requiring explanation that much of what I still wished to write remained in the pen. And, on top of that, so long as I am unsure about when I will finally settle somewhere, I want to avoid all extra baggage.

You shall probably also be surprised that the work will take so much longer than we had thought. I will not see him before February; I mailed a letter by him to Mama, from which you will get a good idea of his present life. For me, the letter was even clearer because I know so very well all the places and people he names.

I am following with interest your experience of visiting the poor and I saw with great pleasure that [Liefdadigheid naar Vermogen] sent an answer so quickly. Now, you will probably be inundated with letters and demands for coupons and, if so, it will be a big comfort to be able to point them toward charity, because only feeling sorry for poor souls is not very satisfactory. Nevertheless, you will still always have the idea that they are very poor, and so you take the chance of being fooled or helping in the wrong way. Did you not find it unnerving in the Tuinstraat,[411] when you heard that noise above the dark stairway? I imagine that you must be very busy with all of your new activities and I feel immensely lazy. All day, I do nothing other than write a few letters and a little walking, chatting with whining acquaintances and bit of reading.

When Mr. Wilkins is on his way again with the mail service, I will go and teach [Kathleen] bread-baking and cooking, and then stay overnight with her to console her in her loneliness. That shall be an enjoyable change.

Bye, dear Willemientje! Many greetings to your Mama and Cor, from your Heleen.

KLAB04554000219-220 [Karel to Wil]
In camp, Crowsnest Pass, January 14, 1892

---

411   The Tuinstraat is a street in Amsterdam, in the Jordaan, then a very poor neighbourhood.

Our Plan in Disarray!

Dearest Wil,

Where in the world would our thoughts cross each other, our wishes meet each other? Somewhere at sea on a roaring winter ocean? Or above the white cloak of the prairie?

I celebrate today in private and, tonight, you are in my thoughts at least. And you? Did you get presents and visits, also from 717? I hope that you will write to me about your day. Your first birthday since we have been engaged, but now so far from each other.

Imagine that due to the dim-wittedness of a Macleod postman (our mail is being withheld instead of sent on) the last of what I have heard from Amsterdam was through the letters from you and Thijs of November 17 and 10! But the carrier, who will take this letter to a nearby farm, shall try to pick up our mail there at the same time because, a week ago, there was a pressing letter written to the negligent postman and we hope that it has helped.

Through a special carrier, our head engineer received "Locate the line [here]" to definitively mark where the rail line shall be built. The day before yesterday, our provisional measuring ended at the highest point of the mountain pass. The water that I saw there, flowing in various streams, speeds westward toward the Pacific Ocean and possibly will one day wash upon the coasts of Japan or Australia.

Without this urgent message, we would now be on our way back to the civilized world and I would soon have been automatically dismissed from my modest job. Now, however, the troop stays together until around the end of April, when the job will now be done. In the meantime, I expect that my high protectors in Montreal will not leave me here so long, but that they will create an opening for a secure future in one way or another. In the letters that I have hitherto written, with reports about my so-much-improved health, and which were probably received on December 26, etc., leaving some room for the busyness of Xmas, I count on receiving an answer by the end of the month.

In the meantime, I am doing well. Winter here is a completely different thing than winter in the Netherlands. It never rains! But, good gracious, can it ever freeze here! You should see me sometime on a cold day, when I am on my way to work or when I come back. Shall I describe my outward appearance? The dark suit that you know, here and there torn but mended, the legs shortened to where the pants become a kind of knickerbocker, thick woollen socks with knee-high, yellow-leather oil-shoes. A wide black belt with a revolver in a holster and a short hatchet called a 'tomahawk'. This is all covered by a light layer of snow, collar up on the coat. A thick woollen muffler, two or three times around the neck. Fur hat pulled down low over the ears. Moustache and (!) beard completely white, stiff, lumpy and frozen so that yawning is very painful. If it gets still colder, then I add a brown overcoat, but that one is seldom necessary now that we walk to work; this is because the mountain pass is impassable for wagons. Every day last week, we had to make a two-hour walk, each morning and each evening. Now, however, we actually work from the summit backward, and every day the distance that separates us from the camp becomes shorter.

The camp is now pitched at the end of the wagon trail, where a landowner from the area has built a hut from tree trunks, which he uses when he goes there to hunt, fish or chop wood. Phooey! That 'hunting' is also sheer humbug. The deer keep to a respectful distance from the mountain pass and we have had nothing worthwhile within shooting range. Once, an antelope, that is all! Brooks (not 'from Sheffield'!) shot at him, but he escaped.

Oh, Wim. I am truly too tired to write something enjoyable. I shall entreat you to still live off little bits from my last one. By the way, I hope Helena will have prepared you for the scarcity of tidings from me. It is so strange to travel through a country with the knowledge that it will undergo, within the year, the formidable change that the railway shall bring to it, and at every new spot, I think: "Shall we ever see it together?" Probably never. But it would be delightful because, oh, it is so beautiful here, and if we are that fortunate, then it would be so enjoyably nostalgic to see the place, where — Stop little man! Future dreaming? Enough! Facts, hard facts!

I am curious about whether, tomorrow, I shall receive the photographs that were promised to me, of you and Nel in cooking costumes; and what you would have said about my Nicolaas surprises; and whether you dined on December 12 at number 717; and how the Kindervoeding suits you, etc., etc., etc. And all of that, I may perhaps come to know tomorrow, and then I cannot answer you for over one month!

This time, I had also wanted to mail a worthy critique of *Two Rings*[412] to you, but I do not feel up to it right now. Goodbye, darling. Your Karel

A32005000422–424, KLAB09193000026 [Father to Heleen]
Amsterdam, January 16, 1892

Dear Helena,

Yesterday, I received your letter of December 28, wherein you spoke so beautifully about Aad Gildemeester,[413] about the befriended ministers, etc., and see, just yesterday in The Hague, I found myself in the midst of these friends.

Mama had already travelled there on Thursday, made many visits to the van Maanens, etc., and dined and stayed with the Piersons. There, she was busy discussing and debating, and afterwards slept peacefully.

I arrived Friday, first made a visit to the Department of Colonies and found our friend van Dedem, who finally had read the postal contract

---

412   Play by Henrik Ibsen, *Fruen fra havet*, 1888, English translation, *The Lady from the Sea*.

413   Adriaan (Aad) Gildemeester (1828–1901): member of Parliament from 1883 to 1891; married to Marguerite Elisabeth de Clercq (1830–1908).

and with whom I could now discuss a few items. I regret to say that I had quite a spat with him because he is even more frugal than the famous Aaltje the kitchenmaid! With great interest, he asked about 'the Canadians'!

Then I went to pick up Mama with a proper 'brommer',[414] but that was not necessary because the carriage of the Piersons had already been fetched. First, we saw [their] house on the Laan van Meerdervoort, a well-laid-out, cheerful house, with all the known paintings and prints, the large bookcases and very nice furniture.

Then we drove to see Mrs. van Tienhoven and Mrs. Tak, both of whom had their 'open house'. We came quite early, so therefore it was not yet busy. It was amusing to see Mrs. van Tienhoven's face change (who was waiting for her visitors all 'dolled up' with lovely gloves) when she saw us coming in. And then, with a happy shriek, "Are you folks here?", she quickly lured us through to see the whole house. A very spacious house with four rooms downstairs, close together, among which is one very light reception hall decorated with Amsterdam-style furniture that looks very good there. Further on, a beautiful dark wooden spiral staircase to the first floor, where one arrives at a landing that gets a lot of light through the coloured windows and looks very nice with old-fashioned cabinets and a lot of Japanese porcelain. On that floor there are a number of bedrooms, I believe about six, and also a cozy study for Mr. van Tienhoven and another for Gerard.[415] Later on, Mrs. van Tienhoven told us, in a very amusing way, all about her French cook and the society of The Hague, and then with *fouetté de cocher* [the whip at our backs] to Mrs. Tak's, who gave a reception along with her daughter, and who was also very pleasant and full of interest in your welfare.

From there on to Mr. and Mrs. Cremer's, who live at the Nassauplein, also with a beautiful house full of Japanese, Chinese and Eastern luxury goods and lovely paintings, among them, from Israëls. Mrs. Cremer received us very charmingly, told a lot about the party at the Royal Court and the amiability of the Queen Regent, who spoke to her right away in English and had made a compliment about her Dutch after she had learned that she also spoke it. Cremer himself also joined us and we talked for a while with each other about business.

Then to [Villa Casanetta] at cousins Aad Gildemeester and Guus, and there we were immediately welcomed with shouts of excitement about the letter from Calgary that he had just received. He had to read it aloud to us, and I have to say that I had some *amour propre d'auteur* (to the second power) when I heard that interesting, excellent return letter by my daughter. He was clearly happy with it and you gave him a lot of pleasure.

The little villa of the Gildemeesters is also very cozy. We sat there chatting very enjoyably. Afterwards, he took us through the completely

---

414 A rental carriage with a uniformed driver.

415 This is likely their son, Pieter Gerhard (Gerbrand) van Tienhoven (1875–1953), director of de Nationale Zee- en Brand Assurantie Maatschappij N.V.; involved in nature conservation; married in 1910 to Cornelia Johanna Marggraff (1883–1919, Pasadena, California, USA).

snow-covered garden to the villa of Mrs. ten Kate Pierson,[416] who was there lying sick with influenza; also her maid [was sick], so that it looked like a real hospital where Mrs. Pierson had come to be of assistance. We awaited the arrival of the doctor and then walked with Mrs. Pierson back to her house through the snow-covered bushes by twilight and with the fading rays of the sun, which still lit everything with a golden tint. Mama enjoyed it beyond description.

Lovely dinner at [Minister Pierson's], who came home by six o'clock. He talked about everything — his experiences; his forthcoming loan; his relationships with his colleagues; and once again, debated strongly about defence (about which, in my view, he was on foreign ground); further about children and friends; and about many Amsterdam memories. With the last train, we arrived home and this time Mama slept very well. In the meantime, the girls had van Eeden over for dinner, who had arrived *à la fortune du pot* and very much regretted having missed us.

Just a moment ago, a big crate of dates again arrived from your friend Dawes.[417] It is a shame that it is a bit too far, otherwise I would have sent some to you in Canada.

On Wil's birthday, I wrote a letter to Karel after a long talk that I had with . . .

KLAB09193000026 [continues on]

. . . Mrs. de Vos. I really value talking to someone when they are prepared to hear what you have to say, and Mrs. de Vos was very sympathetic with Wil (according to her view) about Karel's cooler and detached manner. For me, that moment seemed very suitable to let her know that probably a letter from Karel would soon arrive that would clarify the whole situation for Wil. I have the impression that [Mrs. de Vos] (with *coeur et âme* and with gathering all of her strength) shall cooperate to make sure that everything stays completely between us. That, she also finds very necessary for Wil. What the decision will be, I do not know and I cannot even guess, and at least we now know that we do not have to fear ill-considered steps from [their] side.

The mail is about to close. Many greetings from your loving Father.

A29670000038–41 [Heleen to Li]
Calgary, January 16, 1892

Dear Li,

Yesterday and the day before yesterday, I was at Mrs. Wilkins' and it was a pleasant change to experience her life alongside her. She first went

---

416   Carolina Henriette Constantia ten Kate Pierson (1836–1895): daughter of Jan Lodewijk Gregory Pierson and Ida Oyens; married to Herman Frederik Karel ten Kate (1822–1891).

417   Sir Edwyn Sandys Dawes (1838–1903) of the firm Gray, Dawes & Co., shipping agents; insurance broker and general merchant, London; married in 1859 to Lucy Emily Bagnall (1836–1921).

with me to tea at Mrs. [Snyder's],[418] where the gossip of all those women bored me immensely, and at about 6:00 p.m., we went back to her house and started to prepare dinner. In the meantime, the water was frozen again and we dove into the cellar to defrost it, with the pleasant result that the pipe burst! Luckily, she could get water from the neighbours and the dinner took its course successfully and cozily in the end.

Where the evening went, I do not know. We did something like preparing bread (I mean putting it to rise) and a little bit of unpicking [the seams] on her wedding dress, which she wanted to wear the next day to a 'euchre party', so it was midnight before we were in bed. The next day, I did the housework and she prepared breakfast, and afterwards, I continued working on the wedding dress. She went to the plumber and I remained in complete possession of the house, at least, that is what I thought. But soon I heard a surprising thumping in the kitchen. I stormed out and saw my hostess buried under a number of hard hulks, which soon proved to be frozen sheets and shirts. All of a sudden, an intense wind had started to blow and the wash flew all over the ground! Everything [was] taken inside, with the result being that the little kitchen was chock-full.

When the plumber came, I went into the cellar and sold wisdom, and soon Kathleen came back with the message that I also had to go to the party. We gathered up our stuff, the stove fully stoked up, closed the doors and together went to the hotel to dine and dress for the party. We also pleasantly grumbled about the difficulties of dressing when it is cold, as one has to wear so many heavy things over lovely clothing. One must suffer for beauty.

We walked to Mrs. McCallum's,[419] where there were more than thirty people in the strangest outfits, from grey silk dresses to ball gowns. 'Progressive euchre' (pronounced 'joeker') is an easy card game. All of them played at eight tables, four on each table, from time to time changing partners and tables according to set rules. Then buffet supper in small groups, the ladies sitting and the gents walking and serving. Afterwards, dancing. The 'gentlemen' were pretty annoying; the ladies had schoolgirl fun with each other and about each other, literally no other chatter than gossip. A Mr. Dean[420] was quite friendly, talking about the fourteen farms that he runs, and Dr. Fraser was very friendly and attentive, and danced well. At one o'clock, we walked home (to the hotel) accompanied by Mr. Alman, a nice, decent chap, nicknamed Cupid.

Today, I received a letter from Karel, which I include herewith. You will see that "waiting" is still the message for me and the future — just as uncertain as before. Now he is bothered with asthma again, so I have

---

418   Constance Helen Snyder (née Edmiston) (1865–1914): married to Major Arthur Edward Snyder (1861–1940) of the Northwest Mounted Police, who served in the South African War (or Second Boer War), Lord Strathcona's Horse (Royal Canadians), eventually knighted CBE and awarded MVO. See Carmen Miller, *Painting the Map Red: Canada and the South African War, 1899–1902* (Montreal & Kingston: Canadian War Museum and McGill-Queen's University Press, 1993).

419   Flora McDonald (1848–1923): married to John G. McCallum (1849–1925), building contractor.

420   This is possibly John Dean, the accountant for the Canadian Agriculture, Coal & Colonization Co. Ltd.

no desire to go to Montreal. I would rather stay here. If he should stay longer in the mountains, then I can look him up again. I think that I am already far enough away. Make sure that Wil does not make herself too worried about his health. I am certainly convinced that they will get everything in Pincher Creek, in any case, overshoes, socks and mitts.

January 17: I received your letter of December 27 yesterday, and it gave me a lot of pleasure. It is nice to be kept on top of things so regularly, and you must be so busy. Prepare everyone for fewer letters from me in the future. I have had quite enough of writing and I will stop with it for a while — for the time being. Also, there will not be that much to write about anyway. From Karel, I will hear nothing for a month, and my life here will stay the same.

I am pleased that Dr. [Simon] Frédéricq[421] is married, the duty of every right-minded medical doctor. And now he shall certainly give up his Flemish, not that that would please me, to the contrary. Is our Paul perhaps coming again to Amsterdam? Rather, let Pa Quack talk about him; that interests me more. I remember really enjoying, once, watching Pa Quack's discussion with other gentlemen.

I am pleased for young Dirksen. He has *après tout* received the best that he could wish for!

[Jan Kruseman's] surprising vicissitudes I find more or less mysterious, or, actually, less the circumstances than his situation. What a worry for Aunt Annette and I think that it will also bother Papa.

Earlier, I received a visit from Reverend Smith[422] of Pincher Creek. It was lovely to hear about everyone there and to talk with an old acquaintance. Now, enough!

Many heartfelt greetings to everyone, much love from your Heleen.

A32005000511-514 [Wil to Heleen]
Amsterdam, January 17, 1892

Dearest Heleen!

You particularly spoil me with your joyful letters, now two again, one of which for my birthday, in which you spoke so beautifully to me. Just like you, I have sometimes looked ahead and wondered, how shall the next, and the next, time be? But one becomes wary of looking into the future. Then, coming back to the present, or rather, what has just passed! So, then I have to acknowledge that the day passed much better than I had thought, perhaps since I had so little time to think about myself. After lying in bed awake (which ended with Mama's arrival — she looks just like an angel in her nightgown), the busy morning arrived. The cooking school, the

---

421 Simon Frédéricq (1857–1934): medical doctor; married in 1892 to Louise Beaucarne (1868–1926). He is the brother of Paul (1850–1920), a Belgian scholar and professor of history at the University of Ghent.

422 Reverend Henry Havelock-Smith (1857–1904): minister of St. John's Anglican Church in Pincher Creek; married to Beatrice Balfour Henrietta Miles (1861–1904).

visit from Uncle Jan during coffee time, then quickly changing clothes, and then the whole afternoon making visits. In the evening, we were so tired from talking that Cor and I had a nap and finished a card game with Mama. So, you see, a quiet day, just busy enough not to be sitting still.

Before, I was really dreading it, but Wednesday evening at 717 was very enjoyable and lively, and I left there much more cheerful. You will also hear from Karel [about] how your parents took care of me, because, after all, you two are together now? I am so curious about the next letter, what you two will do now and where you are going to live. I do so much hope that Karel will get work soon. What nasty people those Lougheeds seem to be; had you only stayed with the Wilkinses, but such a young family would perhaps rather be alone.

I can imagine the doctor with the lamp on his lap. For old-fashioned Dutch people like us, it sounds so preposterous to have electric light and then to not have an entrance hall to come into the house — to literally 'fall into the house'. And that [Mr. Wilkins] served at the table! Imagine that Karel would have to do that, even once. He, who always expected that his sisters would wait on him hand and foot.

But one changes so much through circumstances. I had also never thought that I would be cleaning the pots and scrubbing the outside with *Brusselsche aarde*,[423] and that I would enjoy it. But to touch raw veal, and to cut off the skin, was somewhat grisly, just like birds of prey do. The others make me afraid that later on we will also have to pluck birds and skin hares. Yuck! Do you know that Nel and I always work together? We were allowed to choose and so I had asked her about that cute idea. Otherwise, I would have gone with Coba van Eeghen. Last time, we cooked together with Minni Gunning,[424] but three is a bit too much. Nel and I are both left-handed and, therefore, we do not hinder each other while peeling potatoes. The first day, we each cooked five and found it such a large number that I decided to never cook five again. Nel assured me that Karel does not like potatoes in particular, and therefore, we will then each get two and *un pour l'honneur du plat*, or for mashed potatoes the next day. Cleaning salsify is also a very 'enjoyable' job; I am glad that it does not happen every day. And rest assured, Heleentje, that later on, we will also learn to bake bread. Last time, we saw a girl working on a lovely raisin bread. It rose so beautifully, but the kneading was terribly heavy work. Your Aunt Emily, who brought flowers for me on my birthday, is refraining from learning to iron. She said that if one had to do it, one could do it anyway. And since Mama is against it, because of the big change from hot to cold outside of the ironing room, I will follow Aunt E's advice and see how it goes.

I cannot refrain from planning all the time how things will be later on, even though I am not permitted, but it is so difficult not to look at this time as being a time of transition, a means to come to a better

---

423 Fine clay used for polishing metal.

424 Wilhelmina Maria Gunning (1877–1946): married in 1905 to Adrianus Bonebakker (1863–1947), medical doctor.

place. Your having said that you divide the days into 'mail days' and 'no mail days', I can understand so well. It must, therefore, also be so lonely sometimes among all those friends with whom one can never talk about mutual friends or well-known places; never once about something you have experienced together, and seldom able to talk about books. In that respect, I am better off than you are, but I also count the time between one letter from Karel to the next. And the days are certainly going fast, but the weeks creep by.

Up until the new year, we had a point in time to look forward to, then it was there, and already so much time has passed and now, so many long months are looming ahead of us. But again, I am being ungrateful. For example, the cooking school is a fulfilling pastime. Then, at least, I am not fully occupied with Karel's well-being. His letter, with many interesting items, did me good; it came Tuesday. Write something to me about his situation. He does not write anything specific about his health. Is he sometimes still short of breath, or do you believe that his lungs are now healthy?

Oh, Heleentje, do you know that I am 'of age' now? And that I must take care of the bookkeeping myself? I already received a memorandum from Mr. Muysken[425] about a bank draft that he purchased for me and must, for the first time, put my signature as something of value on a receipt, after receiving the money released from the inheritance of my great-grandfather. It is but a small amount, but later on, more will come. Then I have to pay for my lessons, my clothing and everything. Your mother thought that it was also very good that I learn how to do it.

And now, *adieu*, dear Heleentje. Much love to Karel if you are with him, and a warm kiss for yourself from your loving Wil.

P.S. Just a short while ago, a letter came from Jo; she must still be very careful and is not allowed to drive [a carriage], or to bend [over], but the doctor was satisfied. Her address is: Russia, Livonie, Meiershof, Wenden, par Pleskow [Pskov].[426] The house had been painted green and the dogs were sweet; she was happy to be home again. Your mother was very cheered up after her visit at the Piersons'.

---

425 Floris Coenraad Muysken (1833–1919): partner of the financial firm Leembruggen Guépin & Muysken; married to Elizabeth Charlotte Guépin (1835–1929).

426 This area, formerly part of Russia, is now in present-day Latvia, near the city of Cesis, formerly known as Wenden. Pskov is twenty miles east of the Estonian border.

Chapter 9

To a Convent and Dancing in Edmonton

The much-anticipated letter from Van Horne finally makes its way to Karel in the Crowsnest, although it does not bring with it the clarity he had been hoping for. Heleen learns more about Canada's history than she may have anticipated. Jan questions Karel's intentions to go through with his marriage to Wil, while Wil ponders a move to Canada.

A28335001555–56 [Heleen to Mother, fragment]
Calgary [probably the week of January 21, 1892]

What I shall now do with the toys, I do not know yet. One doll, and perhaps the yoke and pails, I shall give to Mrs. McCaul's little girl, a friendly affectionate child of three years, who I enchanted last Sunday, so much that she did not want to be with her father when I was there. I have little pleasure in giving anything to the Lougheed children. They destroy everything immediately, and Mrs. [Lougheed] once again put us into a peculiar situation. She had said that she would really like to go to Edmonton. Mr. Niblock provided me again with a carriage and I invited her to accompany me. Mrs. Trott and her sister were also to come along. Mrs. Lougheed accepted eagerly. The day before our departure, last Sunday, I went to tell her that the carriage was ready and that we would get settled that evening in order to leave early in the morning. Then, she seemed to be doubtful if she would be going, but did not, as usual, want to decide.

    We three of us gathered that evening, but Mrs. Lougheed did not show up. In the meantime, she had let her brother[427] in Edmonton know that

---

427   Mrs. Lougheed's only brother living in Edmonton during this period was George Hardisty (1840–1898).

she would be arriving with companions and he had, therefore, arranged a ball. When it appeared that the company was only two ladies in deep mourning and me, it was a big disappointment. The little widow could not go dancing and it was an amusing thing for the two of us to trot off to a ball with a bunch of strange gentlemen.

All went well and I got a lot of enjoyment from it, but if Mrs. Lougheed had just told me that she didn't want to go, then I would have arranged for another chaperone.

I will send a description of our journey to Wil. I felt comfortable and at home in my carriage, and my travel companions, while perhaps not the most entertaining that one could wish for, were quite bearable. By the end, it started to bore me to hear proclamations of the outstanding qualities of the dead pharmacist (who died due to the consumption of too much whiskey), but the poor soul was satisfied with my sensible comments about clinging to a buried husband and began slowly to find some enjoyment in the free life of a wealthy widow and was sometimes the most cheerful of the three [of us].

She is an oddly shallow, foolish creature, who had before never looked outside of her own pharmacy circle, and now for the first time was starting to see and to think. In Edmonton [actually St. Albert], we visited a convent where neglected mixed-blood children were being nursed and brought up, and to see the life full of hardship and devotion of those nuns impressed her greatly and took away much of the bitterness of her own lot. She looks French, with short black [hair], is lively and claims to have many French affinities, but in fact, she does not understand one word of it. At the convent, I alone had to keep the conversation going with the nuns and the bishop,[428] a very gentle old priest who amused me immensely with his practical remarks about the missionary work and the Indians.

Bye, Mama, many thanks for all your letters, also those in the chest, and a warm kiss from your Helena.

A32074000170-77 [Heleen to Wil]
Calgary, January 21, 1892

Dear Wil,

This week I made a most enjoyable trip to Edmonton, a little town north of Calgary, to where a branch of the CPR has been in operation since August 1890. The train runs twice each week and is used for both passengers and freight. We had to take this normal train and could not go as slowly as [we did] in the mountains, but again, I had my own carriage. We amused ourselves with the wobbling of the plates and dishes. The conductor was

---

428   Bishop Vital-Justin Grandin (1829–1902), of the diocese of St. Albert, served from 1871 to 1902. During his life he was revered; at the present time, his legacy is seriously tarnished as a result of his supporting role in the residential schools for Indigenous children. See also footnote 434.

a friend of Mrs. [Elizabeth] Trott's and was very courteous. Underway, we had a visit from Mr. Becker,[429] who had introduced himself the previous day. He had been very busy telegraphing about a ball that he wanted to throw for us in Edmonton. Afterwards came Mrs. Beck,[430] with a sweet girl of three years old. They were returning to their husband and father, whom they had not seen in seven months. [Mrs. Beck] had gone to Winnipeg for her health, to recuperate. Mrs. Trott enjoyed these new listeners and shared her catastrophes and talked for three hours about the dearly departed pharmacist and his nasty family.

In the meantime, I had such fun with the little girl, who made up long stories, and acted like little brothers or birds and flowers that, for the two of us, became so realistic that the rest of the company looked anxiously into the bedroom, thinking that there were real boys and birds to see.

It was eleven hours on the train, but it did not seem that long. We left the mountains behind us, but then we drew nearer to the forest and, slowly, the track appeared as a long avenue of lit-up birch trunks, high and straight.

January 22: Yesterday, I got no further with writing because Miss Wardlow came to fetch me in order to go to Mrs. Snyder's. [Mrs. Snyder] is Scottish and we met her married brother, Mr. [Edmiston],[431] in Edmonton. There, I met Mrs. Wilkins, who came with me back to the hotel to admire the contents of the chest. She stayed for dinner and, in the evening, brought me along to her house, where I was to alter a black lace dress for her this morning. We both slept in, did not get up until 9:30 a.m.; then it was hurry, hurry in order to get ready before 1:00 p.m., because she had to wear the dress to a luncheon party and had to wash a tablecloth before then.

I lunched back at the hotel and further occupied myself by giving my room a somewhat more pleasant appearance, because with all the stuff from the chest, it was very untidy. I got a plank for the linen cupboard from Mrs. Perley[432] and stored the toys and additional items that I will not need daily, put the chest on its back, and on top and over it some photographs in frames. On the tea tray, I arranged the tea service and put it on the table in front of the window. Now the room is again usable and looks homey with all the well-known faces and the blue porcelain. When I was done, it was time, along with Miss Wardlow, to make a visit that I had promised to Mrs. Macleod, who was so friendly to me in [Fort] Macleod and who is now staying at the house of the bishop here. After

---

429 This is probably Charles D.T. Becker (born Waterford, Ireland; 27 years old): accountant with the Hudson's Bay Co.

430 Mary Ethel Lloyd Beck (1865–1904): married to Nicholas Dubois Dominic Beck, lawyer and jurist at Beck and Emery (1857–1928).

431 William Somerville Edmiston (1857–1903): architect; was the fifth mayor of Edmonton, serving in 1895 and 1896; married to Georgina (Georgie) Annie Eliza Frith (1866–1940).

432 Eliza G. Hammond Perley (1852–1928): married to Henry Allison Perley (1849–1933); owner and operator of the Alberta Hotel.

that, it was dinner time, and now it is close to 7:00 p.m. and I can continue my story.

We arrived in [South] Edmonton [on the south side of the North Saskatchewan River] around 7:00 in the evening. Mrs. Beck was preparing to leave the carriage through one door when, at the other door, there was a knock. When I opened that door, I saw a distinguished stranger in front of me, whom I immediately understood to be Mr. Beck, with his face full of cheerful expectation. Mrs. Beck was called back and [there was] an endearing meeting in the narrow aisle between the couchettes.

In the meantime, the landscape was darkened by what first appeared to us to be a herd of buffaloes. It approached and (after a short wrestle in the narrow aisle) appeared to be the 'coming out' of the *jeunesse flores* of Edmonton in their winter coats! How we sat with twelve of us in the small salon car, on two chairs and one sofa, I leave to your imagination. But it is a fact that all of those folks, of which eight of them were in huge buffalo coats, talked for fifteen minutes most enjoyably, and then they were gone, with us having promised to go on a sleigh ride the next day with one of them, and for all of us to go dancing the next evening. We had great fun looking forward to it and slept the sleep of the righteous.

The sleigh ride was indeed the next morning. Suddenly, the weather had become mild and it was barely freezing; the sky was lightly clouded and we had a delightful trip through the woods. We first had to go down a hill, cross the river and then again up a hill in order to reach the city. But after my Banff experiences, this was child's play. The river was frozen solid, at least three feet of ice, and all of it pure pleasure. Edmonton is not like Calgary, in the valley, but built spread out on a hill, appearing very pleasant in the hazy sunlight.

We drove, or rather glided, on a nice curvy trail through the bushes, which were glowing warm red due to the colourful twigs scattered on the snowy ground. Dick Hardisty[433] drove and we flew along the trail. He is an amiable red-haired young man who has a ranch somewhere and loves to party, and so is mostly in town. *Aux petit souris* for us, very good manners and easy-going, an outstanding driver, twenty-one years old!

[40] **Richard George (Dick) Hardisty**

433   Richard George (Dick) Hardisty, Major (1871–1943): one son of Senator Richard Charles Hardisty (1832–1889) and Eliza Victoria McDougall (1849–1929). He married in 1892 to Margaret Taylor (1873–1901) and in 1908 to Esther B. Kelly (1884–1947). Dick was a veteran of both the Boer War and the First World War. He is also a cousin of Isabella Hardisty (Belle) Lougheed.

The goal of our journey was to be 'The Convent', in other words, 'The Mission',[434] a collection of buildings of the Roman Catholic missionaries, situated at some distance, with Edmonton on the other side of the river on a higher hill. In the convent, a luncheon was ordered for us. The Mother Superior received us most warmly and sent for a beautiful Irish nun to speak with the English [folks]. [The Mother Superior] was French, just like all the others, and guided me around through the hospital, where I was able to console a poor German woman a little bit. She was ill from deprivation; no one understood her language, while neither she nor her husband nor children could understand English.

An Indian woman with beautiful black eyes was dying from tuberculosis.

The sisters mostly dealt with the upbringing of the so-called converted Indians and mixed-blood children. There were almost a hundred there. We saw them reciting verses, rattling off history and geography, but notwithstanding that they pronounced the words very well, it seemed to me that they did not comprehend very much of it. Dick Hardisty contended that the nuns were not doing any good by it and that nothing would ever come of their foster children. The Superior also said something of the sort, but she did not appear to be very concerned about it. She did her duty for the church and, no matter what, earned her place in heaven for it.

Mr. Hardisty was allowed to eat with us in the dining room, but while we toured through the building, he visited the bishop, Monseigneur [Grandin], and we found him there later. In the palace of the bishop, we viewed with interest the furniture, some beautifully carved, and all made by the monks. In a small room downstairs, we spoke with an older gentleman who was confined to his chair as the result of a spinal disease, or something like that. He was from a good family and had been very rich, but was now penniless and helpless and, despite the fact that he is not Catholic, the bishop provides for him.

---

434   The sleigh ride to the "Mission" took Heleen to St. Albert, about 12 km northwest of Edmonton. The mission was founded by Father Albert Lacombe in 1861 and situated on the hilltop overlooking the Sturgeon River. By 1868 the parish had about 699 Métis Catholics. Bishop Grandin was appointed the first Apostolic Vicar in 1871, and the town became an important Oblate centre; by 1879 there was a new church-cathedral, a convent of the Sisters of Charity of Montreal (Grey Nuns), a school (60 children) and orphanage (30 children), and a hospital. It is difficult to distinguish the Oblate school in kind from those which began operating in eastern Canada, spreading westward since 1831. The first residential school for Indigenous children in Alberta was formally established in 1862 in Lac La Biche, north of St. Albert. Not yet formally designated an Indian Residential School, this Oblate school (now referred to as Youville) was already awarded $300 a year in federal funding in 1873, later funded under the Indian Act of 1876. Bishop Grandin (a close friend of Dick Hardisty's father) frequently asked the federal government to increase grants and promoted industrial and residential schools throughout the rest of his life. Youville closed in 1948. The formal era of residential schools in Canada officially ended in 1996, but the tragic aftermath is ongoing. By 2007, 139 residential schools across Canada were formally recognized, 26 in Alberta. The observations made by Dick Hardisty and Heleen Boissevain in January of 1892 would not be out of step with the stories and the current work of the Truth and Reconciliation Commission of Canada. Sources: *https://nctr.ca/residential-schools/alberta/st-albert-youville/* at the University of Manitoba; *https://laclabichemuseum.com/tag/industrial-schools/*; *https://www.teachers.ab.ca/SiteCollectionDocuments/ATA/For%20Members/ProfessionalDevelopment/Walking%20Together/PD-WT-16n%20Residential%20Schools-M%C3%A9tis%20Experience.pdf*.

[41] Mission and convent on the hill in St. Albert

The return trip with the wind was, if possible, even faster and lovelier than the outward one. We dined on the train and at 8:00 p.m. another gentleman, with a sleigh for two persons, arrived to take us to the ball. (The pharmacist's widow, because of mourning, could not go to the ball.)

You do not know what a funny feeling it was, being there at this faraway, strange place, in the starry night, riding in a sleigh to an unknown ball! We got out in front of a small hotel and walked up the wooden stair to the cloakroom. There, the coats and furs were taken off and overshoes and boots changed for shoes, the only sign that my travel clothing had changed into clothing for dancing. In the scarcely lit entrance, one of the buffaloes from the prior evening (now in tails) introduced us to Mrs. Edmiston, a sweet dark-haired little woman in her bridal gown. We followed her to the dance hall downstairs, a long narrow hall with an uneven wooden floor, lit with five petroleum lamps and decorated with buffalo hides on the wall.

The gents stood in a little group by one of the doors while the ladies walked arm in arm, in threes and fours, through the hall. I only became acquainted with the younger sister of Mrs. Beck and a few young girls between seventeen and fourteen years old. Soon, the procession of gentlemen came toward us and then we were waltzing through the hall, some of them dancing very well. Mr. Edmiston gradually gathered a number of his Scottish friends around him and they pleasantly gushed about the Highlands and the lochs, the Isle of Skye and Beauly.

They strongly urged us to stay a few days and to take more sleigh rides. They suggested unhooking the wagon just before the train was to depart, and Mrs. Edmiston asked me to stay on her farm, about twenty miles outside the city. I strongly desired to do that but understood how difficult it would be to persuade Mrs. Trott. That indeed was the case. At 2:00 a.m., we were back in the carriage after a lovely slow ride in the moonlight, because Mrs. Trott did not want to stay.

The train departed at 8:00 a.m. Indeed, a few buffalo-coats came running down [to send us off], but they did not have much fun with it because the curtains were closed; in any event, they did not unhook the wagon. But later at breakfast, when we had already been underway for a few hours, we did get a parting note that they had written at the station.

In Calgary, I was glad not to have stayed away longer, because I had received enjoyable mail about which I could write to Karel, and I could still buy overshoes for him, etc., and pass them on to Mr. Harris,[435] who was to leave the next morning for the camp in the Crowsnest Pass.

No doubt you are sorry that it took so long for Karel to receive your book, *Gedachten*, by Carmen Sylva,[436] but in camp all excess baggage is barred and there is so much chance that it would be damaged by snow or wind, or become lost. It will not take so long anymore, once he returns again to somewhere in the civilized world.

It is nice to know that these letters to you are read by you at home and also by your family; if I had to write everything three times, I could not manage it. Now, Karel also takes up such a large part of my correspondence. I wanted to write to Thijs to thank him for his watercolour, but would you do it for me, now? I am very delighted with it and hung it up in my room right away; every time my eyes fall upon it, it is a new joy. I think that he was very successful with it. The high trees, especially, seem to be livelier than the previous ones and it is once again a joy to see a real, half-lit Dutch sky, with shadows from the clouds.

The carved wooden spoon box is very much admired here. When I am in Montreal, I shall nose around for an agency for it; it would certainly sell well here.

Bye, Willemientje, a warm kiss from your Heleen.

A32005000425-26 [Father to Heleen]
Amsterdam, January 23, 1892

Dear Helena,

---

435   This is likely Michael Harris (1837–1917): engineer and employee at the Dominion Land Titles Office in Calgary.

436   Pauline Elisabeth Ottilie Luise zu Wied (1843–1916): wife of King Carol I of Romania; widely known by her literary name, Carmen Sylva. The book is *Gedachten*, a Dutch translation from the original in German, *Vom Amboss*, by Cornelie Lijdie Huijgens, published by Veen, Amsterdam (1890).

Anna's birthday. I already gave her present to her yesterday because I had to get up early to see the SS *Soenda* off, which left at 9:00 a.m. from the Handelskade so that in the case of a delay due to the ice, it will still arrive on time at IJmuiden. We are managing the ice quite well. I have, by scratching and biting, gathered ƒ5,000 and, with that, I pay a small Rotterdam tow-boat with a 'big nose' that, up to now, keeps the waterway open. The gents Goedkoop[437] were not very amenable, and therefore it was necessary for me to go elsewhere for the services.

Captain Visman[438] was again in full spirits on his small SS *Soenda*, which will be going on an adventure to Java without passengers. He has good lodging on the ship, but it is boring, since he has not much to do with his officers and machinists. He reads a lot and consoles himself with the prospect of once again getting a mail ship.

At 10:00 a.m., I attended a gathering at Aunt Henriette van Heukelom's,[439] where the drawing up of the inventory and apportionment of the estate of Aunt Louise took place. There was something melancholic about the cousins van Heukelom, Beuker,[440] van Houten[441] and me being together for the arrangement of the estate that will occur after the death of Aunt Henriette, who was also present. In short, everything was agreeably arranged; we ate a date from the box that Dawes had sent and we each went again on our own way. You should know that our friend Dawes, with whom we jigged over the heather in the highlands, has sent a crate of dates to me, containing thirty boxes and, after that, I sent small samples to a wide circle of family and friends.

This evening, there will be a gathering of young folks. I think that things are going well between Anna and Nella and that they can invite their mutual friends without any clashing.

Jan Kruseman has returned by sea from Genoa and, in my mind, is doing much better. He is now definitely out of the insurance business and has re-established himself as a lawyer. Still somewhat slow with decision-making, however, he is nonetheless his old self again and not so melancholic anymore.

On Thursday, there was great concern at the van Eeghens' because Willem[442] had coughed up blood again, just on the wedding day of his sister, to Wolterbeek, no less. The symptoms do not seem to be that alarming and he is now reasonably well. Yet it is constantly a big worry and I have a lot of sympathy for these friends.

437 Rederij Goedkoop: a tow-boat company in Amsterdam, operating from 1807 to 1999.

438 Hendrik Sierik Visman (1856–1911): a sea captain; married to Bastiana Petronella Anna Huizer (1866–1949).

439 Henriette Adriana van Heukelom (1816–1894) and her sister Louise (who had recently died) are both unmarried half-sisters of Jan Boissevain's mother.

440 Jan Hendrik Beuker (1831–1905): stockbroker; married to Bartruida van Heukelom (1841–1902).

441 Johan Walraven van Houten (1833–1911): manufacturing director; married to Alida Berendina Langeler (1834–1917).

442 Anne Willem van Eeghen (1860–1938): merchant.

Mia is to go figure skating today with her friend, van Steijn,[443] on the skating rink [at Museumplein, Amsterdam], but it is thawing and therefore I do not know if the competition will go ahead.

The government loan was successful and was oversubscribed, so that the subscribers did not even get half of what they had asked for. This made me very pleased for Minister Pierson, who bypassed the bankers and had directly appealed to the public. Last week in The Hague, I had a long discussion with Minister Tak again, who encouraged me to run as a member of the senate, but at the end, he had to agree with my objections (in other words) that I have to stick to my business so long as I am the manager.

Mama was feeling unwell for a few days, but she kept herself somewhat quiet and I think that she now looks well again. Li is still weak, but I believe on the right track.

Many greetings to you and Karel, from your loving Father.

KLAB04554000223-224 [Karel to Wil]
In camp, Crowsnest Lake: Sunday, January 24, 1892

Dear Wil,

I am permitting myself the luxury of a short supplement to my last short letter, which I fear was put a little bit despondently, therefore quite accurately reflecting my mood from those days. Five weeks without news was somewhat severe for me. You understand well that this is much worse than while I was on board, where I expected frequent, much longer times without news. This time, my scheme had been set, news every fourteen days (sometimes weekly), and then come to find that along with Helena's departure all the dispatches suddenly stopped. Now and then, a single magazine slips through and reaches us and makes me even more confused. Daily expectations and daily disappointments. But now, all is in order. The post office dolt finally sent us the accumulated stockpile. I have you to thank for your letters from December 3, 7, 21.

Lovely news! Oh, my dear, I am so thankful that you keep yourself in good spirits and continue on so bravely and that you come to our house on such friendly terms.

Dear girl, what a difference for you between this winter and the last one! You may now say — and I feel very flattered — that I was the great attrac-tion at the balls; but in any event, so also was waltzing with Notje and dining with Joan Rahusen![444] And flirting with all your other admirers also had its charm; is that not true? And, once in a while, you

---

443 Louisa Charlotte van Steijn (1878–1941): married in 1901 to Jhr. Bertram Philips Sigismund Albrecht Storm van 's-Gravesande (1873–1959), mayor of Bleiswijk from 1906 to 1911, and in 1911 became mayor of Wassenaar.

444 Joan Rahusen (1864–1920): director of the Amsterdam Spaarbank; married to Boudewina de Graaff (1870–1933).

will still feel a small 'pang' at Cor's stories about merry suppers and glorious waltzes, and sigh sometimes as you send her on her way. And that is no more than natural, and you do not have to be ashamed of that, I think. Nevertheless, there is danger (generally speaking) for jealousy to arise in a situation like ours, but this will not be the case for you, of that I am convinced. Mama's older sister, Aunt Anna,[445] who died about twenty years ago from tuberculosis, was a beautiful young girl at that time, who loved to go out but had to give it up after a short period because of her health; and I always found it to be such a lovely trait of hers that, while she could not participate, she very much took pleasure in the outings of Mama and Aunt Helena [Pijnappel]. She had a lot of jewellery, fans, etc., and always gave those to her younger sisters to let them shine where she could not go.

Yes, dear girl, your letter of the 7th was piercingly intimate. It was painful, but a pain that is blissful and that, in the end, should work very well. Oh, if everything would end up well! I am so very happy about the good news about Jo. That is a capital fellow, this Thure Brandt! A fellow to cast in gold. Imagine that dear soul, who even during her own suffering, still had so much concern for me that she wrote a long, lovely letter to me here. I cannot yet answer it, but Helena took it upon herself to do it for me. And will you, once again, thank [Jo] for me when you write to her? The shower of letters gave me such a sweet feeling. All those friends who had me in their thoughts, all the warm love charmed me. That was something comforting, and then I went to work on Saturday with more joy than I had felt for days and days.

One letter that I had expected did not come. It is the call from Mr. Van Horne to come and settle in Montreal for the time being, and from there to look for a regular job. According to the agreement when I left, I was seriously counting on it, very much. Now, I am really taken aback to know that I must keep going with this journey until the end of April. But I would feel so miserable if I had to sit and do nothing for the whole rest of the winter in Montreal that I would much rather prefer to stay here, where I, despite the drawbacks, at least have an occupation.

Sleeping on the ground is not as bad as you may imagine. Think about it — we shovel the snow, or if it is frozen solid, first hack it away. Then we cover the ground with at least a half-foot of spruce branches. Then comes a piece of caoutchouc[446] against the possible damp of the ground, and then I make my bed with the aid of three thick blankets, a travel rug, a fur and a few overcoats. I dare you to match up my comfort and warmth against that of anyone. No, the misery is not so bad, especially not today, now that it is lovely and sunny and I am enjoying my day off.

I must write Heleentje and Mama and would also like to find time for a word to cousin [Cornelis] den Tex and to [Jacobus] Boelen.[447] See also

445 Anna Antonia Brugmans (1835–1874).

446 Natural rubber that has not been vulcanized.

447 Jacobus Boelen (1854–1932): merchant and Amsterdam city counsellor; married to Dorothea Maria Schlette (1853–1931).

my letter to Mama. Bye, my darling, I still have a horrendous amount to say to you in response to your letters, but I may not indulge myself in my letters, so.
    Oh Wim, O Wim . . . ! Your own, Karel

A32074000183–184 [Heleen to Wil]
Calgary, January 25, 1892

Dear Wil,

This morning I received your letter of January 5 and I must thank you right away and answer it — and thank you because you write just the way you feel, even when you go through difficult, doubting days. Karel wrote you a long letter for your birthday and that shall certainly have satisfied the sad longing of the time around the coming of the new year. But those fourteen days shall have weighed heavily, and likely a sombre time and despondent yearning will return. Therefore, with full conviction, I am grateful to reassure you about your involuntary worries that, despite yourself, will almost creep up on you sometimes.
    Last summer, when everything seemed to be so good and promised such a beautiful future, I sometimes looked at Karel and you with apprehension. I knew how instantly intolerable he was, and also what high standards he would expect of his wife, and I feared for the duration of the happiness of both of you. But no matter what grievousness he may inflict during this time of stress and sorrow while so many other influences work upon him, for myself, I have the assurance that you are the master of his whole soul, that the best part of him loves you with all of his heart.
    Do not be afraid that dangers and hardships will cloud your view, but be thankful that the necessary strain of all his tribulations prevents him from admitting to the agonizing thoughts about how much sadness he has caused you. I do not know whether I am doing the right thing by writing in this way, but Karel himself is so afraid to demand too much from you, with following him in this, that he perhaps does not dare to speak his thoughts, out of the fear of tying you too tightly to him. Still, life is difficult enough without making it more burdensome through misunderstandings, and therefore I wanted to relieve you of the unnecessary worries as soon as possible.
    With affectionate love, your Heleen

P.S. Today was a delightful spring day. The snow disappeared as if by magic. The river streamed again playfully and happily and so clearly that we could count the pebbles on the riverbed. It was a pleasure to breathe. I got a letter out of Liverpool from Mr. Ashley Elton, whose sister I had supported a little bit on the train from Lethbridge to Dunmore. A lovely letter of thanks, and to mention the safe arrival of his sister. From your Heleen.

A28335001524 [Heleen to Father, fragment]
Calgary, January 25, 1892

Dear Father,

This morning, I was made very happy by your letter of January 7. I receive letters almost daily and that is much lovelier than in the 'far west' — twenty letters in one day and then three weeks with nothing.

Yesterday, I got a letter from Karel from the camp. Their letters were still missing, but he is doing well. They are at the end of the line, have placed the terminus and begun to 'locate'. That is much slower work than the preliminary survey and he thinks that the camp will now remain for six weeks at the same place. His work remains more or less the same and therefore not very instructive. The day before yesterday, I got a letter from Wil and one from Mr. E.A. Elton, out of Liverpool. Today, your letter and a telegram from Hosmer.

Count Adolphe did not go to Montreal and I did not get in contact with him by telegraph. Therefore, would you please write or speak with him about extending the credit at the Bank of Montreal? Since I last wrote to you about this, I have spent nothing to speak of and the same for Karel, but the bill here at the hotel shall most likely increase. I have agreed to $55.00 for a month — a steep price in Holland, but here, quite normal. If I am away during that time for a week, then it will be subtracted. Since we travel free of charge, there is, therefore, no hurry; perhaps it is easier to wait until I am in Montreal, since I am not sure what my movements will be up to that time. I have no desire to go there on my own. Here, I am closer to Karel and freer than I can be among my prominent 'friends' there.

Here, I am now promoted to 'Countess'. Everyone is amiable and hospitable but, through my frequent absences, no one knows if I am present or not. In that way, I can choose the people that I wish to see for myself and that suits me well, because if the whole bunch of friendly, babbling ladies would like to haul me in, my tribulation would be incalculable.

Sunday, yesterday, was a beautiful spring day and it was a pleasure to be able to leave the heavy winter clothes at home while reading in front of an open window. I tried to pore over *The Divine Comedy*, but it appears that I have left my study-spirit on the other side of the Atlantic. Also, I tried to imprint upon my memory the lessons of my nursing book, but it was in vain. My thoughts are always wandering and I might as well think that looking at the real life around me is just as useful; it is easier, in any case. I closed my book and went to fetch Mrs. Trott, to hear her beloved shepherd, Reverend Cooper,[448] but the Anglican ritual was, for me, unbearably hollow and the bishop, with his phony, sugary tones, annoyed me so that I not in . . . [Ends here]

---

448   Reverend Alfred (Alf) William Cooper (1848–1920): later Anglican Archdeacon of Calgary (1895–1898).

A32005000427-428 [Father to Heleen]
Amsterdam, January 29, 1892

Dear Helena,

Since I wrote to you on Anna's birthday, I have received an enjoyable letter from you dated January [8] and a cordial letter from Mr. Hosmer, from which I saw that the crates finally arrived, that he has a lot of interest in the two of you and that he remains fully attentive. He can see that the great Van Horne and his family are also interested in both of you; Mr. Hosmer believes that Karel's health is doing so well that there could be a chance that he will get a job.

It is a pity that Mama's letter about unnecessary travel brought you into doubt and difficulty just when the trip to Vancouver was to go ahead. *Il faut juger les écrits d'après leur date* and her letter was perhaps written just after we had heard about your accident. Now Mama really regrets that she has hindered you from getting a change [of scenery] from the very monotonous stay in Calgary. This will most likely continue until the beginning of February, since Karel's work in the mountains will take so much longer. I fear that you have sometimes felt lonely and I am sorry that, due to the irregular mail during this season, our letters are not so frequent, or at least have not arrived in as correct a sequence as I had hoped for. It is difficult to connect in this season, overseas as well as overland.

Yesterday, I had a visit from Captain van der Lee,[449] who arrived in London four days ago from Halifax and St. John's with the SS *Celebes* and, during the conversation, he presumed I had known various things that I knew nothing about. Today the mystery will be solved by his letter of January 9, written before his departure from Halifax, now delivered by mail via New York. In Halifax, he met a Dutch vice-consul[450] who had been in the appointment for twenty years and still never had to do anything in his position. He is a practising doctor and was called to attend to one of the crewmen. Then he remembered that he still has something to do with the 'Dutch' and he dug up an old seal to sign off on the ship's certificate of registry.

I find it interesting that you have become impressed with the mighty, giant mountains and that the grandness of nature in the vicinity of Banff left you speechless. It also gives that impression to me, overwhelming. I find the same in the Grimsel region; as soon as one arrives above the vegetation and there is nothing else around you but ice, snow and granite, then one is in awe of the enormous Alpine giants.

The party for Anna's birthday turned out well. I found the young folks quite joyful and the tone was pleasant. I sat beside a Wolterbeek girl,

---

449   Tymon Van der Lee (1851–1917): captain; married to Anna Catharina Wilhelmina Zeilinga (1865–1932).

450   Dr. William Nathan Wickwire (1839–1911): medical doctor and vice-consul in Halifax; married in 1870 to Margaret Louisa Keith (1843–1930).

who spoke very pleasantly. Betsy Röell is maturing very nicely, both inwardly and outwardly. Jo,[451] Ko's daughter, looked very nice and seemed to be very popular with the dancers.

Anna herself was very cheerful and looked quite nice, even though she is missing the talent of looking gracious in full dress. There is always something a bit off-key. Nella looked much more polished. The gents were all contemporaries of Matthijs. Very many salient young men, I did not see. I think that Willem Waller,[452] who is now at the office in Amsterdam after his return from America, is no great addition for the circle.

Our attempts to get the Canadian Insinger, along with his sister [Willy],[453] to visit us have so far failed. I have not yet written to you, I believe, about visiting him. I found him very cooperative and polite, but I have heard absolutely nothing from him that would be useful to me with an eye to where Karel may eventually settle. If he is, perhaps, not doing very well in business, I do not know; everything came down to the fact that, from here, one could say nothing, and that one has to be in the place itself in order to know whether it is a wise place to settle, etc.

Today, we will have Charles and Maria [Boissevain], Cor and Mary [van Eeghen], [David] Fock, and Wil for dinner. I hope that it will be enjoyable, only I do not know exactly what we will do in the evening.

My best greetings, also for Karel, if he is with you. From your loving Father.

A29648000016-18 [Heleen to Thijs]
Calgary, January 31, 1892

Dear Thijs,

Your letter from January 2 to 8 has again considerably perked me up. How nice of the Swiss cousins to remember you for the new year. A lovely memory of joy-filled days!

This morning (coming home from Mrs. McCaul's, who I had been 'protecting' last night because her husband is away in Lethbridge for a few days), I found a page of music addressed to me. It was an Edelweiss waltz and written on the title page was "Would you like me to get you the flower?" I absolutely cannot guess who sent it to me, but I shall try to find out.

I have seen a favourable review of *Edel*,[454] van Bourget, and I would also like to read it if you folks have it at home, but you may have read

---

451   Johanna (Jo) Dorothea Boissevain (1872–1937): daughter of Jacob Pieter (Ko) Boissevain; married in 1906 to Robert von Hemert (1871–1930) partner in the firm Tiedeman & van Kerchem, Batavia; second marriage in 1936 to Josef Heinrich Amrhein (1876–?), a lawyer in Lucerne.

452   Willem Maurits Waller (1873–1945): first marriage to Marion Gibberd (1863–1944); second marriage to Dorothy Mitchell Smith (1898–1983).

453   Wilhelmina (Willy) Jacoba Insinger (1868–1937): married on January 5, 1893, to Carl August Breitenstein (1865–1921), painter.

454   *Edel* is a poem (1878) by Paul Bourget (1852–1935), a French writer.

it in the Leesmuseum.[455] Bourget must indeed have been sometimes burdened by the responsibility of the influence he has had with his books, and therefore, has written *Edel* expressly [because of this].

I hope for you that another treasurer will be found. It is especially difficult with parties, a difficult job that requires a lot of dull work, but if there is no other option, we must console ourselves with the thought that at least it will be useful as a practice in bookkeeping and in the appreciation of reliable payers.

I shall send your letter to Karel. There is now some chance that he will get it in about fourteen days, and with that, I come to the end of your letter and see with horror your closing "*Au revoir!*" You must not be serious about that. You shall, after all, write very often to me before we see each other again. I trust that this is poetic licence, in other words, a disregard of the real word value, and in light of that, I shall not dwell on it. Today it is Sunday, and in any event the weather is too beautiful to do that. I left Mrs. McCaul at the door of the church and then went out on my own to start walking outside of the city, over the furthest bridge (the same one as that which I had written about earlier to Mia), and loved it beyond description.

It had iced over, and over the bridge the white frozen road cut between the hills and meandered upwards. The straight firs, rooted in the shadow of the slope below me, were glorified in their tops by the golden light of the happy sun, which had started to live in the bare crowns of the silver-stemmed birches and every fine twig became alive with dizzying light. On top of the rolling hilltops [was] the beautiful broad view of the friendly, quiet city in Sunday's peace, and the blinking ice-blue mountains, so well known in their contours and seemingly so close by in the unwavering full light, where Karel now also enjoys his well-earned rest. And, around me, the fuzzy, dreamlike, soft and golden-brown prairie, like the skin of a gazelle. I stood for a long time as if captive, listening to the soft moaning of the wind in the firs and following the satisfying movements of the grazing horses in their velvet winter coats. Then suddenly from the foot of the hill, merry, laughing voices rang in the cavernous trail, and when they neared the top, I saw two cowboys trotting by with their jingling spurs, fur coats and broad-brimmed grey hats.

However, it became high time I returned before lunch. I descended carefully over the slippery road and only once met a rancher in his buggy, in buffalo skin and fur hat, who was driving slowly up the road, his two horses harnessed far away from each other. We exchanged a friendly greeting and I descended still further back to the city that was still far away, but from which the laughing voices of children reached my ears. Hesitating, I still continued on. It was as if the high mountaintops and the broad prairie held me prisoner; as if I could always stay on the high hilltop looking toward the far, far world in the valley and the high beautiful mountains so close by!

455 The Leesmuseum was a gentlemen's club from about 1800 to 1930, located on the Rokin in Amsterdam. It was established to provide a place for gentlemen to read both local and foreign newspapers.

Bye, little Thijs! Walking is a lovely thing to do and gives people much pleasure. A warm kiss, from Heleen.

A32005000457-462 [Heleen to 'Pa' Quack]
Calgary, January 31, 1892

Dear Mr. Quack,

I was so happy to receive your book [*De Socialisten*] and your lovely, dear letter to Papa, enclosed within. Far too sweet and too flattering for my modesty this letter would be if I did not know that all the good and beautiful things, which you so readily express, must be attributed more to your way of seeing than to mine.

Your book has been my loyal companion when, in these strange surroundings, I long for a Dutch word and the voice of a friend, because in everything that you write, I always hear your voice; and however much I always liked to hear it at home, here, the pleasure for me was twice as great. After the chatter of my well-meaning but by no means literary Canadians, it is refreshing to hear your lovely Dutch and to revel in the beauty of our language.

And that was not the only enjoyment the book gave me. You think that life here is more spacious and more modern than in the confinement of the crowded cities and daily worries; but the breadth of everyone's horizon is limited through their visual acuity and that does not increase with the large open spaces, but rather through practising and gazing into the beyond. Here, where the winter is so harsh and the services so few, the daily needs of material life show themselves to be merciless; all eyes, by necessity, are oriented to the ground, the ground which gives wood and coal against the cold, and beef and bread against hunger.

When I had stoked the stove, helped to bake the bread here, and from every voice had heard the same melody — how heavy the work was and how expensive the foodstuff is — then I returned with satisfaction to my room, in order to immerse myself in the works and struggles of those who pursue a better future for all, etc. It seemed to me from here, at a distance, as if I could better see the grand direction of all that striving; how the personal deviations of those searching, bringing themselves down, was short-lived, yet the goodness and the truth that they stood for remained alive and flourished.

In the last couple of days, I also received Wibaut's[456] translation of *Socialism* from the Fabian Society[457] and I read the first chapters with great interest. They appear to me to be a big step forward, in particular

---

[456] Dr. Florentinus Marinus (Floor) Wibaut (1859–1936): businessman and socialistic politician; married to Mathilde Berdenis van Berlekom (1862–1952), politician and feminist.

[457] A British socialist organization, 1884, which spawned similar organizations, such as the Douglas-Coldwell Foundation, in Canada, inspired by Tommy Douglas.

when they cleanse socialism of the elements of hate and envy against the *Nieuwenhuizen en Fortuinen*.[458] But it is such a pity that there is nobody here with whom I can exchange views about this, now that Karel is still so far from me.

I am like 'Sister Anna',[459] looking out to see whether the brother would come running at full gallop, but my waiting takes longer. On the other hand, I have no trouble with Bluebeards who pursue me, but my life looks more like that of Snow White being served by the dwarfs. In the hotel, I have all the comforts that I could wish for, and my numerous new friends bestow all the kinds of attention on me that they can think of in this bleak winter.

Perhaps you have heard how regally I travel here, and certainly, it is a great pleasure to travel in that way to see this beautiful country. When I was to come here, I did not think that these months would give me so much enjoyment, or be so relatively carefree, especially because Karel is so much better and stronger than we had dared to hope.

Elisabeth wrote to me about the upcoming wedding of the doctor Frédéricq. Will you be invited to it? When you speak to 'our Paul', please greet him heartily for me. I always think about him and his fight for the Dutch language when I see the difficulties of the mixed French and English population here. It is different here, but the French of the Canadians is just as ugly a language as Flemish, and all the French understand English but no English understand French.

Very much love for Aunt Thérèse,[460] and believe in my heartfelt friendship, sincerely yours, Helena Boissevain

KLAB09193000030-31 [Father to Karel and Heleen]
Amsterdam, February 2, 1892

Dear children,

Just a short chat about finances. First of all, enclosed is a new credit letter so that now, it turns out, you hold a current credit of $1,000.00 at the Bank of Montreal; so, after using the available credit, and each time after the previous is depleted, you will not be short of money. Keep me regularly informed about your balance in order to ensure that any possible misuse (by forging your signature, for example) will immediately be discovered.

Secondly, for each of you is an extract of your account from my piggy bank administration. It is difficult and unprofitable to invest in all kinds of small amounts. Therefore, I have added your funds to that of

---

458   In reference to the large stone houses (Nieuwenhuizen) inhabited by those of great fortunes (Fortuinen).

459   Sister Anna is the heroine of the Bluebeard tales, who is saved from the murderous Bluebeard by her brother.

460   Clasine Thérèse van Heukelom Quack (1841–1923) is a relative of Jan Boissevain's mother and married to Hendrik Peter Godfried (Pa) Quack (1834–1917): professor.

the others, counted all of the coupons together and distributed the interest over each one's holdings. By varied investing, I made quite a good average return.

At the end of the year, I will credit you for the earned return that will be reinvested if it is not used for other purposes. Operating this way, you will keep a very good overview, make a good return, and later, or as soon as you wish, will receive from me your shares along with their offspring.

At any moment, I will be going to London for a conference with Holt and Ruys. Yesterday, I caught the [SS *Prinses Amalia*] from IJmuiden. I am very satisfied with the new machine and boilers from the Schelde [wharf] and think that she will run well.

Our neighbour opposite us, Teding van Berkhout,[461] has died.

Jacoba van Eeghen is engaged to Dirksen, my secretary of Scheepvaartbelangen. At this time, I get along with him pretty well. I find him honest and industrious. I know that the families van Eeghen and den Tex were not very pleased about it.

Yesterday, Elisabeth, in a divine white dress, went to a party at Meindert Waller's,[462] a pinnacle of banality.

Since yesterday, I am taking great pleasure of being in possession of a new winter coat, just as worthy and dignified as it is warm and heavy.

Otherwise, there is absolutely nothing special. Many greetings from your loving Father.

A32005000353-354 [Wil to Heleen]
Amsterdam, February 3 [1892]

Dearest Heleen!

Slowly the time nears that I may expect a letter from Canada again, but I find waiting for a whole month quite long and shall therefore write to you a little bit sooner. Should a letter arrive tomorrow, I could still add a few words to this one.

Any from Karel cannot come sooner than next Tuesday and, since I am aware of this, I am not getting worried about it (maybe, a little bit — about the lack of news from him and from your letters, about which Li has told me). In his last letter to Thijs, Karel wrote that he, I believe, had ridden forty miles to Pincher Creek to pick up the mail and, to his sadness, had found nothing. This, we all find so nasty because there were, in particular, letters from 717, and I had written to him myself on December 3 and December 8, after receiving his St. Nicolaas present, which he should surely have received just before New Year's Day.

---

461 Jhr. Pieter Jacob Teding van Berkhout (1810–1892): judge, politician; married to Baroness Hieronyma Maria Antonia Forunata van Slingelandt (1814–1875).

462 Meindert Johannes Waller (1834–1924): stockbroker; married to Maria Elisabeth Adolpheine Schill (1846–1927).

He also wrote that he had luckily found the way and had arrived in one piece. But now I am so afraid that he has had an accident on the way back and therefore you have not heard anything from him. It is perhaps unfounded, but Li, who I met yesterday on the street, told me that your mother had the same idea and she talked me out of it, a little bit; but one cannot completely reason fear away. Sometimes it grips me, like torture, and shows me nothing other than a big black emptiness in which Karel is no more and I remain behind all alone. Oh, you do not know how horrible that is, but after a while I resist it and try to go on with life again. Nevertheless, I cannot refrain from wondering how I can ever become happy again and not always find myself in excruciating fear. Then, it is a blessing when the tears come. Oh, I long so much for him and I imagine everything, how wonderfully we tried to spend this summer, and sometimes I indulge myself, imagining all kinds of lovely images. But I do not dare to go further, because it is as if something horrible must still happen. How shall all of this end?

Last Friday, I had dinner at your parents', and in the evening, [Li] and I sat in your little room, talking intimately. [David] Fock was also there and had the temerity to ask me in the midst of dinner, "And, when are you going to get married, Miss de Vos, or will you marry by proxy?" I quickly said something like everything was still quite uncertain, but then your parents also said something and I concluded that they did not think that Karel would ever come and fetch me, but if that should happen, I would have to go over there and marry him there. And when I asked [Li] about it, she also spoke along that vein. You see, I had always imagined that we must live at least the first years in Canada, but I had not thought that Karel would not show up even once more before then; that I would not marry in our own house, and that I would not arrive there with him, etc.

Oh, Heleen! Please write what you think sometime. And do you think that it will still take a very, very long time? I do not wish to be childish, and I am doing well enough, but it is still something so horrible, anyway. I sometimes find it humiliating to think that one man has my . . .

A32005000364–365 [continues on]

. . . complete happiness in his hands, or rather, that it is so attached to his, but when I think that it is Karel, then I find it glorious. I believe that I have changed quite a bit, because now I would not find it terrible to always cook and to keep the house myself, so long as I can be with him. But when we talked about it before, in reference to your letter about Mrs. Wilkins, Mama said that she would never wish for me to do everything myself. Now, I believe I would be very tired in the evenings and could not play piano well anymore.

I have now started Chopin's 11th *Nocturne*, which is the third that I now play, and I have not completely finished the 24th *Prélude*, which is a beauty. Mrs. Bosmans says that it is so "intimate," and also that the whole piece is a cry of profound sadness; when one hears it being played, one gets tears in the eyes. I feel it, but cannot play it as I wish to because it is technically so difficult; the runs are so difficult and must be quite quick because it is so passionate. It is wonderful that Karel also loves Chopin so much. You do not know how much the music and the lovely piano gives to me. Once Mrs. Bosmans finds the sonata (that I have struggled through) good enough, then the *Pathétique* will follow, which I am looking forward to. I have also a very nice old French gavotte, which according to Mrs. B., "must be played in the old-fashioned style"; and the *passepied* from Delibes out of *Le roi s'amuse*,[463] true French grace and refinement; but after the prelude from Chopin, the mind eases. That piece is so completely without ulterior motives — he puts all of himself into it.

At your parents' on Friday were also Charles and Maria [Boissevain Pijnappel], Cor and Mary [van Eeghen Boissevain], and Karel Schorer. Mary was adorable in a black lace dress, cut sharply at the neck. That lovely little head was framed so beautifully! Everyone was charmed by her. This was the first, among other things, that your mother spoke of once they had left the room. Maria also talked for a long time with Mary, as did I, and I found Maria much friendlier than I have ever found her, but she also rarely speaks about herself. Li and I had a quite philosopical discussion about Maria's situation and came to the conclusion that it is twins. I found it terrible, but she was not shy (at least not very) — but we were all shy.

Cor very much enjoyed her first 'event', a dinner with dancing afterwards at your parents', [to] which she was also invited. [Cornelis] Röell had asked her for the *souper*, so she had no fear of that and she also danced with others. Röell sent a marine to find out about the colour of her dress; our temporary helper did not understand a thing, the poor [marine] was very shy, but at the end, Lien sorted it all out. At the table, Cor heard an amusing story about the surprise of the marine when he got the order about the ensemble of a lady. With her pink dress, she received lovely pink roses and white lilacs with a long white ribbon.

Saturday, Cor has a dance party and so I will go to your parents' for dinner and stay overnight (!!), and christen my beautiful bag. There will be nineteen girls and twenty gentlemen, Mama and Mrs. J. ter Meulen.[464] Sixteen (!) gentlemen declined, so that Mama could not even ask everyone that she had wanted to invite to come for a visit.

And what do you have to say about the engagement of Coba van Eeghen and Dirksen? They were here yesterday. They were quite relaxed, but it is also unpleasant for them that her parents were initally against it and that it is just now that it is going ahead. They had already agreed about the same time as Karel and I had. After all, everyone has some sorrow along with one's happiness.

---

463 Clément Léo Delibes (1836–1891): French composer; wrote music for this play, which was written by Victor Hugo (1802–1885).

464 Henriette Antoinette Leembruggen (1845–1920): married to Jan ter Meulen (1846–1916), banker.

From Jo (in addition to the roses), I also got permission to choose a present. I ordered Ibsen's *En Folkefiende*,[465] about which Karel had written, and shall still search for something nice from the catalogue; it is so difficult to come by good titles.

My cousin, [Willem] Coster, will be moving; he is now moving to the Prinsengracht near the Leidschestraat, with the office at home. I hope that everything will go well with moving, etc. His sister will come to help him.

Our housemaid is steadily improving. Today, she walked, dressed, to our sitting room, but otherwise she must still stay in the same atmosphere.

And now, dear Heleentje, I will close this one. If you happen to see Karel when you have received this letter, then there is a lot of love enclosed for him. A friendly kiss for you from your loving Wil.

A28335001526-1529 [Heleen to Mother]
Calgary, February 4, 1892

Dear Mother,

Yesterday, a lovely bunch of letters from Papa (Jan. 14), Li and An, and the small book from Coba Reijnvaan[466] arrived. Is it, perhaps, Coba who wrote it? Many thanks to everyone. It is nice to receive answers, but it is a strange feeling that you still think that we are together, while I cannot imagine when I will see Karel again. Wil also asked me about Karel, and I almost know less than she does. I would so much love to be with him when he gets Papa's letter of January 14, and I feel so useless and yet digest so much. If I could only speak with you or Papa for just half an hour. Apart from that, I am doing very well in the hotel and my time is always fully occupied.

The pharmacist's widow is now alone in the hotel, and as much as I can, I try to lift her from her lot and to make her walk or sew; and my friend, Kathleen Wilkins, is always happy when I come, and there is always something to help with.

Last week, I stayed for three nights at Mrs. McCaul's home. Her husband was in Lethbridge for business and she was afraid to stay alone with the children. Her husband is the only one who could be somewhat supportive to me if I needed advice. All of the young women are very sweet and kind to me, but too much occupied with their own worries to imagine themselves in someone else's situation, and so I attach little value to their judgments.

As a matter of fact, they have put me on a pedestal and they look upon me as a phenomenon of wealth, nobility and intelligence, and would

---

465   Henrik Ibsen's *An Enemy of the People* (1882).

466   Jacoba (Coba) Clara Elisabeth Reijnvaan (1851–1926): married in 1891 to Bartout Emerins (1838–1913), substitute clerk of the Supreme Court. The book is *Zuster Clara: Schetsen uit het leven eener verpleegster in een stedelijk gasthuis* (1892, Amsterdam), written by her sister, Johanna Paulina Reijnvaan (1844–1920), stories about the life of a nurse in a city hospital. See also footnote 16.

not dare to contradict me. That is quite flattering, but sometimes also tiresome and upsetting, as when they send reports from charitable institutions with the clear aim to receive a large gift. I dined with the bishop and, yesterday, spent the afternoon at the home of Mrs. McIllree, the wife of the commander of the local police[467] here. She is Irish, with a small streak of megalomania that shows itself in her continual bragging about the wealth and beautiful estate of her father. She showed me numerous photographs of the really princely castle, in sharp contrast with the small wooden houses in the barracks, where she now lives without a maid and with a soldier who does the cooking and is so truly sloppy and dirty that it was an effort to get the grim potatoes and stewed beef down. Her daughter, a lovely child of six, soon became good mates with me. (It appears that the children are so fond of me because they are not used to much attention.)

[42] Caroline Elisabeth (Lily) Humphreys McIllree

I have now given away three dolls and they have brought great pleasure. The one from Marken[468] is christened Dutchie.

I have also made tea. Mrs. Trott has an alcohol lamp to boil water and I bought some good tea. I surprised everyone with the quick service and the delicious tea.

I also opened the box of Marquis[469] and enjoyed them very much.

But I digress, because I wanted to tell you about the end of yesterday. After dinner, while I was getting ready to walk home with Mrs. McIllree, Dr. George[470] came to ask her to come to play whist with them that evening, and I had to go along. Dr. George is an English village doctor from a family of doctors on all sides. He looks like [Dr.] Versteeg, twenty-eight

---

467 Superintendent John Henry McIllree (1849–1925) of the NWMP was a commanding officer at Fort Calgary in 1888 when the barracks were built. In 1884, he married Caroline Elizabeth (Lily) Humphreys (1854–1930). Lily was an accomplished artist and many of her paintings are in the RCMP Museum at Depot Division, Regina, Saskatchewan.

468 Marken is a village in North Holland, and it is likely that the dolls were dressed in the traditional costume.

469 Chocolates from La Maison François Marquis (1818), Paris, France.

470 Dr. Henry George (1864–1932) was an early doctor in Calgary and Innisfail, who wrote authoritatively on the flora and fauna of Alberta and is known for treating Chief Crowfoot during his last illness. He married Barbara Mary Bernard (1867–1936). "The boy" is George Morton Bernard (1874–1960).

[43] Home of Dr. Henry George and family

years old, appears very young and has a dear, simple wife and two children. They live in their own house, larger than most here, four rooms, hall and kitchen downstairs, cheerful, welcoming and squeaky clean. Soon came 'the boy', a brother of Mrs. [George], and four friends looking like garden-variety office clerks. They came to talk about the costume for the carnival the following evening, and they devoted themselves to fixing a sorcerer's cone atop a magic hat. We played whist with enthusiasm and fun, and at 11:00 p.m., four of 'the boys' took me back to the hotel. It looked more like [the towns of] Helmond or Utrecht than 'the Wild Northwest'.

It remains beautiful weather here. Last Monday, Mrs. McIllree came with the police team to pick me up and we drove to a ranch, a long way away. The road was mostly very good — for here — but I believe that you would not have enjoyed it very much, because sometimes the road inclined quite sharply, and at the end, we did not know the way exactly, and went straight through stubble-fields and over low barbed wire.

We were welcomed by Mr. Moore,[471] in a work jersey with short sleeves over a flannel shirt. The living room was cold, and so he led us into the kitchen where it was nice and warm, and served us tea and ginger cake. His mother and sisters were in town. He was a little bit shy but very

---

471 Alexander Ewan Goodrich Moore (1867–1934) was then a twenty four-year-old rancher. He lived with his mother, Mary Ellen Alexander Moore (1846–1912), who was the widow of John Moore (1837–1869), a merchant in India. Alexander's two sisters were Ethel Christiaan (1864–1938), a teacher, and Hellen Lilian (1868–1948). All but Lilian were born in India; she was born on the Isle of Man. See the 1891 Canada Census.

gentlemanly. The house was beautifully situated at a bend in the river, on a hill among bushes.

Just a minute ago, a runaway horse with an empty cart came by. Everyone immediately flew out of their houses and, at the end of the street, the horse was stopped. It is amusing to see how, with the nice weather, everyone is on the street. Between 4:00 p.m. and 5:00 p.m., there are coffee chats. Everybody speaks with everyone else.

Wil sent me her portrait. She looks sad and drawn; the blouse appears smart to me.

Goodbye, dear Mummie, lots of love to everyone. From your Heleen.

A32074000185–190 [Karel to Wil]
In camp, February 8–14, 1892

My dearest Wil,

Les jours se suivent et se ressemblent.
I am starting to get used to the routine; but now I really miss the enjoyment of something new. I notice that there is almost no art in adapting yourself to an unpleasant lot, knowing that it will last only a short time. But the difficulty increases to the second or third power in proportion to the time that it takes. The news of the day for me is embodied in a letter that I received from the hand of my powerful patron, W.C. Van Horne, President of the Canadian Pacific Railway. He has still had little time to occupy himself with my future but will now certainly think about me. For the time being, I should stay where I am. And when this work is finished at the end of April, he will place me on another line of the CPR. Doing what? I have no notion of what that might be.

I still hold the important position of stake-marker, which I took up as a side job in order to have something to do while I was getting my health back. But you understand (most likely very well after what I have written about my activities) that I have no ambition to do this little job for a longer period. The prospect of doing this for even another few months does not sit well with me. My position is also somewhat changed. While in the beginning I was looked upon as a 'gentleman' who was along on the trip for his health and who kept occupied by getting his hands dirty, I am now at the other end. Now, they notice that I remain simply one of the 'men', 'one of the boys', and they expect just as much and just as good of work from me as from anyone else, and they grumble if I fall short.

February 12: Phooey! How grumpy I was when I wrote the above. It is certainly true what is written, but what good does it do to complain? Since then, we had a couple of mild days and the job took us to prairie ground, blown clear of snow. There, I felt good and envied nobody his important and responsible position that binds him to the pressures of an office and prevents him from enjoying this champagne-like air. (You would possibly prefer *champangneuse*, but don't forget the wordplay with *campagnard*!)

While getting up this morning, the weather was so mild that one wondered why the trees were not budding and the birds were not flying. Most of the boys spruced themselves up in summer clothes with hats (instead of toques), pants and less footwear, and so forth. But your humble servant, who is an old hand and has lived in many climates — and not that long ago was cautioned to take good care of himself — did not wear one square inch less animal skin than usual and it suited him very well! *Apropos*, how many different animals have to sell their skins for my present clothing? They were certainly brave animals, who also seemed to have decided at the critical moment to sell their skins very expensively; this, when you see the prices in the stores here:

My fur hat.....otter
My fur.....[coyote]
Gloves.....buckskin
Underwear.....sheep
Shoes.....cattle

Because (I retake the thread that I dropped on the earlier pages under the view of so many deerskins) this afternoon, a fierce wind started up from the east, and this 'miscreant' brought with it a flurry of hail that was so piercingly cold and, as such, not only lashed your face, but more importantly, our view was so hampered that the boss . . .

KLAB04554000225-226 [continues on]

. . . had our observations suspended and we returned to camp around 4:00 p.m. This gave me a good chance to write, an opportunity that I grabbed with both hands (although the right one alone is enough for writing!).

Among the countless novels that circulate in the camp (which are mostly unreadable and badly written), I have finally found one whose story I follow with pleasure. It is called *The Squire's Daughter; or The Mystery of Thorpe Regis*.[472] It sounds a bit old-fashioned with such a double title. And that in America! But the core is better than the wreath on the label; the first half does not taste like the cork, far from it. But it may still be possible that there could, as yet, be a lot of sediment at the end. In it, there appears an otherwise not so unsympathetic couple that, just like another pair (not unknown to you), is in a hurry to marry but is hindered by a shortage of money. Another comparison is that the young gent has a job that he intensely laments. (Here stops the similarity.) He is becoming thinner through his sadness. (Here, he is the opposite of

---

472 The squire's daughter is a character in *Thorpe Regis: A Novel* (1874), by Frances Mary Peard, British author (1835–1923).

the other young gent, who is busy becoming 'as fat as a porpoise', just like Winnie's father.)

Well then, a few nights ago, this young couple delivered to me the dream that I, too, could finally get married. A week before it was to happen, it came to me that the honeymoon would be seven days in total. About a hope chest, there was nothing spoken of, and we spent all of our time studying Hendschel.[473] My fiancée (she was [the fiancée], but it was not really you; I didn't see you, as it usually goes in dreams) wanted absolutely to go to Trieste or 'Terentes', which is a fictional place out of the book and factors, peremptorily, into the whole story. Oh, dreams are deceptive but, nevertheless, I had a happy feeling when I woke up; and when I walked to work in the morning, I allowed my thoughts to be caught up again while walking with this short illusion. I was awakened from my daydreams by the lovely light of the sunrise over the mountains. And when I looked up, the sun had just come up and created such an encouragingly lively glow over the whole of the surroundings that I became involuntarily impressed and thought, "Yes, the day is in the east and night is past." Oh, that is all nonsense of course, however not to the extent that it has influence on someone's moods and, therefore, works for the better!

It is almost about time that I receive a letter from you again, Miss! December 21 was the last one. Methinks that if you had written in mid-January (by now, February 12), I would have again in my possession a lovely small gem, rather than what is now the case; yes, perhaps even an answer to my indiscreet long-chattering letter of mid-December, which mother-in-law probably confiscated — no, that is only silly talk.

KLAB04554000225–226 [continues on]

And are you not content with Sully Prudhomme's title, *Les vaines tendresses*? I would concur with your critique, should the title have read *La vaine tendresse*, but now I think you are touching on all of the little tendernesses to which a great thinker and poet certainly has the right, especially in a title that, even if paradoxical, may use the word *vaines*. Here in the wilderness, I cannot look up which poems he summarized under this title, or whether they reflect on the tenderness with which a young person cares for his growing moustache; or a lieutenant, his epaulette or his sextant; or a schoolgirl, the page of an album that *he* composed for her; or the mother, a lock of hair from her darling boy or the first money earned by her clever son. Perhaps he calls "vaines tendresses" everything that stirs the heart of a poet and expresses itself in measure, or does he truly find a tenderness vain, so long as it does not express itself in deeds or matter?

A32074000188 [continues on]

---

473   This is probably Albert Louis Ulrich Hendschel (1834–1883): German painter and pencil artist.

Only then, shall I agree with you about the conclusion of your tirade.

Mid-February! It will probably be in mid-March or thereabouts before you get this content, so that days of remembering are all that lie in between, eh, Wim? Of sweet remembrance, later perhaps; but of bitter sorrow, now. PARTED! Or not! Let me just say for a moment (and then I shall behave again for three pages) that [despite] how far we are from each other now, we are still really closer than before, yes? How much anxiety during this time! If it had overcome us this winter, it would have been very easy. 1892 is a leap year! Now the girls are permitted to ask the boys. (If they would ever do it!) Then you would have had to make tea-visits and I would have been going out dining across the canal. Therefore, you would have had to come to listen at the Walloon [Church], but certainly not such an irritating service as the one from Mr. van Son,[474] and then you would have arranged a dinner with — I don't know whom — to have the honour of sitting beside [Joan] Rahusen and across from me. Then it would have been a strange world.

From Heleen, I receive a letter faithfully every week. Here in the west, she has turned a lot of heads, but Canadian heads turn slowly and stay on the course, so therefore it is not dangerous. It is the most peculiar life that she is leading these days. Calgary, itself, the place where she has her headquarters, is such a place you cannot categorize, incomprehensible for one who has never seen cities other than a few centuries old. She now benefits from the mild weather, walking in the surrounding area, but feared, when she last wrote to me, that the increasing thaw would, from now on, prevent her from doing it, because if it really thaws, as she wrote in her last letter, "the snowy roads are impassable."

But everything is relative. There was a big thaw in the last days, so the roads which are impassable for pleasure walking are eagerly awaited by the tired legs of an engineer's crew, returning after a day's surveying. Even so, it is acknowledged that the high wet snow is miserable, even though it is not as tiresome to get through as is soft snow with a hard crust. That is the worst form of a road to wade through that you can think of. Just think, the snow does not give way to your legs at all. You must lift up every footstep (say one or two feet) in order to break the crust of frozen snow and then lumber through it in the soft underlayer. Off and on, there is a piece of sturdier crust that carries us and that is a lovely rest, even though it means continually walking tensely.

Up until now, I never fully understood on what sort of soil the road was laid that Fruitje had to follow on her visits to Cateautje. You know that history, don't you? But now I know, and if I ever may tell the story to my children, I will call the *Ort der Handlung*[475] a settlement in Canada's Northwest. In case you are not familiar with the adventures of the proper, energetic Fruitje and the lazy, whining Cateautje, you must sometime ask Papa, who will tell you with charm and grace, and the

---

474   Reverend Pieter van Son (1838–1919).

475   The setting of the story, where it happened.

illustrations, which are the essence of the story, were simply masterly. (In my day! That is, twenty years ago!!!)

Tomorrow, the mail will come. I hope then to be able to follow up with an answer to that one. For the time being, my darling, I have already been sweet for three pages. Yes, it gets closer; so then, I dare to ardently embrace you now in my thoughts, my dear, dear treasure, and for now, to lock you again in my writing folder. Bye, bye!

Saturday morning!!!! [February 13] Do you understand what this — and this!!! means? A half-day vacation. A lovely stroke of luck! After it snowed heavily yesterday, it began to freeze overnight, an extremely sharp frost. The walls of our tent, having become saturated yesterday from the melting snow, are now an ice-crust, stiff as a plank, and the door of my tent (normally a limp piece of canvas that one has to lift or to hold aside like a curtain as you crawl in and out) is now also so stiff that one has difficulty pushing it aside. Every arrival or exit is accompanied by tremendous cracking. Thus, we now live in an igloo with a red-glowing stove in it, four inhabitants on the stove side, roasted, and on the side of the tent wall, frozen! Now, these expressions are a bit exaggerated, but it is no exaggeration to say that, this morning, some of us had frozen ears, cheeks, toes or fingers. We left at 7:30 a.m., a bit later than usual, also due to the cold, because everyone first needed to thaw or to warm the pieces of clothing that they had to put on in front of the stove.

Well, in camp it was somewhat sheltered, but outside on the prairies we caught the full wind that propelled the fresh dry snow through the air, blinding your eyes and lashing your skin. After half an hour of agony against the wicked weather, it was too much for the boss, and at 8:30 a.m. we were already back in camp. The man who would deliver the mail to the 'Springs' most likely will be held up on his way through the snowstorm and will not arrive before the evening. Whatever it may be, we will not go out again in this weather, and must therefore still have a bit of patience. You know what the Springs are, don't you? It is a sulphur spring that originates right in the so-called Gap, the narrowest part of the pass, where the mountains are not 1,000 feet away from each other. There are a few houses and a small hotel, and in summers, rheumatic patients go there for their well-being.

Our camp lies two miles further into the mountains and it takes us about forty-five minutes to walk there. I had arranged with one of the Springs' inhabitants, Jack Willoughby,[476] to meet at Turtle Mountain tomorrow in order to climb one of the walls of the Gap. But after the snowfall from yesterday, it is likely to be impossible. The rail line will, of course, go through the Gap and close by one of the houses. The house and the stable will probably have to be taken down.

---

476 John Milton (Jack) Willoughby (1851–1913), a son-in-law of Samuel Lee, or Old Man Lee, was married in 1894 to Mary Lee (1878–1940). He worked with Lee to build Sulphur Springs' "sanitorium hotel" in 1885, a large log structure, reputedly the first with sulphur baths for cure and rheumatism. See Mary Rose Smith, *Canadian Cattlemen*, June 1949, 12.

By the way, the whole area that we go through shall be destroyed as a result of the construction of the railway. It is such a strange idea, the certainty that every lovely spot in the forest that attracts us and draws us in soon will not exist anymore. On the way in, I sat for a little while on the ground under a gigantic pine tree, whose thick branches and rich foliage had protected the foot of it from the snow. I cut a piece of the bark and wrote my name with the date, "2 Jan 92," to cherish for a moment the illusion that we, one day, [will be here] together — the tree stood a bit away from the 'preliminary line' and I had hoped that the railway would save it. Or rather, I thought nothing about the whole railway, but on the way back along the 'real line', the tree would be passed closely and, during the construction, it will inescapably be felled. And so, it goes on, again and again. The fleeting pipe dream about a lovely place for a picnic and a wonderful seat for the two of us, in contrast with that place overtaken by a railway bridge or that seat taken by a line watchman!

L'appétit vient en mangeant! Since, over the last few days, from time to time, I have put to paper what I would so like to tell you if you were here; every free moment, I desire to bring out my *nécessaire*, that is, to start writing. My tent-mates already ask teasingly, "Add a few lines, Bozzie?", when they see me so often, time and time again, writing a letter for a short time, but it is so enjoyable and enticing. Also, still no mail today, although the work brought us close to the Springs and I went there to inquire about it. If no one else is going there, I shall get on my horse tomorrow and try to capture our mail. I have finished my novel, and the wine was light, so light, just as with very pure water. Nevertheless, there is much good in it. Character description good, dialogue flowing, but the plot meagre; the "I am obliged" is a slip knot and a loose one, too. The writer would probably write a sketch or something like it, with a good result, but a novel is far beyond his ability. Pity, yes? What does 'Thorpe Regis' mean? Has 'Thorpe' something to do with turpitude, and 'Regis' with a 'region'? You, learned linguist, will be able to explain this. Yes?

Today, Sunday [February 14], nothing yet. I must have patience for a week. In the meantime, dear, dear Wil, warmest greetings from your loving, Karel

A32074000191-192 [Heleen to Wil]
Calgary, February 9, 1892

Dear Wil,

I see, to my horror, that it is more than two weeks since I last wrote to you. Here, time goes by so unnoticeably and there are so few things that have happened here worth mentioning. Now, a change will come again for me because I think that I will go to Montreal next week. I am very sorry to be moving so far away from Karel, but there is as yet no prospect that he will soon find another job, and this surveying could go on indefinitely, that is, until the whole railway is finished. Therefore, Karel will stick to it for the time being, until he sees another opening.

Now it becomes pointless to continue to spend my way into poverty, and I hope that in Montreal I can become more useful. It may be to find a position for Karel at an office, or if that does not materialize soon, for the time being, to work in a hospital.

Karel finally received his mail, thirty-four letters (!), and was still a bit bewildered about it. So much he lived over again, especially regarding yourself, through your lovely letters that have stirred and touched him, and for which he is profoundly thankful to you. There were letters from a number of friends, such as Mr. Caird[477] and Kees den Tex, and an especially lovely one from [Jacobus] Boelen, who had sent a bouquet to you. He has already made plans, if it is at all possible, to visit Karel on his way back via New York. I also got a letter from Mrs. Caird that I first had to decipher, which turned out easier than I expected.

I must still also thank you for your letter of January 17. About cleaning wild meat, I can reassure you. The hunters here are so gracious as to deliver wild meat, clean and plucked, to your home. If you buy it at the butcher, you can also get it cleaned. Also, there are always Chinese who can iron for you if you can pay for it. Even Mrs. Wilkins, who must live on $83.00 per month in this expensive country (she pays $15.00 per month for a teensy-weensy house with three little rooms, an alcove and a tiny kitchen), lets her shirts be ironed by the Chinese and only irons the rough goods and the flannel shirts by herself, to save a little bit.

Also, many thanks for your portrait photograph. The blouse appears to me to be a complete success. "Go forward my *kachler* and you shall eat spinach."[478] (Ask Li or Thijs what that means.)

I have noted Jo's address and shall write to her again soon.

Much love to your mother and Cor and a warm kiss for my darling, brave Wil, from your Heleen.

A32005000494-497 [Wil to Heleen]
Amsterdam, February 10, 1892

Dear Sister!

I received three letters from you almost at the same time, and do not know where I shall start with answering them. The one that arrived in the middle, but of the most recent date, attracts me the most. I want to thank you very much for your lovely words about Karel and me, which

---

477   Robert Caird (1851–1915): director of Caird & Co, Greenock; shipbuilder; married to Fiorenza Louisa Kathleen Caird (née Hall) (1851–1892).

478   This is a translation of *Ga zo voort mijn kachler en gij zult spinazie eten*, meaning "keep it up and you will be rewarded for it." Heleen used *kachler*, an Amsterdammer's word for "drunk," in place of "my boy/girl."

gave me courage and lifted me up. Not that I was not reassured about my disappointment over New Year's, but nevertheless, there are other things in your letter that will stay with me for a longer time. And within the phrase where you tell me about your fears this past summer for the duration of our happiness, lay a warning for me. To be honest, I have never doubted our happiness, because then it would have been as if already disrupted, but it did sadden me that the distance would perhaps estrange us for the time being. I feel it myself, how difficult it is to keep his image completely true, completely unspoiled (also morally) when, from time to time, there does not come a refreshing and a revival of impressions.

When one thinks a lot about someone and then one automatically asks oneself, "What would he say about this?" and "How would he find that?", it adds or takes away something of his being. One idolizes, and by doing so, takes away something of the original personality. At least, that is how it is for me. There was, therefore, beyond my disappointment and longing for a letter, a sort of fear for our intimate relationship. I, at least, feel as if I need him so much in order to become as he wishes me to be. However, what you wrote to me did me a lot of good. It is childish, but that is the way of it, that one never gets tired of hearing that he or she, whom one loves also, feels that way and, that Karel, in any case, is not permitted to write about all that, especially for the reasons that you mentioned. But he must really not think that it will be too burdensome for me to follow him over there. I believe that it would be too burdensome for me, later on, to live on without any hope for the future.

Yesterday (Cor was out for dinner), Mama and I talked again, since some time ago, about my possible future in Canada. I know that she finds it so terrible and I always dread bringing up this topic, but now that it had come up, I pleaded my case, which is that I believe that it is my duty, and tried to prevent Mama from saying, "You will never see me there. I am not going overseas!" And I said that when the time comes, I still had as much right to a visit from her as did Jo, since, in the case of health reasons, everyone must keep their objections to themselves. I now hope that Mama will think differently. I can very well imagine a life there, but a year from now, the departure, for example, seems to me to be so unreal, so strange, so intensely unpleasant. I always find it awful to leave somewhere, wherever it may be.

Do you know that I also got a letter from Karel? The letters arrive so irregularly. We think that it was because of the [stranding of] the *Eider*,[479] and that there were letters from you on board. Saturday, your mother received a letter from the 10th, one from the 12th, and another one from the 21st of January, all from you. Saturday evening, I got one from January 12. Sunday morning came one of the same date for Li; Monday

---

479 The SS *Eider*, which was built for the Norddeutscher Lloyd shipping company in 1884, ran aground on the Atherfield Ledge near the Isle of Wight on January 31, 1892.

at breakfast, the one from January 23; and during coffee time, those from the 21st, 22nd; and about 4:00 p.m., one from Karel from the 14th. That one had to make a much longer journey, of course. He wrote to me on my birthday, even though he was so tired after his workday. Sweet of him. He must travel for two hours back and forth to work and it is therefore no surprise that he is really tired in the evening. He had not yet received letters, but hoped that the person who would be delivering my letter would then take his along. Otherwise, he seems to be very well.

And what a delightful letter from you about the trip to Edmonton. On the map, it is an astonishingly long way, and I understand very well that it was eleven hours by train. It is so nice, in some way, to be able to see where you two are. The Crowsnest Pass, where Karel's camp is set up, is also on the map. The 'buffaloes' who came into the train carriages amused us very much.

What a really nasty person Mrs. Lougheed is, to leave you in the lurch so often. I can understand why you did not want to stay there any longer. But it is understandable that they, who have not seen new faces for so long, were half-crazy when there was an opportunity to meet such nice company. What a lot of broken hearts will be left behind! I think that you rescued yourself beautifully from all of those less enjoyable situations. I believe that you are the best chaperone for yourself; as far as I can see, Mrs. Lougheed and [Mrs.] Trott are less adept in this art. So long as the people are friendly or interesting, it is lovely and intriguing to make new acquaintances, but I can imagine that you sometimes get tired when they are boring or negative. One can endure all these things better from older acquaintances than from newer ones. I think that Mrs. Wilkins will bless the fates that brought you to Calgary. For her, it is very comfortable and for you, I am glad that you have found someone with whom you get along and who is more your age.

How relatively quickly the chest arrived; normally parcels go so slowly. The Zandvoort woodcarvers would certainly promote you to patroness should you find a market for their art, because here it seems that there is mediocre interest in it. At least, I know of one supply that was written off because of the low demand.

Cor's party went quite well. Friday, we sorted out our room [and] rearranged just a few things. For example, a small lamp with a red shade on a *guéridon*; two small chairs, in front of the right window; a flower table in front of the mirror was freshened up; and the fairy lamp and so forth were set up. On the landing above, a canapé with a blue Italian throw, with a small table and yet two more chairs; and then a bench made of two peat-chests, along with the other pink throw, *eau de Cologne*, fans and a fairy lamp. A few chairs on a stair landing; the side room divided into small corners with seating places for two; the living room, where the one white rug was stretched out, almost completely cleared; the same for the music room, the piano was shoved over and a canapé put in the corner. Niederländer[480] had promised not to pound too much, and luckily there were no strings broken.

That Saturday, I still had Kindervoeding and singing lessons, which made it a tiring day. My beautiful bag was inaugurated for my stay at 717. Everything in there is so lovely. For example, I have never had such a lovely hairbrush. I slept in [Mia's] bed and Li ensured that there was heating. Your Papa was in England and Li was actually to go to Haarlem that day in order to cheer up Suze [Kruzeman], who was not yet completely better; but she stayed because I would otherwise have been alone with Wallie and Mia, since your Mama had bad headaches, and An had lain in bed that morning for domestic reasons, and Nel went to our place. I felt bad about being a nuisance, but your mama came for lunch in the afternoon, and An had already come out of bed earlier, so therefore, I had actually had no reason [to feel bad]. Your mama looked very tired and drawn, but yesterday, I was there to read Karel's story and she was then completely fine again. It was so nasty that it affected her so much. But you must not worry yourself about it.

On the first of March, there will be a kind of 'fancy fair' in the Concertgebouw for the benefit of the Vacation Colonies [providing a vacation in the outdoors to improve the health of school-age children of poor families]. However, one may not use that name and must speak of 'evening party'. Actually, it will be a 'flirting fair' because, apart from the recitations of van Zuijlen,[481] with separate fee and ditto for the ballroom, nothing will be sold other than champagne, tea, oysters and flowers. Mary van Eeghen will be serving in the one tea booth, where Nel and Jet Schiff will also be serving. Cor was invited by Mrs. Oyens to a different stand. Aunt Su is going, together with Mrs. Rahusen Hooft,[482] to the flower booth along with Jenne,[483] Lou [Biben], Loukie [van Loon],[484] Valérie Hooft,[485] Gie [den Tex] and three others.

It will certainly be a very mundane evening, but they will have a lot of fun, I think. I pity the gents, however, because they shall have to bleed abominably with such an event, which I think is a burden for young folks, in particular. Maria [Boissevain Pijnappel] agreed, and also said

480 Berend Karel Niederländer (1856–1928): piano tuner; married to Catharina Clermont (1861–1904); in 1904, married Rose Barralis (1883–1947).

481 Willem Jacob van Zuijlen (1847–1901): an actor who was the first to perform monologues; married in 1867 to Helena Cornelia Elisabeth van Dijk (c.1845–1902).

482 Anna Louisa Hooft (1867–1948): married in 1889 to David Rahusen (1858–1932), member of the executive committee of De Nederlandsche Bank.

483 Eugenie (Jenne) Hooglandt (1873–1948): niece of Aunt Su; married in 1900 to Johan Anthoni Philipse (1876–1947), banker.

484 Louisa Catharina Antoinetta (Loukie) van Loon (née Borski) (1832–1893): married to Jhr. Hendrik Maurits Jacobus van Loon (1831–1901), banker.

485 Valérie Eugénie Hooft (1872–1936): sister of Anna Louisa Hooft.

[that] they did not go with the idea of doing 'good', but actually went there with the intention of enjoying themselves. Now, if you take it that way and say, "I am going to have fun," but without saying at every moment of pleasure, "What a good cause this is," then that is fine.

Oh, yes. Mrs. Rahusen [Hooft] visted me a while ago when she had a letter of yours. How nice and sweet of her. I did not find her at home yesterday. Aunt [Su] and Uncle [Eugen] are both still at home.

And now I go to the Kindervoeding in a rainshower. Once again, many thanks for all of your friendliness, with a kiss, your Wil. Much love from Mama and Cor.

KLAB09193000031 [Father to Helena]
Amsterdam, February 12, 1892

Dearest Helena,

This morning I received your lovely letter of January 25 from Calgary, with the typical coverage of a Sunday with the Reformed [Church] folks. I have experienced your sensations and placed my whole self in your way of thinking. You would understand better after becoming acquainted with George Eliot's novels about the Presbyterian and puritanical middle class, a strange contrast between sordid observations in daily life and practices from very strict and very difficult to digest (but still exalted) dogmas about the unseen world. Later on, you would not find it so pleasant in such an environment. Now, they will not be paying that much close attention to it, but should you live there, they would soon execrate you.

I can understand that the serious Reverend Gordon[486] reminds you of Robert Elsmere [the hero of Ward's *Robert Elsmere*]. A new novel from Mrs. Humphrey Ward has just been published, on which she worked for five years, and now has also received eleven thousand pounds sterling in royalties from England, America and Tauchnitz[487] together. It is called *The History of David Grieve*.[488] I bought it today in the Tauchnitz edition and in the English edition – it cost nineteen guilders. I fear that the Tauchnitz edition cannot be mailed to Canada. Perhaps you may have a chance to buy or to borrow one at your end, otherwise we will put it in the next crate to be sent.

486 Charles William Gordon (1860–1937), a Presbyterian minister, later of the United Church of Canada, was the first minister in Banff, Alberta, from about 1890 to 1894, serving a large area west of Calgary. He moved to Winnipeg, Manitoba, in the mid-1890s, where he also became a prolific novelist, writing under the pen name of Ralph Connor. He based many early works on the miners, lumbermen and cowboys of western Canada. In 1899, he married Helen King (1876–1961). During the First World War, he served as Senior Protestant Chaplain, with the rank of major. The Ralph Connor Memorial United Church in Canmore, Alberta, is named for him.

487 Tauchnitz Publishers was established in 1796 in Leipzig, Germany, by Carl Christoph Traugott Tauchnitz (1761–1836).

488 *The History of David Grieve* is a novel in three volumes, first published in 1892 by Mary Augusta Ward (1851–1920), under the name Mrs. Humphrey Ward, following her previous novel, *Robert Elsmere*.

I am beginning to long for an answer to my letter to Karel of January 3. In your letter of (?), which I received a few days ago, you wrote to me about things I mentioned to you on the 4th, and my apologies that I did not put a copy of my letter to Karel in yours. At that time, I had hoped that, by the time of receiving my letter, you would already be together, but now, Karel has my letter in the wilderness, without anyone there with whom he can talk.

We have absolutely no clue here about such an irregular mail service. [For that], one must live on Texel during the the winter — which prevents shipping — and so the access to it is on foot over the ice. To me, if I have counted correctly, Karel has been at least five weeks completely deprived of letters, but still two newspapers, the *Hansa*[489] and the [*Algemeen*] *Handelsblad*, came into his possession in two different places. Why is printed matter being forwarded and not letters? *Tout cela me chipoter*. However, I expect that there will soon be an explanation.

In any case, it is good that Karel has planned to leave the outfit and return to the civilized world. Definite plans cannot be made, anyway, before you both have obtained a full notion of any chance of a decent living that could come up for Karel in Canada. I have intentionally given you ample credit, because I believe that with your being together in Montreal at your own cost, you will appreciate that room more than staying with rich friends. Or, I now believe, that it is just possible that I have made a mistake, and therefore you are free to handle things the way you think is best.

The main thing remains — how Karel himself is — how he is doing: if he has faith in the future; if he dares to take on the big responsibility of this lifetime of happiness by committing himself to this sweet, innocent girl. Because of the fact that I have not been in contact with Karel for weeks now, I feel concerned sometimes; but then, each time comes the wish (and the hope above all) that the solitude will give him back to society completely, mentally rejuvenated.

Concerning his health (if we dare to have trust in his health), then the question remains about the 'ways and means' of the budget of the young household. About that, I think that the latter is attainable: Karel, $1,000.00 at his disposal; Wil's income, $1,000.00; contribution from me of $1,000.00. Simple living, preferably outside the city with a kind of outdoor life, with chickens, dogs, etc. It seems to me that that would be attainable in Canada. Please enquire!

In case the plans for the Canadian [Pacific] to create a fast mail-link to Europe goes ahead, perhaps there is a chance for Karel to get a job with the steamship venture. Then he would be again in his element!

Count Adolphe is back again. He had, indeed, not been in Canada and therefore could do nothing for both of you. Perhaps his son, young Do, will come there before long. I shall keep you up to date.

---

489 *Hansa: Zietschrift Für Seewesen,* a periodical published by H.W. Silomon, in Bremen, printed by Aug, Meyer & Dieckmann, Hamburg.

Regarding our discussion about Karel, I have forgotten to mention that I would also, so gladly, wish to know what sort of impression the men at the 'outfit' have of him; if he is taken seriously, that is to say, as a determined young man that one can rely on, or if he is tolerated and treated with sympathy. It is so difficult to get to know what Karel's capacity for work is worth. Neither from the navy, nor from Bakker or Fenenga[490] could I learn something. While, earlier, even in the short time that he worked with them, Wallis and Op ten Noort reported right away about our Gideon, that he was a worker with "potential."

Concerning you, dear child, I shall become sunnily happy, if, after a decision has been made about Karel, you can return to us again. You have been keeping yourself capital, but it is still a true banishment that must not take longer than necessary for the cause. Also, I have taken care to see that you have enough credit for eventual travel money; even though it is now still not plausible, you would then be free to leave when the journey has finished.

Let's assume for a moment that the wedding never takes place; that is also possible. Then Wil must play *le beau rôle*, and Karel will go on with someone who does not take it seriously enough. Hence, Karel remains there, of course, looking for a career in Canada or America, but without having too much haste to find a position which will support a marriage. I remain, of course, willing to help him, but for that, however, he will succeed sooner after you have returned.

I just thought that I would talk with you about everything that often goes through my head and heart. Since I have shared a word with Mrs. de Vos, I am in great suspense and very much long for the final act. Wil knows nothing of this and is, just like a barometer, now on 'lovely weather' and then on 'rain', depending on whether she received a letter or not. From all that is written here, let Karel know nothing more than is necessary. Now you will get a separate sheet with my latest news.

[Part 2] Great events about steam shipping. Last week, I went to London with Ruys. It was poor, misty weather. My travel companion had not been well recently, and therefore we went by Calais-Dover, but I cannot say that it suited me. The only good thing was the lunch in Brussels, in Le Sole d'Or(!), close to Hotel Anspach, but the old *Fawn* is an annoying rocking-boat and the train journeys make you 'land-sick'.

On the boat, we travelled with a Mrs. Osborne, who had stolen horses from her cousin and was being detained on arrival. The next morning, she was brought before the Police Magistrate, where a nasty scene took place, because the Treasury, with her acquisitions, made all sorts of clumsy blunders; as a result, she was first released and then, because of perjury, she was taken into custody all over again. She has a godfather who had already spent £8,000 on this expensive niece, for damages and court costs, and her husband, who was pitied by everyone, remained loyally on her side.

490 Pieter Fenenga (1846–1926): captain in the merchant navy; married to Margaretha Imke Bengen (1850–1923).

We stayed in the Royal Hotel and the next morning had a conference in the Euston Hotel with Alfred Holt and Crompton. We hit the nail on the head and reached an agreement. Afterwards, a conference with [Thomas] Wallis, who was as clear as ever, but exhausted through and through because he had spent three days and three nights in a coastal hut at the beach on Wight, where the *Eider*, a beautiful ship of the Norddeutsche Lloyd of Bremen, had been lost. Director Lohmann[491] died of a stroke yesterday. It could be in relation to the disaster, but it could also be purely physical. It is a horrendous blow for the company, which bore the entire risk (two million Deutschmarks). The assurance fund is not large and they were used to paying dividends from the premiums. The big question (during our conversation with Holt) was "Will it give us something as long as the Germans are still operating?" My answer to that was always "They will not last long anymore."

Yesterday, from a good source, it was communicated that the Soenda Lijn will definitely take her last journey, and that her three remaining ships will go up for sale and the [line] will liquidate.

I will soon go to Hamburg in order to organize a sizeable service line via Amsterdam and, if necessary, with extra ships (off and on direct), and also in order to ensure that the Hamburg exporters to Java do not settle in countries of other [exporters].

Incidentally, I had a pleasant travel companion in Ruys, with whom I talked about many matters. We dined together at the London Krasnapolsky, a beautiful building, but not very cozy, like [the one] in the Warmoesstraat.

Immediately after returning from London, there was a sitting of the Provincial Council about the election of a member of the senate for the vacancy of Akerlaken.[492] During the preliminary meeting, at the request of Mr. van Dedem, I nominated as a candidate Mr. de Jong[493] from Hoorn (the father of your neighbour at the table), but he did not belong to those in the highest tax bracket! Your friend, van Dedem, has shown to have had more distractions, such as when he donned the jacket of Tak [van Poortvliet]. But I will forgive him his strange behaviour so long as he introduces the post contract, and there does seem to be a chance for that.

Everything is fine with us. Anna and Nella are currently on an outing. Grandmama is quite well. Uncle Sebald will dine with us today.

Many greetings, from your loving Father.

---

491   Johan Georg Lohmann (1830–1892): Director of the Norddeutscher Lloyd, 1877–1892; married to Clarissa Frost (1838–1920).

492   Jhr. Dirk van Akerlaken (1815–1892): judge, politician; married in 1841 to Christina Johanna de Vicq (1820–1860); second marriage in 1862 to Jkvr. Johanna Godardina Laurentia van Doorn (1838–1912).

493   Melchert (Melchior) de Jong (1840–1914): merchant, politician; married to Johanna de Vries (1834–1889).

A29670000050–53 [Heleen to Li]
Calgary, February 14, 1892

Dear Li,

Many letters are still lying here waiting to be answered, and yesterday I received again a lovely shipment of letters from Papa, you, Tol, Antoinette and Mrs. Pierson, with portraits of herself and her husband. Very lovely, and I rush to answer yours. I can envision the party of January 28 in front of me, and am glad to hear your impressions of the 'Karels', and can imagine the whole evening of getting acquainted and being reacquainted with each other. For me, Mary [Boissevan-van Eeghen] is a sort of Roman heroine who I know very well and love very much, but she does not mean anything to my life and it shall never be so. It would not surprise me if it goes no further than one evening, and yes, that after the dinner at our house, you have seen little of her again. I am very curious about how you liked the evening at our house, if Cor and Fock got along well, [if] Wil was charmed by Mary, and whether Fock could be decent and normal.

    Here, I have been to a ball with 130 people! Among the guests were the owner and manager of the hotel, and I danced with the sales clerk from the drapery store! The house of Mrs. Lougheed was wonderfully spacious, but some things were comical. In the dancing room was one sofa and the unlucky wallflowers sat there, eleven packed together, with sour faces the whole evening and without anyone speaking with them. Upstairs were two small salons, very nicely decorated, but almost nobody had the wherewithal to go there, so that most of the time, my 'gentlemen' and I had the place all to ourselves. I went there with Mr. and Mrs. Wilkins. After breakfast, I walked over to their house for just a moment to see if her dress was still not too short in the front. It was very mild weather, but I was barely there when we heard the wind howling in the distance, and soon an intense dust storm started up, followed by a fierce blizzard. I stayed the whole day with them and, to pass the time, played two of Mendelssohn's quartets (98 pages!) with Mr. Wilkins. When the weather calmed down a bit, I went to the hotel to get my white dress. When I came back, Kathleen had fallen asleep, and therefore I hurried to start getting the dinner ready (beef steak, turnips, potatoes and rice pudding).

    It was 7:00 p.m. before we began, and after dinner, we cleaned the plates, pans and bowls while he got dressed. By the time we were ready after that, it was quite late (the ball started at 8:30), but we had so much fun about all kinds of small mishaps that we did not worry about arriving late, and with verve (into our overshoes, fur capes and so forth) we walked to the Lougheeds'. We had to go through the ballroom, where the dance was fully underway, to reach the stairway to the bedroom, where we took off our things. There were many ladies still busy taking off their over-socks and flannel pantaloons.

When we had finally come down, ready for dancing, the fourth dance was going on. Nevertheless, we still had twenty dances and six extras, and in a wink, our ball-books were fully subscribed. I met a couple of old friends from Edmonton and one from Macleod, who all insisted that I stay at the ranches with their mothers or sisters. About the Edelweiss, I heard nothing, and I think that it must be one of the others from Edmonton, who had not been invited to the ball. The waltz is the only dance that is danced in the same way as at home. The rest are all double-quick; if you do not want to dance the polka as fast as a fiery Esmeralda, you do not dance. Dancing the lancers,[494] everyone is continuously spinning around.

There were seven unmarried ladies, of which four were over thirty, but the married ones also danced along just as lustily. At 2:00 a.m., we hauled ourselves again into heavy clothing, said thanks for the good time and took the way back against the blizzard. I had promised to sleep at the Wilkinses' and was glad to not have to go any further.

We made a bed for Mr. Wilkins on the sofa in the dining room and talked comfortably afterwards. We slept like roses, but the next morning there was a lot of conversation through the wall before we could decide to get up. Furthermore, it was a dilemma over how he could come into the bedroom to dress himself without being seen by me. The solution was that he would go back to bed. In the meantime, he had put on the fire and put the porridge on the stove.

While I was away, the mail had come, which brought me a letter from Karel along with one from Mr. Van Horne, one from Papa, one from *Fräulein* [Eva Ketjen], and one from Annie den Tex.[495] Would you thank the last two very much for me? How well An already writes! It must have been a lot of work for her. It was as if I saw her and heard her and it gave me very much pleasure. It is getting close to 1:00 a.m. and I shall now go to bed. I had to write a lot to Karel, in answering his letter, and enjoyed the quiet evening. The hotel is full again and I seldom have a quiet moment for correspondence.

Much love to everyone at home, from your Heleen.

A28335001530-31 [Heleen to Father]
Calgary, February 16, 1892

Dear Father,

Just now, I received your letter of February 1, and I thank you very much for the letter of credit and taking care of our costs. I copied it for Karel and will keep the original with the other papers. I did not think that I would receive so much in interest for 1891, but a portion of it is certainly from the legacy of Uncle Toon.

494   A quadrille for eight or sixteen pairs.
495   Jkvr. Anna Mathilda den Tex (1861–1944): married to Adriaan Jacob Paul Metelerkamp (1856–1920), colonel.

I fear that the crop from my savings bank will not be very abundant because I am a terrible spendthrift; and all of the socialistic ideas with which I have been fed, nowadays, make me think that it seems wrong to gain capital from interest while I do not lift a finger. Li wrote to me that Liefdadigheid cannot take over her hospital commitments and I would gladly set aside one hundred guilders of my interest from 1891 if she can use it for her discharged patients. I fear that it might muddle your calculations a bit, when you had already recorded the amount as capital in your books. But charity work is so demoralizing when one has to be so frugal, and now that I can do nothing else from here, I want very much to help Li with this.

Lovely that the dinner with [Uncle] Charles, Emily and Mary went so well. It is wonderful to be kept so well informed about everything in Amsterdam. I can see Nel genuinely enjoying the outings. Life in Amsterdam seems so busy and fast. I can already talk about the Pentecost plans. (Very nice plans, I hope that something will come out of it.) And here we are, in the midst of winter, and it seems to me such a short time ago that I arrived here — three and a half months ago.

The day before yesterday, I had a very enjoyable dinner at Mrs. Dean's,[496] with a doctor from Chicago. Over dinner, we had a lively discussion about marriage. The doctor had been married for nineteen years and his appreciation for his wife increased day by day. But he needed four years to get to know her. In the evening, a fun euchre party.

It gave me a lot of pleasure to hear something about Captain Visman. When will the new boat be ordered; is it also waiting for the new post contract? I hope that the small Rotterdam boat stays tough enough and performs better than those wretched little tow-boats from last year that spent more time in the docks than in the ice.

This morning was 20° below zero Fahrenheit, but the Calgarians still praise their mild winter, because in Edmonton it was minus 34° and minus 43° in Winnipeg.

Much love to everyone at home, from your Helena.

---

496   Mrs. Dean may be the wife of John Dean, an accountant for the Canadian Agriculture, Coal & Colonization Co. Ltd., in Calgary.

Chapter 10

The Benevolence of Bigwigs

In the absence of information regarding the future of Karel's work in the Crowsnest, Jan hears of an opportunity in Canada, somewhere, that may change the fate of all involved.

A29670000054–55 [Heleen to Li]
Calgary, February 19, 1892

Dear Li,

Last time, you asked me how I did my hair and now the question comes to me while I have a pen in my hand. I shall just tell you right away that I wear it normally and with a braid on the top of my head. By the way, I look rosy and portly, becoming heavier every day, to the surprise of the observers, since all of the toiling ladies here shrivel in no time and their hair becomes grey because of the alkali in the water. I regret that the photographer is so bad, and expensive, and slow. Otherwise, I would have let myself be photographed, but now that I am always expecting that I will soon go to Montreal, I shall wait. My nose (no more like the once thin, lovely nose) has appropriated a larger place (since my fall) than was granted to it by nature. My frequent manipulation was accredited and I do suspect the upper cartilage had been broken. The direction, however, has not changed. Therefore, I expect (despite running horses and other hindrances) to be following my nose to get home again, but not before a longer time has passed.

For a change, I shall now tell you what I have done today. For that, you should first know that yesterday evening I went with Kathleen to her house. She went to bed early and I remained awake reading a book from the reading circle that must go back today (*Cecil's Tryst*[497] by James Payne). In the morning, I was up first at 8:30 and sped to the freezing kitchen to put the fire on. Dressing myself with fur hat, collar and lined gloves, and with coal bucket in hand, I went to the shed at the back of the yard. When I had brought back the second pail, my hands were at the point of freezing and Kathleen (who had also dressed in the meantime and had put the porridge on to boil), said that it was enough. At least I could fill up the stove in the dining room. After breakfast, the unavoidable washing up, doing the bedroom, dusting and, after that, ironing. At first, Kathleen would not let me do that, but while she was busy thawing the last pieces in front of the stove in the dining room, I began to iron the handkerchiefs and, when she saw that I could do it, she was glad and went to the neighbour to borrow a few more irons so that we could do it together. It was a wash of the last fourteen days, four sheets, six pillowcases, numerous towels, polishing rags, clothing, etc.; and we ironed as fast as possible without worrying about straight seams or lace.

In the meantime, I had decided to cook dinner and, in particular, to make *hutspot*, and when the ironing started to progress somewhat, I dove into the cellar to pick some frozen carrots out of a crate of sad vegetables, as well as some potatoes and onions. Where the petroleum lantern shone, I saw a bone, not from the chimney and no human bone, but a piece of beef bone, good for *hutspot*.

A28335001535-38 [continues on]

While that mixture was cooking, I helped again, skilfully ironing until the neighbour needed the iron herself. That was quite sad, especially since Kathleen did not want to quit, even though she was very tired. Then, there was nothing for me to do in the kitchen other than to watch the potatoes, which were far from being cooked, and to remind Kathleen of that fact. Then, I played a tremendous waltz by Chopin (the first). That helped. When I returned to the kitchen, she let herself be led to a chair to sit quietly and permitted me to iron the last sheets.

She also watched intensely while I, with much wisdom, stirred together the half-cooked potatoes and carrots and put them on the stove with a little butter. Now, surely you think that I had forgotten the salt. To the contrary, at the right time, I had also even put in pepper. I do not know if they do that at home, but here pepper goes in all the vegetables. Then, I quickly made a hot dish from cold rice, fried bacon and set the table. Seldom have I had such fulfilling satisfaction from eating my own dinner. We ate everything up and had a lot of fun. We no longer noticed the cold. I even got so warm that I put on one of Kathleen's cotton

---

497   James Payne (1830–1898): English author of *Cecil's Tryst*, published in 1872.

blouses. When the pans and the dishes were clean again, we dressed up and went out to make some visits.

I went first to Mrs. George's, whose baby was ill, but who still wished to give me tea and also called her brother, Mr. Bernard,[498] to help keep me company while she went to comfort her crying child. At Mrs. McIllree's, I again found Kathleen, who was extremely astonished about the 'Irish pigsty' in which this sprig from distinguished lineage lived. Then, [we went] together into a store to buy cooking apples and to go to Mrs. Braithwaite's,[499] the young, beautiful, slim and distinguished wife of the banker, who was very much condemned by the Calgarian public because of her modern clothing. She lives above the bank. The drawing room is spacious and very cozy — two Japanese screens, canapé angled before the hearth, piano, etc. She has a kitchen maid and a nanny for two children (of three and six years), still bakes and often cooks herself, and sews everything for the children. I brought Kathleen and her apples home, while a fine snow started and a clear rainbow appeared around the descending sun, a quite surprising spectacle here.

The days are getting appealingly longer. It was barely twilight at quarter to seven, when I came back to the hotel. I found an invitation from Mrs. McCarthy for a dance this coming Thursday, February 25, that I have accepted. They live in another stone house near Mrs. Lougheed with two adult daughters, of which one is engaged and nicknamed The Ha-Has, because of her loud laughing at the slightest inducement.

Lastly, I ate alone in the hotel (Mrs. Trott was not home), and I am now doing some writing in my room because the parlour became unsafe, due to a woman of ill repute who lives somewhere on a ranch and who sometimes comes into town to meet her many friends. Also, without giving too much credit to the gossip, the large gathering of gentlemen in the parlour now makes it a less desirable reading and writing room.

A long account of an important day. But you see now how I get through this waiting period and how life here takes up my time. It is so lovely to sympathize with Kathleen, which takes me out of my lonely worries; such a pleasant, friendly babbler, she tells me all of her experiences, which are [both] more and sadder than I thought. She is now much more cheerful than two months ago and has had no crying fit in a long time, and he is also much gentler and more patient with her.

From my letter to Papa, you can see that I received your letter of February 1, but what I really wish to tell you is that it gave me a lot of pleasure. It is so enjoyable to hear about everything, dinners, your new dress, Norwegian, the Salvation Army, etc.

Now that everything is again going normally at home, I am not regretful that I am somewhere else this winter, and however much I long to see and

---

498 William Leigh Bernard (1845–1911): lawyer and owner of the *Daily Tribune*; married to Mary Morton (1840–1929).

499 Marjory Margaret Walker Hendrie (1867–1930): married to Arthur Douglas Braithwaite (1856–1934), the first manager of the Bank of Montreal in Calgary.

[44] Alberta Hotel, Calgary, 1890

talk with everyone at home, I still would not want to start again with the old life. If I go to Montreal soon, I shall try to make myself useful in a hospital for a while.

Much love for everyone, from your Heleen.

A32074000020-23 [Heleen to Wil]
Calgary, February 22, 1892

Dear Wil,

My sweet, unable to think clearly, anxious little woman, phooey, phooey! How many worries and doubts, and for little reason? I just received your letter of February 3, and I was saddened to see that from the lack of news from Karel, you formed so many bleak impressions of the situation. Karel is as healthy as a fish and his biggest sorrow is that he is the cause of such a long, lonely time for you.

It is true that I said nothing about him because I had no information and, especially here, it is the reality. No news is good news; because if an accident had happened, they would have immediately sent a man on horseback from the camp to Macleod to telegraph. Then I would have the news within three days, and you, in four, hence long before you got any letters. That, you must never forget.

I will confess, though, that I was not completely without worry about that story of his trip to the camp, and I had expected to be without news from him for a whole month. Happily, I got news after fourteen days, but in that time, I had already prepared telegrams in my head, in case of any unfortunate events. I could only comfort myself alone with the thoughts that the accidents one worries about in advance never happen, and then I was thankful in the hope that you would not have that fear; it was a disappointment for me to see that you had been worrying anyway.

I can understand, a little bit, that you sometimes feel quite lonely, and then somehow look for a reason for your intense sadness and fear, and you worry because of the lack of news. But really, darling, you must not do that again. It may still happen, every so often, that Karel cannot send any news for weeks, and it would be too nasty for me to always be thinking that you spend that time with horrid fears. Love gives hope to all things, as you have read many times in the beautiful chapter of the letter to the Corinthians, but nowhere did I see "love frightens all things."

I understand that the more time passes without making future plans, the more difficult life becomes, while your life in Amsterdam must sometimes seem so unreal for you. I would give my everything in order to write to you: "Karel has a nice job in Montreal. All concerns have been cleared up. Please, all of you, come over as soon as possible to help to marry our two." Still, I do hope that it will not take so much longer. Perhaps it will not be a nice job and not in Montreal. But while the exact time is still uncertain, I would advise you to not constantly wait and long for it, and to accept the situation as it is now. I fear that I have started preaching and I really do not mean that, because I know that you are constantly doing your best, and how difficult it must be to put on a brave face. I was only afraid that you would reproach yourself for your cheerfulness, while [in truth] it is certainly better for Karel if he may think that this time is not too burdensome for you.

If I could only once talk with you, just as I did with Mrs. Trott a little while ago. You know that the poor soul lost both her husband and child two months ago, and now, actually alone, stares aimlessly at the world. Her only friend is Mrs. Lougheed, and you understand that, at the moment, she is of very little value. For my Dutch reserve, there is something childish in her need to constantly air her sorrow to everyone (the cleaning lady, every new acquaintance in the hotel, Mrs. Lougheed's driver, etc.), and now I allow her to lament only every other day and to cry only once each week. She is also now much stronger than in the beginning and has no more nervous attacks, eats regular meals and sometimes tries to keep herself busy. She has a strong heliotrope odour that makes me faint and, since she is more often in my room than on her own, that is certainly a bit unpleasant.

Today, an acquaintance of hers was in the hotel and I was able to get out of the hotel on my own, taking advantage of the time to have a long walk to my comforting hill over the river and far from the city. It was again a beautiful spring day, surprising after the fierce cold of the previous week. I lay down for a while in the dry grass, gazing at the blue mountains and listening to the far sounds of the city.

From letters to home, you have certainly heard that I had news last week from Karel regarding the letter of Mr. Van Horne, and the result that he, most likely, will stay at work until the end of April. He had visited a cave in the mountains that Sunday and was doing very well.

With a warm kiss, your Heleen.

A32005000429-430 [Father to Heleen]
Amsterdam, February 23, 1892

Dearest Leentje,

En route from Hamburg, on my way to The Hague, I do not have the time to write. However, I do not want to omit sending mail in order to tell you the following: next week, Count Adolphe is going to America again, and is thinking about going to Montreal, perhaps for only one day. His address is:

    A.A.H. Boissevain, Esq.
    Wilkes Building
    Broadstreet Corner
    Wall Street, New York

Get into contact with him, now. Write him a letter right away, that he will find upon his arrival. Keep him up to date with your plans and where you are staying. He is willing to support you with advice and assistance, and to see if he can also give Karel a 'push' in one direction or another. Since it will take so terribly long before Karel comes back from the Rocky Mountains, I hope and expect that you have already gone to Montreal. I think that there, you will be more useful than in Calgary.

Adolphe also spoke with me about Vancouver and British Columbia. He thought that Wil had quite a fortune and was of the opinion that one could have a lovely life on a 'farm' in British Columbia. But I believe that Karel would not feel happy there, when he would be able to do nothing other than overseeing the farming. I know a number of people who would find themselves content with that, and supposedly happy, but Karel has a lot of ambition and a restless nature.

Adolphe was very pessimistic about the chance of Karel getting a job with the Canadian Pacific Railway. He also talked of a 'station master'! Regarding the head office, he thought that was very unlikely. I admit that the prospects are not bright. If Karel cannot find what he likes, he will not want to marry, relying on the income of his wife and the allowance from his father. The feeling that would prompt him to refuse is respectable — yes, nothing other is left than a long engagement, unless they give each other their freedom back.

Can you still support him with these difficulties and final decision? Then that would be very pleasant for us, but for that matter, I believe that you can consider your 'task' as finished, and can come back to us in the spring. Adolphe will gladly accompany you on the return trip, and in case you should wish to go before him (he returns not sooner than May), he shall find a good escort for you.

Everything is going well for us. I hope to soon send you a letter about how I fared in Hamburg and Bremen.

Pierson's tax plans were formally announced yesterday!

Warm greetings from your loving Father.

A32005000490-492 [Wil to Heleen]
Amsterdam, February 24, 1892

Dear Heleen!

How horrible for you to still be in that unpleasant Calgary and unable to do so little of what you had planned for yourself. Your mama also found it so nasty and, I believe, has advised Karel that he might as well leave. I can also certainly understand and appreciate this idea, but he will of course do nothing against the wishes of Mr. Van Horne, but that does not mean that it is not a hard thing for you. We cannot even form an impression about your life over there and, even though I do my best, it is difficult to imagine what you are thinking and to put myself in your situation.

Certainly, you will feel lonely from time to time and think, "Why, actually, did I come along?", but in the beginning, you were of so much value and use to Karel and, after all, that should give some consolation. And even when there is to be a change, he will still need you. Your mother also spoke about encouraging you to return. Perhaps you could then be a travel companion to your Cousin Adolphe, she thought.

Friday, I hope I shall hear more about everything. Then, I will be dining at 717 and your papa, who I have not seen for a long time (because he was in England and Hamburg), shall likewise give his opinion. For Karel, I also find it difficult that Mr. Van Horne did not send him an answer; perhaps however it will still arrive. Karel seemed to feel very good after he received thirty-eight (!) letters, of which three were mine, and I got yet another from him, a supplement to his last letter. One could tell that the arrival of the letters had perked him up. It appeared to be much more like the old Karel. I am very curious to know what you will think of him when you next see him.

Would you also let me know about the prices of a few things in Canada sometime? You should not find this strange; I know very well that I still have to wait for a long time, but nevertheless, it would interest me very much to know a little bit more about it, for example, if you could find out how much money Mrs. Wilkins has to manage her household. It is necessary, in any event, that I have some small idea about it. The prices here, even though I faithfully record them on the cooking school recipes, would help little over there, and can, at best, only serve as a starting point and, who knows, perhaps not even that. What is always the most expensive here are the expenditures that one does not count on, such as subscriptions or membership fees, gifts, tips, travel. I must now, of course, pay the last two, having reached the age of majority, but Mama treats me very reasonably. I am quickly learning about how money flies, because it is so long ago since I had money for clothes, and now there is so much going on that I previously had never dealt with.

Do you know what activity I have now taken on? You will never guess it and I would have never thought that I would ever dare to do it. For a few months, I will take over a Sunday school class. It is the one of Coba van Eeghen, in the Mennonite Sunday School (Sweelinckstraat, at the corner of Govert Flinckstraat), quite far away. That is why Mama found it only so-so, going through wind and weather and to be tied up on Sundays, but we let our concerns go for other thoughts. Coba could never walk with Dirksen on Sundays, or at least only for a short time, and she saw him so little otherwise. At first, I was so very anxious. Coba and Jetje Muller[500] (who runs the other [Sunday School] outside the Haarlemmerpoort[501]) asked me about it while at the cooking school. When I came home, it seemed less dreadful to me and now I am quite encouraged, even though the next few times it will be as if I must go to the dentist. Last Sunday, I sat in during Coba's lesson. The school is large, the classrooms, standard. There was another much larger class in the same room, where children from six to seven years old, who were very naughty and playful, were standing on the benches and putting each other's hats on. A young lady, who was just reading out loud instead of talking about the stories, could not keep any order.

First, the dividing doors were opened and all of the children, I think about 100, sang together. There was no organ nor piano, so that sometimes it went quite off-key. I hope to study the songs to some extent, because it is still too difficult to sing without the support of the sheet music. I sang along, but very softly. After that, the other children went upstairs, the door was closed and Coba started her class of about twenty with a short prayer. You see, I find that awful to do. It is so intimate, so holy, and to do that now for all those children that you do not know. I have already thought once about what I shall say, but I think that for me it will not be like real praying. When Coba did it, it was done so softly that I didn't understand any of it. She also felt nervous about it. Then she requested the pennies that the children had brought along, tested them on their passages that they rushed through, of which

500   Henriette Sophia (Jetje) Muller (1868–1935): married in 1893 to Dr. Reverend Abraham Kornelis Kuiper (1864–1944).

501   The Haarlemmerpoort is the gatehouse of the old wall around Amsterdam.

I believe that they did not understand any, gave them new ones to learn and asked whether they had any questions about the previous lesson.

They spoke very nicely and simply, and some of the children, in particular the boys, understood the text well, but they stayed quite playful. When she asked them if they knew what embalming was (it was about Joseph), one said, "Yes, then they take all the stuff out, and then inject him." Another one remarked that the King was also embalmed. Next Sunday, I have to test them about Moses, up to his flight, and then continue the story.

This afternoon, there is a meeting at Miss van Eeghen's (Herengracht) where ds. Leendertz,[502] who established the school, will discuss with us what we have to discuss the next time, because we only come together every two weeks, on Wednesdays. I will be going with Jetje Muller, but it is still a bit scary. I only hope that he will not ask me any questions. Right now, it is very good that we have the biblical stories firmly instilled in our minds again, because, after a while, so much is forgotten; for example, names are a weak point for me. I am very anxious to know how my first lesson will turn out. The [children] were not happy that Coba was to leave, and they may well not be very quiet about it. If I had not first had the experience with the Kindervoeding, I would never have gone this far. I am still very shy around children.

Poor Willem Coster is still staying at Mr. Kalff's, as long as the move takes. However, he is too weak and has pain in his back again. The house is ready and is waiting for him. Mama spoke with my cousin there and said that it was such a pity to see the new rugs and furniture, and to know that he may be there for only a few weeks. It is really horrendous to be moving when one is in such a condition. But the sick always want to make plans and changes, and many like to do just what they want.

Thursday, February 25: That is all that I could do yesterday. It was a busy day, since after the reading, which was quite customary, I had to quickly go home to eat. A short nap, and in the evening, we were at Mr. and Mrs. van Eeghen de Clercq's,[503] where we, among others, saw the most charming family portraits, almost all drawings of the old Mr. van Eeghen.

This morning, we also had some amusement at the cooking school. The butcher came with Willem, his volunteer, along with a quarter of beef and both of the hind legs with a lot of meat on them. We saw the fat, with the kidney in the middle, the filet, the pieces for steak, rump, the silverside, and so forth, being cut up. Willem put up a real hangman-face during this demonstration. His eyes rolled out of his head. The boss said a lot that was certainly very interesting, and one could see that he was very well informed about his trade. I kept a faint impression of the location of the various parts and a firm intention, namely, that I never wish to become a butcher.

---

502   Willem Izaak Leendertz (1850–1917): Mennonite minister; married in 1879 to Geertruida Kops (1853–1941).

503   Pieter van Eeghen (1844–1907): partner of Van Eeghen & Co. and city counsellor, Amsterdam; married to Maria de Clercq (1844–1897).

We got three tickets for the recital of the students of Miss Berghuijs.[504] You know that she gave us singing lessons? I very much look forward to such a wonderful evening with nothing other than singing and hope to be able to understand what they are saying. There are also three of her own compositions on the program.

And now, dear Heleen, I stop. Today, I longed so much for Karel and do not have anything more to write. Many greetings from Mama and Cor, and a kiss from your Wil.

P.S. Tuesday, Mama has a dinner for elderly folks and she would like it if Cor and I would be there. At first, I thought it unpleasant, but will do it anyway. I shall again, since quite a while, be in a light dress. It is the same one that I was wearing while with Karel at Maria and Charles'.

KLAB09193000036–38 [Father to Karel and Heleen]
Amsterdam, February 26, 1892

Dear children,

I am writing this letter to both of you because I do not know for sure whether you will be together when it arrives, and it is of importance that the chance of working at the phosphate mine[505] (about which I will write later) becomes known to both of you as soon as possible.

The letter from Karel to Mama from the camp and the letter from Helena dated February 8 from Calgary, in which she let us know that she will be leaving for Montreal soon — much to my great pleasure — have been received, and you will see from this letter that notice was taken of the contents.

I agree that by initially participating with the survey crew as a volunteer (as was the case), there is no career for Karel to be expected. We must appreciate that he had the opportunity to test the strength of his physique and morale, but that is not where his future lies.

The benevolence of the 'bigwigs' does not go further than to offer an opportunity to put one's foot in the stirrup. And Hosmer's advice "to keep your eyes open" in order to see if there is a position here or there that you might readily like to occupy, and then to let the influential friends use their best efforts [to open the door], is 'sound advice'.

A while ago Eugen Bunge told me about a phosphate mine that is owned by Dutch gentlemen, located in the region near Ottawa. Their most important mine is in Florida [USA] and is profitable, but this one in Canada is going poorly. They have now delegated Mr. Beenhouwer[506] to assess the

---

504   Elizabeth (Elise) Berghuijs (1858–1939): singing teacher; married to Wouter van Haften (1871–1940), clergyman.

505   Nederlandsche Phosfaat Maatschappij owned a phosphate mine in Canada, named the Amsterdam Mine, in the Buckingham area of Quebec.

506   Joseph Beenhouwer (1871–1940): commercial agent; married to Johanna Speijer (1878–1934).

business. This is a young Dutchman who is commercially (not technically or chemically) familiar with this product. He works for Mr. J. Kogel,[507] a stockbroker here who, along with [David] Fock and Bunge, has interests in this company.

This Mr. Beenhouwer departs for Canada in the next few days and shall ask of Hosmer in Montreal about Karel's address. He gets the task of contacting Karel to invite him to spend time at the mine (for example, for fourteen days) while he, Beenhouwer, is also there. Probably the current agent will be let go and Beenhouwer, who can only stay a few months, must appoint another agent. Now it is possible that such an opening could be available for Karel. In any case, it is worthwhile to look into it. Keep your eyes wide open. Beenhouwer, I do not know. Kogel is an honest man, but very shallow, easily wound up by smooth talkers and not discerning in his choice of people.

Cousin Adolphe Boissevain is also going to America one of these days and will, as I have already written to Helena, perhaps be in Montreal for a day. His address in New York is:

A.A.H. Boissevain, Esq.
Wilkes Building
Broadstreet Corner
Wall Street, New York

I consider it advisable that you write to him and let him know your plans and future prospects. I am convinced that he, especially, will be a very shrewd and concerned adviser on the establishing of one or the other businesses.

I had this on my heart and now close this letter, since I would love for it to go with the mail today. In case I still find some time, then I will add something to it.

Your loving Father.

P.S. Everything is going fine with us. Today, Wil and Ko den Tex, along with the children, will come to dine with us.

Following, February 26, after the stock market closing: I spoke to Cousin Adolphe, who once again pressed upon my heart that you must write to him soon at his address in New York about plans and prospects, because he probably will be in touch with Mr. Van Horne quite soon.

Enclosed is a notice about the Nederlandsche Phosphaat Mijn, which appeared in the issue of public limited liability companies. From that, it shows that the paid-up capital was initially ƒ200,000. I do not know if, since then, there have been still more funds provided. Mr. Beenhouwer is to come here tomorrow. I will give him an introduction [letter] intended for Mr. Hosmer, whom he will meet up with at your address.

---

507 Jacob Matthijs Koegel (aka Jacques Kogel) (1835–1907): stockbroker; married first to Sara Solomon (1852–1885); second marriage in 1889 to Fanny Henriette Enthoven (1854–1940).

I understand, from Helena's as well as from Karel's letters, that you are both somewhat preoccupied with the expenses of your stay in Canada. This is very respectful and I appreciate it very much, but I find it necessary to tell you directly what I think about it. At the moment, we are working on a task, the result of which both families depend upon. In the event that Karel gets honest work that gives him a chance for happiness, where his facilities can develop, any sacrifices being made will, therefore, not count. I have all the Canadian expenses recorded in books under "Expenses." *A chaque annis suffit sa peines*, I can pay them without going downhill. Therefore, I also include all of your equipment, etc. Karel's piggy bank must be available to him until he can make good use of it for his own establishment. When you have expenses now, you can ask yourself about whether it is advisable in reaching that goal. It is probably more expensive to live in Montreal than in the interior, but there, you have more chances to reach your goal. And enough about this topic.

We are doing well at home. Anna and Nella are going out quite a bit and so they seem to amuse themselves. Matthijs remains jolly and pleasant. Wallie and Mia are attentive in their respective schools and, at home, are also jolly and are nice to talk with. Mia keeps amusing us with her original opinions. Elisabeth is staying in Haarlem at the moment, with the Krusemans. I find it quite a chore for her, but she finds that she is useful and, therefore, I can do nothing about it. Mama is doing really well, but I would really like to think about a diversion for her once again. She is now very preoccupied about the possibilities of reciprocation with Mrs. de Vos, and I believe, therefore, that it is necessary that we soon get some clarity with mother and daughter.

Goodbye and fare thee well, always your loving Father.

A32074000193-94 [Heleen to Wil]
Calgary, February 27, 1892

Dear Wil,

Now the wall of silence has fallen; now the worst has come to you and I shudder to think what you have gone through. Can you ever forgive us, and will you still listen to me? The one that helped to mislead you in order to fuel your love, when it would perhaps have been better to put an end to it at once.

Oh, Wil, believe me that that was the worst for us, that in all this sadness that you were dragged into, in which we saw you worried about his health, to constantly have led you down the garden path knowing that so much more sorrow was to come for you. And I still believe that it will be all right because I cannot think that it will be a parting. I have no right to influence your decision and which ones you make. I shall accept them and remain thankful for all that you have offered to Karel, when you did not know how big the disappointment was that he was preparing you for.

Do not consider yourself as bound by what came before. That, Karel has also said, and certainly also Papa, and if it has to be a farewell, do not read on, because I cannot imagine you other than forgiving and trusting, and I hope so much that we are allowed to try to make good on all the suffering that is now part of you.

When I said goodbye in October, I could not have said the words that I am now writing. But Karel has become so different during these months that I have faith in him again, more so than ever before. You have also granted me a peek into the depths of your devotion and love; and even your own shattering grief will not prevent you from suffering under his remorse and struggle. I do not know what he has written to you, but Papa will tell you for sure how much could be ascribed to his physical situation, his slack life in Indonesia and on board, and where Karel perhaps blamed himself too harshly. In that, you will recognize him — in his drive to be true. When the first heavy shock is over, you will perhaps allow a smile at this new life, based on truth and mutual trust, more than the old dream-image, the haziness of which made you sometimes afraid.

Wil, Wil, life is more serious than we could have guessed last summer, but I see the day coming for you and Karel, a day of happiness so great that the autumn days at Teylingerbosch will look small and superficial by comparison.

You will now, more than ever before, long for news, and I hope that the mail from the mountains will come regularly, but the drawbacks of writing and mailing were not known in advance. Do not become anxious, therefore, if further letters fail to appear. We shall do our best.

With a warm kiss, your deeply loving Heleen.

Images List

Cover
"Canadian Pacific Railway survey team, Palliser, British Columbia.", 1884, (CU1106748) by Unknown. Courtesy of Libraries and Cultural Resources Digital Collections, University of Calgary

Front Matter
Letter from Jan Boissevain to Charles R Hosmer
Stadsarchief Amsterdam

[1] Photograph of A. Adolphe H. Boissevain
Athanase Adolphe Henri Boissevain, Atelier J. Merkelbach. Stadsarchief Amsterdam

[2] The Boissevain children: (standing, L–R) An, Karel, Heleen; (sitting, L–R) Thijs, Nel, Li, Mia; (reclining) Wallie
Stadsarchief Amsterdam

[3] Jan Boissevain and Petronella (Nella) Boissevain née Brugmans
Stadsarchief Amsterdam

[4] Helena (Heleen) Boissevain, wearing the fur hat
William Notman, Montreal. Stadsarchief Amsterdam

[5] Willemina (Wil) de Vos and Charles D.W. (Karel) Boissevain
Woodbury & Page, Amsterdam. Stadsarchief Amsterdam

[6] Dr. Constant C. Delprat and Catharina (Coba) Elisabeth Reijnvaan
Stadsarchief Amsterdam

[7] Map: Amsterdam–Vlissingen–Liverpool
Courtesy of Ted Bal, Calgary, Alberta

[8] Dr. Ernest Black
From a photograph by Pioneer Studio (Norseman, W.A.), published in the *Western Mail*, 27 May 1898 (BA1263). State Library of Western Australia, Perth

[9] Citadel from harbour, Quebec City, QC, about 1890
McCord Museum (View-2784-P2)

[10] Boissevain home: Keizersgracht 717
Stadsarchief Amsterdam

[11] Noel Edgell Brooks, seated left
"Noel Brooks, Ernest Brooks, Meredyth B. Hallowell", Sherbrooke, Quebec, 1893. Eastern Townships Resource Centre Archives, Minnie H. Bowen fonds

[12] Alberta Hotel arrivals, *Calgary Daily Herald*, Nov 2, 1891

[13] John Niblock, president of hospital board (1890)
Esplanade Arts & Heritage Centre, Medicine Hat, Alberta (accession no. 0180.00024)

[14] Map showing Calgary and rail lines to towns in southern Alberta
Courtesy of Ted Bal, Calgary, Alberta

[15] Lethbridge House Hotel
Hotel Lethbridge, 1885-1904. Galt Museum & Archives, Lethbridge, Alberta (accession no. 19640158000)

[16] Lethbridge House letterhead with Karel's diagram of train car

[17] Survey wagons in Oldman River, Alberta
"Survey wagons in Oldman River, Alberta.", summer 1895, (CU182258) by Unknown. Courtesy of Libraries and Cultural Resources Digital Collections, University of Calgary

[18] Macleod Hotel, Fort Macleod, Alberta
"Macleod Hotel, Fort Macleod, Alberta.", 1890-12-10, (CU141313) by Gourley, William. Courtesy of Libraries and Cultural Resources Digital Collections, University of Calgary

[19] Women of the Kainai Nation (Blood Tribe) on travois, Ft. Macleod
"Blood women on travois, Fort Macleod, Alberta.", [c. 1890s], (CU1156839) by Steele and Company. Courtesy of Libraries and Cultural Resources Digital Collections, University of Calgary

[20] Heleen's drawing of a map of the Bow River in Calgary for Miep
Stadsarchief Amsterdam

[21] Alberta Hotel in Pincher Creek: white building behind the Union Bank
"Union Bank building, Pincher Creek, Alberta.", [c. 1905], (CU186752) by Unknown. Courtesy of Libraries and Cultural Resources Digital Collections, University of Calgary

[22] Mary Macleod
"Mrs. James F. (Mary) Macleod.", [c. 1880], (CU1153176) by Unknown. Courtesy of Libraries and Cultural Resources Digital Collections, University of Calgary

[23] Diagram of CPR survey camp tent, drawn by Karel
Stadsarchief Amsterdam

Images List 265

[24] Elizabeth S. White Fraser
c. 1920. McCord Museum (00583065)

[25] Inspector M.H. White Fraser of the NWMP
c. 1920. McCord Museum (00583045)

[26] Augustus Jacob
My Jacob Family: https://www.myjacobfamily.com/
Permission granted by Kenneth Jacob

[27] Pincher Creek polo team: (L–R) William Humfrey, Louis Garnett, Dr. Herbert Rimington Mead, Jack Garnett
"Pincher Creek polo team.", 1892, (CU1126004) by Unknown. Courtesy of Libraries and Cultural Resources Digital Collections, University of Calgary.

[28] The Grange Ranch, west of Pincher Creek
"'The Grange' ranch, southern Alberta", [c. 1885-1894], (CU1218472) by Smyth, S.A. Courtesy of Libraries and Cultural Resources Digital Collections, University of Calgary.

[29] Diagram by Karel of Oldman River with wagon
Stadsarchief Amsterdam

[30] Jonas Jones
President of the South-Western Stock Association, organized in Fort Macleod in 1883. Galt Museum & Archives, Lethbridge, Alberta (accession no. 19770285005)

[31] Maude Elton
"Maude Elton, Pincher Creek, Alberta.", 1895-1907, (CU1157293) by Army and Navy Co-op Society. Courtesy of Libraries and Cultural Resources Digital Collections, University of Calgary

[32] Lougheed Mansion
"Residence of Senator James Lougheed, Calgary, Alberta.", [c. 1903], (CU1155102) by Unknown. Courtesy of Libraries and Cultural Resources Digital Collections, University of Calgary

[33] Karel's diagram of the distances measured following the river
Stadsarchief Amsterdam

[34] Karel's sketch of line elevation
Stadsarchief Amsterdam

[35] Kathleen Hollingsworth Wilkins, c. 1920
City of Wetaskiwin Archives

[36] Ernest Drummond Hay Wilkins, c. 1920
City of Wetaskiwin Archives

[37] Isabella (Belle) Lougheed and son Clarence
  "Isabella and Clarence Lougheed", from the Lougheed House Conservation Society Photo Collection, Calgary, Alberta

[38] View of Calgary, c. 1890
  "Calgary, Alberta.", 1890, (CU187425) by Mather, T.H. Courtesy of Libraries and Cultural Resources Digital Collections, University of Calgary

[39] "Old Auntie" Annie Saunders, Pincher Creek
  "'Old Auntie', Pincher Creek, Alberta.", [c. 1890], (CU1154664) by Wilmot, E.M. Courtesy of Libraries and Cultural Resources Digital Collections, University of Calgary

[40] Richard George (Dick) Hardisty
  Edmonton City Archives (EA-10-669-119)

[41] Mission and convent on the hill in St. Albert
  "St. Albert, Alberta.", [c. 1892], (CU1110736) by Boorne and May. Courtesy of Libraries and Cultural Resources Digital Collections, University of Calgary

[42] Caroline Elisabeth (Lily) Humphreys McIllree
  (c. 1875-1935). Whyte Museum of the Canadian Rockies, Banff. Brett Family fonds, image no. 133, Whyte.org

[43] Home of Dr. Henry George and family
  "Home of Doctor Henry George, Calgary, Alberta", [c. 1885-1894], (CU1156341) by Smyth, S.A. Courtesy of Libraries and Cultural Resources Digital Collections, University of Calgary

[44] Alberta Hotel, Calgary, 1890
  "Alberta Hotel, Calgary, Alberta.", [c. 1890], (CU1220801) by Boorne and May. Courtesy of Libraries and Cultural Resources Digital Collections, University of Calgary

Cover for Book 2
Hallway, Van Horne House, Montreal, QC, 1920
McCord Museum (view 19337)

Archive Inventory List

Stadsarchief Amsterdam, the Netherlands, inventory number 394-4
"Boissevain family and related families"

1.24   Jan (1836—1904) X Petronella Johanna Gerarda Brugmans (1838—1905)

    1.24.1.1
    335: From children
    A28335000707—A28335001538

    1.23.1.12
    Copybook of Jan Inv. Nrs. 344—352 to children in Canada
    KLAB09193000004—47

1.44   Elisabeth (Li) Antonia (1864—1906) X Johannes Hermanus Gunning (1859—1951)

    609: Letters from Heleen to Li
    A29670000013—57

    610: Letter from Jan and Nella to the children
    A29624000002—11

1.45   Charles Daniel (Karel) Walrave (1866—1944) X Willemina (Wil) de Vos (1869—1951)

    1.45.1.1
    613: Letters to Wil from Karel
    KLAB00455400083—84, 171—226, 288—289,
    A32074000185—190

    615: Letters to Karel and Wil from their parents
    A29589000995—998

    620: Letters to Wil from Heleen
    A32074000020—245

    639: A07095000001—4

1.46   Helena Mensina (1867—1946)

    1.46.1.1
    684: Letters to Heleen
    32005000337—338 + 32005000345—430

1.47   Matthijs (Thijs) Gideon Jan (1870—1941)

    1.47.1
    705: Letters to Matthijs (Thijs)
    29648000011—12 + 29—34

1.48   Anna (An) Maria (1872—1924) X Gideon Mari Den Tex (1870—1916)

    714: Letters to An, and Mia (Miep)
    A29662000033—52

2.18.6.11.14—1095   Letter to Grandmother Brugmans from granddaughter Helena
                      A33091000001—03

Bibliography

Newspapers, Australia
Sydney Morning Herald, New South Wales
The West Australian, Perth

Newspapers, Canada
Calgary Daily Herald, Calgary, Alberta
The Gazette, Montreal, Quebec
The Macleod Gazette, Fort Macleod, Alberta

Newspapers, Netherlands
Delpher.nl

References
Lovell's Directory
Henderson's Directory
Dictionary of Canadian Biography

Genealogical sources online
Ancestry.com
Boissevain Stichting: https://www.boissevain.org/
Census: Government of Canada, Library and Archives Canada
Centrum voor familie geschiedenis: https://cbg.nl/
https://www.familysearch.org
https://www.findagrave.com
https://www.geni.com

Websites and web sources
Boissevain, Robert Lucas, "Boissevains as founders of prominent banks," Boissevain Bulletin 1999, no. 10: http://members.ziggo.nl/boissevain/Boissevain/EN/frames/bulletinen1999.htm

Connolly Brothers, Alberta Hotel, Pincher Creek, http://www.crowsnest-highway.ca/cgi-bin/citypage.pl?city=PINCHER_CREEK

dbNL digitaal bibliotheek voor de Nederlandse letteren: https://www.dbnl.org

Books, magazines and articles
Aberdeen and Temair, Ishbel Maria Marjoribanks Gordon, marchioness of. *Through Canada with a Kodak*. Edinburgh: W.H. White & Co., 1893.

Andra-Warner, Elle. *James Macleod: The Red Coats' First True Leader*. Victoria: Heritage House Publishing, 2014.

Birkwood, Susan M. "Different sides of the picture: Four Women's Views of Canada (1816-1838)" (PhD diss., The University of Western Ontario, 1997).

Boissevain, Charles F.C.G. *Zeilvaart op Nederlands-Indië: Boissevain & Co. (1836-1882)*. Zutphen: Walburg Pers, 2015.

Boissevain, Mia. *Een Amsterdamse Familie: Autobiographie over de periode 1883-1914*. Typewritten copy, c. 1940.

Borgstede, Arlene. *The Black Robe's Vision: A History of St. Albert and District*. 2 vol. St. Albert: St. Albert Historical Society, 1985.

Brado, Edward. *Cattle Kingdom: Early Ranching in Alberta*. Vancouver: Douglas and McIntyre, 1984.

Bruin, Kees. *Een herenwereld ontleed: Over Amsterdamse oude en nieuwe elites in de tweede helft van de negentiende eeuw*. Amsterdam: Sociologisch Instituut, 1980.

Carter, Sarah and Lesley Erickson, editors. *Unsettled Pasts: Reconceiving the West Through Women's History*. Calgary: University of Calgary Press, 2005.

Colmjon, Gerben. *De beweging van tachtig: Een cultuurhistorisch verkenning in de negentiende eeuw*. Utrecht, Antwerpen: Aula boeken, 1963.

De Vries, Boudien. *Electoraat en Elite: Sociale structuur en sociale mobiliteit in Amsterdam, 1855-1895*. Amsterdam: De Bataafsche Leeuw, 1986.

Eggermont-Molenaar, Mary and Paul Callens, editors. *Missionaries among Miners, Migrants & Blackfoot: The Van Tighem Brothers Diaries, Alberta 1875-1917*. Calgary: University of Calgary Press, 2007.

Felius van, H. and H.J. Metselaars. *Noordhollandse Statenleden 1840-1919*. 's-Gravenhage: Stichting Hollandse Historische Reeks, no. 21.

Fort Macleod Historical Association, officers for. *Fort Macleod: The Story of the Mounted Police*. Fort Macleod: Fort Macleod Historical Association, 1970.

Herk van, Aritha. *Mavericks: An Incorrigible History of Alberta*. Toronto: Penguin Canada, 2001.

Herbert, Rachel. *Ranching Women in Southern Alberta*. Calgary: University of Calgary Press, 2017.

Historical Society, Pincher Creek. *Prairie grass to mountain pass: History of the pioneers of Pincher Creek and district*. Pincher Creek, Alberta: Pincher Creek Historical Society, 1974.

Hofland, Peter. *Leden van de Raad: De Amsterdamse Gemeenteraad 1814-1941*. Amsterdam: de Stichting H.J. Duyvisfonds no. 26, 1998.

Hoyle, Mickey. "Levensgenot en dolce far niënte in onze eeuw van haast en agitatie: De ervaring van binnenlandse plezierreisjes door de Amsterdamse elite (casus Jan Boissevain, 1865)." *De Negentiende Eeuw* 37, no. 4 (2013): 312-330.

Kessel van, Ineke. *Zwarte Hollanders: Afrikaanse Soldaten in Nederlands-Indië*. Amsterdam: KIT Publishers, 2005.

Kistenmaker, Renée and Martha Bakker. *Amsterdam in de Tweede Gouden Eeuw*. Bussum: Thoth Uitgeverij, 2000.

Klassen, H.C. *Eye on the Future: Business People in Calgary and the Bow Valley, 1870-1900*. Calgary: University of Calgary Press, 2002.

Klassen, H.C. "Social Troubles in Calgary in the Mid-1890's." *Urban History Review/Revue d'Histoire Urbaine* 74, no. 3 (1975): 8-16.

Koning de, Willemijn. "De Boissevains in Brieven: A case study about the relations between fathers and sons of the upper class in 19th-century Amsterdam." *Skript Historisch Tijdschrift* 32, no. 3 (2010): 144-156.

Krijff, Jan Th. J. *100 Years Ago: Dutch Immigration to Manitoba in 1893*. Windsor: Electa Press, 1993.

Krijff, Jan Th. J. *Een Aengenaeme Vrientschap (An Amicable Friendship): A collection of historical events between the Netherlands and Canada from 1862-1914*. Toronto: Abbeyfield Publishers, 2003.

Krijff, Jan and Herman Ganzevoort. *Dutch Gentlemen Adventurers in Canada: 1811-1893*. Vancouver: Granville Island Publishing, 2013.

Lamb, W. Kaye. *History of the Canadian Pacific Railway*. New York: Macmillan, 1977.

Macpherson, Gerardine Bate. *Memoirs of the Life of Anna Jameson*. Boston, Roberts Bros., 1878.

Marsh, Christopher James. "Scouts and Seizers: Community-Oriented Policing in Blackfoot (Niitsitapi) Communities of Southern Alberta, 1874-1919." (PhD diss., University of Saskatchewan, 2020).

Miller, Carmen. *Painting the Map Red: Canada and the South African War, 1899-1902*. Montreal & Kingston: Canadian War Museum and McGill-Queen's University Press, 1993.

Moes, Jaap. *Onder Aristocraten: Over hegemonie, welstand en aanzien van adel, patriciaat en andere notabelen in Nederland, 1848-1914*. Adelgeschiedenis, 9. Hilversum: Verloren, 2012.

Monto, Tom and Lawrence Randy. *Old Strathcona: Edmonton's South Side Roots*. 2nd ed. Edmonton: Crang Publishing, 2011.

Nienhuys, Klarissa. "Dr. Mia Boissevain (1878-1959)." *Boissevain Bulletin* 17, Christmas, 2006.

Palmer, Howard and Tamara Palmer, editors. *Peoples of Alberta: Portraits of Cultural Diversity*. Saskatoon: Western Producer Prairie Books, 1985.

Pierson, J.L. *Sir William Van Horne en de Canadian Pacific spoorweg*. Leiden: N.V. Boekhandel en Drukkerij voorheen E. J. Brill, 1925.

Rasporich, A.W. and Henry Klassen. *Frontier Calgary: Town, City, and Region, 1875–1914*. Calgary: McLelland and Stewart West, 1975.

Reynaerts, Jenny. *Speigel van de Werkelijkheid: 19de eeuwse Schilderkunst in Nederland*. Herent: Exhibition International, 2020.

Rikxoort van, Ronald and Nico Guns. *Stoomvaart Maatschappij Nederland: Schepen van de 'Nederland' in beeld*. Zutphen: Walberg Pers, 2015.

Schijf, H. "Wonen op Stand in de Negentiende-eeuws Amsterdam." *Sociologisch Tijdschrift* 14, no. 4 (1988): 596.

Stephen, George. *Officieele Mededeeling: Omtrent den toestand en vooruitzichten van Canadian Pacific Spoorweg*. Amsterdam: Canadian Pacific Railway, 1882.

Santen van, Caroline. "Een Zeeuwse rancher in Canada." *Archief: Mededelingen van het Koninklijk Zeeuwsch genootschap der wetenschappen*. Middelburg: Koninklijk Zeeuwsch genootschap der wetenschappen, 2010.

Smith, Mary Rose. "80 years on the Plains." *Canadian Cattlemen*, June 1949, installment V, chapter IX: 12.

Tex den, Ursula. *Erfgenamen: Het verhaal van een Nederlandse familie van aanzien en vermogen*. Amsterdam: Uitgeverij Balance, 2009.

Tolton, Gordon E. *The Cowboy Cavalry: The Story of the Rocky Mountain Rangers*. Vancouver: Heritage House Publishing, 2011.

Veenendaal, Augustus J., Jr. *Slow Train to Paradise: How Dutch Investment Helped Build American Railroads*. Stanford: Stanford University Press, 1996.

Vonderen van, Barbara. *Deftig en Ondernemend: Amsterdam 1870-1910*. Amsterdam: Meulenhof, 2013.

Vorsterman van Oyen, A.A. *Geslachtlijst der Familie Toe Laer*. 's-Gravenhage: Genealogisch-Heraldisch Archief, 1890.

Vroom Ellis, Bessie. *The Vrooms of the Foothills: Ranching, the Real West*, vol. 4. Victoria: Friesen Press, 2013.

Index

A

Aceh (Atjeh) War, xxiii*n*17, 167
Adolphe Boissevain & Co., xix–xx
Alberta Hotel
    in Calgary, xiv, xxvii, *41*, 49, 149–50, 190, 196, 220, 225, *252*, 325
    Edmonton, 211–12
    Pincher Creek, *82*, 97–98, 107–8, 141
Alberta landscapes, 152–53
Algemeen Handelsblad, 25
Algemeen Werklieden Vereniging, 122
Alman, Mr., 205
Amsterdam, xviii, 5, 25, 161–62
Amsterdam Centraal train station, xviii
Amsterdam City Archives, xiv
An Amicable Friendship (Krijff), xiv
Anderson, Arthur Scott, 22
Angus, James Alexander, 145
Angus, Mary Anne, 22–23
Angus, Richard Bladworth, 22*n*75, 27, 32
archives, changing access to, xiv
art, xviii, 31*nn*90–95, 32*nn*98–100, 96*n*233, 230*n*467, 234*n*473
    mentioned, 10, 31–32, 37–38, 45, 59, 62, 88–89, 98, 105, 203, 215
    by Thijs, 22–23, 26, 205, 215

B

Baden-Powell, Sir George, 38
baggage, 21–23, 26, 37
Baker, Montague, 104
Bakker, Captain Teunis, 61*n*159, 95, 124
balls/parties, 83, 85, 131, 193–94, 199, 205, 210–11, 214, 217–18, 228, 240–41, 246–47
Banff, 182–83
Bank of Montreal, xx, 220, 225, 251*n*499
Beck, Mary Ethel Lloyd, 211–12, 214
Becker, Charles D. T., 211
Beenhouwer, Joseph, 258–59
Berg, Jkvr. Pauline, 40
Berghuijs, Elizabeth (Elise), 258
Berlin (ship), 135*n*302
Bernard, George Morton, 230*n*470, 251
Bernardo, Thomas, 9
Beuker, Jan Hendrik, 216
Beuker, Jeanne Marie Louise Petronella van Rossum, 111

Biben, Angelique Charlotte (Lou), 181, 184*n*384, 241
Biben, Evline, 184
Bicker, Jkvr. Daniëlle Augusta (Lilly), 171*nn*367
Bienfait, Antoine Charles, xx
Bienfait, John, 108
Bigelow, Clara Jane, 20*n*70
Billiton, 143
Black, Dr. Ernest, *10*, 19–20, 28, 35–36, 95–96, 175
blacksmithing, 20
Blijdenstein, Maria, 132
Boelen, Jacobus, 218
Boissevain, A. Adolphe H., *xix*, xx, 6, 22–23, 26–27, 30, 53, 95, 99, 192*n*399, 220, 243, 254–55, 259
Boissevain, Alfred Gideon, 174
Boissevain, Anna (An), *xxi*, 74*n*178
    letters to, 65–72, 88–89, 138–40, 189–90
    mentioned, 29, 80, 128, 185, 187–88, 195, 216, 221–22, 241, 245, 247, 260
Boissevain Brugmans, Petronella (Nella), xvii–xviii, xxi, *xxii*, 44, 94
    in Heleen's letters, 6, 198
    Heleen's letters to, 9–10, 19–22, 35, 46–51, 58–59, 80, 99–104, 115–17, 119–21, 144–46, 163–67, 196–98, 209–10, 229–32
    in Jan's letters, 44, 53, 202–4, 217, 221, 245, 260
    in Karel's letters, 2–3, 12, 155
    Karel's letters to, 25–31, *136*, 137–38
    letters from, xxvi–xxvii, 187–89
Boissevain, Caroline Augusta Antoinette Sophie, 192*n*399
Boissevain, Dr. Charles Ernest Henri (married to Maria Barbara Pijnappel), 75*n*188, 95, 222, 228, 258
Boissevain, Charles (Karel) D. W., xiv, xvii, *xxi*
    dreams, 234
    health of, xvii, 1–2, 7–8, 10–11, 16, 23, 33, 41–43, 46–47, 51, 72, 99–100, 137, 196, 198, 205–6
    Jan on, 243–44, 254, 260

mentioned by Wil, 16, 72, 110, 129, 160, 207, 226–27, 240
Naval years, xxiii–xxiv
relationship with Wil, *xxiv*, 185, 219, 226–27, 235, 238–39, 243–44, 253, 260–61
Sardinian notes, 11, 14–16
travels, xxv, 4, 6, 8, 11–12, 23
working with CPR, xxv, 152–59, 175–79, 218, 232
and writing, xxiii, xxv

Boissevain, Charles (Karel) D. W. —
letters to Heleen, 175–79, 195–96
from Jan, 43–46, 52–55, 61–62, 109–10, 151, 167–69, 172–75, 225–26, 258–60
mentioning Heleen, 12, 25–26, 41, 43, 235
to parents, 25–31, 123–24, *136*, 137–38
to Wil, 1–6, 8, 11–14, 31–34, 39–43, 59, *60*, 61, 86–87, 151–59, 200–202, 217–19, 232–37

Boissevain, Charles (Uncle Karel) (married to Emily H. Macdonnell (Aunt Emily)), 10n51, 76n191, 95, 174, 248

Boissevain, Daniel (Daan) Gideon, 6n39, 44, 53

Boissevain, Daniel (Do) Adolphe, 168–69, 243

Boissevain, Daniel François, xxi

Boissevain, Elisabeth (Li), xxi
letters to, 6–7, 37–39, 81–85, 104–9, 127–28, 147–51, 181–84, 198–99, 204–6, 246–47, 249–52
mentioned, 8, 26, 29, 34, 73, 111, 130, 187, 192, 225–28, 241, 248, 260

Boissevain, Emily (Aunt Emily), 10n51, 76n191, 95, 132, 174n374, 207, 248

Boissevain family
background, xix, xxi
home, 16, *17*, 145
house planning, 44

Boissevain, Gideon, xxin14, 189, 244

Boissevain, Gideon Jeremie, xxii

Boissevain, Gideon Maria (Gie Mie/Uncle Gi), 192

Boissevain, Helena (Heleen/Leentje), xiv, xvii, xxi, xxiii, 213n434
in Alberta, xxv–xxvii, 29, 37, 110
appearance, 249
birthday, 129
childhood, xxiii
coach tumble, 101–2, 108, 114, 116, 120, 132, 187, 197
education, xxiii

Karel on, 12, 25–26, 33, 41, 43, 59–60, 137–38, 154–55, 235
riding, 36, 108, 138–39
travels, 7–8, 16, 50
unpleasant travelling encounters, 70–71

Boissevain, Helena (Heleen/Leentje) — letters, xxvi
to Anna, 65–72, 88–89, 138–40, 189–90
to Grandmother Brugmans, 79–80
from Jan, 43–46, 52–55, 61–62, 93–95, 98–99, 124–25, 132–35, 142–44, 172–75, 191–94, 202–4, 215–17, 221–22, 225–26, 242–45, 254–55, 258–60
to Jan, 46–51, 90–93, 103–4, 194–95, 220, 247–48
from Karel, 175–79, 195–96
to Li, 6–7, 37–39, 81–85, 104–9, 127–28, 147–51, 181–84, 198–99, 204–6, 246–47, 249–52
mentioning Karel, 7, 47–49, 103, 114–15, 194, 198, 205–7, 215, 237–38, 252–53
mentioning Wil, 206, 229, 232
to Mia/Miep, 76, 77, 78
from Nella, 187–89
to Nella, 19–22, 58–59, 80, 99–103, 115–17, 119–21, 144–46, 163–67, 196–98, 209–10, 229–32
to 'Pa' Quack, 224–25
to parents, 9–10, 35–37
to Thijs, 96–98, 121–23, 170–71, 222–24
on travel, 35–36
from Wil, 16–18, 72–76, 110–14, 129–32, 159–63, 184–87, 206–8, 226–29, 238–42, 255–58
to Wil, xxvii, 4, 8, 22–25, 51–52, 62–65, 89–90, 114–15, 125–26, 140–42, 169–72, 199–200, 210–15, 219, 237–38, 252–54, 260–61

Boissevain, Henriette, 173

Boissevain, Jacob Pieter (Ko), 173

Boissevain, Jan, xvii–xviii, xxi, xxii, xxvi–xxvii
letters from Heleen, 9–10, 35–37, 46–51, 90–93, 103–4, 194–95, 220, 247–48
letters to Heleen, xxii–xxiii, xxvii, 52–55, 61–62, 93–95, 98–99, 124–25, 132–35, 142–44, 172–75, 191–94, 202–4, 215–17, 221–22, 225–26, 242–45, 254–55, 258–60
letters from Karel, 25–31, 136, 137–38
letters to Karel, xxii–xxiii, 43–46, 52–55, 61–62, 109–10, 123–24, 151, 167–69, 172–75, 225–26, 258–60

mentioned, 6, 12–13, 138, 197
  travelling to England, 13, 61–62, 93, 95, 124, 134, 226, 244–45
Boissevain, Johanna Dorothea (Jo), 222
Boissevain, Johannes (Jan) Arnold (Faber), 7
Boissevain, Maria (Mary) (married to Cornelis van Eeghen), 52, 112n262, 222, 228, 241–42
Boissevain, Maria (Mia/Miep), xxi, 106
  letters to, 76, 77, 78
  mentioned, 130, 144, 187, 192, 217, 241, 260
Boissevain, Matthijs (Thijs), xxi, 117
  art by, 22–23, 26, 205, 215
  letters to, 96–98, 121–23, 170–71, 222–24
  mentioned, 8, 10, 22–23, 74, 94, 111, 129–30, 175, 188–89, 260
Boissevain, Olga, 76n191
Boissevain, Petronella (Nel), xxi, 105
  mentioned, 26, 55, 73, 187, 241, 248, 260
Boissevain Pijnappel, Maria Barbara (married to Charles Ernst Henri Boissevain), 75, 241
Boissevain, Robert Walrave, 174
Boissevain, Rutger Jan Gideon (Tin), 74
Boissevain, Walrave (Wallie), xxi
Bonebakker, Dr. Adrianus, 110
books. see novels/books
Booth, Anna, 26n81
Bos, Dr. Johannes Jacobus, 93
Bosmans-Benedicts, Sarah, 18
Bosmans, Mrs., 113, 227–28
Bourget, Paul, 222–23
Bouyssavy, Lucas, xix
Bow River, 76, 77, 78
Braithwaite, Marjory Margaret Walker Hendrie, 251
Brandt, Marten Thure Emil, 113, 131, 160
Breitner, George Hendrik, xviii
Briet, Mrs., 100–101
Brooks, Noel Edgell, 29, 30, 33, 36, 38, 42, 47–48, 64
Browning, John M., 145
Brugmans, Anna Antonia, 218
Brugmans, Anthonie, xxi
Brugmans, Pibo Antonius (Toon), 53, 61, 73, 79, 93–94, 99, 104–5, 110, 125, 134–35, 138, 140, 175, 192, 247
Brugmans, Sebaldus Justinus, 54, 135, 245
Brugmans van Maanen, Elisabeth Susanne Gerardine (Grandmother), xxi, 48n136, 79–80, 93–94, 111

Bundten, Jeannette Geertruida, 163
Bunge, Eugen Carl Gustav, 92n210, 258–59
Burgemeester den Tex (ship), 55
Burns, Patrick (Pat), 71

C
Caird, Robert, 238
Calgary, 44, 53, 57, *190*, 212, 235, 248
  Alberta Hotel, xiv, xxvii, 220, 225, 252
  Heleen in, xxvii, 46, 48, 76, 77, 78, 164, 169, 196, 220, 223, 225
  travel to, 33, 40–41
  travelling from, 181–83
Calgary Daily Herald, xiv, 41
Canada, 35–36, 44
  in Heleen's letters, 7
  travelling to, xxv, 6, 8, 11–12, 22–23
  see also *specific locations*
Canadian Pacific Railway (CPR), xx, 7n41
  construction plans, 28, 201
  to Edmonton, 210–11
  telegraph, 21
  see also train routes
Canadian Pacific Steamship Company (CPSC), 7n41, 23n76, 243
Celebes (ship), 61, 95, 124, 221
chaining, 100
checkers games, 148–49
church services, 12–13, 15, 24
Clarke, Mr., 155
Clarkson, Nellie Humphrey, 126
Clarkson, Robert Barton (Chappie), 126n284
Clercks, Mr., 42
clothing, 30, 35, 37, 195, 246
  indigenous, 49, 68
  ironing, 207
  Karel's, 201, 233
  for riding, 29, 35, 37
  sewing, 126, 142, 196, 205, 211
Cnoop Koopmans, Wilhelm, 94
coach travel, 62–63, 65, 70, 79, 81–82, 101, 121, 144, 146–48
coal mines, 62
Concertgebouw, xviii
Connelly, Albert Charles, 82n198
Connelly, Alfred Thomas, 82n198
Conrad, Jan Frederik Willem, 167n354
cooking, 207, 246, 250
Cooper, Alfred William (Alf), 220
Coster, Willem, 76, 154–55, 162, 186–87, 229, 257
Couchon, Nalon, 49
coyotes, 154

CPR survey crews/camps, xxv, *64*, *87*, 115, 140–41, 152–53, 177
   crew, 42, 64, 116
   living conditions, 38–39, 67–68, 89–92, 100, 159, 201–2, 218, 236
   locations, 38–39, 64, 79, 176, 215, 220
   work, 91–92, 116, 133, 136–37, 154, 156–58, 175–76, 195, 201, 220, 237
   see also *specific individuals*
Cremer, Jacob Theodoor, 45, 203
Cremer, Mrs., 203
Crompton, Albert, 174, 245
Crowsnest Pass, 215, 237, 240
Cruys, Susanna Catharina (Aunt Su), 92, 97, 106, 135, 242

D

da Costa, Isaac, 74
Dawes, Sir Edwyn Sandys, 204, 216
de Bordes, Woutrina Johanna Jacoba, 6n39
de Bosch Kemper, Jhr. Gerrit, 94
de Clerq, Gideon Stephanus, 192n399
De Doofpot, 44, 113
De Grondwet, 192n400
De Ijsploeg (ship), 169
de Jong, Melchert (Melchior), 245
de Jonge, van Ellemeet, Jhr. Henri, 46
De Morgenster, 152
De Nieuwe Gids, 171
De Socialisten, 197
De Stoomvaart Maatschappij Nederland (SMN), xxii
de Vos & Zoon, xxiv
de Vos, Cor, xxiv, 130, 142, 207, 218, 239–40
de Vos, Hendrik, xxiv
de Vos, Jo, xxiv, 17, 40, 42, 52, 105, 113, 130–31, 160–61, 169, 195, 208, 218
de Vos, Johanna Jacoba (Caro), 75, 204
de Vos Leembruggen, Cornelia, xxiv
de Vos, Willemina (Wil/Wim), xvii, *xxiv*
   birthday, 206–8
   daily life, 17–18
   early years, xxiv
   on finance, 255–56
   health, 161, 185–86
   letters from Heleen, xxvii, 4, 8, 51–52, 62–65, 89–90, 114–15, 125–26, 140–42, 169–72, 199–200, 210–15, 219, 237–38, 252–54, 260–61
   letters to Heleen, 16–18, 72–76, 110–14, 129–32, 159–63, 184–87, 206–8, 226–29, 238–42, 255–58
   letters from Karel, 1–3, 8, 11–14, 31–34, 39–43, 59, *60*, 61, 86–87, 151–59, 200–202, 217–19, 232–37
   letters to Karel, 39
   mentioned by Heleen, 206, 229, 232
   mentioned by Jan, 45, 55, 133, 191–92, 222, 243–44
   relationship with Karel, 185, 219, 226–27, 235, 238–39, 243–44, 252–53, 260–61
   teaching Sunday school, 256–57
de Vries, Jeronimo, 94
de Vries, Willem Marie, 173
Dean, John, 205n420, 248n496
Dean, Mrs., 248
Delbet, Dr. Pierre, 131, 170
Delprat, Dr. Constant Charles, xvii, xxv, 2, 95, 125, 133, 187
den Tex Biben, Cateau, 174
den Tex Boissevain, Hester, 44, 95, 160, 173, 189
den Tex, Cornelis Anne (Kees), 52, 55
den Tex, Gideon Mari (Gi), 74, 95, 140, 160, 241
den Tex, Jhr. Cornelis Jacob (Coo/Ko), 45, 106, 111, 135, 172–73, 218, 259
den Tex, Jhr. Gerrit, 128
den Tex, Jkvr. Anna Mathilda, 247
den Tex, Karel, 173
den Tex, Nicolaas Jacob (Uncle Nic/Niek), 25, 97
den Tex, Paul, 173
Denny, Sir Cecil Edward, 67, 69, 83
Déroulède, Paul, 40
des Amorie vander Hoeven, Henrietta (Jet), 184
Dirken, Marinus, 97
Dirksen, Jan Cornelis, 168
dolls, 230
Doude van Troostwijk, Wilhelmina Louisa, 74n180
Drever, Mary Isabella, 83n199, 84
Drinkwater, Charles, 27, 32
Drury, Edmund Hazen, 42, 48–49
Duinlust (country house), 74–75
Duncan, Dr. George Cuthbertson, 10, 19, 23–24, 28, 73
Dunmore, 183
Dutch East Indies, 134
Dutch Gentlemen Adventurers (Krijff), xiv

E

Eddy, Wallace Thurston, 178
Edel (poem), 222–23
Edmiston, Mrs., 214

Edmiston, William Somerville, 211, 214
Edmonton, 209–13, 214
Eider (ship), 239n479, 245
Elias, Wouter Hendrik, 94
Elsmere, Robert (character), 242
Elton, Edmund Ashley, 141n308, 144–45, 219–20
Elton, Maude, 141, 142, 144, 150–51
Elton, Mrs A., 141n308, 184
Eman, Anna Elizabeth, 171
euchre party, 205

F
Fabian Society, 224
family finances, xvii, 21, 99, 125, 134–35, 192, 220, 225–26, 237, 243–44, 247–48, 260
Fawn (ship), 244
Fenenga, Pieter, 244
Fenwick, Dr. George Edgeworth, 28
Fock, David, 222, 227, 246, 259
Fock, Jacob, 135
Fort MacLeod, xxv, 37–39, 53, 57, *66*, 83n199, 195, 201
Fraser, Samuel Martin, 196, 205
Fraser's Magazine, 123
Frédéricq, Dr. Simon, 206, 225
Fruin, Elizabeth Anna (Antoinette), 174, 184
Fruin, Georgina Antoinette, 7
Fruitje (character), 235–36

G
Galt, Evelyn Cartier, 69n170
Ganzevoort, Herman, xiii
Garnett, Alice Mary Leslie-Smith, 119, 128, 140, 148–49, 178, 189, 191
Garnett, John, 108, 151, 179
Garnett, Louis Osmond, 119n271, 126, 128
Garnett Ranch (The Grange), 119n271, 120, 121–22, 126–27, 191
Garnett, Walter Emilius, 119n271, 121
George, Dr. Henry, 230n470, 231
George family, 230, 231
George, Mrs., 251
Gigot, Edward-Francis, 78–79
Gildemeester, Adriaan (Aad), 202–3
Gildemeester, Guus, 203
Gordon, Charles William, 242
Gordon, J. E., 9
Grandin, Vital-Justin, 210n428, 213n434
Greenwood, Frances, 41n114
Gunning, Anna, 110
Gunning, Wilhelmina Maria, 207

H
Hardenbroek van Lockhorst des Tombe, Baroness Jeanne, 18, 117
Hardisty, George, 209n427, 210
Hardisty, Richard George, 212, 213n434
Harris, Michael, 215
Havelaar, Carel Eduard, 45
Havelock-Smith, Henry, 206n422
The History of David Grieve (Ward), 242
Hofstede, Joan Pieter, 143
Hogg, Mr., 42, 47, 90–91, 116, 155
Hollandsche Manege, 179
Holt, Alfred, 26n81, 245
Holt, Philip Henry, 26n81
"home child" movement, 9
Hooft Graafland, Jhr. Ferdinand, 27n86
Hooft, Valérie Eugénie, 241
Hooglandt, Eugenie (Jenne), 241
horse-theft case, 83–84
horses, 139
Hosmer, Charles, 20–21, 23–26, 30, 33, 43, 61, 90, 132, 145–46, 149, 164, 169, 190, 195, 220–21, 258
letter to, x–xi
Hudson's Bay Company, 165
100 Years Ago: Dutch Immigration to Manitoba in 1893 (Krijff), xiv
hunting, 120

I
Indigenous peoples, 3, 42, 49, 50n139, 68, *69*, 70, 83–84, 150n326, 195, 198, 213
Insinger, Frederik Robbert, 168n358
Insinger, Maurits Herman, 54
Insinger, Wilhelmina (Willy) Jacoba, 222n453
International Congress of Women (1915), xxii
Ipsen, Peter Alfred Buntzen, 161–62
Italian, 24

J
Jacob, Augustus, 96, *97*
Jameson, Anna Brownell Murphy, xxvi
Janssen, Folmina Margaretha (Mien), 131
Janssen-Rehbock, Anna, 164
Joker (dog), 153–54
Jones, Jonas, *141*
Jones, Tom, 97

K
Kalff, J.H.A.A., 163, 257
Kam, Marie, 111

Keizersgracht 717, 16, *17*
Keller, Gerard, 40
Keuss, Cornelis Henricus, 45
Kindervoeding, 18*n*60, 40, 111–12, 161–63, 187, 195, 202, 241–42, 257
Kingsley, Charles, 92
Kingsmill, Maude Grange, 19
Kipling, Rudyard, 123, 139
Kloos, Willem, 171
Koch, Jan Hendrik Zeno, 25*n*78
Kogel, Jacob Matthijs, 259
Koningin Emma (ship), 22, 168
Kremers, Catharina Johanna (Toos), 107
Kruseman, Annette, 111
Kruseman, Gideon, 188
Kruseman, Jan, 125, 135, 162, 168, 187, 206, 216
Kruseman, Suze, 111

L

La Grandeur, Moise (Mose), 100*n*239
Lachapelle, Eugenie Marie, 41*n*114
Lanting, Dieuwke, 80, 186, 188
Lastdrager, Sophia Clara Emilia, 26*n*82
laundry
   costs of, 21, 197
   doing, 192–93, 250
Lee, William Samuel, 178*n*377
Leembruggen, Caroline Cecilia, 130
Leembruggen, Johannes, 18
Leembruggen, Marinus, 74–75
Leendertz, Willem Izaak, 257
Leesmuseum, 223
Lely, Dr. Cornelis, 167*n*352
Lethbridge, *57–58*, 59
letter-writing, discussions of, 206
Liedermooy, Catharine, 162–63
Liefdadigheid Circulaire, 128
Livermore, Julie, 100*n*239
Lohmann, Johan Georg, 245
Lombok, 134
London & China Telegraph, 55
Long, Catherine, 26*n*81
Lougheed, Clarence, 165, 166
Lougheed House, 150, 196, 246
Lougheed, Mrs. Isabella, 27*n*84, 149–50, 165, *166*, 169, 181–82, 184, 207, 209–10, 212*n*433, 240, 251, 253
Lougheed, Sir James Alexander, 47*n*134, 165–67, 169, 207
Lower Waldron Ranch, 100
Lycklama à Nijeholt, Petrus, 45

M

McCallum, Flora McDonald, 205
McCarthy, Mrs., 251
McCarthy, Peter, 199
McCaul, Charles Coursolles, 41*n*114, 51–52, 76, 199
McCaul, Frances Greenwood, 41, 51–52, 209, 222–23, 229
Macdonell, Alexander Roderick, 85*n*204
McGillis, Mary Sophia, 85*n*204
McIllree, Caroline Elisabeth Humphreys (Lily), *230*, 231, 251
McIllree, John Henry, 230*n*467
MacKenzie, Jack, 153
Mackinnon, Sir William, 9
Macleod Hotel, *66*, 71
Macleod, James Farquharson, 83
MacLeod, Mrs., 211
mail, 116, 126–27, 156, 163–64, 172, 179, 184–86, 195, 198, 201, 203, 208, 217, 220–21, 226–27, 229, 234–40, 243, 246–47, 255
maps, 3
   rail lines, 57
Marken, 230*n*468
Maud (maid), 197
Mead, Dr. Herbert Rimington, 103–4, 198
Medicine Hat, 147–48
Meijboom, Margaretha (Marg) Anna Sophia, 133
Meijer, Clasine Elisabeth (Klaartje), 186–87
Menalda, Anneus, 105
Meredith, Frederick Edmund, 20*n*68, 27
Meredith, William Collis, 20, 26
Meredith, William Henry, 20*n*68
Mills, Caroline Emily, 178*n*378
Mills, George Ashby, 178*n*378
Mingelen, Geverdina Johanna, 192
Mitchell, Edward James, 117*n*270
Montreal, 26–28, 220
   and the Boissevain name, xx
   Heleen in, 237–38, 252
   Karel in, 12, 27, 31–32
Montreal Gazette, xiv
Moore, Alexander Ewan Goodrich, 231–32
Moore, Ethel Christiaan, 231*n*471
Moore, Hellen Lilian, 231*n*471
Moore, Mary Ellen Alexander, 231*n*471
More, Sir Thomas, 12
Motley, John Lothrop, 38*n*104
Muller, Henriette Sophia (Jetje), 256
music, 9, 41, 49, 52, 113, 132, 197, 199, 227–28, 250

Musset-Pathay, Alfred Louis Charles de, 13
Muysken, Floris Coenraad, 208

N
Naber, Henri Adrien, 122
Napoleonic War (1803-1815), xviii–xix
National Review, 146
Nederlandsche Phosfaat Maatschappij, 258*n*505, 259
Nelson, Augustus Jacob, 178
Nereus, 122
Ness, Rosina, 78*n*194, 79
Netherlands, municipal governance in, xix
Nettleton, Julia, 168*n*358
newspapers, 243
    requests for, 25
    see also *specific publications*
Niblock, John, 47, 140, 145, 147–48, 181–83, 194, 209
Niederländer, Berend Karel, 241
The Nineteenth Century (magazine), 12
Noltenius, Herman Heinrich, 6
Noordhoorn, Jacob, 188*n*390
North Bay, 38
North Holland province, ice clearing, 54
novels/books, 8, 13, 19–20, 37, 38*n*104, 51, 79, 96, 129–30, 133, 139, 148, 159, 161–62, 169, 171, 174–75, 193, 198, 215, 220, 224–25, 229, 233–34, 237, 242, 250

O
Old Establishment, xiii
Oldman River, xxv, 63, *64*, *136*, 152, 157
Oort, Egbert, 120
Osborne, Mrs., 244
Oyens, Mrs., 113

P
'Pa' Quack. see Quack, Hendrick Peter Godfried
Paterson, William Brockie, 24
Patti, Adelina, 63
Percy (cook), 194
Perk, Cornelis Egbertus, 167*n*356
Perley, Eliza G. Hammond, 211
Philips, August, 174
phosphate mines, 258
Piers, Arthur, 23, 28
Pierson, Mr., 160, 204, 217, 255
Pierson, Mrs., 107, 110, 143, 160, 204, 246
Pijnappel, Elisabeth Antonia (Lies), 186
Pijnappel, Helena, 218
Pijnappel, Menso Johannes, 79, 93–94, 99, 144, 192
Pijnappel, Pibo Antonius (Toon), 95
Pincher Creek, 91, 96, 125–26, 140, 151, 163–64, 169, 172, 178–79, 197
    Alberta Hotel, *82*, 97–98, 107–8, 141
    mail addressed to, 195, 226–27
    polo team, *102*
Pinkham, William Cyprian, 140*n*306
Pollones, Jean Charles Gerard, 192
Pompe, Adriaan Anne, 142
Posthumus Meyjes, Reinier, 67*n*169
prairie fires, 109
Prins Alexander (ship), 144
Prins, Carel Julius, xxiv*n*21
Prins van Oranje (ship), 168
Prinses Amalia (ship), 226
Prudhomme, René François Armand (Sully), 129–30, 134, 234
Punt, Huyberdina Gerarda, 48*n*137
Puss in Boots, 82*n*197

Q
Quack, Hendrick Peter Godfried, 44, 93–94, 105, 133, 167, 206, 224–25
Quebec City, *14*, 20–21, 26

R
racism, 50*n*139
Rahusen, Eduard Nicolaas, 94, 99
Rahusen Hooft, Anna Louisa, 241–42
Rahusen, Joan, 217, 235
Rederij Goedkoop, 216*n*437
Reijnvaan, Catharina (Coba) Elisabeth, 2
Reijnvaan, Jacoba Clara Elisabeth (Coba), 229
residential schools, 210*n*428, 213*n*434
Retallack, Francis, 71*n*173
Reverend G., 15–16
Richard, Jacobus Jeremias, 105
Rijksmuseum, xviii
Robert Elsmere (Ward), 15*n*56
Röell, Jhr. Cornelis, 193, 228
Röell, Jkvr. Elisabeth (Betsy), 188, 222
Roodenburg, Johanna Heilina, 167*n*353
Ross, James, 29, 195
Routledge, James T. (Jimmy), 92
Routledge, Jimmy, 127–28
Rutgers van Rozenburg, Jhr. J.W.H., 167*n*355
Ruys, Willem Willemsz, 45, 244–45

S

St. Albert, convent in, 210, 213–14
St. James Club, 26
St. Nicholas day, 124–25, 129–30
Salonica fire, 39
Sanders, Caroline A., 84
Sardinian (ship), 8–16
Saunders, "Auntie" Annie, 197n409, *198*
Schiff, Agatha Henriette Charlotte Maria (Jet), 74, 241
Schmidt, Andries Christiaan Nicolaas, 54–55
Schoening, Charles Conrad (Karl), 106
Schorer, Jhr. Karel Johan, 105, 228
Schwartze, Thérèse, 31
sewing, 126, 142, 196, 205, 211
Sillem, Jerome Alexander, 94
'Sister Anna' (character), 225
Sisters of Charity of Montreal, 213n434
sleigh rides, 212–15
Slotemaker, Adrianus, 40n108
Smith, Sir Donald Alexander, 27–28, 27n84, 30–31, 38
snow, 37, 46, 49, 59, 65, 67–68, 79, 89, 103, 114, 121, 139, 152–53, 175–76, 182, 219, 235–36
    see also winter storms
Snyder, Constance Helen, 205, 211
Sociëteit Het Casino, 193
Sociologische Club, 122
Soenda Lijn, 245
Soenda (ship), 216
Spot (dog), 153–54
Sprenger, Meinard, xxvii
Springett, Arthur Richard, 69
Steele, Samuel Benfield, 66n167
Stephen, Sir George, xx
Strauss, Richard, 113
Suwerkrop, Claus August Wilhelm, 93
"Swijght Utrecht", 171
Sylva, Carmen, 215

T

Tachtigers, xviii
Tak, Mr., 217
Tak, Mrs., 203
Tauchnitz Publishers, 242
Teding van Berkhout, Jhr. Pieter Jacob, 226
telegrams, 172–73
ten Kate Pierson, Carolina Henriette Constantia, 204
ter Meulen, Agnes, 112
ter Meulen, Jan, 75n187
ter Meulen, Mrs. J., 228
The Light That Failed (Kipling), 139
Thénard, Jenny, 73–74
Thorpe Regis: A Novel (Peard), 233–34, 237
Tideman, Peter (Pet), 171
Tiedeman, Nicolaas Jacob, 45–46
Tilanus, Catharina (Cateau) Johanna, 25, 184
Tindal, Baron George August, 32
toe Laer, Ottoline, xx
toe Laer, René R. H., xx–xxi
Tollens, Hendrik, 154n331
train routes, xxv, 37, 49, 53n146, 62, 148–49
    maps, 57
    planning process, 91, 157–59, 176–77, 237
    to the survey camp, 42
    see also Canadian Pacific Railway (CPR)
trains
    travel conditions on, 38–41, 46–48, 58–59, *60*
    and travel distances, 137
    travel from Calgary, 181–83
Trakranen, Antonia Elisabeth, 75
translation process, xiv–xv
Treaty 7, 150n326
Trott, Bruce Wardlow, 189n395
Trott, Elisabeth Jane (Wardlow), 189, 209–11, 215, 220, 230, 240, 251, 253
Trott, Samuel William, 189n395

V

van Akerlaken, Jhr. Dirk, 245
van Dedem, Baron Willem Karel, 134, 202–3, 245
van den Berg, Cardina Frederika Holle, 186
van der Hoop, Johanna, 130
van der Lee, Tymon, 221
van der Weijde, Mrs., 188
van Deventer, Jacob, 94
van Eeden, Dr. Frederik, 161–62, 171, 204
van Eeghen, Anne Willem, 44, 216
van Eeghen Boissevain, Mary, 52n145, 112, 222, 228, 241, 246
Van Eeghen, Cornelis (Cor), 52n145, 222, 228
van Eeghen, Jacoba (Coba) Hermina, 168n357, 207, 226, 228, 256
van Eeghen, Jan, 53, 72–73, 182
van Eeghen, Petronella Clasina (Nel), 193n401
van Eeghen, Pieter, 257
van Gendt, Adolf Leonard (Dolf), 54n153

van Gijn, Simon Marius Hugo (Hugo), 167n353
van Gogh, Vincent, xviii
van Gorkum, Sara Jacoba Susanne Caroline, 40
van Hall, Debora, 9
van Hall, Suze, 18, 40
van Heukelom, Henriette, 216
van Heukelom, Louise Victoire, 99
van Heukelom, Maria, xxii
van Heukelom Quack, Clasine Thérèse, 225
van Hoëvell, Baron Wolter Robert, 155n32
Van Horne, Addie, 32–33, 37, 92, 106, 125, 190
Van Horne family, 31–32, 37–38
Van Horne, William Cornelius, xiv, xx–xxi, 27, 37, 124, 145, 177, 183, 195, 198, 247, 259
    and Karel, 20, 24, 137, 195, 218, 232, 254–55
van Houten, Johan Walraven, 216
Van Houten's Chocolate Factory, 63n165
van Jorksveld, Steven Jansen, 66n166
van Kerkwijk, Sara Antonia, 167n354
van Loon Borski, Louisa Catharina Antoinetta (Loukie), 241
van Loon, Jkvr. Henriëtte Agnes, 54n153
van Maanen, Agnes Catherina Angelique, 188
van Maanen, Cornelis Felix, xxi, 94, 188
van Maanen, Martine Margaretha Jacoba, 188–89
van Maanen, Otto, 94
van Marle, Jan Constant, 74
van Notten, Unico Hendrik (Notje), 74
van Ogtrop, Lambertus Johannes Gerardus, 53–54
van Oosterwijk Bruijn, Pieter Adolf, 53–54
van Rhemen, Baroness Johanna Cecilia Elisabeth, 130
van Scherpenberg, Maria Cornelia, 88
van Son, Pieter, 235
van Steijn, Louisa Charlotte, 217
van Stockum, Abraham Jacob (Bram), 76
van Stockum, Dirk Johannes, 26n82
van Tienhoven, Gijsbert, 94, 171, 203
van Tienhoven Hacke, Anna Sara Maria, 94, 173–74, 203
van Tienhoven, Pieter Gerhard (Gerbrand), 203n415
van Veen, Anna Christina, 193
van Zuijlen, Willem Jacob, 241
Vancouver
    Heleen's travel plans to, 103, 109, 116, 138, 145, 164, 197–98, 221, 254
    rail to Calgary, 37
    shipping via, 7
Veenenburg (country house), 74
Vening Meinesz den tex, Jkvr. Cornelia Anna Jacoba Clasina, 45n122
Vening Meinesz, Sjoerd Anne, 45n122
Verheij, Neeltje, 61n159
Verlaine, Paul Marie, 12
Viruly Ledeboer, Aegida Johanna Elizabeth, 17
Viruly, Theodorus Pieter, 17n57
Visman, Hendrik Sierik, 216n438, 248
Vogelenzang, 20
von Möller, Friedrich Nikolai Otto, xxivn20
von Schiller, Elvira Thekla, 6n39
V.O.N.D.E.L, 74n184
Voorwaarts (ship), 174
Voûte, Dr. Alexander, 161, 185

W

Waller, Catharina (Cateau) Rutgera, 45
Waller, Catharina Rutgera (Tol), 18, 22, 184, 197, 246
Waller, Meindert Johannes, 226
Waller, Willem Maurits, 222
Wallis, Thomas, 95, 162, 245
Walloon Church, 62
Ward, Mrs. Humphrey, 242
Wardlow, Mary Louise, 181, 183, 211
wealth taxes, 195
Wertheim, Abraham Carel (A.C.), 54, 143, 194
Wertheim family, 105
Wertheim, Rosalie Marie, 54n152
Wetterstrand, Otto George, 160n335
White Fraser, Elizabeth Sage Retallack, 71n173, 85, 88, 89, 92, 97–98, 105, 108, 116, 120, 132, 169, 179, 198–99
White Fraser house, 98, 108, 172
White Fraser, Montague Henry, 71n173, 88, 89–90, 97–98, 100, 103–5, 108
Wibaut, Florentinus Marinus (Floor), 224
Wickwire, Dr. William Nathan, 221
wildflowers, 88–89
Wilhelmina (Queen of the Netherlands), 193n405
Wilkens, Mrs., 144
Wilkins, Ernest Drummond Hay, 164, *165*, 199, 207, 246
Wilkins, Kathleen, xxvi, 164, *165*, 171–72, 196–97, 199, 204–5, 207, 211, 227, 229, 238, 246, 250–51, 255
Willink, Heer van Bennebroek, David Arnoud, 168

Willoughby, John Milton (Jack), 236
Wilson, Frances, 38n105
Windsor Hotel, 12, 19–21, 28, 37
Winnipeg, 40
Winnipeg Free Press, 177
winter storms, 102, 127, 137, 140–41, 191, 195, 233, 246–47
  see also snow
Wolterbeek, Jacob Cornelis, 193n401
Wragge, Edmund Carlyon, 19n65

Z

Zandvoort woodcarvers, 240
Zeeman, Dr. Johannes, 94
Zimmerman, Bertha, 75n189
Zimmerman, van Rhemen van Rhemenhuizen, Baroness Jacoba Elisabeth (Line), 75n190

Amsterdam's Boissevain Family Letters, Part 2

The fates have been cast, but not very decisively. The contrast between Quebec and the North-West Territories shows ever more starkly when the lifestyles of Heleen and Karel change radically as Montreal becomes their new home, for as long as that may be.

Pictures by Verbeek Fotografie, Hoofddorp

Jan Krijff

Born in the Netherlands, Jan received a BA in economics from the University of Calgary. Soon afterwards he signed up with the CIBC and worked in various branches, spending one memorable year in Resolute Bay, Nunavut (then the Northwest Territories.) Later on, he earned an MA in history from the University of Leiden, in the Netherlands. He has been exploring relations between Holland and Canada, especially in the relatively unexplored period before the end of World War I. He is the author of several books on the subject and co-author, with Karen Green, of *Greetings from Canada, 1884-1915*, which received an honorable mention from the IndieFab Awards.

Karen Green

Karen was born in southern Alberta and earned her BA and LLB from the University of Alberta in Edmonton. She focused on labour and employment law, working with municipal governments, and later provided HR training courses at various institutions. For twelve years she served as a part-time chair of review panels with the BC Mental Health Review Board. After retiring from BC Hydro in 2012, she moved from Vancouver to the Netherlands with her husband, Jan, where she is trying to learn Dutch and other languages.

www.ingramcontent.com/pod-product-compliance
Lightning Source LLC
Chambersburg PA
CBHW081914170426
43200CB00014B/2728